1 FLANDERS AND THE NETHERLANDS
Miles
0 20 40 60 80
Texel I.
Helder
The Marsdiep
Camperdown
Hoorn
Zuyder Zee
Alkmaar
Haarlem
Amsterdam
UNITED NETHERLANDS
Ysel
The Hague
Belvoetsluys
Waal
Clacton Beach
Boxtel
Walcheren
Flushing
Bergen
The Nore
Dommel
Rhine
Canterbury
Deal
Walmer Cas.
Ostend
Nieuport
Furnes
Bruges
Antwerp
Dunkirk
Calais
Ghent
Scheldt
Meuse
Cologne
Bergues
Hondschoote
Ypres
AUSTRIAN NETHERLANDS
Brussels
Maestricht
Menin
Courtrai
Boulogne
M.St Jean
Neerwinden
Tourcoing
Tournai
Lille
Condé
Fleurus
Vicogne
Charleroi
Sambre
Beaumont
Valenciennes
Le Quesnoy
Maubeuge
Wattignies
Cambrai
Le Cateau
Landrecies
Amiens
FRANCE
SWEDEN
Reval
RUSSIA
BALTIC SEA
Riga
POLAND
Galicia
Vienna
Leoben
Hungary
BLACK SEA
Dalmatia
TURKISH EMPIRE
Constantinople
Brindisi
Taranto
Otranto
Corfu
Ionian Is. (Ven.)
Calabria
MOREA
Dardanelles
Aleppo
Syria
Messina
Syracuse
C. Passero
G. of Koron
Marmaris B.
G. of Alexandretta
Damascus
Crete
Acre
Derna

THE YEARS OF ENDURANCE

By the Same Author

Collins

ENGLISH SAGA 1840-1940

Cambridge University Press

SAMUEL PEPYS:

THE MAN IN THE MAKING

THE YEARS OF PERIL

THE SAVIOUR OF THE NAVY

Longmans

CHARLES II

THE ENGLAND OF CHARLES II

POSTMAN'S HORN

THE NATIONAL CHARACTER

THE AMERICAN IDEAL

Peter Davies and Nelson

MACAULAY

ETC. ETC.

ARTHUR BRYANT

THE YEARS OF ENDURANCE

1793-1802

COLLINS
48 PALL MALL LONDON

THIS BOOK IS SET IN FONTANA, A NEW TYPE FACE DESIGNED FOR THE EXCLUSIVE USE OF THE HOUSE OF COLLINS, AND PRINTED BY THEM IN GREAT BRITAIN

First Impression - - - November, 1942
Second ,, - - - December, 1942
Third ,, - - - March, 1944

COLLINS CLEAR-TYPE PRESS : LONDON AND GLASGOW

TO

A. L. ROWSE

IN COMMON DEVOTION

TO THE ENGLISH PAST

"I am not at all afraid for England;
we shall stand till the day of judgment."

Pitt.

CONTENTS

LIST OF MAPS

PREFACE

THE British fight against the attempt of a revolutionary France to dominate the world lasted twenty-two years. It began in 1793 when men who had set eyes on Protector Richard Cromwell were still living, and ended in 1815 when others who were to know the youth of Adolf Hitler were already born. It saw the end of an old age and the beginning of a new.

In that struggle there were only two constant factors. One was the French resolve to create a New Order; the other was the British refusal to admit any Order not based on law. Other nations were tossed in and out of the storm like leaves. Only Britain, though she bent, never broke. For a generation, sometimes with powerful allies but as often alone, she fought on against a nation with twice her population and animated by a strange revolutionary fanaticism which gave its devotees the strength of a man in delirium. Such was its power that at times Britain found herself fighting almost the whole of Europe, including her former allies, without, apparently, the slightest chance of victory and with very little of survival.

Yet her patient, rock-like people never compromised, never gave in, never despaired. They had no Churchill to lead them, for Pitt—the pilot who weathered the early storms—was Chatham's son only in his faith and fortitude but by no means in his understanding of war, in which at first he was the veriest bungler. After three years in which Britain lost almost all her allies and reached the verge of bankruptcy, her enemy threw up the greatest military genius the world had known. For thirteen years, until Sir John Moore twisted his tail in Spain, no soldier got the better of Napoleon or, save for the stubborn Russians for a few months in the Polish mud of 1806, was even able to stand up to him. "The in-isled Ararat, on which the ark of the hopes of Europe and of civilisation rested," alone survived.

. . . .

Survived and triumphed. "Amid the wreck and misery of nations it is our joint exaltation that we have continued superior to all that ambition and despotism could effect; and our still higher exaltation ought to be that we provide not only for our own safety but hold out a prospect to nations now bending under the iron yoke of tyranny what the exertions of a free people can effect." The voice is not Churchill's but Pitt's: the year not 1940 but 1804.

For this is not the first time Britain has faced a Continent overrun by a tyrant or seen her allies, one by one, beaten out of the field by seemingly omnipotent force. When France collapsed in 1940 and her coasts became Hitler's, some, remembering how desperately we fought in 1914 and 1918 to save the Channel ports, felt that our case was desperate. It was happy for England that at that hour she had as Prime Minister a man who was not only a master orator but also an historian, and who knew that the lonely and desolate place in which his country stood was one in which she had stood before. He saw her, awakened and restored by adversity, fulfilling her supreme historic function: the faithful custodian of human law and liberty in the hour when others fell or slept. Until younger nations should awake to join her, he gave her the faith to endure.

. . . .

It is to enshrine the lessons of that earlier war that I have written this book. The present volume covers only its first decade: that which ended with the Peace of Amiens. But it is the part of the war about which least is generally known and that to which our own struggle has borne till now the closest affinity. Trafalgar and Waterloo were so engraved on the mind of the nineteenth century that men forgot what preceded them and alone made them possible.

I have tried to portray the British people on their long pilgrimage of endurance and to show, shining through all their mistakes, what Pitt called "the virtues of adversity endured and adversity resisted, of adversity encountered and adversity surmounted." Because the duration of the conflict robbed it of unity, I have not attempted to compass it in a single volume. It was two wars, not one. In the first the combatants only reached the stage at which a final victory for Britain became possible by fighting themselves to a temporary standstill. They had to pause in order to be able to go on at all. Few British statesmen imagined that the truce of exhaustion negotiated at Amiens could be anything but temporary. But it was necessary to prove to a war-worn people that, though revolutionary France had ostensibly changed its rulers and principles and substituted the despotism of a professional soldier for that of political dictators, it was still a State with which it was impossible to remain at peace. Like ourselves after Munich, our ancestors tried the experiment of living with and letting live a Europe in which there was no balance of power but only unilateral force. Within a year the experiment had failed. When the war began again it was a new war. Yet the foundations of victory—the theme of my sequel—had already been laid.

. . . .

This is the story of how they were laid. They were compounded of errors and follies, of failures and recoveries, of bitter disappointments bravely borne, of experience and dawning realisation, above all of courage, resolution and endurance. The scene of battle ranged from the swamps of the Caribbean to the sands of the Egyptian desert, from the dark waters of Lough Swilly and the Sound to the blue of the Malacca Straits and the Indian Ocean. The mechanical and tactical devices of war were utterly different from those of to-day; the human and strategical problems strangely similar. Weapons and methods of manufacture and transport change much in five generations. Human and national characteristics, geography and the laws of war change little.

Within these pages the reader will find many of the familiar phenomena of our own troubled time. He will see on the Continent the corruption and final breakdown of an outworn society, and the emergence from its collapse of a dynamic and revolutionary force operating not in the peaceful vacuum of a university classroom but in the most powerful military nation in Europe. He will see the early enthusiasm to which that national rebirth gave rise turned into a terrible instrument of force by the cruel and purposeful men who rose on its waves to power. He will see the proscription, imprisonment and murder of political opponents, the denial—in the name of liberty and patriotism—of all freedom of speech and, as the appetite for blood grew, an orgy of sadistic cruelty, indulged not only as a deliberate instrument of policy but, by the baser sort of Jacobin, for its own sake. He will see mass hatred employed as a motive force and ideological ends held out as justifying every means, however base and destructive. He will see a "Great Nation" denying all morality but the pursuit of its own interests and using, as part of its technique of conquest, a propaganda appealing to diametrically contradictory interests and a diplomacy which pretended peace while planning war and which overran its victims' territories by hordes of agents acting as the advance guard of armies. He will see its unconscious allies or dupes in every decaying eighteenth-century State turned by war into "fifth columnists" and by defeat into "quislings."

It would be easy to carry the parallel too far. The French Revolution was marked in its early stages by nobility and generosity: it was inspired by a creed not of hatred and racial discrimination but of love and brotherhood. In the long run it permanently broadened the horizons of mankind. It is remembered to-day for the residue of what was good in its fiery vitality after it had been confined within lawful bounds by the resistance of Britain. Yet without that resistance it would have consumed the earth and, under the little gang of tyrants into whose keeping the French people had committed their bodies and souls, would have perpetuated a tyranny more awful than the corrupt inertia it destroyed. Revolutionary force can seem very harmless in a school text-book after the lapse of a hundred years. We who have seen the unloosed surge of Nazi fanaticism and the Panzers breaking down the dams of civilisation are better able than our immediate predecessors to understand what the generation of Pitt and Nelson had to resist.

. . . .

It remains to express my debt to those who have helped me: to Milton Waldman, Henry Newnham and H. J. Massingham, who have placed at my disposal their knowledge and judgment of books; to Lord Queenborough, who, in addition to valuable criticism, has allowed me to reproduce the battle-piece on the dust-wrapper and whose gallant grandfather and great-uncle figure in these pages; to Eric Gillett, who has generously given me leave to quote from the unpublished MS., *Autobiography of Elizabeth Ham*; to Colonel Alfred Burne, to whom I owe a soldier's scholarship as well as two brilliant studies of the Helder campaign in the *Army Quarterly* and *Fighting Forces*; and to Francis McMurtrie, who has checked my imperfect pages by his own immense maritime lore, largely, I believe, in the hours of fire-watching: an activity which afforded in the still hours of the night part of the inspiration of this book. Without their help, and that of my wife who typed it, my work could not have been completed in so difficult a time.

As my aim has been to present not new facts but old ones focused in the light of present experience, I have, on account of the paper shortage, omitted both bibliography and appendix of references, contenting myself with occasional footnotes. A list follows of abbreviations used in these.

June, 1942. ARTHUR BRYANT.

LIST OF ABBREVIATIONS

Add. MSS.—Additional MSS., British Museum.
Alison—Sir A. Alison, *History of Europe* (1849 ed.).
Ann. Reg.—Annual Register.
Bamford.—*Dear Miss Heber* (ed. F. Bamford), 1936.
Bonner Smith.—D. Bonner Smith, *The Naval Mutinies of 1797*; *Mariner's Mirror*, XXI.
B.M.—British Museum.
Bunbury.—Sir. H. Bunbury, *Narrative of Certain Passages in the late War with France*, 1852.
Calvert.—*The Journals and Correspondence of Sir Harry Calvert* (ed. Verney), 1853.
C.H.B.E.—*Cambridge History of the British Empire*, Vol. II, 1940.
Cockburn.—H. Cockburn, *Memorials of His Time*, 1856.
Colchester.—*Diary and Correspondence of Charles Abbot, Lord Colchester*, 1861.
Collingwood.—*A Selection from the Correspondence of Vice-Admiral Lord Collingwood*, 1828.
C.J.—*Commons' Journals.*
Cornwallis.—*Correspondence of Charles, First Marquis Cornwallis* (ed. C. Ross), 1859.
Crabb Robinson.—*Diary of Henry Crabb Robinson*, 1869.
D'Arblay.—*The Diary and Letters of Madame D'Arblay.*
Dropmore.—*Historical Manuscript Commission*, Report on the Manuscripts of J. B. Fortescue, Esq., preserved at Dropmore.
Dyott.—*Diary of William Dyott* (ed. R. W. Jefferey), 1907.
Eden.—Sir F. Eden, *State of the Poor*, 1797.
Espriella.—(R. Southey.) *Letters from England by Don Manuel Alvarez Espriella*, 1807.
Farington.—*The Farington Diary*, 1922-6.
Fortescue.—Hon. Sir J. Fortescue, *History of the British Army*, IV., 1906.
Friend, The.—S. T. Coleridge, *The Friend* (1890 ed.).
Fremantle.—E. A. Fremantle, *England in the Nineteenth Century*, 1929.
Frischauer.—P. Frischauer, *England's Years of Danger*, 1938.
Gardner.—*Recollections of James Anthony Gardner* (ed. Sir R. V. Hamilton and J. K. Laughton, Navy Records Society), 1906.
Ham. MS.—*MS. Autobiography of Elizabeth Ham.*
Hannah More.—*Memoirs of the Life of Mrs. Hannah More* (ed. W. Roberts), 1836.
Hester Stanhope.—*The Memoirs of Lady Hester Stanhope*, 1845.
H.M.C.—*Historical Manuscripts Commission.*
James.—James, W., *Naval History*, 1837.
Jomini.—Baron A. H. de Jomini, *Histoire des Guerres de la Revolution*, Paris, 1824.
Lecky.—Lecky, *History of Ireland in the Eighteenth Century*, 1892. ed.
Lennox.—*Life and Letters of Lady Sarah Lennox* (ed. Countess of Ilchester and Lord Stavordale), 1901.

Lloyd's Evening Post.—*Lloyd's Evening Post and British Chronicle*, 1798:
Long.—W. H. Long, *Naval Yarns*, 1899.
Lynedoch.—A. M. Delavoye, *Life of Lord Lynedoch*, 1899.
MacRitchie.—W. MacRitchie, *Diary of a Tour through Great Britain*, 1795.
Madelin.—L. Madelin, *The French Revolution*, 1916.
Mahan, Nelson.—A. T. Mahan, *Life of Nelson*, 1899.
Mahan, Sea Power.—A. T. Mahan, *The Influence of Sea Power upon the French Revolution and Empire*, 1892.
Malmesbury.—*Diaries of the First Earl of Malmesbury*, 1845.
Manwaring and Dobrée.—G. E. Manwaring and B. Dobrée, *The Floating Republic*, 1935.
Martin.—*Journals and Letters of Admiral of the Fleet Sir Thomas Byam Martin* (Navy Records Society, ed. Sir R. V. Hamilton), 1900-2.
Mathieson.—W. L. Mathieson, *England in Transition*, 1920.
Minto.—*Life and Letters of Sir Gilbert Elliot, First Earl of Minto*, 1874.
Moore.—*Diary of Sir John Moore* (ed. Sir F. Maurice), 1904.
Morris.—Gouverneur Morris, *A Diary of the French Revolution*, 1939.
Nicolas.—*Despatches and Letters of Lord Nelson* (ed. Nicolas), 1844-6.
Parlt. Hist.—Parliamentary History.
Pitt and the Great War.—J. Holland Rose, *William Pitt and the Great War*, 1911.
Reflections.—E. Burke, *Reflections on the Revolution in France* (Works, 1867 ed.)
Rochefoucauld.—*A Frenchman in England* (ed. J. Marchand), 1933.
Rose.—*The Diaries and Correspondence of the Right Honourable George Rose*, 1860.
Spencer Papers.—*The Spencer Papers* (Navy Records Society), Vols. III & IV, 1924.
Stanhope.—Earl Stanhope, *Life of William Pitt*, 1862.
Times.—*The Times.*
Torrington.—*The Torrington Diaries* (ed. C. B. Andrews), 1934-8.
War Speeches.—*The War Speeches of William Pitt the Younger* (ed. R. Coupland), 1940.
Wheeler & Broadley.—H. F. B. Wheeler and A. M. Broadley, *Napoleon and the Invasion of England*, 1908.
Windham Papers.—*The Windham Papers*, 1913.
Woodforde.—J. Woodforde, *Diary of a Country Parson* (ed. J. D. Beresford), 1924-31.
Wynne Diaries.—*The Wynne Diaries* (ed. A. Fremantle), 1935-40.

PUBLISHERS' NOTE.

For kind permission to use certain copyright extracts the Publishers are indebted to:

Messrs. Constable for an extract from Mr. Christopher Hobhouse's biography of *Fox:* Messrs. Macmillan for an extract from the late Sir John Fortescue's *History of the British Army:* the executors of the late Sir Henry Newbolt for a stanza from the poem *Admirals All* reprinted from Sir Henry Newbolt's *Poems New and Old*, published by Messrs. John Murray.

CHAPTER ONE

Freedom's Own Island

"Our good old island now possesses an accumulation of prosperity beyond any example in the history of the world."
Lord Auckland to Lord Grenville, 3rd July, 1792.

"Good and evil will grow up in the world together; and they who complain, in peace, of the insolence of the populace, must remember that their insolence in peace is bravery in war."
Dr. Johnson.

A LITTLE before it grew light on a cold February morning in 1793, a crowd began to gather on the parade ground at Whitehall. Against the seventeenth-century façade of the Treasury and the grey classic stone of Kent's Horse Guards, the first battalions of the three regiments of Foot Guards were drawn up in long lines of scarlet and white. At seven o'clock precisely, a cortège of officers appeared riding down the Mall from the direction of Buckingham House. At their head was King George III. of England with his two elder sons, the Prince of Wales and the Duke of York.

Mounted on a white charger, in General's uniform, the little, erect, blue-eyed man who represented in his person the idea of England rode down the lines. Then the men marched past in companies, moving in slow time. Two thousand strong, they swung out of Storey's Gate and crossing Westminster Bridge took the road to Greenwich, the King and the officers of his staff riding for a time after them and the Queen and the Princesses following in carriages. All the way through the southern suburbs the troops were accompanied by a vast, enthusiastic crowd, who so overwhelmed the rearguard with embraces and loyal potations that many fell by the way and had to finish their journey in carts. Next day they embarked under the royal eye for Holland in overcrowded, unseaworthy transports, without stores, medical appliances or reserves of ammunition. So the first expeditionary force of the longest war in Britain's history passed beyond seas.

No man living could have guessed its duration. Before it was to end at Waterloo the youngest survivor of those who sailed that day was to be in his forties. The nature and purpose of the struggle were to change out of all recognition; those who were Britain's allies were to become vassals of her terrible adversary and to be aligned against her, and yet more than once, fired by her example, to shake off their chains and range themselves again by her side against the tyrant. Once, for a short while, Britain herself, victor on her chosen element the sea but wearied by the unending conflict, was to temporise with a momentarily exhausted foe, only to renew the fight within a few months when the faith reposed in despotic power had been violated. Only one thing was to remain constant: the dogged resolution of the British people and their leaders to restore the rule of law in Europe, and to go on till they had done so. But on that cold February day nothing of this could be foreseen.

. . . .

To the island State, which with scarcely half France's population took up her gage of battle, had come during the past century the most astonishing prosperity. Divided a century before by violent political and religious controversies which on more than one occasion had degenerated into civil strife, she had achieved enduring unity with the Revolution of 1688. This had placed a Dutchman and later a dynasty of German princes on the throne, but had given the real direction of the kingdom to the greater owners of land. Wiser than the Stuarts they had overthrown, they exercised power by shunning its outward forms. They governed in the King's name and legislated through an assembly of country gentlemen, lawyers and placeholders, more than equal to their own hereditary chamber in status but subject to their social and territorial influence. In this they showed their shrewdness. For the English people did not like the appearance of power.

Nor did these supremely fortunate creatures exercise power for its own sake—these Russells and Grenvilles, Cavendishes, Talbots and Howards with their scores of thousands of acres, their hereditary titles and offices, their State sinecures and pensions for their younger sons and cousins and retainers.[1] During their rule they evinced little desire to oppress their fellow subjects. Such activity was alien to their character. They sought honours and riches with avidity and retained them with firm grasp, securing their continued enjoyment by elaborate entails on their elder children. But they valued them almost entirely for what they brought in freedom and ease to themselves. They extended and improved their domains and cheated the King's Exchequer for the glorious privilege of being independent. This they achieved on a scale formerly unknown to any society.

[1] At the beginning of George III.'s reign there were only 174 British peers.

The countryside was dotted with their lovely palaces and noble avenues, the fields and woods of the whole kingdom were open to their horses and hounds, the genius of man, past and present, was brought to decorate their houses and gardens, to fill their libraries with the masterpieces of the classical and modern mind in bindings worthy of them, to cover their walls with paintings and tapestries, and adorn their tables with exquisite silver and porcelain. Theirs was an ample and splendid design for living. Nor was it a purely material one. For such was the subtlety of their intelligences that they instinctively refused to be chained by their possessions and comforts. They encouraged freedom of expression and diversity of behaviour, preferring a vigorous existence and the society of their equals to a hot-house tended by serfs. They sent their sons to rough, libertarian schools where strawberry leaves were no talisman against the rod[1] and afterwards to the House of Commons where men used plain words and likewise suffered them. And if by their English law of primogeniture they transmitted to their firstborn a wealth and freedom equal and if possible superior to their own, the same law endowed their younger sons with incentive and scope for action and adventure. They left the doors of opportunity open.

Nor did they ignore nature. They made no extravagant attempt to secure exclusive privilege for their blood, but frankly recognised the principle of change. They were realists. Though possessing almost unlimited power, the English aristocracy never attempted to make itself a rigid caste. The younger sons of a Duke or Marquis were by courtesy entitled Lords; the younger sons of a Viscount or Baron, Honourables. There their transmitted dignities ended. Save for the eldest male their grandchildren were all commoners with the same prefix as groom and gamekeeper. Kinship with the great, though a social asset, was no defence to breach of the law: a man might be hanged though he were cousin to a Marquis with 80,000 acres. The great lords looked after themselves and their immediate kin: they refused to endanger their privilege by extending it too widely.

Within the confines of their sensible ambition there was no limit but the laws they made to their personal power and enjoyment. When Lord Plymouth, passing through a country town, took a fancy to an itinerant Punch and Judy show—a novelty to him—he bought it, proprietor and all. The Duke of Devonshire, a quiet man who gave no trouble to any one, kept house at Chatsworth for a hundred and eighty persons, killed on an average five bullocks and fifteen

[1] At Harrow the Duke of Dorset was always beaten twice; once for the offence and once for being a Duke.

sheep a week for their sustenance and paid £5 a year in pensions to every poor family in the neighbourhood. If such great ones liked formality, they dined like Lord Darnley with Chaplain and Tutor in their appointed places, or shot like the Marquis of Abercorn in the ribbon of the Garter: if they preferred obscurity, they enjoyed that too like that easy-going member of the Beauclerk tribe who was "filthy in his person and generated vermin."

They did as they pleased. The world was their park and pleasaunce, and they never doubted their right to make themselves at home in it. "Mr. Dundas!" cried the Duchess of Gordon to the Home Secretary at an Assembly, "you are used to speak in public—will you call my servant"; Lord Stafford paid a later Home Secretary a private retaining fee of £2000 a year to do his accounts.[1] And if they chose to be naughty, naughty they were: his Grace of Norfolk—"Jockey of Norfolk"—who looked like a barrel and reeled like a drunken faun, broke up a fashionable dance he was attending by ringing the church bells and distributing cider to a mob under the ballroom windows to celebrate a false rumour that a fellow "Radical" had won the Middlesex election.

Because they enjoyed life and seldom stood deliberately in the way of others doing the same, they were popular. They took part in the nation's amusements and mixed freely with their neighbours. They were healthy, gregarious and generous, and had little fear in their make-up. They governed England without a police force, without a Bastille and virtually without a Civil Service, by sheer assurance and personality. When the Norfolk Militia refused to march to a field day unless a guinea a man were first distributed, their colonel, William Windham, strode up to the ringleader and, calmly ignoring their oaths and raised muskets, carried him to the guardhouse, standing at the door with a drawn sword and swearing to the rude and liberty-loving mob about him that while he lived the man should not go free.

Wishing to be *primi inter pares* and not solitary despots, the higher aristocracy merged imperceptibly into the country gentry. The Marquis of Buckingham in his white pillared palace at Stowe was only the first gentleman in Buckinghamshire, the social equal if political superior of the Verneys, Chetwodes, Drakes, Purefoys and other humbler squires. They went to the same schools, sat round the same convivial tables, rode together in the hunting field and took

[1] "If I were a great nobleman I should come at once to a distinct understanding with my steward, auditors, etc., that they should upon no account take places in the Cabinet under pain of not being received again in my service, since such a practice, if encouraged, might occasion to me great loss and hindrance of business."—John Ward to Mrs. Dugald Stewart, Oct., 1809, *Letters to Ivy*, 85.

counsel with one another at Quarter Sessions. In each family the elder son was the independent lord of his own little world whether it was a couple of thousand homely acres or a broad province such as fell to the lot of a Fitzwilliam or a Northumberland. The younger sons and their younger sons after them quickly shaded off into the general body of lawyers and clergymen, Navy and Army officers, bankers and merchants. Proud blood and breeding flowed in a broad unimpeded current through the nation's veins.

So did the desire to live well: to dine and hunt and lord it like an elder son. The English, despite inequalities of wealth and status, preserved a remarkable unity of social purpose. Even in their most snobbish occasions—and in their veneration for the "quality" they were snobs to a man—there was something of a family atmosphere. On the Continent, where noble blood was a fetish and caste a horizontal dividing line, a nobleman's house tended to be a vast barracks rising out of a desert and set against a cowed background of miserable hovels in which ragged creatures of a different species lived an animal, servile existence. But in England even the costliest mansion soon mellowed into something cosy and homely: more modest, more human than anything dreamed of by Polish count or German baron. French princes and princesses at Versailles built themselves sham cottages in their grounds and dressed up as shepherds and shepherdesses to feed their starved palates on homely pleasures: in England simplicity, with sturdy mien and broad bucolic joke, was never far off. The cottage, snug and thatched with its porch, oven and tank and its garden warm with peonies and rambler roses, stood four-square against the mansion gates. In *The Deserted Village* Goldsmith, by describing what sweet Auburn had been before the east wind of enclosure struck its Christian polity, idealised yet painted from a still living model the English hamlet as our forbears knew it. It was something common to England alone:

> "How often have I loitered o'er thy green,
> Where humble happiness endeared each scene!
> How often have I paused on every charm,
> The sheltered cot, the cultivated farm,
> The never-failing brook, the busy mill,
> The decent church that topped the neighbouring hill,
> The hawthorn bush, with seats beneath the shade,
> For talking age and whispering lovers made."
>
> . . . .

The thing that first struck foreigners about England was its look of prosperity. "As always," wrote the young Comte de la Rochefoucauld of a Norfolk journey in 1784, "I admired the way in which in all these little villages the houses are clean and have an appearance of cosiness in which ours in France are lacking. There is some indefinable quality about the arrangement of these houses which makes them appear better than they actually are." The English perpetually emulated the good living of their richer neighbours. The larger farmers rode three or four times a week with the squire's harriers, kept a decanter of wine on the sideboard to impress strangers, and a neat parlour wainscoted in oak and furnished with good mahogany. In the same county every weaver's house had its flower garden and grandfather clock and a good open fire round which on winter evening's rosy-faced wives and children sat with beaming faces spinning wool. Houses were still cheap: a good cottage could be built for £50, and William and Dorothy Wordsworth in 1797 were able to rent an ancient mansion in Somerset with a deer park for £30 a year and live there very handsomely on a legacy of £900.

Poverty there often was and injustice—in many cases and even districts harsh, bleak and grinding. With the coming of large-scale enclosure in the seventeen 'sixties and 'seventies they began to increase fast, for the new methods of farming and land tenure brought wealth to the few but debasement and suffering to the many. But in 1789 the process was still comparatively young. Though men were everywhere being dispossessed by mysterious parliamentary and legal processes beyond their understanding of rights their forebears had enjoyed, the countryside as a whole retained the air of well-being that had pervaded it for the past hundred years. The landless householder was still the exception rather than the rule. The predominant type, soon to become a minority, was the cottager who laboured three or four days a week on his richer neighbour's land and two or three on his own, who worked far longer hours than his descendant to-day but did so with a freedom of method now unknown. He still regarded the larger farmer who was beginning to be his employer as an equal: had lived in his house in his bachelor days as an unmarried farm servant, had perhaps aspired to his daughter, and had shared his bread and cheese at the long oaken board and drunk his home-brewed beer or cider round his winter ingle-nook. In an unenclosed village he farmed three or four acres of his own in the common fields, holding them by a tenure—a copyhold or perhaps a lease for the longest survivor of three or more lives—which made him something more than a cap-touching tenant dependent on another man's will and gave him social rights founded on the needs and affections of human nature.

Such men could afford to feel independent: they were. "If you offer them work," wrote an improving farmer, "they will tell you that they must go to look up their sheep, cut furzes, get their cow out of the pound or, perhaps, say that they must take their horse to be shod that he may carry them to the horse-race or a cricket-match." It was, indeed, this independence[1] that caused their better-to-do neighbours to disregard them in their attempt to enlarge their own freedom by opening new avenues to wealth. The tragedy of the enclosures is not that they changed the older basis of farming and land tenure, which was ill-suited to the needs of a growing country, but that they did so without making provision for that continuing stake in the soil for the majority which had made the English a nation of freemen. When the Parliamentary Commissioners offered a poor commoner a few years' purchase for his hereditary rights of grazing and turfing, they were depriving unborn generations of their economic liberty. This was forgotten by a vigorous gentry exercising untrammelled legislative power in Parliament and possessed by an enlightened if selfish desire not only to enrich themselves but to improve on the wasteful and obstructionist farming methods of the past. In their impatience they overlooked the fact that freedom—their own most prized privilege—generally appears inefficient in the short run.

At George III.'s accession half the cultivated land of England was still farmed on the old open-field system. But during the last forty years of the century, nearly three million acres were subjected to Enclosure Acts and at an ever-accelerating rate. The shadow of an acquisitive society was falling fast on the old world of status and inalienable peasant right. The loss in general social prosperity of an enclosed village was as marked as the ground landlord's gain in freeing his land from antiquated restrictions. In the former, farms were few and large. In the latter, the small farmer still predominated. In one typical enclosed village the labourer's wages had dropped to 7/- a week and poor rates had risen to 5/2 in the pound: in an unenclosed village a few miles away a labourer could earn from 1/3 to 1/6 a day at piece rates as well as the perquisites—

[1] The great agricultural innovator, Jethro Tull of Hungerford, complained that serious farming was often made impossible by the independence and excessive conservatism of the English peasant. "The deflection of labourers is such that few gentlemen can keep their lands in their own hands but let them for a little to tenants who can bear to be insulted, assaulted, kicked, cuffed and Bridewelled with more patience than gentlemen are provided with. . . . It were more easy to teach the beasts of the field than to drive the ploughman out of his way."—*Horse-Houghing Husbandry* (1731).

butter, eggs, cheese, milk, poultry and fuel—of his common rights, while poor rates were only 3/4.[1]

In the decade before the start of the great wars the new rural poverty had still not banished good living from a great and perhaps the greater part of rural England. Coming home through Hampshire after foreign travel, George Rose in 1783 sought refuge from a shower in a small public-house, "the extreme neatness of which I could not help contrasting with the dirt and inconvenience of the houses by the roads on the Continent. The parlour in which the family were going to sit down to dinner was as clean and neat as possible; and on the table were a nice piece of roasted beef and a plum pudding—articles I had not seen for a long time." He would have seen them at the same hour in the corresponding place in most English parishes.

For, though decline and decay had set in, the average eighteenth-century village had not yet become a rigid community with a sprinkling of gentry and tenant farmers and a mass of landless labourers. It was still a little microcosm of the greater England of which it was a part, whose members included every social type from the squire who administered the law to the barber who cupped veins and drew the rustic tooth. Here was the blacksmith whose smithy was at once the ironmongery of the community and the wayside repair-station of an equestrian age, the wheelwright with his cunning craft, the clockmaker, the tailor seeking orders from door to door, the upholsterer, glazier, miller, cobbler, farrier, maltster, reddleman and tranter. Arthur Young, writing in 1789, enumerated in a Norfolk parish of 231 families 38 husbandmen, 26 spinners, 12 farmers, 12 publicans, 8 carpenters, with a total of 57 different classes of employment. Here was a closely-associated community rich in diversity, and because in diversity in vital and self-renewing life.

Such employments were intricately interwoven. The farrier, the miller and the maltster generally also held or rented farms; each village craftsman had his garden and, in an unenclosed village, his holding in the common fields. Few were solely dependent on their craft. The rustic world, by geographical measure, was narrow, but there was choice in it. In many counties a subsidiary form of employment was afforded by the cloth industry, then scattered throughout the rural counties of Norfolk, Suffolk, Yorkshire, Lancashire, Gloucestershire, Wiltshire, Somerset and Devon. Like other local crafts such as the cottage lace industry and straw plaiting

[1] The comparison is taken from the North Buckinghamshire villages of Winslow, enclosed in 1766, and Maid's Morton, still unenclosed in 1800.—Fremantle, I, 33.

of Buckinghamshire, it afforded domestic occupation and employment not only to men, but to women and children, endowing every member of the family with a measure of independence. The wealth thus acquired and diffused, as Wilberforce said, was not obtained at the expense of domestic happiness but in the employment of it. Such trades had their ups and downs, and with the rapid expansion of machinery it was soon to be mostly downs. But in the last decade before the great war, the weavers of the North Country were doing well, often employing journeymen and apprentices in addition to their families. The new mechanical spinning frames gave them cheap and plentiful supplies of yarn. They enjoyed well-furnished dwellings bright with clocks, prints, mahogany furniture and Staffordshire ware, and plenty of butcher's meat, oatmeal and potatoes cooked as only the housewives of the North know how.

Good fare was still regarded as the Englishman's birthright. In many counties a gallon of beer a day was not thought an excessive allowance for a working man. Men still lived on the fresh fruits of the earth they tilled: the germ of the wheat remained in the bread, the waste of man and beast went back into the soil and the healthy cycle of nature was unbroken. Every substantial cottage had its flitches of home-cured bacon hanging from the smoky beam and its copper for brewing ale. Eggs, geese, poultry and rabbits abounded, though the wild game which in earlier days had come easily to the peasant's pot was disappearing with enclosures and the growing passion of the rich for the chase. But although a term was being set to all this prosperity and a stormier horizon lay in the path of the poor, the age of comparative rustic plenty lingered into the 'eighties of the Hanoverian century. Rochefoucauld in 1784 noted how much greater the consumption of meat was in England than in any other country and even claimed that in East Anglia the labourer enjoyed butcher's meat every day.[1] This was almost certainly an exaggeration: but in France such a claim would have seemed fantastic.

How much well-to-do folk contrived to eat staggers the modern imagination. With transport still predominantly dependent on the beast and the soft cart-track, the bulk of what was raised could only be consumed locally. Every place and season had its own peculiar delicacies. Our stout forbears, reckless of pot-belly and rubicund countenance, took care that they were not wasted. "My dinner (I love to repeat good ones)," wrote John Byng over his slippered ease in his inn at nightfall, "consisted of spitchcock'd eel, roasted

[1] On one of Coke of Holkham's farms he was told that the harvesters had meat three times a day and as much small beer as they could drink.—*Rochefoucauld*, 230.

pidgeons, a loyn of pork roasted, with tarts, jellies and custards." Woodforde, a Norfolk parson with a modest living, entertained his neighbours to such fare as "fish and oyster sauce, a nice piece of boiled beef, a fine neck of pork roasted and apple sauce, some hashed turkey, mutton stakes, salad, etc., a wild duck roasted, fried rabbits, a plumb pudding and some tartlets, desert, some olives, nuts, almonds and raisins and apples." "The whole company," he added apologetically, "was pleased with their dinner, and considering we had not above three hour's notice of their coming, we did very well in that short time." Nor was such feasting confined to the days when the good parson entertained. He and his niece Nancy, and one can be sure his domestics below stairs, did themselves almost equally well on ordinary days. "We returned home about three o'clock to dinner. Dinner to-day boiled chicken and a pig's face, a bullock's heart roasted and a rich plumb pudding." Small wonder that Nancy sometimes felt ill of an afternoon "with a pain within her, blown up as if poisoned"; that the parson was forced to complain after a somewhat restless night "mince pie rose oft"; and that itinerant Torrington after his inn fare found himself so frequently battling—with true English stubbornness—against post-prandial slumber.

They drank as deep: even when it was only tea. Miss Burney's mother once made Dr. Johnson twenty-one cups in succession. After dinner, bottles of spirits of various kinds—brandy, rum, shrub—moved in ceaseless procession round the table. At Squire Gray's—"a fine jolly old sportsman"—the cloth was not cleared until a bottle of port had been laid down before a mighty silver fox's head, out of which the squire filled a bumper and drank to fox-hunting preparatory to passing it about.[1] Parson Woodforde did not scruple to entertain five fellow-clergymen with eight bottles of port and one of Madeira besides arrack punch, beer and cider.

It was the hallmark of your true Englishman that he "loved his can of flip." In London alone there were more than five thousand licensed houses within the Bills of Mortality. From the Royal Family to the poor labourer "being in beer"—a state so habitual that it was ordinarily held to excuse almost any excess[2]—there was a general contempt for heeltaps: the King's sailor son, the Duke of Clarence, whenever one of his guests stopped drinking, would call out, "I see some daylight in that glass, sir: banish it." "We made him welcome," wrote Ramblin' Jack of the fo'c'sle, "as all Englishmen do their friends, damnabell Drunk, and saw him safe home to Dean's

[1] *Dyott*, I, 17.

[2] Mr. Newton, Secretary of the Royal Academy, dining with some friends in Somerset and being "a little affected by liquor," found his coachman and footman much more so, so put them into the carriage and himself mounted the coachbox.—*Farington*, I, 68.

Square, Ratclife way."[1] Even the livestock on occasion seemed to partake of the national passion: a clergyman noted how two of his pigs, drinking some of the beer grounds out of one of his home-brewed barrels, got so drunk that they were not able to stand and remained like dead things all night: "I never saw pigs so drunk in my life."

Foreigners, less blessed with plenty, were profoundly impressed, if sometimes a little appalled. All this exuberant grossness seemed part of the genius of England: these robust islanders, with their guzzling and swilling, were like so many pieces of animated roast beef with their veins full of ale. It appeared a point of pride with them—a mark of their superiority to other starveling nations—to fill themselves up. A farmer at the Wheel at Hackington Fen ate for a wager two dozen penny mutton pies and drank half a gallon of ale in half an hour: then, remarking that he had had but a scanty supper, went on for the sheer love of the thing and consumed a 3d. loaf, a pound of cheese and a leg of pork. "Sir," said the great Dr. Johnson, the very embodiment of England, "I mind my belly very studiously, for I look upon it that he who will not mind his belly will scarcely mind anything else."

. . . .

The foundation of this good living was the wealth of the English soil. Few countries were more blest by nature: in none had nature been turned to such advantage by the cultivator. Since the Revolutionary settlement a succession of remarkable men—aristocrats, hedge squires and farmers—had devoted their lives to the improvement of crops and livestock. Bakewell's new breed of Leicester sheep in the 'sixties and 'seventies were said to have given his country two pounds of mutton where she had one before. In 1776 young Thomas Coke began his great work of transforming the Holkham estate from a sandy desert into the agricultural Mecca of Europe. It was due to such efforts that England in the grim years ahead was able to sustain the long burden of blockade and feed her industrial population.

In the two decades before the war with revolutionary France farming was the first hobby of educated Englishmen. From the King—"Varmer George"—who contributed to the *Agricultural Magazine* under the pseudonym of Robinson and carried a copy of Arthur Young's *Farmer's Letters* on all his journeys—to Parson Woodforde, who recorded daily his horticultural activities and his observations on the weather, the pursuit of husbandry gripped their eminently practical minds. Great lords would pay £400 or more for

[1] *Ramblin' Jack* (ed. R. R. Bellamy), 204.

the hire of one of Mr. Bakewell's rams, and yeomen would club together to establish cart-horse and ploughing tests. The country gentleman who did not look after his estate lost as much caste as he who shirked his fences in the hunting field. Practical, hardy, realist, the landowners of England were a source of astonishment to their Continental neighbours, who did not know at which to wonder more: aristocratic absorption in clovers and fat cattle or the intelligence with which farmers and peasants, who abroad would have been regarded as no better than beasts of burden, conversed on the principles of their calling.[1]

This common passion had one important political consequence. It helped to unify the nation and, by accustoming men of all classes to act together, gave them cohesion in time of trial. It made not for theoretical but for practical equality. It was one of the influences that constantly tempered the aristocratic government of the country. Too many currents of robust popular air broke in on the senate and salons of eighteenth-century England for the atmosphere to remain hot-house.

They blew not only from the field, but from the jury-box, the hustings and the counting-house. In this land of paradox a lord might find his right to lands or goods questioned by process of law in courts where the final word lay with the decision of twelve fellow-countrymen chosen from the general body of the nation. Strong though the opportunities of blood were, there was no profession to which a man of humble birth might not aspire. Dr. Moore, Archbishop of Canterbury from 1783 to 1805, was the son of a grazier: Lord Eldon, Lord Chancellor with one brief break from 1801 to 1827, the son of a coal-factor's apprentice.

The way these strange islanders chose their rulers outraged alike foreign prejudice and logical formulas. An English election had to be seen to be believed. It was not that the political constitution of the country was democratic: it was on the face of it overwhelmingly aristocratic. The House of Lords was hereditary. Of 558 members of the House of Commons, 294—a majority—were returned by constituencies with less than 250 members. Many of the newer and larger centres of population had no representation at

[1] "Captain Fremantle drove me in his gig to see Mr. Wenar's farm and his famous fat oxen for which he every year gets two or three prizes—he was not at home, but his daughter as fat as the cattle, tho' a civil girl, did the honours of the mansion which is a very ancient half-ruined house—she showed me the fat beasts which are fed some on oil cake and some on turnips, and look like elephants. It is only in this country that one may see a man like Mr. Wenar, who is visited and courted by Dukes and Peers, dines at their table, and returns their dinners, and all this because he can fatten oxen better than his brethren, the other farmers. A German Baron could hardly believe this."—*Wynne Diaries*, III, 72.

all, while an under-populated county like Cornwall still returned a tenth of the English and Welsh members. 157 M.P.'s were nominated by 84 local proprietors, mostly peers, and 150 more on the recommendation of another 70.

Yet the curious fact remained that the English parliaments of the eighteenth century represented not inaccurately the trend of popular political feeling. Not all the power and bribery of a few great lords, who regarded the Whig rule of England as something permanently ordained by heaven, could prevent the younger Pitt from carrying the country against the prevailing parliamentary majority in the famous election of 1784. The effect of corruption, openly acknowledged and shamelessly displayed, largely cancelled itself out. Those who sought entry to Parliament, being English, were individualists to a man. They were there for their careers or local prestige, or out of a sense of personal duty. They were seldom much interested in abstract ideas nor inclined to press them to inhuman extremes. They were often childishly sensitive to what their fellow-countrymen—and particularly their neighbours—thought of them. The very illogicality of the electoral system inclined them to bow to any unmistakable expression of public opinion; unlike both ideological despots and the representatives of a more rational democracy they felt the intellectual weakness of their position and claimed no sanctity for their point of view.

An example of this was the regard paid to county as opposed to borough elections. The 92 Knights of the Shire were the élite of the House and carried far more weight than could be explained by their numbers. When they were united—an event however which only happened in a time of national emergency—no government could long withstand their opposition. This was because their election by forty-shilling freeholders gave them a real right to speak for England: they represented the substance of her dominant interest and industry. They were no placemen or carpet-baggers but independent gentlemen openly competing with their equals for the suffrages of their neighbours—of those, that is, best fitted to judge their character and stewardship. Before a county election sturdy freeholders rode into the shire town from every side to hear speeches from the rival candidates, to be canvassed by them in market hall and street, to march in bannered and cockaded processions behind bands of music, and to eat and drink at their expense in the leading inns and taverns. The most important of all county elections—because it represented the largest constituency—was that of the great province of Yorkshire: on the result of this the eyes of Ministers and even of European statesmen were fixed.

In such contests, and even in those of the close borough, there was a wealth of homely plain speaking and even homelier conduct. The candidates, however splendid their lineage and estates, had to take their turn of lampoons, brutal jests and rotten eggs and run the gauntlet of a fighting, drunken, cheering, jeering crowd before they could hope to enter the portals of Westminster. One did not have to be an alderman or an hereditary burgess or even a forty-shilling freeholder to fling a dead cat at the hustings. The right to do so during an election was regarded as an inalienable privilege of every Englishman: the only check the right of every other subject to return the compliment. At the Wycombe election in 1794 Lord Wycombe was thrown down in the mud and Squire Dashwood, another candidate, lost his hat and almost his life. "Elections are certainly of some use," wrote radical John Byng, "as affording lessons of humility and civility to a proud lord and a steeped lordling."

The rowdiest of all elections was that of Westminster. Here, by one of the incalculable illogicalities of the English constitution, something approaching manhood suffrage prevailed. Every adult male with his own doorway and a fireplace on which to boil his pot had the right to record his vote. Like Yorkshire Westminster was regarded by statesmen as a political test: in its noisy humours—its riots, its stuffed effigies, its grand ladies cajoling porters and draymen with kisses—one could feel the pulse of England.

But perhaps the most startling manifestation of English licence was the power of the mob. England had no police force, and it was regarded as a mark of effeminate namby-pambyism to wish there to be one. Facing a mob was like facing a fence or standing up to an enemy in the ring: a thing a gentleman took in his stride. One did it with courage and good humour, and then the monster—which, being English itself, respected courage and good nature—did no great harm. True in 1780 the London mob surrounded the Houses of Parliament, took drunken control of the capital for four days and burnt about a tenth of it down. But even this excess was regarded as part of the price of popular freedom. And in its crude, barbarous way the mob did—under guidance—act as a kind of rough watchdog of the national liberties and even, on occasion, of morality. Thus, when the House of Commons in its dislike of the disreputable John Wilkes outraged the principles of freedom of choice and speech which it was its duty to uphold, it was the constancy of the mob to the cause which had brought Strafford to the scaffold that shamed and finally defeated the advocates of despotism. And when an aspiring lady of the frail sisterhood buried her cat in hallowed ground, it was not a dignitary of the church but the hand of the London mob which rebuked her, noisily flinging the corpse back through her window within two hours of its interment.

Liberty outside Parliament was reflected by liberty within. For all the power of the great nominating lords and borough-mongers and the allurements of the Treasury, there were more independent members in the House than is possible under the rigid Party machinery of to-day. In a major issue it was not the Whips but men's consciences that turned the scale in the lobbies. Minorities could make themselves felt. A great speech could still decide a hard-fought debate: members were not the tied advocates of particular interests obeying mandates issued in advance. They gave their constituents not so much rigid obedience as unfettered judgment.

Nor did the complexion of the House discount the rise of talent. Within its narrow range the old parliamentary system fostered it. Again and again it recruited to the country's service the strongest motive power in the world—the force of genius untrammelled by the rule of mediocrity. A young man of brilliance, who had the good fortune to attract the notice of some great peer, might be set on the high road to the Front Bench at an age when his counterpart to-day is laboriously overloading his brain and memory to satisfy the Civil Service Commissioners. Pitt with £300 a year was Prime Minister at twenty-four. Probably at no other time in British history could Edmund Burke, a man of genius without any of the arts of the demagogue and lacking both birth and independent fortune, have become a lifelong legislator. Like Macaulay and Gladstone after him he entered Parliament by the back door of a rotten borough and a discerning aristocrat's approval.

. . . .

Behind every English exercise of liberty was the underlying conception of law. It was because the law was there, guaranteeing the freedom of every man against every other, that the English were able to allow and take so much licence. The law did not coerce a man from acting as he pleased: it only afforded redress to others if in doing so he outraged their rightful liberty or the peace of the community. Every man could appeal to the law: no man could legally evade it. Not even the King: perhaps it would be truest to say in the eighteenth century, least of all the King. The squire who rebuked George III—a very popular monarch—for trespassing on his land became a national legend.

In England there was no *droit administratif*: no sacred principle of state with which to crush the cantankerous subject. The official had to produce the warrant of law to justify his every action. If he exceeded his authority, whatever his motives, he suffered the same penalty as though he had acted as a private citizen. There was no escape from the law: it was like divine retribution and might overtake the transgressor at any moment of his life. Joseph Wall, for all his fine connections, was hanged at Newgate in front of a cheering mob for having twenty years before, while Governor of Goree, sentenced a mutinous sergeant to an unlawful flogging that caused death.

Trial by law was conducted in public. Judges were appointed for life and were irremovable save for gross misconduct. Issues of fact were decided by a jury of common citizens. Any man arrested could apply to the Courts for an immediate writ of *Habeas Corpus* calling on his custodian to show legal cause why he should be detained. In all doubtful cases the prisoner was given the benefit of the doubt and acquitted. These were the main pillars of English justice, together with an unpaid magistracy of local worthies, the absence of a paid constabulary and a traditional distrust of the standing army which was always kept by Parliament—alone capable of voting funds for its maintenance—at the lowest strength compatible with national safety, and often a good deal lower. The duties of police were performed by the general body of citizens serving in turn as constables on a compulsory parish rota or paying substitutes to deputise for them during their year of office. In the larger towns this ancient system had long broken down. But the national distrust of despotism long made reform impossible.[1]

There was another principle of freedom scrupulously honoured in England. It was the legal sanctity of property. It was individual ownership, it was held, that enabled a man to defy excessive authority. Without a competence of his own to fall back on the subject could be bribed or intimidated: a John Hampden without an estate seemed impracticable to the English mind.[2] The guardians of English liberty were the gentlemen of England whose hereditary independence protected them from the threats and guiles of despotism. They were tyrant-proof. That men might be rendered servile through wealth as well as through poverty had not yet dawned on them.

[1] In London a small patrol of less than fifty mounted men was maintained to guard its highwayman-infested approaches, while a handful of professional Bow Street Runners —popularly known as "redbreasts" on account of their scarlet waistcoats—occasionally patrolled the more lawless districts. For the rest the public order of the capital was left to the medieval constables of the parishes assisted by a race of venerable watchmen or "Charlies" with traditional staffs, lanterns and rattles.

[2] This was also the belief of the great libertarian pioneers of the United States. To Washington and Jefferson property and democracy were synonymous: their ideal was the small freeholder scorning all tyrants, political and economic, and dispensing almost with government itself.

Any interference with a man's property by the State was regarded as pernicious. Freemen were supposed to be free to do as they liked with their own. Taxation had, therefore, to be kept as low as possible and the extent of a man's contribution to the upkeep of the State left wherever practicable to his own choice. "No taxation without representation" was the oldest battle-cry in the armoury of English freedom: it dominated the whole constitution. Those assembled in Parliament did not represent numbers but property: the greater landowners in the House of Lords, the lesser in the Commons, side by side with the burgesses who represented the nation's mercantile interest.

Such an assembly was naturally tender to the taxpayer and unsympathetic to the Executive. In the seventeenth century it had made government virtually impossible, and England had only been saved from a second civil war by vesting the King's executive power in a Cabinet of Ministers who commanded the support of a majority in the House of Commons. But though the expenses of government steadily rose with the growing complexity of civilisation, taxation continued to be kept as low as possible. Direct taxation was regarded as repugnant to English principles both on account of its compulsion and of the odious power of inquisition it involved. The taxpayer was given the option of declining to purchase the taxed article and so of avoiding the tax. For this reason many antiquated tariff barriers which would otherwise have been swept away in the rising tide of free trade were retained for revenue purposes. Anything which infringed what an eighteenth-century correspondent called "the sweet majesty of private life" was discouraged.

Because of this, administration and justice were supported more cheaply than in any other country of equivalent size and importance in Europe. The cost of administration in Prussia was twice as much, in France many times that of Britain. The chief civil expenses were the sinecures and pensions which the ruling aristocracy, usurping the former perquisites of the Court, lavished on their relations and supporters. The Army was pared to the bone: so in time of peace was the Navy, especially in the matter of seamen's pay. Yet economy on the Navy was at least kept within limits, for two centuries of experience had taught the English that their commercial wealth depended on their fleet.

. . . .

For more than a century and a half trade had played an increasing part in the direction of English policy. Commerce was the activity by which younger sons and their progeny sought to raise themselves to the same standard of wealth and independence enjoyed by their elder brothers. The richer the latter under entail and primogeniture, the greater became the desire to emulate them.

The development of British commerce during the eighteenth century was immense. Population was rising, and the luxuries of one generation became the necessities of the next. In 1720 the value of British imports was just over £6,000,000. By 1760 it was nearly £10,000,000, by 1789 over £37,000,000. During these years tea, coffee and West Indian sugar became part of the staple dietary of the people. Everything conspired to further this process: natural health and vigour, free institutions, aptitude for seamanship and colonisation and a unique geographical position.

It brought the British a great Empire, acquired not by any design of imperial conquest but through the individual's search for trade. The fight to maintain it against their rivals, the French, placed them in the middle years of the century on a pinnacle of unprecedented glory. Under the leadership of the elder Pitt, they gained supremacy in India and a new dominion in Canada.

Before Clive's victory at Plassey in 1757 the British had only been casual factors trading from isolated coastal ports in the anarchical Indian peninsula by precarious leave of native princes and in armed rivalry with other European trading companies. But in the second half of the century the East India Company of London found itself administering possessions many times the size of England. At first it merely regarded this unlooked-for dominion as a windfall for its factors and shareholders: the imagination of Leadenhall Street could stretch no further.

It was not only in India that a race of sober farmers and shop-keepers failed to visualise the magnitude of their opportunity. Along the eastern seaboard of North America, now freed from fear of French aggression by the conquest of Canada, lived two million British settlers. These a patronising Court and Parliament treated as if they lacked the stubborn independence of their kinsfolk at home. The result was a quarrel, persisted in with all the ferocious obstinacy and moral rectitude of the race until no alternatives remained but either a systematic conquest of the colonies by British soldiers or the end of the imperial connection.

The issue was still undecided when Britain's outdistanced competitors in the race for empire seized their opportunity for revenge. France, Spain, and Holland—the three chief maritime powers of the Continent—supported by Russia, Sweden and Denmark, joined hands with the colonists. With her fleets outnumbered and her finances in ruin, Britain seemed beaten. Then the brilliance of her seamen and the stubborn defence of Gibraltar turned the scale. A disastrous war dwindled away into stalemate. The British faced the facts and in 1783 made peace. Their former colonies became the United States of America.

But unperceived by the islanders, who thought their imperial heritage lost for ever,[1] the process which had made the first empire continued, and at an accelerated pace. What had happened before happened again. In every corner of the world where ships could sail appeared enterprising Britons, begging concessions, planting factories and on occasion hoisting the imperial flag as a protection for their ventures. No sooner, in the poet Cowper's phrase, had the jewel been picked from England's crown, than new jewels blazed in the empty sockets. Within five years of the final loss of the American colonies, Captain Phillip had established the first British settlement on the Continent of Australia. An even vaster new Britain in America took embryonic shape amid the snows of Canada where 140,000 defeated French, 60,000 migrant loyalists from the United States and a few thousand rough Scottish emigrants contrived to live together under King George's writ. Elsewhere a chain of forts, naval bases and sugar and spice islands continued to afford the traders of Britain springboards of opportunity.

For the moment the chief imperial field for the aspirant to wealth was India, which was beginning to take the place of the West Indies. From this oriental El Dorado flowed an ever-widening stream of spices, indigo, ivory, sugar, tea, ebony, sandalwood, saltpetre, cotton, silks and calicoes and fabulously rich merchants who bought up English estates and rotten boroughs, married their children into the aristocracy and received from their less fortunate countrymen the envious name of nabob. It was due to them that Britain first became conscious of its eastern possession and began to assume a direct responsibility for its government. The India Act of 1784, subordinating the political power of the Directors of the East India Company to a Board of Control appointed by the Crown, and the impeachment of Warren Hastings in 1787 were symptoms of this new interest, half-humanitarian and half-imperial.

. . . .

The commercial aptitude of the nation perpetually modified its habits. It was not only to be seen in the spread of new luxuries into farm and cottage[2] and the splendour of the metropolis, an eighteenth-century imperial Rome whose red brick houses marched

[1] Parliament in its gloom abolished the third Secretaryship of State (for the Colonies) and the Board of Trade.—C.H.B.E. II, 1.

[2] Rochefoucauld (p. 23) noted that the humblest peasant had his tea twice a day just like the rich man.

in shapely ranks under the dome of St. Paul's, with its dazzling shops—"drapers, stationers, confectioners, printsellers, hosiers, fruiterers, china-sellers, one close to another without intermission, a shop to every house, street after street and mile after mile." The race was setting out on its long trek from country to town. Already London had more than three-quarters of a million inhabitants with a circuit of twenty miles from Millbank in the west to Limehouse and Poplar hamlet in the east and from Islington in the north to Newington in the south.[1] Elsewhere population was concentrating itself in urban entities of a kind unknown to the civic culture of the past. By 1790 Manchester had 80,000 inhabitants, Liverpool and Birmingham over 70,000 and Leeds 50,000. The population of Lancashire, hitherto one of the most barren areas of England, had grown to 600,000.

For here on that humid western slope of England an industry had arisen to rival the cloth trade of Yorkshire. It had grown out of the demand for the bright cotton goods of India. Raw cotton, it was found, could be grown with slave labour on the plantations of the southern American colonies. The traditional skill of English spinners and weavers and the astonishing ingenuity of British inventors did the rest. In 1771 Richard Arkwright, a Bolton barber, improving on the earlier work of the handloom weaver, Hargreaves of Blackburn, set up the first water-propelled spinning frame in Derbyshire: eight years later Samuel Crompton, a Lancashire farmer and weaver, invented his spinning mule. These changed the entire nature of the industry and ultimately of British domestic life. The factory with its myriad turning machines took the place of the cottage spinning wheel. In 1741 Britain exported £20,000 worth of cotton goods; in 1790 £1,662,369 worth.

The northern deserts with their water power and coal-seams became transformed. Gaunt buildings with rows of windows rose like giant wraiths on the wild Matlock hills and in the misty Lancashire valleys under the Pennines, and around them rows of cheerless, squalid little houses. Within a few years quiet old market towns like Rochdale swelled into noisy, straggling cities, filled with unwashed, pagan spinners and weavers: they seemed to a Tory of the old school "insolent, abandoned and drunk half the week." The capital of this area, now given over to the service of Mammon, was the old Jacobite town of Manchester, whose new population huddled together in damp, stinking cellars. Its port, importing corn and

[1] Gouverneur Morris reported in 1790 that from the western gateway of Hyde Park Corner to Chiswick village there was an almost continuous suburban highway running through the Middlesex meadows and market gardens: "should the peace be preserved for twenty years this overgrown capital would become immense." Morris I, 556.

raw cotton, was upstart Liverpool, home of the West Indian trade and its scandalous offspring, the slave trade, with windmills and warehouses full of flies, rum and sugar crowding for a mile along the northern bank of the Mersey.

Farther south in a formerly wild countryside another industrial area was growing up round the coal and iron-fields of Staffordshire and north Warwickshire. This was the Black Country—by 1790 a land of forges, collieries and canals with grimy trees and hedges. The traveller, venturing into this little-trodden, satanic region, saw rows of blackened hovels swarming with ragged children, and instead of church spires tall chimneys belching metallic vapours and at night lit by flames. At its southern extremity was Birmingham—a squalid village afflicted with elephantiasis where "crusty knaves that scud the streets in aprons seemed ever ready to exclaim, 'Be busy and grow rich!'" and where the head grew dizzy with the hammering of presses, the clatter of engines and the whirling of wheels. Here almost every man in the cobbled streets stank of train oil, and many had red eyes and hair bleached green by the brass foundries.

A few miles from Birmingham, the "toyshop of Europe," lay the great Soho manufactory of Boulton & Watt. Here over his own works lived the princely capitalist who in the course of thirty virtuous and laborious years turned the creative genius of a Scottish engineer, James Watt, into a dynamic force to refashion the world. Here the first practical cylindrical steam-engines were placed on the market, and manufacturers, statesmen and princes flocked to see the first wonder of Europe and buy the commodity which all the world of Mammon needed—"power." Such men as Boulton were pioneers of a new race, serving and exploiting the needs of their fellow-creatures with an energy and disregard for all other objects that make them loom through the mists of time like Titans. John Horrocks, the Quaker spinner, beginning work in a horse quarry, within fifteen years amassed a fortune of three-quarters of a million and entered Parliament as member for his native town. Josiah Wedgwood of Etruria, exploiting the contemporary love for the ceramic art, made £500,000 out of pottery and transformed a wild moorland into a hive of smoking ovens trodden by thousands of horses and donkeys laden with panniers and by men and women with faces whitened with potter's powder. Far below them in the social scale but travelling the same adventurous road were newer and ever newer capitalists: dispossessed yeomen venturing their little all in the fierce industrial hurly-burly, or spinners earning, perhaps, 35/- a week, working what would be regarded to-day as inconceivable hours[1] and denying themselves every comfort to purchase a mill where others should work as hard for them in their turn.

Moralists deplored what was happening and in the spread of depravity and atheism predicted revolution. Instead of thinking of national well-being, statesmen and men of substance, they argued, were becoming obsessed with sordid considerations of profit-making. By 1798 there were 100,000 men and women and 60,000 children working in the cotton mills, many of the latter indentured by Poor Law Guardians to masters who treated them little better than slaves. Yet the national conscience was not asleep but only overwhelmed by a multiplicity of new activities and openings for money-making. A great people, firmly launched on the ocean of untrammelled enterprise, was bound to commit errors, even crimes. Liberty had her economic gales as well as political. Yet the sea of endeavour was wide, and it was open. There was room to correct mistakes.

For all the while an eternal transformation was taking place. As popular energy, overwhelming the barriers of restriction, swept away obstructions to the free flow of trade and talent[2] the competition of ruder types tended to outproduce and undersell those already established. The genteel merchants of Bristol, mellowed by a hundred years of wealth and refinement, were no match for the products of pushing, hungry Liverpool, whose merchant captains were content with a seventh of the wages paid to their haughtier rivals. Those who had their way to make by a natural process caught up and ultimately outdistanced those with an inherited start. At first sight this seemed to threaten a progressive debasement of culture and social standards: the tough and the shover ever tending to shoulder out the gentleman and the fair dealer. Yet, as one bucket in the well of commerce fell, the other rose: the national passion for emulation constantly replanted the standards of quality in fresh soil; the greasy, aproned, clog-footed mechanic of one generation became the worthy merchant of the next. And if the process of cultural rise was not so quick as that of fall, the artistic and intellec-

[1] Some kept themselves awake at night by singing "Christians Awake!"—Fremantle, I, 51.

[2] The strength of the popular tide that was flowing towards complete freedom of trade is illustrated by a letter written in 1767 by Lord Kinnoul to a young Scottish laird, Thomas Graham of Balgowan, destined many years later to become Wellington's right-hand man in Spain. "We see by daily experience the fatal effects of politics upon industry and manufactures; and the great towns of Birmingham, Sheffield and Manchester feel the superior advantage of not sending members to Parliament, and likewise that of not being hampered with the fetters of the exclusive privileges which corporations enjoy. By these means genius has free scope, and industry is exerted to the utmost without control, check, or interruption."—*Lynedoch*, 4.

tual reserves of society were so vast that they could afford a good deal of dilution.

For in culture England had never stood higher, not even in the age of Shakespeare or that of Wren and Newton. Samuel Johnson had died in 1784 and Goldsmith ten years earlier. But in 1790 Reynolds, Romney, Gainsborough, Opie, Rowlandson, Stubbs and the young Lawrence were all painting. Cowper, Crabbe and Blake were writing poetry, Boswell was putting the last touches to the greatest biography in the language, and Gibbon had two years before finished its grandest history. Wordsworth was born in 1770, Coleridge in 1772, Turner, Jane Austen and Charles Lamb in 1775, Constable in 1776, Hazlitt in 1778, de Quincey in 1785 and Byron in 1788. Shelley was still to be born in 1792 and Keats in 1795. North of the border, where Adam Smith of Glasgow had established an international reputation as the first political economist of the age, Edinburgh was just entering upon her brief but glorious flowering of native wit as the northern Athens. Raeburn was beginning to paint, Dugald Stewart to lecture, Walter Scott was studying the romantic lore of his country and an Ayrshire ploughman, by name Robert Burns, had published his first volume. And in the realm of science the achievements of late eighteenth-century Britain were equally remarkable. Joseph Black, the chemist, Hunter the founder of scientific surgery, Priestley the discoverer of oxygen, and Jenner who conquered the scourge of smallpox, are among its great names. It was an age of gold that had the Adam brothers as its architects, Cosway as its miniaturist, Hepplewhite and Sheraton as its cabinet-makers. In the drawing-rooms of London and of the lovely pastoral mansions that looked out on to the dreaming gardens of Repton and Capability Brown[1] a society moved, brocaded, white-stockinged and bewigged, more gracious, more subtle, more exquisitely balanced than any seen on earth since the days of ancient Greece.

Yet this society was governed by no fixed and absolute laws, confined by no insurmountable barriers. Under its delicate polish lay a heart of stout and, as the event was to prove, impenetrable oak. Its people were tough to the core. "I shall be conquered, I will not capitulate," cried Dr. Johnson as he wrestled with death, guiding the surgeon's blade with his own hand. The Duke of Portland at 68 underwent an operation for the stone and was seven minutes under the knife without a murmur. Diminutive Jacob Bryant, the great classical antiquary, asked by his sovereign what branch of

[1] "The laying out of the ground in a natural way is carried to greater perfection in England than in any part of Europe. In foreign countries . . . the taste of gardening is forced and unnatural. . . . They constrain and counteract nature; we endeavour to humour and assist her."—Lord Kinnoul to Thos. Graham, *Lynedoch*, 5.

activity he was most noted for at Eton, answered to the astonishment of his auditor: "Cudgelling, sir, I was most famous for that." Young girls wore sticks of holly in their bosoms to teach them to hold their heads high, old Edge of Macclesfield at 62 walked 172 miles in under fifty hours for a bet; the King rose daily at 4 a.m. and spent three hours on the government dispatch boxes before taking his morning ride in Windsor Park. And the common people were tougher, if it were possible, than their betters. At Shirley village in Bedfordshire the penny barber told a traveller that he never used a brush since his customers, complaining of the tickling, preferred to be shaved dry.

They were fighters to a man: a race as game as the cocks they backed in the crowded, stinking pits of Jewin Street and Hockcliffe. When challenged they fought to the death. "Look, you, sir," cried old General Sherbrooke to a fellow-officer who had offended him, "my hands are now behind my back, and I advise you to leave the room before they are brought forward, for if they once are, I will break every bone in your body." "Why, my little man," asked one of the East India Directors of twelve-year-old John Malcolm at his interview for a commission, "what would you do if you met Hyder Ali?" "Cut off his heid," came the instant reply.

Boxing was the favourite pastime of the nation: all seemed ready at a moment's notice to roll up their sleeves for a mill as they had done on the sward under the billyard at Harrow or behind the church wall in the village at home. The last years of the eighteenth century saw the classic age of the Fancy: of John Gully and Robert Gregson, the Lancashire giant, Cribb and Belcher and Gentleman Jackson: the ringside under the open sky with its packed, democratic crowd lying, squatting and kneeling around it and the top-hatted seconds shadowing the combatants in their shirt-sleeves. The young lordlings of the day were never so proud as when they forgathered with their favourite champions at Zimmer's Hotel or took their lessons in the manly pastime in Gentleman Jackson's rooms in Bond Street. When the Jew Mendoza on April 17th, 1787, beat Martin in the presence of the Prince of Wales he was brought back to London with lighted torches and to the strains of Handel's "See the Conquering Hero Comes."

Yet in all this brutal bruising—and in those days of gloveless, timeless contests a dead man sometimes lay on the sward before the sport was done—there was curiously little bullying. "In England," wrote Southey's visiting Spaniard, "a boxing match settles all disputes among the lower classes, and when it is over they shake hands and are friends. Another equally beneficial effect is the security to the weaker by the laws of honour which forbid all undue advantages; the man who should aim a blow below the waist, who should kick his antagonist, strike him when he is down or attempt to injure him after he had yielded, would be sure to experience the resentment of the mob who on such occasions always assemble to see what they call fair play which they enforce as rigidly as the Knights of the Round Table and the laws of Chivalry."[1] It was not unfitting that this intensely individualistic, quarrelsome and stubborn race should have this rough and equalitarian sport to even harsh tempers and teach the sobering lessons of defeat.

At the heart of the English character lay a fund of kindliness. Though in the mass rough and often cruel, and passionately addicted to barbarous sports like bull-baiting and cock-fighting, they led the world in humanitarian endeavour. It was an Englishman who in the 'seventies and 'eighties, at extreme risk and personal inconvenience, travelled 50,000 miles visiting the putrid, typhus-ridden jails of Europe; and it was Englishmen who at the close of the century first instituted organised opposition to cruelty to children and animals. But nothing so well illustrates the slow but persistent national impulse to mitigate inhumanity as the popular condemnation of the slave trade. This movement ran directly counter to the immediate material interests of the country; it none the less steadily gained strength from its inception by a handful of Quakers in the 'sixties until at the end of the century it was espoused by the Prime Minister himself and the overwhelming majority of thinking Englishmen.

The transatlantic slave trade had grown up to meet the needs of Britain's plantations in the West Indies and American colonies. Its headquarters was Liverpool, whose merchants imported seven-eighths of the negroes brought from Africa to America. In return for the slaves sold to the planters, they brought back to England sugar, rum, cotton, coffee. Thus the whole of the country indirectly benefited from this horrible traffic. The slaves, many of whom were kidnapped, were taken from the West African coast across the "Middle Passage" to the West Indies in crowded slavers, loaded three slaves to a ton, the poor chained wretches being packed so tightly between decks that they were often forced to lie on top of one another. The mortality both of seamen and human cargo was appalling, but the smaller the consignment of slaves that arrived, the better the price paid for the remainder. For the laws of supply and demand, when allowed to find their true level, always operated beneficially!

[1] *Espriella*, III, 311.

As is the way with conservative-minded people whose interests are vested in an abuse, every reason was found to justify the continuance of the traffic.[1] Liverpool merchants and their parliamentary representatives declared that, were a measure passed to regulate the miseries of the Middle Passage, the West Indian trade would be ruined, Britain's commercial supremacy lost and the Navy be left denuded of trained seamen.

Yet having once been brought to the not very observant notice of the British people, the slave trade was doomed. For with all its barbaric survivals, Britain was a land of decent folk: of men and women with conscience. And because of the blend of freedom with order in British political institutions, the dictates of that conscience, though slow to mature, were ultimately given effect. Barbarous laws and customs[2]—men hanged in public for petty crimes, lunatics chained to the wall knee-deep in verminous straw, animals tortured at Smithfield and in the bull-ring—of these and their like there were plenty, but they were continually being ameliorated by the advancing pressure of public opinion. Gradually but instinctively a nation of freemen turned towards the light. That age-long process was the justification of their freedom.

For by freedom the English meant something more than freedom for themselves, though they certainly meant that. Conventional and conservative in their prejudices, often thoughtless and mentally lazy, they yet genuinely valued freedom for its own sake: for others, that is, as well as for themselves. And their ideal of liberty was never an abstraction. It was based not on generalising but on measuring: on an impartial calculation of the comparative rights and wrongs of every individual case. Burke's dictum, "If I cannot reform with equity, I will not reform at all," was a curiously English saying for an Irishman. It expressed the intensely personal interpretation of the national conception of freedom.

It derived from the Christian faith acknowledged by the peoples of all the other lands of Europe save those of the Turk. Heretics in Catholic eyes, backsliders in those of Geneva, the rustic English by the very freedom of their beliefs kept perhaps nearer to the Christian pattern of life than any other people. Dogma counted

[1] Boswell in his *Life of Johnson* went so far as to claim that "to abolish a status which in all ages God has sanctioned and man has continued, would not only be robbery to an innumerable class of our fellow subjects, but it would be extreme cruelty to the African savages, a portion of whom it saves from massacre or intolerable bondage in their own country and introduces into a much happier state of life. . . . To abolish that trade would be to 'shut the gates of mercy on mankind.'" Many honourable men at the time agreed with him.

[2] Rochefoucauld (p. 31) noted with astonishment that the sideboards of the most aristocratic houses were furnished with chamberpots which, after the departure of the ladies, were resorted to freely by the gentlemen as the drink circulated.

less for them than fair dealing, ritual than honesty. By their laws neither priest nor king had any power to constrain the individual conscience, for such constraint seemed to them unjust. Save for Holland, England was the only European country in which men might worship God in any way they pleased. The multiplicity of their beliefs was bewildering. A French visitor thought that the only point in which they agreed was in every Englishman believing in some particular peculiar to himself alone.

It was true that there was a State Church to which the majority of Englishmen still belonged and whose membership conferred civic privilege. But this was regarded not so much as a religious matter as one of political convenience, and was partly aimed at stopping clerical power from falling into the hands of those less tolerantly inclined.[1] The Church of England was supported by Parliament not because it had a monopoly of truth but because it was thought the most suitable medium for promulgating Christian teaching. "Gentlemen," said Lord Chancellor Thurlow to the deputation of Nonconformists which waited on him in 1788 to ask for a repeal of the Corporation and Test Acts, "I'm against you, by God. I am for the Established Church, damme! Not that I have any more regard for the Established Church than for any other Church, but because it is established. And if you can get your damned religion established, I'll be for that too!"[2]

After a century's monopoly of the loaves and fishes it cannot be said that the Church of England was in a very flourishing state. There was a good deal of pluralism, in some cases amounting to downright scandal, much neglect both of church and parishioner and a general atmosphere of comfortable complacency. Almost a quarter of the nine thousand parishes were without resident incumbents, and in many churches there was an uninspiring atmosphere of damp and decay: weeds grew in the graveyard and small boys played fives in the shady corner under the belfry. And the new classes which commerce was creating in place of the old world of status were little regarded by comfortable clergymen obsessed by thoughts of tithes and good living.

Yet here also the fidelity of the English to the principles of freedom came to their aid. Those whom the Church neglected, the rejected of the Church cared for. The missionary journeys of the early Methodists among the pagan outcasts of industrial Britain

[1] The denial of political rights to the small Catholic minority in England, which in Ireland amounted to a grave social injustice, was persisted in from a widespread belief that Catholics used political power to establish religious despotism. The most popular British festivals were those that celebrated past escapes from "Popish tyranny."

[2] Crabb Robinson, *Diary*, I, 378.

evoked a Christian revival in the quarter where it was least expected and most needed. Wesleyans and Evangelicals, Nonconformists of the older denominations and Quakers stepped in and did God's work where well-endowed complacency failed. Among the roughest of the rough—the lonely weavers of Yorkshire and Lancashire and the foul-mouthed miners of Durham and Cornwall—thousands of men were to be found practising a faith as pure as that taught by Christ to the fishermen of Galilee and using with quaint but moving effect the phraseology of the Bible. This noble work of reconversion—the supreme triumph of eighteenth-century English individualism—served not only spiritual but political ends. As much as any other single factor the faith and discipline of Methodism helped to save Britain from the fate of revolutionary France.

This may be claiming too much. England with her solid heart of sober, quiet folk had such reserves of strength that it is hard to estimate her breaking point. The living oak could carry an astonishing burden of dead wood. To comprehend the real England one must probe beneath the rich variegated surface—the splendours of aristocratic salons and provincial parks and palaces, the gambling dens and cockpits of the metropolis, the grim sores of factory and foetid slum—and seek her in the calm continuity of family life. The lessons handed down from mother to daughter, the hereditary craft taught the boy at his father's knee, the sturdy children playing together in the orchard, the clean-dressed, home-spun village people taking the road to church on Sunday morning, here were the enduring roots of national life. It was of these that the Anglican creed was the decorous, devout expression, commemorating the virtues of the past and consecrating the aspirations of the present. The highest tribute ever paid the Establishment was that of the Duke of Wellington, who, looking back over a quarter of a century of war and revolution, declared with whatever exaggeration: "It is the Church of England that has made England what she is—a nation of honest men."

. . . .

In the pages of John Nyren's *The Cricketers of My Time*, published in 1833, the author recalled the men of Hambledon with whom he had grown up in the 'seventies and 'eighties of the previous century. In his gallery of cricketing heroes we see the fathers of the men who tended the guns at Trafalgar and manned the squares at Waterloo. We can watch them over his old shoulders, making their way with curved bat and eager eye up the woodland road from Hambledon village to the downland pitch at Broad-Halfpenny on the first Tuesday in May. The dew is still on the grass and the sun is shining high over "Old Winchester" as they take the field against All England. Here is little George Lear, the famous long-stop, so sure that he might have been a sand-bank, and his friend, Tom Sueter, the wicket-keeper who loved to join him in a glee at the "Bat and Ball"; Lambert, "the little farmer" whose teasing art, so fatal to the Kent and Surrey men, had been mastered in solitude by bowling away hours together at a hurdle while tending his father's sheep; and "those anointed clod-stumpers, the Walkers, Tom and Harry" with their wilted, apple-john faces and long spidery legs as thick at the ankles as at the hips. "Tom was the driest and most rigid-limbed chap; . . . his skin was like the rind of an old oak, and as sapless. . . . He moved like the rude machinery of a steam-engine in the infancy of construction, and when he ran, every member seemed ready to fly to the four winds. He toiled like a tar on horseback."

What Wellington became to his Peninsula veterans and "Daddy" Hill to Wellington, Richard Nyren was to the Hambledon cricketers and John Small to Nyren. "I never saw," his son recorded, "a finer specimen of the thoroughbred old English yeoman than Richard Nyren. He was a good face-to-face, unflinching, uncompromising independent man. He placed a full and just value upon the station he held in society and maintained it without insolence or assumption. He could differ with a superior, without trenching upon *his* dignity or losing his own." And his *fidus Achates*, yeoman Small, was worthy of him. He loved music, was an adept at the fiddle and taught himself the double bass. He once calmed a bull by taking out his instrument and playing it in the middle of a field. His fellow-cricketer, the Duke of Dorset, hearing of his musical talent, sent him a handsome violin and paid the carriage. "Small, like a true and simple-hearted Englishman, returned the compliment by sending his Grace two bats and balls, also paying the carriage."

In the English memory there are few lovelier scenes than that famous pitch on the Hampshire down. When "Silver Billy" Beldham—the first bat of the age—was in or runs were hard to get and the finish close, Sir Horace Mann, that stalwart patron of the game, would pace about outside the ground cutting down the daisies with his stick in his agitation and the old farmers under the trees would lean forward upon their tall staves, silent. "Oh! it was a heart-stirring sight to witness the multitude forming a complete and dense circle round that noble green. Half the county would be present, and all their hearts with us.—Little Hambledon, pitted against All England, was a proud thought for the Hampshire men. Defeat was glory in such a struggle—Victory, indeed, made us only 'a little lower than angels.' How those fine brawn-faced fellows of farmers would drink to our success! And then what stuff they had to drink! Punch!—not your new *Ponche à la Romaine*, or *Ponche à la Groseille*, or your modern cat-lap milk punch—punch be-deviled; but good, unsophisticated, John Bull stuff—stark! that would stand on end—punch that would make a cat speak! . . . Ale that would flare like turpentine—genuine Boniface!"

"There would this company, consisting most likely of some thousands, remain patiently and anxiously watching every turn of fate in the game, as if the event had been the meeting of two armies to decide their liberty. And whenever a Hambledon man made a good hit, worth four or five runs, you would hear the deep mouths of the whole multitude baying away in pure Hampshire—'Go hard!—Go hard!—*Tich* and turn!—*tich* and turn!' To the honour of my countrymen . . . I cannot call to recollection an instance of their wilfully stopping a ball that had been hit out among them by one of our opponents. Like *true* Englishmen, they would give an enemy fair play. How strongly are all those scenes, of fifty years by-gone, painted in my memory!—and the smell of that ale comes upon me as freshly as the new May flowers."

The words of Mercury are harsh after the songs of Apollo. From the high hill which rose out of the woods beyond the pitch one could see on clear days half southern England—valley and down and forest. Over that wide countryside the sea winds never ceased to blow from every point of the compass, free as the hearts of oak the land bred. Waving trees and smoke fluttering like a ragged banner, feathery heath, lonely cottages at the edge of moor and forest, ragged cows and geese and ponies pasturing in the wild by ancient prescribed rights. Tidal rivers flowing through marshes to the ocean with black cattle grazing at their salt edges and wooden cobles and crab-boats tossing on their silver bosom, land of semi-nomads, gatherers of shellfish, fowlers, longshore fishermen and armed smugglers—of Slip-jibbet and Moonshine Buck tip-trotting by in the dark with tubs of Geneva for the parson and "baccy for the Clerk." Sometimes travellers and shepherds near the coast would see the fleet of England riding at Spithead in one of the broad bays of the Channel shore; "pleasant and wonderful was the sight as seen from Ridgeway Hill, with the West Bay and the Isle of Portland and Weymouth and Melcombe Regis, all lying in the calm sunshine," wrote Elizabeth Ham in after years, "I see it now."[1]

Further inland were the familiar objects of the country scene: the reapers in the golden field, the cottages of wattle and timber with their massive brick chimneys and deep-abiding thatch, the mill

[1] MS. *Diary of Elizabeth Ham.*

with its weather-boarded walls and throbbing wheel amid willows and alders, the saw pit with sweating craftsmen and stacked timber, the leafy lane with the great hairy-footed horses drawing home the wain laden with hay and laughing children. Along the high roads bright liveried postilions glinted like jewels before swaying post-chaises, and postmen riding or mounted high on coaches passed in the scarlet livery of England. With infinite slowness, soon overtaken by these fast-moving ones, a vast tilted stage-waggon crawled like a snail behind its eight horses, their neck bells making discordant music while the carrier trudged beside idly cracking his whip in the air. Along the road were haymakers at their work, mansions with ancient trees and cropping deer, and at every village the blacksmith's forge with old Vulcan looking out from his open door, "grey and hairy as any badger." And perhaps as it grew dark and the lights were lit on the coaches, the traveller might overtake a neighbouring gentleman's hounds, as John Byng did one May evening, coming home from an airing.

Within the candle-lit windows of the wayside cottage and the farmhouse on the hill, old John Bull would sit dozing with his pot beside the kitchen fire, the dog and cat asleep at his feet, the good wife at her wheel, the pretty maid his daughter coming in with her pail, the children playing with the caged bird, the tinder-box on the shelf, the onions and flitches hanging from the ceiling. From this home he was presently to go out to face and tame a world in arms. For the moment he was content and at his ease, perhaps more so than was good for his continuing soul. In the tavern down in the village old England still lived on where over their pipes and bowls, gathered round the bare rude table, the local worthies with russet, weather-beaten faces cracked their joke and trolled their song. Though their summer was brief, before winter aches and penury encompassed them, they knew how to be merry. Cricket matches and fives playing, the crowd at the fair gathered round the cudgellers' high wooden stage, the squeak of a fiddle or the shrill cry of a mountebank with his Merry Andrew on the village green on a warm summer evening, the carolers and the mumming players coming out of the Christmas snows, these were the outward symbols of a race of freemen taking their pleasures in their own way as their fathers had done before them. It seemed a far cry from these peaceful scenes to the rough humours and turbulent racket of London—the butchers of Sheppards' Market and May Fair elbowing their way through the dirty streets to a hanging at Tyburn, the footpads in the shadows of Park Lane, the foetid cells of Newgate—or the restless, sullen money-making of Manchester and Birmingham. Yet all were part of an English whole whose meaning it was hard to compass in a word, but whose people were in a greater or lesser degree adherents of two dominant ideals—justice and their own freedom.

> "The nations not so blessed as thee,
> Must in their turn to tyrants fall;
> While thou shalt flourish great and free,
> The dread and envy of them all."

So sang the islanders in their favourite "Rule Britannia," and the words expressed their firm, unalterable conviction. Their very versatility was part of their heritage of liberty. "Now in as hot a climate as that of the East or West Indies and sometimes in winter feel the cold of Greenland," wrote John Byng, "up and down; hence we are precarious, uncertain, wild, enduring mortals. And may we so endowed continue, the wonder and balance of the universe."

CHAPTER TWO

The Gates of Brass

1789

"Liberty, like happiness, is most perfect when least remarked. As most misery is caused by the pursuit of an abstract happiness, distinct from the occupations that make men happy, so most tyranny springs from the struggle for an abstract liberty, distinct from the laws and institutions that make men free."

Christopher Hobhouse, *Fox.*

ON Tuesday, 14th July, 1789—more than three years before the event described at the beginning of this book—a great multitude of men and women assembled in front of the Bastille, the old royal fortress of Paris. They were in a state of intense excitement. They demanded that the governor, de Launey, who held the place for the young King of France, should hand it over to the representatives of the people. The governor, whose command consisted of eighty old pensioners and thirty Swiss Guards, did his best to appease them: showed them the emptiness of the fortress and had the ancient guns, long used only for ceremonial purposes, pulled back from the embrasures. But the crowd was in no mood for reason. Behind it all Paris, surging through narrow, cobbled streets, was in revolution, the tocsin was tinging from every tower and a great flag, which was not the flag of the French monarchy, was being borne above a raging, shouting, trampling human river.

As the pressure grew the governor, who had admitted the crowd into the outer courtyard, had the drawbridge leading to the inner court raised. Then someone severed the chains of the bridge with an axe and it dropped, letting the mob into the heart of the castle. Firing began, and for four hours the people, delirious with rage and excitement, hurled themselves at the walls. During these hours the Bastille, with its high antique towers flickering crimson, became the symbol of a dying society: its death throes the commemoration of the birth of a new force in the world, terrible to all who opposed it, full of mysterious hope to those who accepted it.

A few minutes before the great clock of the Bastille tolled five someone in the garrison raised a white flag. There was some parleying through a porthole, a hasty promise of parole by an unofficial spokesman and then as the doors were unbolted all Hell let loose. For an hour the multitude from the medieval streets swarmed through the fortress howling for blood. Old de Launey and his officers were torn to pieces and their heads mounted on pikes. The dazed prisoners—four coiners, a sadistic debauchee and two madmen—were let out into the glare and sulphurous air of the new freedom. Then the mob poured back into the city, bearing aloft the dripping heads like banners, to murder the chief magistrate in the Hotel-de-Ville.

. . . .

The storming of the Bastille told the world that the greatest nation in Europe was in revolution. It shattered the stagnant calm of the eighteenth century. It announced that Frenchmen were no longer prepared to accept the social beliefs on which public order depended.

For the foundation which supported those beliefs had ceased to exist. The basis of the feudal polity of Christian Europe, evolved gradually out of the anarchy that followed the fall of Rome, was that the enjoyment of property and privilege involved the fulfilment of social duty. The Knight and Baron held their lands by tenure of caring for them and those who lived on them: of affording to the cultivator the protection of law and order and defence against aggressor, robber and wild beast. The lord fought, hunted and gave law for all and the peasant ploughed for all, and in a primitive age when all occupation was hereditary both transmitted their obligations to their children. This compact of mutual security ran in an ascending scale through all the stages of society, each petty lord securing his peace and property by vassalage to some more powerful lord. Kings and princes paid fealty to a supreme "Emperor," elected for life from their number and wielding in theory the vanished authority of the Roman Empire and Charlemagne. Binding them all in one faith and morality was the universal or Catholic Church with its great underlying principle that all men's souls were equal in the fatherhood of God. While the lord fought for all and the husbandman ploughed for all, the priest prayed for all. The tithes and endowments of the medieval Church were the price paid by the community for this service.

The grandeur of its Gothic cathedrals, its achievements in agriculture and the arts, its triumphs in arms testified Europe's debt to the system of Christian feudalism. But save in isolated corners its practice had long ceased to bear any relation to its theory. Those in whose hands the sword was placed used it not as a trust but as a means of aggrandisement, those who held land by tenure of service treated it as their absolute property, those who administered pious endowments converted them to their own use. And though everywhere men still confessed and called themselves Christians, the unity and faith had gone out of Christendom. Instead of an indivisible Catholic Church there was an anarchy of warring sects and dogmas. Instead of a united Christian polity there was a discord of national States—France, Spain, Austria, Russia, Prussia—whose rulers seemed absorbed in outwitting one another and adding to their territories. The smaller units of Christendom were everywhere threatened by the lack of principle of the powerful. They only survived at all through Britain's age-long opposition to unbalanced power and because of the chronic financial embarrassment of their larger neighbours.

For from one end of the Continent to the other, bankruptcy impended. To the monarchies of the eighteenth century it was what unemployment became to the democracies of the twentieth. Behind the costly splendour of their palladian palaces, gilded clothes and aristocratic elegance leered the same shocking spectre. The trim, butterfly-coloured, goose-stepping armies, the crowded, resounding Courts, the picturesque schemes of public improvement with which enlightened monarchs endeavoured to immortalise their names wanted paying for. And despite crushing taxation and every ingenious expedient known to spendthrifts and borrowers, there was never enough to balance accounts. The higher the taxation, the poorer became everybody but a few. So desperate was the task of raising the wind, that many statesmen pinned their hopes on alchemy and the mystical researches of the Rosicrucians. In the whole of Europe only Pitt's England and the great banking republic of Holland remained solvent.

The causes of this were not understood. Men saw clearly enough that the old system for initiating and directing human enterprise had ceased to work. What they failed to comprehend was that a new economic power had risen in its place whose machinery, unable to operate in the outworn conditions of a fundamentally different society, only aggravated the situation. The original basis of the feudal system was Christian responsibility. The original basis of medieval creative art was the glory of God. When these ceased to provide motive power for economic activity, their place was taken by usury. But usury could not keep the wheels of society turning if the continuous material development, which was essential to pay perpetual interest on capital, was impeded by a static system of law and status.

But though the professional financier was forthcoming to advance capital to earth's titular rulers, the latter, hampered by restrictive laws and customs devised for an opposite ideal of life, were unable to increase the productivity of their domains fast enough to pay the interest. Borrowing lavishly to meet the requirements of an increasingly complex and luxurious civilisation, they were constantly on the verge of default, and were driven to ever fresh borrowings at still more exorbitant rates. To meet these commitments and finance their costly wars they sought to exact more in taxes from their subjects—or from such of them as they could legally tax—than the latter were able to pay. In Brandenburg eight out of nine and three-quarter crowns—the annual yield of a thirty-acre peasant holding—were taken by the State. The contradiction between two conflicting conceptions of society created a mathematical impossibility. The new freedom of finance, loosed from the fetters of Canon law, was not matched by freedom of trade, labour and contract. The result was universal frustration. Britain and Holland—though it cost the former her American empire—escaped disaster because in both countries with their more elastic constitutions the feudal system had been gradually modified in the interests of commerce. Here alone a system of cheap State borrowing had been erected on a popular basis of funded property and rationally-appropriated taxation.

Such were the causes of the poverty which, despite splendid Courts, noble culture and skilful journeymen, hung like a miasma over a rich continent. The peasants ground down by State taxes, feudal dues and tithes, lived scarcely better than the beasts they tended. Throughout Germany, Italy, Spain and eastern Europe they were still serfs, tied by status to the land and without equality of legal rights. The mutual services they should have received from their feudal overlords were no longer paid. Their bowed backs bore the burden of an ever-growing number of idle nobles and clerics endowed by their ancestors and the pious benefactors of past ages with the fruits of the soil for all time.

The evil was cumulative. The rights exacted from society by the aristocrat, like those of the usurer, were perpetual. On the Continent, not only the eldest son but the entire family of the man ennobled became hereditary nobles down to the last generation. There was no moderation in this conception of aristocracy. These privileged creatures, themselves mostly impecunious on account of their expanding numbers, were exempted from every new burden of a more complicated social life, including taxation. They existed partly by scrambling for the public sinecures which were reserved for their kind and partly by the feudal dues levied on the cultivator.

The state of the cities was little better. The larger kind of merchant, with the capital to finance the bad debts of his noble clients, could make fortunes out of their extravagance and ineptitude. But the journeyman, who bore the ultimate shock of unpaid bills, chaotic finances and recurrent wars, was desperate. The streets of every Continental town swarmed with beggars. "The people of this place," wrote an English girl of Piave, "have a frightful aspect: they looked more like beasts than men, and they were so nasty and dirty that I could not stay a moment without being tormented with the idea of catching some nastiness or other." A traveller in 1768 noted that, compared with the inns between Naples and Rome, the worst Highland alehouse was a palace.

. . . .

The absurdity of the universal contrast between poverty and plenty stared the thinker and philosopher in the face. The system on which the life of Europe depended was outworn, its underlying thesis become ridiculous. It was absurd for the working part of mankind which lived in hovels and had not enough to eat to pay for the maintenance of an aristocracy which had ceased to perform any of the duties for which it was designed. It was equally absurd for men to scrape and starve in order to support in un-Christian ostentation bishops and abbots who neglected their spiritual charge for dicing and love-making. Society could only be freed by shaking off its ancient shackles. A new social contract was needed.

So writers and philosophers preached throughout the eighteenth century, ridiculing the absurdities of the old system and extolling the virtues of an Utopian age of reason which would presently succeed it. Human reason, they felt, when released from outworn prejudice, was capable of solving every terrestial problem. In France a succession of brilliant men led the revolt of the mind against the tyranny of custom. They claimed that the universe was governed by certain simple and logical laws: that on their observance human happiness depended and that it was within the power of reason to discover and apply them. Some—the Physiocrats—confined their efforts to seeking a natural economic law and found it in the removal of the unnatural barriers that feudal moralists had erected to regulate the flow of commerce. "*Laissez faire et laissez passer*," was their open sesame. Others sought a political solution: a revolutionary law or constitution true for all ages and countries.

The philosophers, who were only expressing what every one felt, won supporters even among kings and princes. Struggling to govern in a tangle of dead wood and irrational aristocratic and clerical privilege and immunity, many of them welcomed these heralds of a simpler and—as it was hoped—more solvent order. Catherine the Great of Russia, Charles III of Spain, Frederick the Great of Prussia, Joseph II of Austria and Leopold of Tuscany were all enlightened rulers who patronised the fashionable French philosophers and Encyclopædists and endeavoured to put their theories into practice. In doing so they fell, to a greater or lesser degree, foul of the rights of the old order. Aristocrats, clerics, lawyers and city fathers and conservative folk generally united against them to defend their privileges. Thus the liberal-minded Joseph of Austria had to face a rebellion of his Belgian subjects; and even the autocrat of all the Russias discovered the necessity of going slow in enforcing the rule of reason on an unreasonable realm.

Thus, though the greater part of Europe was at one time or another governed by innovating royal despots or their Ministers, the age of gold tarried in coming. Peasants still died of hunger in ditches, beggars exhibited their sores in cathedral squares and State treasuries remained empty. And the useless nobles and priests, condemned in theory by every rational being, including their own more enlightened members, continued to enjoy indefensible privilege. Nor was it only their opposition which defeated the hopes of the philosopher kings. There seemed, for all their high and unquestionable intentions, to be something wrong with the kings themselves. They were logical and enlightened and clear-headed, but they were also greedy, vain and arrogant. In other words they were men and women. Frederick the Great might correspond with Voltaire, but he left his subjects cowed and stupid—"one cane to every seven men"—and his neighbours, who had suffered from his enlightened aggressions, fearful and suspicious. Kings with the power of reason were not uncommon, but they lacked morality. Moreover they were too often succeeded by half-wits and weaklings. Reason was not hereditary.

When the dream of regenerating society by a few "wise reigns" died, the greater part of Europe sank back into apathy. Courtiers and prelates continued to fritter away their time and rentals on good music and amoral conduct, burghers to stagnate and the "swinish multitude" to suffer. Only in France did hope survive. Here in the most brilliant Court and capital in the world the philosophers and their innumerable aristocratic and middle-class disciples continued to maintain that society could be regenerated and that man was not only perfectible but inherently good. He was merely corrupted by unreasonable laws, customs, and superstitions. If kings could not unloose these rusty chains, man by combining could cast them off himself. The nation had only to resume control of its own destiny, the people to renew with one another the natural contract of a just and rational society. The millennium was round the corner.

. . . .

France was the most powerful nation in Europe, with a population three times as big as that of England and nearly double that of the British Isles, and boasting a record of splendid achievement in arms, learning and the arts. Under Louis XIV she had threatened to establish a suzerainty over the whole Continent. Her advance had only been checked by the resolution of William III, who had marshalled the Powers of Europe and the genius of Marlborough against her. From those twenty years of aggression her finances had never recovered. Though her trade since 1713 had multiplied fivefold, she had never been able to shake off the burden of debt. The usurer's stranglehold frustrated instead of stimulating economic activity. A great nation was reduced to chronic impotence. A titanic exercise of energy was needed to break the vicious circle of bankruptcy and stagnation.

Though, with her virile, ingenious people, France's capacity to recover financial equilibrium seemed self-evident, her every effort to do so failed. The blame was laid at the door of the aristocrats whose irrational privileges alone appeared to stand between the nation and a happier future. Theoretically all power was centred in the throne, and the once-turbulent nobles of France had been reduced to an idle concourse of spineless courtiers, living lives of graceful dissipation around the palace of Versailles. Yet a weak King—and both the successors of Louis XIV were nonentities—exercised authority through those who surrounded him. These were the men of birth—the representatives of an exclusive hereditary corporation of about a quarter of a million persons—with a leaven of financiers, wits and adventurers who were admitted, on terms, into the charmed circle.

Increased privilege was the price which the sovereigns of France had paid the nobility for the loss of ancient powers—privilege not to do but to receive. The aristocrats who monopolised the first-fruits of French agriculture were exempted by perpetual Court attendance both from the local duties for which those first-fruits were paid and the taxes which maintained the public services. Every attempt to rationalise taxation—the only way in which bankruptcy could be averted—was opposed by their interest. Many nobles—for eighteenth-century France sparkled with enlightenment—sympathised with reform. But with swarms of needy and idle relations to support, few were in a position to waive their rights to fiscal immunity. Every Minister who tried to modify them was met by a dead-weight of obstruction. And in a Court where the lightest word of an irresolute King had power and where petticoat influence—legitimate and illegitimate—flourished, intrigues could wreck the plans of the most capable Minister. In theory the Government of France was despotic: in practice it had become almost the weakest in Europe. The dead hand of the past lay heavy on all: on the aristocrat who was the slave of his upbringing, on the government which was helpless in the face of feudal and local privilege, on the King who was only the chief slave of a nation enslaved to venerable inertia. Everything was discussed: nothing constructive ever done.

The aristocracy, debarred from activity and common contacts in the artificial air of Versailles, became, for all its wit and graceful breeding, anaemic and effete. It was a society that within its narrow range had much that was exquisite and lovely. Talleyrand in after years used to say that those who had not known it had not lived. But its members had lost the sense of social responsibility. A habit of all taking and no giving had made them inconsequent. As patrons of the philosophers they were the first to join in the fashionable intellectual derision of their own illogical privileges. Yet they did nothing to forgo or modify them. They scorned to unbend to the eager, middle-class *arrivistes* who pressed at their crimson heels. A little timely sacrifice of vanity might have saved them, their country and the world from untold suffering. They remained incurably frivolous.

The middle-class of France—alert and intelligent—was not frivolous. Debarred from all responsibility by its lack of quarterings, it was politically both ambitious and inexperienced. It devoured the work of the philosophers and longed for the day when its own natural intelligence and virtue would be employed to regenerate society. Because the aristocracy whose manners it aped stood in the way, because the aristocracy patronised, laughed at and ignored it, because the aristocracy had not a tenth of its talent and pent-up energy, it hated the aristocracy. It asked, in Figaro's rhetorical challenge, what the aristocrats had done to deserve so many good things and answered with embittered irony, "You have given yourselves the trouble of being born." It bowed enviously to, but sneered at, their titles, stars and sacred genealogical tables. Bankers and rich merchants and lawyers and their aspiring sons chafed at the elegant, haughty, insouciant creatures whose ancestors had been "*gentilhommes*" in the reign of Philip II and who treated them, when they called on business, in the steward's room. In their impotent wrath they turned not only against the aristocracy but against Church and King who supported the useless encumbrance with their authority. Holbach, the banker, in his salon said many witty, bitter things "*à faire tomber la tonnere sur sa maison.*" Diderot, the philosopher, wished to see "the last king strangled with the entrails of the last priest."

. . . .

The embittered bourgeois had urgent allies. The dumb millions, who did not read the Encyclopædists or mind whether their wives were received by the great ladies of the Court, were also growing restless. The unreason of France's administrative anarchy did not offend their pride or their intellect but something more serious—their stomach.

For the frugal and hard-working peasants wanted their land freed from the seignorial dues, tolls and services which kept the noble in ribbons and stars, gold louis for the faro table and jewels for his wife and mistresses. By incredible frugality they had acquired ownership of a third of the soil of France. And on this third, owing to the fiscal exemption of the nobility, the whole burden of taxation fell. The land which they had tilled so industriously and saved up with such fierce self-denial to buy was starved by the absentee landlords who should have been its custodians. The Court and the cities drained the countryside dry.

In bad years the French people went hungry. When there was no bread in the hovels of the wintry villages, the poorer peasants flocked to the towns where they joined the workless journeymen and the mob that lived on the middens and refuse-bins. In these seasons rumblings of the storm which was soon to break reached the ears of the rich. The nobility who had lost contact with reality paid little heed. The bourgeois, waiting his chance and the dawn of a golden future for humanity, saw in those pallid, drawn faces a challenge and an opportunity.

Such a season of hunger came with the winter of 1788-9. The financial impasse had been growing steadily worse since the war to help Britain's revolted colonies. Every fiscal device had been tried in turn to save the State's credit except the one fateful expedient: equalisation of taxation. But on that rock every reformer had broken.

. . . .

It was the paradox of France on the eve of storm that while her people's minds were full of fear, their hearts were full of hope. From the contemplation of the abyss that opened at their feet they looked across to a radiant vision of human perfection and happiness conjured up for them by the philosophers. Voltaire once observed that Rousseau's picture of the golden age was such that it made one want to walk on all fours. To the great Swiss writer who had inflamed the minds of educated France, the problems of the universe —so complex and daunting to the statesman—were clad in a divine simplicity. There was a key to the universe and its secrets that, used aright, would restore mankind to its primitive heritage of innocent peace and joy. That key was the human reason.

For on the elemental truth that reason was sacred and that every man, possessing reason, partook of the divine, Rousseau had erected an airy superstructure so flattering to human nature that its appeal to those conscious of the misgovernment of eighteenth-century France was irresistible. Since all men enjoyed reason and reason was divine, all men—in their exercise of reason—were equal in potential wisdom. To substitute Utopia for chaos and frustration it was only necessary to frame a constitution in which the dictates of individual reason and the laws of the State were the same. Somewhere, discoverable by the statesman, was *la Volonté Génerale*—a General Will expressing the aggregate reason of everyman. It was the same as the will of God. Every antiquated, irrational law of King, Priest or Noble that stood in its way was blasphemy.

Such a doctrine was as heartening as it was flattering. It offered an immediate hope that the weight could be lifted from all shoulders. It told everyman that he was what he believed himself to be: a creature of godlike reason, virtuous instinct and generous intention; if not perfect, easily perfectible. It was only bad, outworn law, custom and superstition that had made him less than himself: abolish them and he would discard like a disused skin the meanness, greed and cruelty that disfigured his nature. He need no longer grovel before the priests and precepts of an abstract morality, for true religion was in his own heart. God and man were synonymous. All that was wanted to build heaven on earth was to ascertain the General Will: to assemble the representatives of the People and give them power.

That was why the first of January, 1789, seemed to France like the first streak of dawn after a long, dark night. For on that day the King, confronted by a ruined harvest, an empty Treasury and streets full of hungry, shivering wretches, took a step that promised to fulfil the dreams of the philosophers. Advised by Necker, the Swiss banker, he summoned the States General to meet at Versailles. After two centuries of absolute monarchy, the nation was to devise the means of its own regeneration. The godlike power of reason was to be allowed free play.

France went mad with delight. In every pulpit "the divine rescript" was read "bathed in the tears of the people." Even the aristocracy rejoiced. Only those who watched the hungry, ignorant, brutalised poor in the squalid faubourgs and snowy fields and knew something of the ambitions of politicians and the greed of speculators and monopolists, had their doubts.[1] For human nature might be perfectible, but it had still to be perfected.

It revealed itself at once in the character of the States General. For the deputies lacking political experience were impractical and irresponsible. To show its good faith the Crown had doubled the representation of the popular or Third Estate, making the number of its delegates equal to those elected both by Priests and Nobles, the two other traditional Estates of the realm. But it left the decision whether they should vote together or sit in separate assemblies to their own judgment. On this elementary point no agreement could be reached. The opening weeks of the session which was to have seen the formulation of a new social contract—a lucid, rational, written constitution enthroning reason and the national will—were spent in a long, unseemly wrangle between the three Estates. It was only ended by the Third Estate, under the lead of a renegade nobleman, the Comte de Mirabeau, declaring itself the sole constituent Assembly and defying both the Crown to dissolve it or its fellow Estates to act apart from it. "We are met together by the National Will," Mirabeau declared, "force shall alone disperse us."

Thus the first act of the new deal or Revolution which was to restore France to its primitive basis of national virtue was not one of reasoned agreement but of unilateral violence. The next was the storming of the Bastille. For, confronted by delays and contradictions, the People grew impatient and suspicious. Some malignant influence was keeping them back from the paradise they had been promised. In Paris they were not only distrustful but hungry. The monopolists of grain saw to that. And the politically ambitious and the speculators who thrive by fluctuation and uncertainty whenever the ordinary processes of production cease to be profitable saw to it that the people had plenty of rumours and provocations to make them restless. With the summer heats came vague unaccountable fears—tales of bands of robbers and murderers pouring in from the provinces and of military massacres planned by an Austrian Queen. They were the presage of revolutionary change;

[1] "The Tiers Etat by their nature and their occupations must ever be strangers to political passions. Their intelligence and goodness of disposition are a sufficient guarantee against all the apprehensions at present entertained at their excesses."—Mem. de Necker, cited Alison, I, 404.

of society dragging at its anchors. On July 11th, on news that the King had dismissed Necker, the mob rose. On the 13th, joined by many of the soldiers, it seized the arms in the great arsenal of the Invalides. Next day it stormed the Bastille.

The submerged tenth of Paris bore little resemblance to that shining and virtuous Humanity acclaimed by the Philosophers. It was obscene, destructive and, once it had tasted blood, sadistically cruel. But there was no mistaking the terrible authenticity of its voice. Before it the easy-going, good-natured King surrendered. He rode humbly into Paris and made his peace with the illegally constituted Municipality. On the balcony of the Hotel de Ville he donned the revolutionary tricolour. "Sire," cried an onlooker, "with that cockade and the Third Estate, you will conquer Europe."

A confused period of fear and popular tumult followed. The anchor of the *ancien régime* had gone. In the provinces reactionary noblemen were chased by mobs down sunlit streets or fled across the frontiers while behind them the funeral pyre of their chateaux and muniment rooms, stuffed with ancient servile charters, lit up the August sky. All one delirious night in the National Assembly an excited handful of nobles and churchmen who had thrown in their lot with the Third Estate rose amid cheering and weeping to propose the surrender of one after another of their venerable privileges. In the colder light of dawn a new France of social and political equality was born. The feudal system had been abolished overnight.

France in those autumn months of 1789 seemed like a giant awakening from sleep. Her people were gripped by a strange fanatic fervour. "The public highways were crowded with enthusiasts, some shouting the watchwords of the Revolution, others disputing on the most abstract principles of the universal constitution which they fully believed that all the nations of the earth were shortly to adopt: the most ignorant among them confident of his fitness for the highest duties of a legislator and all prepared to shed their blood in the defence of the inalienable sovereignty of the self-governed people."[1] Nothing like it had been seen on earth since the day when the English Fifth Monarchists had hailed the imminent advent of Christ. "We desire," cried one deputy, "to make a Declaration for all men, for all times, for every country, that will be an example to the whole world." The first of the human species outside France to acclaim the Rights of Man were the negro slaves of Santo Domingo, who under its influence rose and massacred their French masters.

[1] S. T. Coleridge, *The Friend*, Section I., Essay III. In the light of later experience this early adherent of the Revolution gave it as his opinion that a "constitution equally suited to China and America or to Russia and Great Britain must be equally unfit for both."

For from the start the Revolution was dogged by an evil fatality. It arose from an inherent conflict between the ideal the revolutionary theorists pursued and the human reality in which their lot was cast. The men who orated so splendidly at Versailles or debated in the Paris democratic clubs on how to make a new France were not statesmen carefully navigating the ship of state through the shifting political and economic facts of the hour. They were dreamers who had seen a vision, sleepwalkers without eyes for the obstacles at their feet. They thought that men were just and rational instead of violent, unreasoning and passionate creatures; that they were swayed solely by love of the commonwealth instead of by greed and self-interest. But the ignorance of the multitude and harsh economic reality did not disappear merely because the representatives of the People had abolished a few irrational laws.

During the summer and autumn of 1789 Paris, its population swollen by political excitement, became ever shorter of bread. The forestallers of wheat, aided by the weakening of the executive power, drove the price up to new and dangerous levels. On October 5th an armed mob, incited by the orators of the Palais Royal, set out to cover the thirteen miles to Versailles. It was partly composed of women, many of them showing masculine legs striding beneath their petticoats. The King returning from hunting in the forest found his Palace surrounded. While the Court debated the pros and cons of flight, the Guard was relieved by the half-trained Citizen Army which under the liberal Marquis de Lafayette had followed the crowd out from the capital. In the early hours of the 6th a mob broke into the Queen's bedchamber: hurried flight down a secret passage alone averted tragedy. Presently an unappeasable clamour arose demanding the seizure of the Royal Family—the "baker" and the "baker's wife." A little before two, the King's coach, surrounded by drunken fishwives and mysteriously followed by laden grain waggons, set out for the capital. For seven hours the bacchanalian rout continued amid obscene jests and threats of "*A la lanterne*," until the sweating captives were deposited at the Hotel de Ville. Thence they were consigned by the city fathers to the palace of the Tuileries.

. . . .

These events caused much astonishment in England. The meeting of the States General had at first been greeted with general sympathy. France, it was felt, was following the British example. Whig magnates and parliamentary lawyers imagined they were witnessing a repetition of the "glorious" Revolution of 1688: Dissenters and Protestants hailed an end of Popish superstition and wooden shoes. The age of reason which William III had established in England seemed to be dawning across the Channel: henceforward the two great nations of the West would lead the world hand in hand. A treaty of commerce with France concluded a few years before by the young Tory Prime Minister, William Pitt, which had been much criticised by the Whigs—a party traditionally hostile to Bourbon and military France—was now universally acclaimed as a far-sighted act of statesmanship. Pitt assured the new French Ambassador "that France and England had the same principles, namely, not to aggrandise themselves and to oppose aggrandisement in others."

Some went further. The leader of the Opposition, Charles James Fox, in his generous enthusiasm described the fall of the Bastille as the greatest and best event that had ever happened. And all who felt that the libertarian tradition of England was not yet liberal enough—Dissenters who wanted the last religious disabilities repealed, parliamentary reformers who wished to see Manchester and Birmingham enfranchised, freethinkers and Unitarians who hated the Church monopoly of education—applauded the lofty sentiments of French orators who in the course of a few weeks seemed to have advanced further on the democratic road than slow-moving England in a century. Most enthusiastic of all were the young: those who like Wordsworth "approached the shield of human nature from the golden side" and sensed the love of humanity that was coursing like an intoxication through the veins of a great people waking from sleep:

> "France standing on the top of golden hours
> And human nature seeming born again."

Many, unwisely as it afterwards turned out, crossed the Channel and imbibed at the source new and generous sympathies.

. . . .

But, when the Paris mob threatened the life of the Queen and insulted the King, sober Britons began to have their doubts. The King of England was no genius. But his people were genuinely fond of him and looked on a decent respect for the throne as a sign of good citizenship. Old Nobbs, as they called him, had been reigning for nearly thirty years, and, though he had had his full and often deserved share of unpopularity and troubles, his natural friendliness and good humour and the personal integrity of his life had finally turned him into a national institution. Since the end of the American War and the revival of prosperity under the brilliant young Minister whom he had so boldly placed in office, George III's popularity had risen by leaps and bounds. Not even the extravagance and indiscretions of his eldest son were able to detract from it: indeed by contrast they enhanced it. When in the autumn of 1788 the King's natural "rapid and rambling volubility" degenerated under the strain of insomnia into insanity, there was widespread grief and alarm.

He recovered suddenly at a time when hope had been almost abandoned. While the States General was meeting at Versailles, England was giving itself up to a round of thanksgiving services, illuminations and roasted oxen. That summer the royal holiday pilgrimage to Weymouth became a triumph, his Majesty driving through flower-strewn villages and grassy forest rides lined with cheering multitudes: the country folk turning out with artless loyalty in their broadcloth, loose white frocks and neckcloths, while chariots, chaises, landaus, carts, waggons, gigs and phaetons, drawn up in democratic disarray under the trees, shimmered with fluttering handkerchiefs. At Lyndhurst the King on an evening walk was accompanied by the entire village repeatedly singing the National Anthem.

This loyalty of the rustic English to the Crown afforded a curious contrast to the uneasy splendours of the French monarchy. At the time of the storming of the Bastille, Britain's sovereign was peacefully taking the sea waters under the delighted eyes of a proprietary multitude, a band concealed in a bathing machine striking up "God save great George our King" as the "Royal one entered the water."[1] Wherever he went the same spontaneous acclamations attended him: "the greatest conqueror," wrote Fanny Burney, "could never pass through his dominions with fuller acclamations of joy from his devoted subjects than George III experienced, simply from having won their love by the even tenor of an unspotted life." It was a loyalty founded on nature by a people who gave him their hearts, not because he was their sovereign but because, being what they wanted their sovereign to be, he deserved them.

For he was as natural as they. In his familiar Windsor uniform—the broadskirted blue frockcoat with its scarlet collar and cuffs—and round hat he looked what he was, an English country gentleman. He liked farming, the routine of his duties, but most of all the human beings about him. He talked incessantly, to every one, pouring out good-humoured comments and questions, such as how the apple got into the dumpling, and answering them mostly

[1] *D'Arblay*, II, 316.

himself with a volley of hoarse "Tut! Tuts!" and "What! Whats!" which somehow removed all sense of ceremony and superiority.

Like his "cousin" of France, King George was a family man, but, unlike Louis, happy in being so since this was what the English, with their strong sense of the realities of life, wanted their sovereign to be. The Queen might be an over-frugal *hausfrau*, but Royal George was a faithful husband and a devoted father, and in his feckless eldest son an injured one, and his subjects loved him for it. They knew that he had a good heart. Nothing so won their affection as his manifest delight in children. When middle-class Dorothy Wordsworth accompanied her uncle and his family to one of the familiar summer evening parades on the terrace at Windsor, the old King stopped in front of little Christopher and Mary Wordsworth and allowed them to play with his stick. And when a day or two later Mary was wearing a new hat, the old man was quick to notice it. "Ah, Mary," says he, "that's a pretty hat! that's a pretty hat!"

Because of these things and because, despite black spots in the national existence, most Englishmen were tolerably satisfied with their lot, King George's subjects echoed Parson Woodforde's prayer:

> "And may so good a King long live to reign over us—and pray God that his amiable and beloved Queen Charlotte may now enjoy again every happiness this world can afford with so good a man, and may it long, very long continue with them both here and eternal happiness hereafter."

They could not follow events across the Channel without their viewpoint being affected by such personal considerations: and when the French people rose in their majesty and established liberty by flinging drunken insults at their sovereign and butchering his retainers, they refused to approve such goings-on. Liberty was one thing: "anarchy and confusion" another. Even John Wilkes, that tried champion of the populace's right to do as it pleased, observed that the new France was not a democracy but a mobocracy.

Not that Britons wished to interfere with their neighbour's concerns. The best of them continued to believe that good would come out of evil and that the licence which despotism had begotten would be succeeded by ordered freedom. For they knew that the French—that effervescent people—must be given time to learn the sober lessons which their own sane land had only mastered in the course of many centuries.

CHAPTER THREE

The Failure of Appeasement

1790-3

"This country and Holland ought to remain quiet as long as it is possible to do so."

Lord Grenville, November, 1792.

For a time it looked as though the first nation in Europe—formerly the terror of her neighbours—might prefer the road of peaceful evolution to that of revolutionary violence. The clamour of the angry fishwives on the march from Versailles was followed by a reaction: the upper middle-class and the more liberal of the nobility assumed a kind of loose control. A business government of rich men dedicated to the proposition of liberty for the talents irrespective of birth temporarily took the place of the old aristocratic muddle and inertia of Versailles. The King to all appearance accepted his new situation as the first clerk of the nation. A man of genius with one foot in both camps, Mirabeau—a rebel who understood the necessity of order and an aristocrat who was also a demagogue—kept liaison between King and Assembly. So long as he lived there was reasonable hope that the French Revolution would take the steady and decent course that every British lover of freedom wanted to see it take.

No one was more convinced that it would than the Prime Minister. A reformer and a lover of peace, William Pitt at 30, after six years as the youngest Premier in English history, was a living example of the triumph of reason. He had apparently no passions, no prejudices and, save for a liking for port, scarcely any weaknesses. By his industry, sound judgment and financial acumen he had raised his country in a few years from the despairing aftermath of a ruinous war to a prosperity unrivalled in the world. He had restored her finances, liberalised her commercial system and begun to rationalise her laws and parliamentary system. Without humiliating his sovereign, he had reduced the undue influence of the Crown and simultaneously ended the long political monopoly of the great Whig families. Instead he had set up a liberal "Tory" government representing the smaller squires and the commercial classes and legislating not for an hereditary clique but for the nation as a whole. He had done, in fact, or begun to do all those practical things about which the French theoretical philosophers and politicians never tired of talking.

The last thing he wanted was to quarrel with them: unlike his father, Chatham, he loathed the very thought of war. In the King's Speeches of 1789 and 1790 Pitt scrupulously refrained from stressing the disorders across the Channel. "The present convulsions in France," he told the House, "must sooner or later culminate in general harmony and regular order, and thus circumstanced France will stand forth as one of the most brilliant Powers of Europe. She will enjoy just that kind of liberty which I venerate."

But one of his auditors, at least, did not share his optimism. After a quarter of a century in Parliament, Edmund Burke, though slightly discounted at home by a certain Hibernian vehemence of speech,[1] had established a great international reputation as a political philosopher and the enemy of every kind of oppression. During the war with the Colonies he had boldly stood out against the popular view and denounced in language which is part of human literature the senseless tyranny that had alienated British America from Britain. More recently he had taken the lead in the impeachment of the great Indian proconsul, Warren Hastings.

In November, 1790, Burke took a momentous step. For some time he had been corresponding with a young Parisian who had begged for his reflections on the happenings in his country. Irritated by the extravagant praise lavished on these by a handful of British cranks, he published his *Reflections on the Revolution*. With splendid eloquence he analysed the divergence between French rhetoric and practice. Irish in his passion and excessive emphasis, Burke was never more English than when he applied to every principle of the revolutionary philosophers the evidence carefully collected from France of what had actually happened when it had been put into effect.

Yet it was Burke's Irish logic that enabled him to see more clearly than any Englishman the unreality of the childlike discussions which were going on in the National Assembly about theoretical systems and constitutions. An Englishman would not have troubled about them at all until their practical effects had begun to touch him directly. Burke knew that those effects would be a universal conflagration. He saw at once the flaw in the reformers' philosophy: that it could not be applied to the world about them without disaster. It was all very well to talk about the divinity

[1] Wilkes unkindly said of him that, just as the Venus of Appelles suggested milk and honey, so Burke's oratory was reminiscent of whisky and potatoes.—Sir Charles Petrie, *When Britain Saved Europe*, 88.

of reason and the General Will, but how was the reason of any man, let alone of a concourse or mob, to be distinguished from his baser passions and selfish desires? For these just as much as intellect were an inherent part of human nature. To assume that the votes of an assembly or the acclamations of a crowd must be synonymous with the will of God was merely to condone despotism which was as evil when practised by a mob as by a king. Burke always insisted on testing the pretence of liberty by the reality. Before he could approve high-sounding generalisations he wanted to know how they accorded with stable government and justice, with the subordination of the military arm to the civil, with prosperous commerce and agriculture, with peace and order, with the security of property and private rights, with morality and religion, with learning and the arts, with social manners, in a word with civilisation. "All these in their way are good things, too," he wrote, "and without them liberty is not a benefit while it lasts and is not likely to continue long."

Liberty to Burke had to be a practical thing. A nation in which a community of nuns could be dragged by a mob from a hospital in which they were nursing and scourged naked down the street was not redeemed from despotism because its national assembly had pronounced its own tolerance to be perfect, inalienable and absolute. Liberty to have any meaning had to be based on law, and law in its turn on morality: that is, on justice. For Burke brought to the French Revolution the historic English touchstone of every political pretension: its compatability with fair and kindly dealing. "Whenever a separation is made between liberty and justice," he wrote, "neither is safe."

Unerringly Burke put his finger on the central weakness of the French philosophy: that in its passion for logical abstractions it did not recognise the existence of religion and morality. It boldly assumed that these were identical with the General Will: the popular vote or other mechanical manifestation of democracy that in some mysterious way embodied the aggregate of human reason and virtue while discarding human folly and passion. The French reformers, who had disestablished their Church, thought that under a perfect constitution men would have no need for religion because the ideal State would automatically create the ideal man. Burke knew that this was putting the cart before the horse: that in practice the ideal State could only grow out of the ideal man. Good men were not to be made merely by laws which relied for their sanction on force but only by religion and morality, which appealed to the conscience. Only when the people, he wrote, had emptied themselves of all the lust of selfish will—and without religion it was impossible they should—could absolute power be safely entrusted to the State.

Burke foresaw that by worshipping an abstract ideal of the Popular Will and calling it liberty, the revolutionary philosophers were unconsciously preparing the way for an intolerable tyranny. "If the present project of a Republic should fail," he predicted, "all security to a moderate freedom must fail with it. All the indirect restraints which mitigate despotism are removed: insomuch that, if monarchy should ever again obtain an entire ascendancy in France under this or any other dynasty, it will probably be the most completely arbitrary power that ever appeared on earth." Looking up the long avenue of promise which led through the self-worship of the State and nation to the precipitous final crag of the Dictator and the national storm-trooper, the eager, beak-nosed, bespectacled seer foretold the course of the Revolution: the pitiless elimination of everything that could withstand the will of centralised despotism, followed, after the rise of a military dictator to save the nation from its own anarchy, by an epoch of world-wide aggression. What some thought the dawn of Utopia and others a harmless exhibition of French enthusiasm, Burke denounced in 1790 as a tornado about "to burst like a levanter and sweep the earth with its hurricane."

His contempt for the slick arrogance of what he called the "philosophy of vanity," his profound historical sense and hatred of the shallow pedantry that viewed the enduring community—the delicate and mysterious growth of centuries—as something to be constantly remodelled according to the floating fancies or fashion of the hour; his strong, masculine realisation of the necessity of some restraint on the passions[1] caused Burke to be less than just to the Revolution. He overlooked the stagnation and corruption which had given rise to the fallacies he denounced, and in an over-idealised picture of France under the *ancien régime* pitied, as Tom Paine said, "the plumage and forgot the dying bird." He missed the tremendous and ultimately healing power of unloosed energy. In his alarm at the dangers he foresaw, he unconsciously helped to bring them nearer. By sounding too powerful an alarm, Burke alienated his countrymen from France at the very moment when their sanity and long political experience might have exercised a restraining influence. Pitt wisely said that he wished Burke had confined himself to praising the British Constitution instead of abusing the French. There were powerful elements in the new

[1] "Government is a contrivance of human wisdom to provide for human *wants*. Men have a right that these wants should be provided for by this wisdom. Among these wants is to be reckoned the want, out of civil society, of a sufficient restraint upon their passions." —*Reflections*, 333.

France, particularly in the provinces, which might have responded to a generous hand from England. There were many good Englishmen who would willingly have extended it. Burke caused them to hesitate.

For the *Reflections*, as almost any book of genius will when written with burning sincerity on a topical subject, had an immense success. Within a year it had sold the unprecedented number of 32,000 copies. And though at first the bulk of Englishmen continued to regard Burke as a violent Irishman apt to be run away with by his feelings and more remarkable for the vividness of his imagery than for sober statesmanship, there was something so striking in what he had written that there was no forgetting it. And as one after another of his gloomy predictions were fulfilled by events across the Channel, the conviction grew that the old Whig hack was not an unpractical visionary after all but an inspired prophet. The effect on the pragmatical English mind was tremendous.

For moderate and liberal-minded men who felt generously towards the new France, including the majority of Burke's own Whig friends, drew back when they saw how Gallic practice of what seemed at first their own principles was accompanied by violence, illegality and cruelty. Every excess of the French mob confirmed what Burke had foretold. The sympathy of educated Englishmen for the Revolution was frozen in its tracks. As it froze, the extremer elements in France seemed increasingly to prevail over the moderate. In May, 1791, Mirabeau died: the one man who possessed both the magnetism to lead assemblies and the statesmanship to avoid a violent breach with the past. Henceforward power passed from the Assembly to the irresponsible republican clubs who controlled the mob. By June King Louis, alarmed by the rising tide of anarchy, had attempted flight, only to be caught on the road to the frontier and brought back in sordid ignominy to his capital.

These events, reinforced by Burke's constantly reiterated plea, thundered in the Commons, broadcast in pamphlets and repeated in every company, "to fly the French Revolution," not only split his own party but awoke the instinctive suspicion of innovation of the English people. He himself had praised their "sullen resistance of innovation," "their unalterable perseverance in the wisdom of ancient prejudice." The dumb Tory majority, which had hitherto regarded Burke with profound distrust, now praised him with more vehemence than intelligence. The more violent the proceedings in France, the more tightly did they shut their minds to anything savouring of novelty. The liberal tide which had been flowing in England since the American war began to ebb fast. A modest measure of electoral reform—no more than Pitt himself had advocated a few years earlier—was rejected by the Commons at the instance of the charming but alarmist William Windham, hitherto an ardent Liberal, on the ground that it was insanity to repair one's house in the hurricane season. Even Wilberforce's annual motion for the abolition of the slave trade—now at last on the verge of triumph—was unexpectedly defeated in 1791 owing to the panic caused by the rising of the French slaves in Santo Domingo.

These alarms were fanned by the uncritical enthusiasm for the Revolution of a small but very vocal minority which identified it with its own hopes and ambitions. In England it was drawn mainly from the middle-class urban Dissenters who welcomed the French doctrine of civil and religious equality and were more accustomed to—and therefore less suspicious of—abstract generalisations than the mass of their rustic countrymen. In imitation of Parisian models these worthy people formed "Constitutional" and "Corresponding" Societies in various parts of the country which earnestly debated French principles, urged their adoption in England and exchanged fraternal greetings with their apostles across the Channel. They did little harm beyond encouraging the more foolish French politicians to imagine that they represented British opinion. But the topics they discussed so loudly deeply alarmed their conservative neighbours. With King Louis a prisoner in his palace and French seigneurs and priests fleeing for their lives from mob violence, it was disturbing to learn that Mr. Price, the eloquent Dissenting preacher, had told the London Revolutionary Society that the British people might also depose their King and nobles and remodel the Church and State. The religious strifes of the seventeenth century were not wholly forgotten: there were still men living whose grandfathers had suffered proscription for the Anglican faith. They viewed the harmless Dissenting controversialists of their own day as descendants of the fanatics who had sent the King to the scaffold, plundered the cathedrals and set up the ugly tyranny of the Saints and Major Generals.

Feeling was aggravated by a spate of pamphlets. Burke's *Reflections* provoked no less than thirty-eight replies.[1] The most famous of these was *The Rights of Man*, the work of an ex-staymaker named Tom Paine who had taken part in the American rebellion and had now thrown in his lot with the French. Forcibly argued and lucidly written, it was suited to simple intelligences unable to

[1] The most important was Sir James Mackintosh's scholarly *Vindiciae Gallicae* in which he prophesied that an attempt of foreign kings to crush the revolution in France would recoil on their own heads.

grasp Burke's profounder points, with which—particularly with his high-flown passages—it made admirable sport. Much of it was good sense: "the vanity and presumption of governing beyond the grave," Paine wrote of Burke's historical polemics, "is the most ridiculous and insolent of all tyrannies." One of his great points was that the Revolution, being directed not against persons but against principles, had been attended by very little bloodshed: "among the few that fell there do not appear to be any that were intentionally singled out. . . . Whom has the National Assembly brought to the scaffold?" he asked.

Circulated by the Constitutional Societies at 6d. and even less, and dedicated to the great though—in England—suspect name of Washington, *The Rights of Man* had an immense sale and helped to stimulate the formation of radical clubs in a lower strata of society than had hitherto been touched by political controversy. The appearance of a workmen's club in a Westminster alehouse at the beginning of 1792 and of another at Sheffield caused a stir utterly disproportionate to the numbers engaged.[1] Here, solid Englishmen reflected of Paine's attack on the Constitution, was a fellow—a Radical, an atheist and perhaps worse—preaching that every violent act committed by a lot of excitable, bloodthirsty Frenchmen was right and demanding that England should throw over the sober gains of centuries, which he had the impertinence to refer to as badges of Norman servitude. The insular hackles rose.

The unreflecting multitude, in whom anti-Gallican feeling was never far from the surface, was quick to respond. When on July 14th, 1791, some middle-class sympathisers with France organised public dinners to celebrate the anniversary of the fall of the Bastille, there were riots in the provincial towns. At Birmingham, where provocative handbills had been scattered through the streets and a church chalked "This barn to let," the mob rose in all its ignorant savagery, wrecked Dissenting meeting houses and burnt the house and library of the famous scientist, Dr. Priestley. For four days the whole of the loyal, royal west midlands was in a tumult, till the 15th Dragoons, covering fifty-six miles in a day, rode into Birmingham amid multitudes shouting "Down with the Rump!" "No philosophers!" "Church and King!" The Government, faced by that infectious violence which revolutionary ideology always provokes in both sides and wishing to preserve order at home and peace abroad,

[1] These were trifling. As Burke pointed out in his *Reflections*, the attention drawn to themselves by the agitators was misleading. "Because half a dozen grasshoppers under a fern make the field ring with their importunate chink whilst thousands of great cattle, reposed beneath the shadow of the British oak, chew the cud and are silent, pray do not imagine that those who make the noise are the only inhabitants of the field."

abhorred the idea of an ideological front against the Revolution.[1] But the danger of such a front, with its threat to the tranquillity of Europe, was growing.

. . . .

In May, 1790, the new rulers of France professing peace and retrenchment—principles which naturally endeared them to Pitt—solemnly renounced war and aggression for ever. One deputy, Maximilien Robespierre, went so far as to declare that France regarded her existing frontiers as fixed by an eternal destiny. But those who, relying on this, hoped that the Revolution was not for export were soon disillusioned. That autumn at Avignon—a little enclave of Papal territory surviving from the Middle Ages—the people, catching the reforming fervour, rose and offered themselves to France. The Assembly accepted the offer and sent troops to take over the territory. It was argued that there was no "conquest" since the consent of the inhabitants had been secured. Yet it was significant that that consent had been expressed not by ballot but by a riot. It was still more so that the foreign sovereign dispossessed was never consulted.

Thereafter "ambassadors of the human species"—in other words gentlemen who for some reason or another were at divergence with their own rulers—began to arrive in Paris and to offer their respective countries to France. The Assembly in its mood of boundless benevolence towards humanity applauded their flattering confidence. It all seemed innocent enough: statesmen, it was felt, need not take these Gallic ebullitions very seriously.

Yet there were many who did. The strictures of the revolutionaries against princes and nobles were too sweeping to be comfortably received in a monarchical and aristocratic continent. Paris was not a remote academy for the discussion of abstract principles but the capital of the first military power in Europe. In Germany in particular, with its innumerable petty Courts and principalities, the democratic frenzy was regarded with acute distrust. Many of the Imperial princes, who still possessed estates in former German provinces conquered by France, had been directly hit by the abolition of feudal dues. All had a lively recollection of the French invasions of Germany during the past hundred and fifty years. It was all very well for France to renounce aggression, but Teutons brought up on stories of the Thirty Years War and the ravages of Louis XIV's armies asked incredulously if the tiger could change his stripes.

The largest Teuton rulers, better able to protect themselves, took

[1] Grenville, the Foreign Secretary, wrote: "I do not admire riots in favour of government much more than riots against it."—*Pitt and the Great War*, 19.

a calmer view of the situation. The Emperor Leopold and the King of Prussia had nothing to fear from an army whose officers were daily fleeing their country and whose discipline had been undermined by the folly of their civil rulers. As a concession to the smaller princes of the Reich and to the hysterical French refugees who were sheltering from the revolution on German soil they made a vague agreement to keep an eye on their volatile western neighbour. But they were far more distrustful of one another and interested in the situation which was developing on their eastern frontiers. For here the ancient kingdom of Poland, long torn by feudal dissensions, was on the verge of final collapse. Fifteen years before, Austria, Russia and Prussia had helped themselves to the outlying parts of its territories. Now under the lead of the Empress Catherine of Russia they were contemplating a new partition. Alarmed by an eleventh-hour attempt of the more patriotic Polish nobles to save their country by reforming its anarchical constitution, the insatiable old woman affected a violent horror of the French Revolution whose subversive influences she pretended to see at work in Poland. It was as the alleged champion of order against anarchy that she prepared to invade that country while urging Austria and Prussia to do the same thing in France.

. . . .

Such was the position at the time of the flight to Varennes in the summer of 1791. The insults to his sister, Marie Antoinette, placed Leopold of Austria—a sensible and moderate man—in a dilemma. Wishing to be free to watch Russia and Prussia, he did not want to become embroiled with France. On the other hand, he could not wholly ignore what was happening in the west. For Leopold was not only hereditary ruler of the twenty million inhabitants of the Hapsburg dominions in Austria, Hungary, Bohemia, Belgium and Lombardy. He was also as Holy Roman Emperor the elected protector of the three hundred and fifty-eight minor German States in the centre of Europe. He could not wholly ignore the wishes and fears of their rulers. He was also a Catholic sovereign, subject to the influence of the Pope, who was deeply hurt by the annexation of Avignon, the disestablishment of the Church of France and the expulsion of his Legate from Paris. Under these influences Leopold issued on July 6th a circular letter to his fellow-sovereigns suggesting some kind of joint European action to secure the release from restraint of the Most Christian King and his Queen.

The British Government, as was expected, declined this invitation. It expressed sympathy with the French Royal Family but made the possibility of British co-operation dependent on a general European settlement guaranteeing the future integrity of Poland and Turkey —both threatened by Russia and Austria—and the restoration of the balance of power. Britain was not interested in ideological fronts or the internal affairs of other countries.[1] Under these circumstances the furthest step which Leopold would take was a joint Declaration with Prussia, issued at Pillnitz on August 27th, expressing the hope that the European nations would act together to place the King of France in a position in harmony with the rights of sovereigns and the well-being of his people. But as Britain would not co-operate, the Declaration was a mere farce.

In September Leopold, hearing that his brother-in-law had accepted the new Constitution forced on him by the Assembly, informed the Powers that the obligations at Pillnitz had been achieved and that the coalition was at an end. His relief was apparent. But he had reckoned without the temper of the French politicians, the excited state of France and the increasingly provocative behaviour of an army of *émigré* nobles, whom the Elector of Trier had most injudiciously invited to his dominions and who, seeing in a European war their one chance of restoration, kept up a shrill chorus of threats against their countrymen. The latter's fears played into the hands of the Party extremists. The baleful influence of the exiles helped to turn an ideological into a national quarrel.

The members of the Legislative Assembly who met under the terms of the new Constitution on October 1st, 1791, were all untried men. More than half were under thirty. They tended, despite their goloshes and umbrellas, to be romantic idealists, nursed in the fashionable classicism of the time and full of windy eloquence about Aristides, Cato and other heroes of antique democracy. The most eloquent hailed from Bordeaux and were known as Girondins—sallow, excitable men hungering for applause and with a genius for self-dramatisation. There seemed no limit to the violence of their splendid enthusiasms. They at once confiscated the property of the *émigrés* and soon afterwards passed sentence of death on all who should fail to return to France by the end of the year. A fortnight before Christmas they made Louis inform the Elector of Trier that, unless the royalists in his dominions were expelled, France would invade his territory.

The Emperor Leopold could scarcely permit the invasion of any part of the Empire without going to war. Yet this, so long as

[1] Though, of course, British policy was viewed on the Continent as purely cynical and Machiavellian. "The worst obstacles," wrote the Austrian Ambassador in Paris, "will always come from England, which wishes to prolong the horrors of France and ruin her."

Britain remained neutral, he was anxious not to do. He therefore, while warning France that he would resist if Trier was invaded, brought pressure to bear on the *émigrés* to remove elsewhere. This evoked a renewed clamour in the French Chamber for strong measures. For the Girondins saw their way to power on the back of a European war. It was the shortest cut to a dictatorship. Popular interest in the Revolution was beginning to flag;[1] hostility was aroused by interference with religion, administrative anarchy and the inflation caused by a reckless issue of paper *assignats* on confiscated church lands. Only hatred of the foreigner could reunite the country behind the Revolution. A crusade against the Austrian despot was the Girondins' trump card. "War," cried their leader, Brissot, "is a national benefit: the only calamity to be dreaded is that we should have no war." On January 11th, 1792, amid shouts of "Liberty or death!" the Assembly voted that the Emperor should renounce his project of a European *démarche* against France or face invasion.

Confronted by this threat, the Emperor signed a defensive alliance with Prussia in which he promised to indemnify that very exacting State for its military expenses. For in view of their rivalry in the east he could not afford to act without it. Unlike Leopold, the King of Prussia had no objection to war provided it could be conducted without expense. He disliked the Revolution and, having been bribed by Russia with a promise of Polish territory at the expense of Austria, wanted to commit the latter's armies to a struggle in the west. The first brunt of war would fall on the Austrian Netherlands; it would then be easy to invent an excuse for husbanding his own armies.

Yet so long as Leopold lived there was still hope of peace. His sudden death on March 1st destroyed it. His successor, Francis II, was a narrow, pedantic young man of reactionary views, much in the hands of the *émigrés* who at once raised their tone. This was just what the war party in Paris wanted. On March 23rd the French Feuillant Government fell and was succeeded by a Girondin Ministry committed up to the hilt to war. Its leader was the vain, eloquent Brissot: its Foreign Minister a military adventurer, General Dumouriez, who had made himself the champion of a plausible but very dangerous idea—"the natural frontiers of France." These, ignoring the rights of her neighbours, he defined as the Pyrenees, Alps and Rhine. His first act was to dispatch agents into the Netherlands to stir up rebellion against the Austrians. His second

[1] In the recent mayoral election in Paris only 6,600 out of 80,000 electors had recorded their votes.

was to send an ultimatum to Vienna demanding the immediate suspension of the Prussian alliance.

The chief obstacle to similar French designs in the past had been the opposition of Britain. It was the belief in Paris that, if France could keep that country neutral, she could manage the rest of Europe. At the beginning of the year a French mission had therefore been sent to London. Though the *émigrés* had done their best to prejudice its reception by spreading atrocity stories about its members and inserting premature press notices that Pitt had snubbed it, the British Government refused to be deflected from its pacific policy. The Foreign Secretary told the Duc de Biron and his unofficial adviser, Talleyrand, that both on political and commercial grounds Britain wished for nothing so much as a happy issue to France's troubles. In his Budget speech of February 17th, Pitt declared his belief that Europe was on the threshold of a long period of peace and prosperity. "I am not," he said, "presumptuous enough to suppose that, when I name fifteen years, I am not naming a period in which events may arise which human foresight cannot reach and which may baffle all our conjectures. . . . But unquestionably there never was a time in the history of this country when, from the situation of Europe, we might more reasonably expect fifteen years of peace, than we may at the present moment." To prove his good faith he made new economies in the Fighting Services.

. . . .

For Pitt, having established his country's prosperity on peace, scouted the idea of war. It seemed to him the last refuge of unreason. Britain in his view had nothing to fear from France, which through the indiscipline of her fleets and armies had become an object of compassion rather than a rival. Her internal affairs were purely her own concern. When representatives of the royalist planters of French Santo Domingo, to avert a massacre at the hands of their slaves, offered the coveted colony to Britain, Pitt refused it as incompatible with neutrality.

On taking office the Brissotin Ministry sent Talleyrand back to London under a new ambassador, the Marquis de Chauvelin, a vain and tactless young demagogue. Their instructions were to secure Britain's continued neutrality and to offer the return of the West Indian island of Tobago, taken during the American war, for a guaranteed loan of £4,000,000 on the London market. France, they were to explain, was bound to dominate Central Europe; should Britain throw in her weight on her side and neutralise her former allies, Prussia and Holland, the two "free" Powers of the west would "become arbiters of peace or war for the whole world." A hint was also to be dropped that France by fomenting a second transatlantic revolution had it in her power to transfer the commerce of Spanish South America to Britain.

But the latter's most vital interest, as Dumouriez knew, was the security of the Low Countries. For this she had gone to war both against Philip of Spain and Louis XIV. The retention of Belgian and Dutch harbours in friendly hands had always been a cardinal point for England: their use by a great military power her age-long nightmare. Chauvelin and Talleyrand were therefore to impress the British Government with the idea that the invasion of the Austrian Netherlands was only a temporary measure for the security of the struggling French State.

To the positive part of this Pitt—courteous but cold—turned a deaf ear: to the negative, still believing that France's interests were as pacific as Britain's, he tacitly agreed. The ideological war he had tried to avert was now inevitable: the only course left was to keep out of it and limit its consequences. He refused any formal declaration of neutrality lest it should encourage the French extremists. But, on the understanding given by Dumouriez that the Belgic provinces should be restored to Austria after the war, Pitt adopted a policy of non-intervention.

In this unknowingly he was contending against history and fate. Already the Revolution had begun to impinge on Britain's internal affairs. In Ireland the French example had aroused the Noncomformist minority of the north. The second anniversary of the Bastille's fall had been celebrated by the people of Ulster with almost military pomp. That September a young lawyer named Wolfe Tone published a pamphlet, *The Northern Whig*, advocating an alliance of Protestant and Catholic Irish to shake off the rule of Dublin Castle. This was followed by the formation in Belfast of the Society of United Irishmen. Under Tone's lead it repudiated the patriot Grattan's moderate programme of Irish reform and advocated revolutionary measures—manhood suffrage, equal electoral districts and annual elections. It even started to raise volunteers for a "National Guard" and to dress them in French uniforms.

At this point the Government intervened and suppressed them. But the disordered state of Ireland made it a dangerous breeding-ground for revolutionary ideas. At the same time both in England and Scotland there was a marked spread of revolutionary propaganda. Working men's clubs debated such perilous matters as the price of provisions and "the lavish of the public property by placemen, pensioners, luxury and debauchery." As these petty societies multiplied there was even talk of suspending Parliament by a General Convention on the French model—"one grand and extensive Union for all the friends of liberty."

The more timorous souls in Church and State, confronted with this radical fermentation, became increasingly agitated. There was no police force, the manners of the people were rough and violent, and the blood-stained example of France was fresh in every mind. The language of the Corresponding Societies was ominously reminiscent of the Jacobin clubs which had terrorised the French Assembly and roused the Paris mob. Englishmen recalled what their own mob had done at the time of the Gordon riots—a glimpse into the abyss which had shaken even their strong nerves. And the artificial concentration of a new kind of population in the industrial towns presented social problems which Government had not even begun to tackle. John Byng, uncompromising champion of the rights of the rustic poor, travelling through the manufacturing districts that summer, was filled with foreboding.

. . . .

Not every aristocrat shut his eyes to the virtues of the new France. A little group, conspicuous in Parliament and the fashionable Whig salons, shut theirs to her vices. To the supercilious, dashing old Etonians who gambled all night at Brooks's, shared the dubious intimacy of the Prince of Wales and worshipped at Fox's political shrine, the red cap of Liberty became the symbol of an imaginary Utopia—the more attractive because it so enraged respectable opponents. In April, 1792, a Whig group formed a club at the Freemason's Tavern called The Friends of the People. Among its members were Charles Grey, Erskine, John Lambton, Lord Lauderdale, Sheridan, Lord Edward Fitzgerald and the young brewer, Sam Whitbread. Their idol Fox would neither join nor disown them. With characteristic irresponsibility he allowed them to drift into what later became an impossible position and in which, being then unable to extricate them, he was out of equally characteristic good nature to join them. Burke and the more mature Whigs, who under the Duke of Portland had till now followed Fox's brilliant star, were horrified.

Pitt as a good politician accepted the growing conservatism of the country. In April he opposed Grey's motion for electoral reform which that ardent young man was to carry forty years later as Prime Minister, declaring it to be productive at such a time only of "anarchy and confusion." In May he spoke against any relaxation of the penal laws against Nonconformity. He also modified his plans for making concessions to the Irish Catholics. Pitt took his stand on the necessity for giving, as he put it, "permanence to that which we actually enjoy rather than to remove subsisting grievances." His policy, after eight years of liberalising reform, now shrank to a single word—security.

For the English instinct, confronted by something new and violent in the world, was ceasing to be tolerant: it sensed danger. Subconsciously it narrowed its vision, and bent its energies to screwing down the hatches before the hurricane. "I shuddered at Grey's motion," wrote the historian Gibbon from Lausanne, "disliked the half-support of Fox, and excused the usual intemperance of Burke. . . . Do not suffer yourselves to be lulled into a false security; remember the proud fabric of the French Monarchy. Not four years ago it stood founded, as it might seem, on the triple Aristocracy of the Church, the Nobility and the Parliaments. They are crumbled into dust; they are vanished from the earth. If this tremendous warning has no effect on the men of property in England; if it does not open every eye and raise every arm, you will deserve your fate."

Yet though Pitt put away his dreams of reform at home, he stubbornly refused to abandon his policy of peace abroad. If France and her eastern neighbours chose to waste their blood and substance in war, that was their concern, not Britain's. When Burke, accorded an interview, urged intervention, he found as always a certain "deadness." The Prime Minister seemed more concerned in saving Poland from Russia, even in dispatching a commercial embassy to China, than in nipping world revolution in the bud. For his policy of security was as dependent on keeping the country out of Continental adventures as on averting doctrinal revolution.

. . . .

On April 20th the French Assembly declared war on Austria. The little group which under the Jacobin clubman, Robespierre, opposed hostilities on the ground that they would favour the growth of tyranny was swept aside by Girondin eloquence. "The people," cried Mailhe, "desire war; make haste to give way to its just and generous impatience. You are perhaps about to decree the liberty of the whole world."

The demagogues of the Gironde imagined that revolutionary fervour would make their armies invincible. They were mistaken. With the inconsequence of their kind, while clamouring for war they had tampered with military discipline in order to discredit their predecessors. The red woollen nightcaps of the Nancy military mutineers, released from prison in their convicts' garb and given the honours of the Legislative Assembly, had been acclaimed as Caps of Liberty—the approved headwear henceforward of every patriot. France had now to pay the price for such folly. The troops who swarmed into Belgium were a mere rabble. At the first sight of an Austrian they ran away and murdered their own general. The greatest war in French history began, as it ended, with shouts of *Sauve qui peut*!

The hideous rout that scrambled back over the frontier did not make a favourable impression. Europe breathed a sigh of relief. England laughed. "A strange reverse," was the caption of Gillray's next cartoon:

> "The democrats display
> And prove the Rights of Man—to run away."

Anti-Gallican feeling stiffened. The King was particularly contemptuous. When Chauvelin protested at a royal proclamation against seditious writings, the Foreign Secretary coldly intimated that he should mind his own business.

The Austrians did not follow up their victory. They had more pressing concerns. That May the Russian Empress's savage soldiery marched across the Polish frontier. The Poles took up arms, some under Kosciusko to repel the invader, others according to ancient Polish custom to serve their faction at the expense of their country. Their Prussian allies, bribed in advance by Russia, threatened them from the rear. Not for the last time the waters of barbarism closed over the Polish plain.

Meanwhile in Paris the parties of the Left were bidding against one another for the favour of the mob by the vehemence of their abuse of King and foreigner. The Clubs forced a decree through the Assembly disbanding the sovereign's Constitutional Guard. The Girondins summoned a meeting of 20,000 armed "Federates" from the provincial Cantons to the national feast on July 14th.

In June King Louis, relying on the reviving conservatism and religious sense of the country, vetoed a bill for banishing non-juring priests and dismissed the Girondin Ministry. But the royalist counter-attack, though nearly successful, failed through the divisions of its supporters. In the face of common danger, Jacobin and Girondin united. Their self-chosen leader was a rough provincial lawyer from Champagne: a pock-marked, passionate, impulsive man of 32 named Danton, whose name is stained by great crimes but who loved France more than anything in the world.

On July 11th, the Left struck. The Assembly, itself assuming the government, declared the country in danger and called on every able-bodied citizen to defend the frontiers. At the national festival on the Champs de Mars the King was hooted and jostled by the assembled "Federates"—the ragged, sweat-stained, angry men of the provincial slums. "The Tarquins," the cry went up, "must be driven out!"

Five days later the Emperor Francis and the King of Prussia met at Mainz amid a gleaming shoal of German Princes and Electors. They were still in no hurry to march for they felt certain of their prey. France, once so mighty, was dissolving into anarchy. They had only to drive the rabble before them and divide the spoil at leisure. On the 24th, having settled the question of indemnities, Prussia openly threw in her lot with Austria and declared war. The Commander-in-Chief of the Prussian Army, the veteran Duke of Brunswick, issued a manifesto to the French people. All who had "rebelled" since 1789 were to submit unconditionally and Paris was to be gutted if a hair of the King's head was touched.

The fruits of German diplomacy never vary. Before this masterpiece of tactlessness reached Paris on August 3rd, the Marseilles "Federates" had marched into the capital: five hundred ruffians "who knew how to die" and how to kill too, and singing a new song bearing their name. They were greeted by the Clubs with ominous enthusiasm and promptly liquidated an officer of the National Guard.

Next day Brunswick's manifesto arrived. That night, while a proud people simmered with rage, the great bell of the Cordeliers began to toll. It was the signal that Danton had seized the Hotel de Ville preparatory to attacking the Palace. All next morning a sulky little captain of artillery, who was trying in that starving time to write a history of his native Corsica, watched the mob storming the Tuileries. The Royal Family fled to the Assembly and the Swiss Guards were massacred. Before night fell Louis—no longer a King—was a close prisoner in a little cell while children in the streets played football with human heads.

Meanwhile the Prussians were marching. With the harsh halo of the great Frederick's victories about them they crossed the frontier, boasting that in a month they would sup in the Palais Royal. On August 20th they took Longwy and twelve days later Verdun. Between them and Paris was only an army of shabby and ill-disciplined Frenchmen, inferior in numbers, with grubby uniforms and officers branded with the memory of the flight from Belgium.

Yet in those ragged ranks a new spirit was stirring. The courage and daemonic energy of Danton—the very personification of France—ran through their veins like an electric current. In their blue jackets and wooden sabots—the "blue earthenware" of the *émigrés*' contemptuous phrase—the men encamped under Dumouriez at Sedan and Kellermann at Metz prepared to put the "Marseillaise" into action. Among those they elected for their colonels were seven future Napoleonic Marshals and a quarter of the Imperial Generals of Division. "We lived," wrote one of them long afterwards, "in an atmosphere of light: I feel its heat and power now at 55, just as I felt it on the first day."

On the day that Verdun surrendered, Danton, calling for volunteers to man the ragged battalions, made his great speech on the Champs de Mars: "De l'audace, et encore de l'audace, et toujours de l'audace—et la France est sauvée!" While he was speaking ruffians paid by the Paris Commune were beginning a massacre in the crowded prisons. In that bestial slaughter 1600 victims perished, mostly aristocrats of the more liberal kind who had stayed to share the fortunes of their country, among them two former Foreign Ministers of France. With their screams ringing in its ears, Paris voted *en masse* for the Jacobins. Only the provinces dared return the men of the Gironde.

On the failing frontiers the unborn Republic faced her enemies. On the 19th France learnt that the Prussians had forced the last defiles of the Argonnes and were debouching into the great plain on which Paris lies. Next day the Constituent Assembly sat for the last time. Miles away to the eastward the guns of Valmy were firing in the drizzling rain. When evening fell the feeble Prussian attack was spent, and Brunswick, cursing the rain and the mud and the sickness and divisions in his army, called off his men. Goethe, accompanying the German Army, alone had the vision to see the blinding truth through the mists of that sordid, petty encounter on the Champagne plain. "From this day and this hour dates a new epoch in the history of the world."

On the morrow of the battle, still ignorant of its fate, the Convention met in haste to make a new France. It decreed that there should be no more Kings and that the Republic was one and indivisible. The provincial elections had given the Girondins a majority, but the masters of the Convention were now the Jacobins. The "Mountain," as they were called from their seats in the Assembly, stood for a collective dictatorship, the crushing of all opposition and a permanent state of siege enforced by mob terror. They had three allies—the foreigner, the stars in their courses and Catherine of Russia. All that September, while the volunteers shambled over the cobblestones in a thousand little towns and the rain fell on the encamped armies on "the plains of lousy Champagne," the Prussians hesitated. On the last day of the month, clogged with mud and emaciated by dysentery brought on by excessive eating of grapes—"*la courée prussienne*"—they began to retreat to their own frontiers. For the Russian Empress had again drawn the attention of Berlin from the birth of the French Republic to the death agonies of Poland.

As the Allies fell back the French advanced. On the 28th Custine entered the Rhineland, moving swiftly on Speyer and Worms while princes, bishops and nobles fled before his dreadful battlecry of "War to the tyrant's palace! Peace to the poor man's cottage!" At the same time another French army, bubbling over with the frenzied enthusiasm of the hour, poured into Savoy, forcing back the Piedmontese over the mountains. Dumouriez's natural frontiers of France—a mirage in the spring—suddenly seemed to be becoming a reality.

. . . .

These events were witnessed by Englishmen with growing bewilderment. Those, who from the first had regarded the Revolution as a disaster, saw in the September massacres not only the fulfilment of their predictions but a call to arms. Burke was beside himself with prophetic rage and terror. He bombarded the Foreign Secretary with letters, demanding immediate intervention. "It is not the enmity but the friendship of France that is truly terrible. Her intercourse, her example and the spread of her doctrines are the most dreadful of her arms." Every day more and more of his countrymen were coming to agree with him. "How," wrote the generous and liberal-minded Romilly, "could we ever be so deceived in the character of the French nation as to think them capable of liberty?" As thousands of poor refugees poured into England with ghastly tales on their lips, a kindly people who were hereditary foes to oppression and cruelty could not conceal their anger. Eastbourne and Rye were full of penniless seigneurs and priests and forlorn women, and waggon-loads of misery rumbled ceaselessly over the London bridges. Such horrors recalled the massacre of St. Bartholomew and Louis XIV's persecution of the Huguenots.

By a familiar paradox this French influx intensified popular hatred of the French race. Spy mania swept the southern counties. With tales spreading of revolutionary "banditti," armed with daggers and disguised as refugees, pressure on the Government to do something grew hourly.

The Prime Minister preserved a wonderful calm. "No hour of Pitt's life," wrote John Richard Green, "was so great as that in which he stood lonely and passionless before the growth of national passion and refused to bow to the gathering cry for war." Neither in his official utterances nor in his correspondence did he comment on the events of August and September. After the massacre at the Tuileries the British Ambassador, Lord Gower, was recalled from Paris on the ground that the life of an aristocrat was no longer safe there and that the Government to which he had been accredited had ceased to exist. But on September 20th Pitt refused a request of the Austrian and Neapolitan ambassadors that Britain should exclude from its territories the representatives of those guilty of attack on the French Royal Family. It was not the business of Britain, he maintained, to take sides in the internal concerns of other countries.

. . . .

For Pitt's steadfast vision was still fixed on England and not on Europe. He was conscious that the harvest had failed after the wettest summer in recent memory, that there was food shortage and rioting in the manufacturing towns and that under such circumstances peace was essential if the growing industrial population was not to go hungry. And for all the rising indignation of the propertied classes, his Home Office reports warned him that the country was not yet united in its attitude to the Revolution. However much the facts belied them, the promises of the French politicians seemed to many to offer hopes of a freer and happier life. The Irish republicans and the radical clubmen in England and Scotland rejoiced over the events of that autumn as milestones on the road to human emancipation. Their eyes were so dazzled by the sunrise of freedom that they could not see the cruel, blood-stained foreground. The Irish volunteers adopted a crownless harp surmounted by a cap of liberty as their emblem: Tom Paine was elected member for Calais in the French Convention and crossed over to his constituency amid the hisses of the good people of Dover.[1]

Pitt was above all things a practising statesman. He was an innovator, trained in the scientific principles of the new economics, who cared nothing for theory, everything for measurable results. A self-appointed committee of ignorant journeymen, passing omniscient resolutions on far-reaching issues of which they knew nothing, or a mob wreaking the basest passions of human nature on society to square the theories of excitable orators, were not, according to his scheme of things, likely to advance the course of rational progress. He was the parent of more practical reforms in administration and political economy than almost any other English statesman:

[1] Looking, as one of his fellow passengers described him, "the very picture of a journeyman tailor who has been drunk and playing at ninepins for the first three days of the week and is returning to his work on Thursday."—*H. M. C. Dropmore*, II, 316.

free trade; a statistical franchise; the Sinking Fund; the Income Tax and the fiscal principle of graduation; national insurance and family allowances; the abolition of slavery and the end of religious disability can all in part trace their ancestry to him. But he approached them with his eye, not on the horizon like a man of the study, but always on the treacherous and broken ground at his feet. He was wholly out of sympathy with what he once described as "the vain and false philosophy . . . which refers all things to theory, nothing to practice—which rejects experience, which substitutes visionary hypotheses for the solid test of experience, and bewilders the human mind in a maze of opinions when it should be employed in directing to action."

He was confronted with the spectacle of frenzied enthusiasts—men foolish or bad or both—who wanted to jeopardise all his careful, hard-wrought progress and the peaceful and stable society of which he was the trustee for the sake of general propositions which to his empirical mind were almost without meaning. At that very moment Chauvelin, the agent of the French Government in England, was appeasing his new masters in Paris by fomenting plots among British malcontents to seize the Tower, arm the mob and proclaim English and Irish republics in dependence on France. Across the Channel the Convention—a body whose extravagant language appeared to Pitt frequently to verge on lunacy—was giving an enthusiastic reception to the complimentary Addresses sent it by British Corresponding Societies. Its President had declared that Britons, once the masters of the French in the social arts, were now their disciples and, treading in their steps, would shortly strike a blow that would resound to the extremities of Asia.

Pitt had good ground for fearing the spread of revolutionary doctrines among the poorer classes. In the country men faced a hungry winter over blackened crops: in the towns, where there was a mysterious commercial crisis, the price of bread rose alarmingly. An epidemic of strikes, food riots and wild talk in taverns had broken out, fomented, it was believed, by French agents. At Manchester and Sheffield disaffection was even reported among the troops. Nor was the language of a little section of ambitious aristocrats out of office, who pictured Carlton House as a second Palais Royal and themselves as Tribunes of the People, calculated to allay unrest.

It was on a Britain so divided that the news burst of the sudden French advance. On the 24th October rough old Custine—"General Moustache"—captured Mainz and, striking terror into the Rhineland, advanced swiftly on Frankfurt. Four days later

Dumouriez, sweeping back the Austrians from the long-beleagured fortresses of the north, entered Belgium at the head of more than 70,000 men. On November 6th he won the first great victory of the Republic at Jemappes as a cloud of skirmishers, followed by columns of ragged fanatics chanting the "Marseillaise," drove the white-coated Austrians from the low heights near Mons. A week later they were in Brussels.

The politicians in Paris went mad with joy. Suddenly the whole earth seemed to be coming their way. Nothing could now stop the advance of their armies and of their apocalyptic creed: nothing should be allowed to. On November 16th an excited Convention passed two Decrees, the first empowering their generals to follow the flying foe into neutral territory, the other declaring the navigation of the Scheldt estuary—granted exclusively to Holland by a long series of international agreements—open to all nations by the Law of Nature. This was followed by the appearance of French gunboats in the river on their way to reduce Antwerp.

Britain was the principal guarantor of the Scheldt treaties. She was also the United Netherlands' ally. Only three days before, the Dutch Ambassador had asked London for an assurance that Britain would honour her pledge in the event of a French invasion. Pitt, whose historic conception of European peace was founded on respect for international obligations, could only agree. "However unfortunate it would be to find this country in any shape committed," he wrote, "it seems absolutely impossible to hesitate as to supporting our ally in case of necessity." But he added that he hoped for an opportunity to reconcile Continental differences and so end the war, leaving France to arrange her internal affairs in her own way. For he and his Government still clung to their policy of appeasement. As late as November 6th, the Foreign Secretary wrote that his chief ambition was to know that he had kept England from sharing in the evils that surrounded her. "I am more than convinced that this can only be done by keeping wholly and entirely aloof."

It was one thing to wish to keep aloof: another to do so. In the van of the French armies moved a swarm of French agents preparing a "liberating" road for them. A number of these gentlemen were hard at work in Holland where they had long been sowing trouble in a fertile soil. In the middle of November the British Ambassador at the Hague reported that there was scarcely a village without a seditious club and a travelling Jacobin. It was obvious that the French meant to follow up ideological infiltration with an invasion. It was equally plain that the Dutch plutocracy was incapable of stopping either.

The rulers of Holland, a rich and timorous merchant oligarchy, did everything within their power to avoid inflaming their powerful neighbour. As long as it was possible they refrained from formally asking Britain to fulfil her treaty obligations. But after the fall of Antwerp on November 28th and a peremptory ultimatum demanding the passage of French troops through the frontier fortress of Maestricht, they begged that a British squadron should be assembled in the Downs. An intercepted letter from Dumouriez to the French envoy at the Hague made that general's aggressive intentions unmistakable.

Pitt was thus faced with the fact that the war he had struggled so hard to avoid was inevitable unless the Convention relinquished its designs on Holland. The retention of the Dutch coastline and the great anchorages of the Scheldt in friendly hands was a vital British interest: the Dutch alliance the keystone of his foreign policy. He could not abandon them at the dictates of frenzied demagogues and of an imaginary "Law of Nature" enforced by French guns. No such canon of law—let alone the exclusive right of French politicians to interpret it—was recognised by his country.

On November 29th Grenville had a conversation with Chauvelin It was a chilling interview,[1] for the Foreign Office with characteristic pedantry refused to admit the French Ambassador's official status, the royal government which had sent him to London no longer existing. At Grenville's request Chauvelin affirmed, not very convincingly, his government's desire to respect Dutch neutrality. Three days later on the suggestion of a well-meaning Member of Parliament Pitt gave an informal interview to Maret, a French diplomat then on a private visit to England.[2] The conversation was friendly, but the Prime Minister warned the would-be appeaser that any act of aggression against Holland would lead to immediate war. When Maret's account of the interview was published in Paris, this warning was deliberately suppressed.

For though a few of the wiser Revolutionary leaders still wanted Anglo-French friendship, others had made up their minds that a war with Britain was necessary. In their view France's interest was not peace but conquest as a Revolutionary instrument. Without it the dictatorship would lose its *raison d'être*. Even the Jacobin Robespierre, who had first opposed a European war out of fear of a counter-revolutionary dictatorship, now advocated its extension. To preserve their monopoly of power, the Party chiefs had to con-

[1] It opened with the Foreign Secretary motioning Chauvelin to the smallest chair in the room and the latter promptly occupying the largest.

[2] Afterwards, as Duc de Bassano, Napoleon's Foreign Minister.

tinue down the bloody slope or be overwhelmed by the forces they had aroused. The ease with which victory had so far crowned their audacity encouraged them to go on: to unloose the Terror of the armed mob beyond the frontiers and again conquer. Aggression, too, was needed to replenish their coffers and recoup the money-lenders and stock-jobbers. War against Holland, with its international banks and gold reserves, offered a wonderful opportunity.

Success depended on the ruling class of every nation proving as weak and irresolute as those of France's immediate neighbours. But an unpleasant shock was now administered to the Revolutionary statesmen by England, which their agents and the Gallophil enthusiasts of the Corresponding Societies had painted as ripe for revolution. For foreign criticism of British institutions instead of dividing the nation united it: foreign victories instead of intimidating aroused it. That eternally recurrent spectacle took every one, even Englishmen, by surprise.

For from every county there suddenly poured in resolutions by spontaneous "Loyal Associations" of yeomen, gentry and shopkeepers, promising the Government their support to maintain the rights and liberties of Englishmen. When Pitt on December 1st, at last openly declaring that nothing but readiness for war could preserve peace, issued a Proclamation calling out two-thirds of the Militia and summoned Parliament to meet in a fortnight, he was universally applauded.

The half-baked enthusiasts, who a few weeks earlier had been acclaiming French victories and penning fraternal greetings to the Convention, now found themselves in a hopeless minority, scorned by their neighbours and threatened by the magistrates. The hour had struck, as often before in her history, when Britain with a single voice resolved to:

> "Stand by the Church and the King and the Laws;
> The old Lion still has his teeth and his claws.
> Let Britain still rule in the midst of her waves,
> And chastise all those foes who dare call her sons slaves."

Chauvelin could scarcely believe his ears. The English, he reported to his Government, were hardly recognisable.

It was this transformation which alone averted war in December. Faced with the certainty of British intervention, the French Government instructed Dumouriez to postpone the invasion of Holland. But nothing could stop the unreasoning course of violence in Paris. The statesman who paused on the downward slope soon heard the yell of the mob and the click of the guillotine behind him. On December 15th a resolution was forced through the Convention that France would regard any nation as hostile that dared preserve its Sovereign and privileged Orders.

When the British Parliament met on December 13th it approved the Government's resolve to strengthen the forces by an overwhelming majority. In the nation's need for unity Whig and Tory had become in Gibbon's phrase, "obsolete odious words." Unfortunately Fox, who had declared in private that Britain was bound to fight if Holland were attacked, took the occasion to divide the House. With the curious political irresponsibility that marred his generous and lovable character he made a violent attack on Pitt's foreign policy. Only a handful of his former supporters followed him into the lobby, and but for personal loyalty and affection they would have been even fewer. But the effect of this futile division was to encourage the war party in the Convention. The French extremists were strengthened in their delusion that they had to deal only with a ruling clique and not a nation.

Immediate security measures were now taken by Parliament. 17,000 additional soldiers were voted and 9000 seamen, raising the personnel of the Navy to 25,000 or about a quarter of its American war figure. A Bill was also introduced to subject foreign refugees to more stringent supervision. The debate was enlivened by Burke, who, exposing a Jacobin conspiracy to arm the mob of Birmingham, astonished the House by flinging down a dagger on the floor. Sheridan spoilt the effect by asking where the fork was.

These proceedings were magnified in Paris by those who wanted war. Chauvelin was instructed to ask in peremptory language whether Britain was hostile or neutral. This was the same technique that had brought about the rupture with Austria. It was regarded by Pitt and Grenville as an ultimatum. The latter informed Chauvelin that the Government wholly rejected the Convention's claim that its unilateral denunciation of the Scheldt treaties was a purely French concern. With his natural frigidity stiffened by his race's traditional self-justification when it stands on its rights, the Foreign Secretary recalled that his Government had always desired to preserve neutrality but denied that she could watch with indifference any nation make herself "sovereign of the Low Countries or general arbitress of the rights and liberties of Europe."

After this there was little hope. On Christmas Day Parson Woodforde, representing an older England soon to spend herself in Herculean labours and in spending herself to pass away, administered the sacrament at Weston Church and afterwards entertained at his house five old men to each of whom he gave a traditional gift of money and a dinner of roast beef and plum pudding. Next day Louis was brought to his trial and the French Ministers discussed a plan for the invasion of England. "We will make a descent on the island," cried the Minister of Marine, "we will lodge there 50,000 caps of Liberty. . . . The tyranny of their government will soon be destroyed."

When Chauvelin on January 7th, 1793, pressed a new demand for the immediate repeal of the Aliens' Bill, the Foreign Office refused to receive it. True to the English habit in the final vigil before contest, Grenville took his stand on the rigid letter of the law. As a matter of equity Chauvelin had some reason to feel aggrieved, for the Act had already been put into force against his unofficial adviser, Talleyrand—the chief remaining advocate of Anglo-French understanding. Yet even while his Foreign Secretary was administering this pedantic rebuff to the French Ambassador, Pitt was still pathetically exploring possibilities of peace. For everything he counted dear in the world depended on it. Resolved to show no weakness in any direct negotiations with France, he still clung to his old idea of a general European settlement.

In this he hoped not only to avert war for his own country but to save Poland from its fate at the hands of Russia and Prussia. He therefore sent the Russian Government a proposal that all the European nations not at war should offer their mediation to France on the following terms:

> "The withdrawing of their armies within the limits of the French territory: the abandoning their conquests; the rescinding any acts injurious to the sovereignty or rights of any other nations; and the giving, in some public and unequivocal manner, a pledge of their intention no longer to foment troubles and to excite disturbances against their own Governments. In return for these stipulations the different Powers of Europe who should be parties to this measure might engage to abandon all measures or views of hostility against France or interference in her internal affairs."[1]

But Pitt was peddling dreams. Even had there been time for their consideration, such proposals had little chance of acceptance either in Europe or France. The allied sovereigns had no intention of laying down their arms until they had obtained "indemnities" for their losses. The Emperor, bound by his relationship to the

[1] B. M. Add. MSS. 34446, Grenville to Whitworth, 29th Dec., 1792.

French Queen, insisted on the restoration of the monarchy—a point on which he was encouraged for reasons of her own by Catherine of Russia. As for the French democrats, they became daily more intransigent. Pitt was haughtily told by the Convention orators that he deceived himself, "for that France should receive laws only from herself." The first cannon fired at sea would simultaneously free Holland, Spain and America.

For, like others before and after them, the men of the Revolution believed that Britain's strength was a web of gossamer. They supposed, as it was not spun of armies, that it would break at a touch. They thought it depended on banknotes. They had only to cut off the trade of the London plutocrats and their power would vanish in a night. Revolution in the countries with which they traded would soon bring them to their knees. The people would then rise and massacre them and welcome the French invaders. France would then "regulate the destiny of nations and found the liberty of the world."

Such men were incapable of understanding the secret sources of England's power. They could no more gauge the islanders' tenacity than those stubborn pragmatists could themselves conceive the *credo* of faith and destruction with which the revolutionaries confronted the complacent *status quo*. Goethe's phrase: "I love the man who wants the impossible!" was to provide the violent *motif* of the next twenty-two years of European history. It was to transform the world and bring it for a time to the edge of ruin. On that narrow verge between humanity and the abyss was to stand for many years nothing but the tried bulwark of Pitt's England.

. . . .

On January 10th the French Executive Council ordered General Miranda to prepare for the immediate invasion of the United Netherlands. Meanwhile Chauvelin was to seek another interview with Grenville in order to lull him into false security. But though Grenville promptly received him, and unofficial negotiations were still pursued through subordinate intermediaries, the British Government was not to be caught off its guard. Instead it gave orders to stop cargoes of grain that might be used by Miranda's invading army. When Chauvelin protested, Grenville refused to discuss the matter.

On both sides the momentum of military preparations was now moving irresistibly towards war. On the 12th Dundas, the Secretary of State, acceding at last to the offers of royalist planters to transfer the province of Santo Domingo to Britain, sent instructions to the Governor of Jamaica "to extend to them the protection of His

Majesty's arms" in the event of war. On the same day the French Government commissioned thirty ships of the line and twenty frigates. Down in Norfolk Captain Horatio Nelson, promised a ship at last after five years' half-pay, was jubilant: "everything indicates war," he wrote; "one of our ships looking into Brest has been fired into." On January 20th, 1793, the Cabinet opened overtures for concerted action with Austria and Prussia.

Three days later London learnt of the French King's execution on the 21st. The news was received with an almost hysterical indignation. At the theatres the curtains were run down, and the Palace was surrounded by crowds shouting for war. The peacemaker Maret, still delaying in London, dared not show his face in the streets for fear of "insults and ignorant ferocity." In the midst of all this anger Pitt—a lonely and tragic figure—waited wearily like a man in a dream. He had given up hope now: on the day before Louis was guillotined, he told a friend that war was inevitable, and the sooner it was begun, the better. Yet the very tenacity of his reason made the triumph of all this violence and unreason seem unthinkable.

On January 24th, the day after his recall had been ordered in Paris, the Government requested Chauvelin to leave the country.[1] A week later, while a French appeaser in London was still assuring an English opposite number that it was the intention of his countrymen to give up all their conquests, Danton swept the Convention into a unanimous vote annexing Belgium. "The coalesced Kings threaten us!" his great voice boomed, "let us hurl at their feet as gage of battle the head of a King!" On February 1st the Republic declared war on Great Britain and Holland.

Far away, under the great chandelier of the old House of Commons, Pitt was quietly speaking, the pale wintry sunlight falling on his paler face and the packed benches around him. "They will not accept, under the name of liberty, any model of government but that which is conformable to their own opinions and ideas; and all men must learn from the mouth of their cannon the propagation of their system. . . . They have stated that they would organise every country by a disorganising principle; and afterwards they tell you all this is done by the will of the people. And then comes this plain question, what is the will of the people? It is the power of the French. . . . This has given a more fatal blow to the liberties of

[1] The diplomatic *impasse* reached by this time is illustrated by a dispatch from Lord St. Helens to Grenville. "It would be extremely difficult to draw one up so as to meet the ideas of the two parties or even to *name* the actual French Government without giving it some appellation which would be either too honourable for its members to wear or too coarse for His Majesty to use."—*H. M. C. Dropmore*, II, 374.

mankind than any they have suffered, even from the boldest attempts of the most aspiring monarch."

Therefore, Pitt went on, England must face the issue. "Unless we wish to stand by, and to suffer State after State to be subverted under the power of France, we must now declare our firm resolution effectually to oppose those principles of ambition and aggrandisement which have for their object the destruction of England, of Europe and of the world. . . . If France is really desirous of maintaining friendship and peace with England, she must show herself disposed to renounce her views of aggression and aggrandisement, and to confine herself within her own territory without insulting other governments, without disturbing their tranquillity, without violating their rights. And unless she consents to these terms, whatever may be our wishes for peace, the final issue must be war."

CHAPTER FOUR

The War of Inaction

1793

> "Our first and great object ought to be to destroy the Convention, and it appears to me that if we are materially diverted from that object by the pursuits of conquests, whether on the continent of Europe or in the East or West Indies, we risk the fate of the whole war and of the existing race of mankind."
>
> *Lord Auckland*, 7 *Nov.*, 1793;

> "The principal object is to have what is wanted and to have it in time."
>
> *General Sir James Murray.*

THERE was nothing unusual in Britain finding herself at war with France. Six times in just over a century had the summons come and always against the same foe. At such moments the ordinary Englishman instinctively obeyed the precept Captain Nelson taught his midshipmen: to hate a Frenchman like the devil.

Because the French were republicans the English, who themselves had once been republican, became filled with an intense loathing for republicans. "All the Kings are dead!" cried a Marseillaise on the night Louis was beheaded. But in the London streets the boys sang:

> "Thus in famed ninety-three
> Shall all Britons agree,
> While with one heart and voice in loud chorus they sing,
> To improve 'Ça ira' into 'God Save the King'!"

At the pantomime on February 5th, the whole house including their Majesties joined in the loyal chorus. At the Opera House the management converted the National Anthem into a Pas de Trois and introduced it into the ballet. A people more given to criticising their rulers than any in Europe suddenly presented an uncompromisingly united front to their enemies. In the general hatred of France one noble Lord even went so far as to propose that the customary Norman French should be dropped from the Royal assent to Acts of Parliament.

A few held out—Fox and his devoted handful in the Commons and those radical clubmen who had committed themselves so far to the foreigner's cause that pride forbade them to turn back. But they were insignificant in numbers and damned by their former association with the enemy. After the first debate of the war the entire Opposition in the Upper House went home in a single coach.[1] The bulk of the Whigs followed the Duke of Portland into a kind of grieved retirement: too loyal to principle to coalesce with Pitt and too patriotic to have anything but detestation for their old chief's views.

Yet Britons, though unanimous in their resolve to fight, were far from so about their war aims. To Pitt England was fighting to honour her word, to combat the view that international treaties could be treated as waste paper and to prevent the domination of the Low Countries: in other words for "security" which without these did not exist for her. In the royal message to Parliament on February 11th, he declared that the King had taken up arms against "wanton and unprovoked aggression . . . to oppose an effectual barrier to the further progress of a system which struck at the security and peace of all independent nations and was pursued in open defiance of every principle of moderation, good faith and justice."

The official attitude did not meet the views of Burke. "A war for the Scheldt!" he cried when the news was brought to him: "a war for a chamber pot!" With his heated but historic imagination he saw before him the last Christian crusade: a civil conflict transcending international frontiers between the forces of righteousness and evil on which everything must be staked. To him the French Royalists were outraged allies to be avenged, the Republicans alone the enemy. The King, on the other hand, regarded it as something simpler: a necessary campaign to punish regicides, atheists and robbers. This was the view of the bulk of his more conservative and unreflecting subjects.[2] As for the man in the alehouse, he accepted

[1] A few aristocrats like Lady Sarah Napier, mother of three of Wellington's future heroes, did not even at this hour lose faith in Fox but saw him "more glorious than ever, with a *few* friends upholding his well-founded opinions in the midst of the confusion of prejudices, frights and abuse and resisting all temptation to fall from his noble height of principle into mean power and adulation." "I abhor," she wrote a few weeks later, "300 and odd of the French murderers, I pity the rest who are slaves to tyrants; I pity the deluded multitude and I wish them success at home but ruin if they go one step out of France. I think our war, the King's war, very wrong and very foolish, but still I wish it success."—*Lennox*, II, 89, 92.

[2] Good Mrs. Drake of Hillingdon well expressed it in a letter of February 17th: "The horrid doings that have been going on for some time in France, and which does not even stop with the murder of the poor King, appears to me like a fabulous story, for one can hardly credit it possible for human beings to be so cruel as those Barbarians have been and still continue to be, but I hope now that they will soon be crushed, for never before was a war so much approved of by all ranks of people as this."—Bamford 146.

the fight as something ordained by nature: another scrap to put Johnny Crapaud in his place.

Yet underlying these divergent views England's aim was that which had inspired all her greater wars. She was answering a challenge. That challenge was the claim of violence to override law: the dominance of the unbridled will. The French were seeking to impose a new order on the world, not by reason and precept but by force. England was not, as Burke had wished, denying the validity of that new order: that was a matter for philosophers and orators to debate and future generations to decide. For three years, for all the great Irishman's eloquence, she had stolidly refused to do anything of the sort. She had even been dimly aware that there was something necessary and even good in the changes in France. What she was defying was not the Revolution but the right of Jacobin politicians to dictate what mankind should believe and do. England did not say that the ideas of Rousseau, Diderot and Tom Paine were wrong. What she did say, and with all her historic emphasis, was that there could be no peace or progress in the world until those who had seized power by appealing to those ideas had learnt an elementary lesson in decency and fair dealing. Again and again she had given warning that she would oppose unilateral breaches of international law. That warning had been disregarded by the headstrong men in Paris. Instinctively she was taking up arms against the most dangerous thing in the world: the lust for tyrannic power which grows on what it consumes.

That England was unprepared for war did not trouble her people at all. Neither they nor their Government had given a thought to the question of what was necessary to ensure success. The English never prepared for war. Yet they never doubted that they would be victorious.

As a land power Britain was contemptible. Compared with France with half a million out of her twenty-five millions in arms or learning to bear arms, the United Kingdom supported at home an effective strength of less than 15,000 troops. Its line regiments, long reduced by peace-time economy, were skeletons with a cadre of regular officers and a rank and file of ragged recruits. The rest of the Army—another 30,000—was scattered about the world, mostly in remote and unhealthy stations which constantly called for new drafts.

Though a force with fine fighting traditions which once under Marlborough had won a European reputation, this little Army typified the unmilitary character of libertarian and aristocratic Britain. Its officers were gentlemen who paid for their commissions and regarded them as their private property. Its rank and file were unemployed artisans, jailbirds and village bad-hats who had exhausted every other resource but enlistment in a despised calling. Many others were drawn, as the Duke of Wellington said later, from the scum of the earth and enlisted only for drink. They had no continuity of employment, no interest in their profession save regimental pride and little hope of gratitude from the community they served. For England still regarded with jealousy a force which might be used to increase the power of the Executive.[1] It was always kept as small as possible and its existence only renewed from year to year by parliamentary vote.

In earlier times, before the menace of Louis XIV had wrung a standing army out of a reluctant people, England had relied for defence on a territorial levy of landowners and peasants who turned out annually for a few days' perfunctory training. Militia service had long ceased to be universal, but it survived for purposes of home defence. The force was commanded by the Lord-Lieutenants of the counties and officered by country gentlemen. Every year, after Parliament had fixed the quota of men required from each county, a ballot was held of all capable of bearing arms. Those who were unlucky enough to be drawn enjoyed a freeman's option of paying a substitute. This had the effect of deflecting recruits from the regular Army since the private bounty money offered for Militia deputies tended to exceed the Government's more parsimonious rate.

On the outbreak of war Pitt introduced a Bill for raising 25,000 recruits for the Army and embodying 19,000 additional men in the Militia. But, as he shrank from compulsion, the former were easier to vote than to raise. And the Militia, being only liable to home service, failed wholly to meet the nation's need for a striking force. For this auxiliaries had to be sought from the smaller states of Germany. According to custom 14,000 troops from the King's hereditary Electorate of Hanover were therefore taken on the pay-roll and another 8000 hired, after much preliminary haggling, from the Prince of Hesse-Darmstadt.

. . . .

Had Britain had to rely on land power alone, her effort in a European war would have been negligible. But though in 1792 only twelve battleships were in actual commission and there was no ship of the line either in the Mediterranean or West Indies, the Navy remained what it had been since Pepys had made it so a century before—the first in the world. Against France's seventy-six battle-

[1] For this reason soldiers, until almost the end of the century, were billeted in alehouses instead of being concentrated in barracks.

ships with an aggregate broadside of 74,000 lbs., Britain had a hundred and thirteen with a broadside of 89,000 lbs. Schooled by the anxious memories of his youth when the fleets of all Europe had united against Britain, Pitt—peace-lover though he was—had never neglected the Navy. During the decade in which he was restoring the country's finances after the American war, he had still found money to build thirty-three new ships of the line and to repair sixty others. Advised by the great naval administrator, Sir Charles Middleton, he took particular care of the arsenals and dockyards. Fanny Burney, who visited Plymouth in 1789, where many of the great ships were laid up in harbour, paid a glowing tribute to their preparedness; "a noble and tremendous sight, it was a sort of sighing satisfaction to see such numerous stores of war's alarms!" A plan of Middleton's for allocating to each vessel a reserve of stores now proved remarkably effective in mobilisation. Within a few weeks fifty-four of the great ships were in commission, and thirty-nine more fit for immediate service.

The difficulty was to get the men to man them. It was the custom at the end of every war for a Government dependent on a Parliament of taxpayers to discharge the bulk of the seamen. Only the officers—a corps of the highest professional skill—were retained permanently. The lower deck was recruited, as occasion required, from the merchant and fishing fleets, whose hereditary craftsmen supported by their labours and simple virtues the nation's maritime wealth and strength.

The sailor's calling was not looked down upon like that of the private soldier. Britons were proud of their Navy and felt no jealousy of it, for they knew it could never be the instrument of arbitrary power. They loved to sing songs extolling the virtues of the honest, manly tars who served it. Dibdin's "Tom Bowling" was a national favourite. But he was not paid or treated like one. So long as he served on a merchantman he could earn good wages. In the King's Navy he got little but wounds and glory. Owing to the excessive conservatism of the race, the rate of naval pay remained what it had been in the days of Charles II. Discipline was stern and cruel, food conditions bad, leave almost non-existent.

Therefore, though British seamen were loyal and brave, they did not volunteer with alacrity. In time of war the nation resorted to a device which savoured more of some oriental despotism than a free constitution. By immemorial custom pressgangs roved the streets and waterways of the coastal towns and districts, seizing at will any young man bred to the sea or who looked like a sailor. Certain classes were exempted, and a gentleman stood in little danger of being "pressed." But though liability to impress was theoretically limited to seafaring men, many a likely looking young landsman in London and the seaports found himself trepanned and hauled aboard one of his Majesty's tenders bound for the fleet. Smollett in *Roderick Random* has left a vivid picture of the press-gang's operations: the "squat tawny fellow with the hanger by his side and a cudgel in his hand" and his genial "Yo ho! brother, you must come along with me!"; the gang with their drawn cutlasses, the stinking hold packed with weeping wretches, the stench of the tender; the undressed wounds of those who had made a fight for liberty; the bumboat women and the gin, the brutal midshipman who squirted a mouthful of dissolved tobacco through the grating on the crowded captives. There was no appeal and no redress.

In 1792 the personnel of the Navy, which had been 110,000 at the end of the American war, was only 16,000. Though an Act for enlarging the fleet was passed in December, up to the outbreak of the war recruiting was conducted through normal channels. Certain cities like London and Rochester offered bounties to volunteers, which, joined to the knowledge that compulsion must follow, speeded things up a little. But it was not till the second half of February that the dreaded Press broke out on the River and several thousand seamen were dragged from incoming merchantmen and colliers. After that the work of manning the King's ships went on smartly. Yet months elapsed before the battle fleet was ready.[1] In the meantime the country had to rely on its frigates.

Fortunately, for the moment the enemy was not formidable at sea. A dozen years before the Royal Navy of France had proved a worthy adversary. But now, though eight of its ships mounted 110 guns or more to the 100 of the largest British class, the Revolutionary cant of "incivism" had deprived it of its best officers and reduced its crews to unruly mobs incapable of the intricate skill and unquestioning discipline needed to bring squadrons of large sailing vessels into action. Even the rank of sea-gunners—the old *corps d'élite* of the French lower deck—was done away with by the Naval Committee of the Convention on the ground that it savoured of aristocracy. The rot which had begun in the dockyard towns soon spread to the magazines and ships: responsibility passed from the worker and the technician to the demagogue. By the second year of the Revolution mutiny was the only sure avenue to promotion. The ships were dirty and neglected: the men remained in port and never went to sea. When the Convention ordered them out to

[1] At the end of the first year of war only 56,337 men had been added to the establishment.—C.H.B.E., II, 39.

fight, it found that the "audacity" it shrilly demanded was a poor substitute for seamanship.

. . . .

Such considerations caused Pitt to hope that the war he had striven so hard to avoid might not be so serious a matter after all. To the eye of reason the French were doing almost everything calculated to destroy their own country. They had slain or banished their leaders, alienated every friendly state in Europe, undermined the discipline of their defenders and neglected the arts of life for windy abstractions. Their frantic boasts that they were about to "dictate peace on the ruins of the Tower of London" and show up the weakness of Britain's "corrupting wealth" did not impress Pitt. It was indeed on this very wealth that he relied. As the first financial statesman of the age, he had nothing but contempt for the reckless way in which the Jacobins were destroying France's credit and commerce. The Republic was already on the high road to bankruptcy. Britain, thanks to his prudent management, was richer than ever in her history. Despite the bad harvests revenue was again buoyant and trade expanding. An economic victory seemed assured.

It was the measure of Pitt's ignorance of war that he put his trust in such a consideration. He was a noble creature with all his father's courage and patriotism and rather more than his sincerity. But cast straight from Cambridge into the Commons and thence, with scarcely a pause, into Downing Street, he was still at 33, after nine years of supreme office, austerely ignorant of the world. A master of figures and blue books, he was not yet a master of men. Inexperienced and unread in warlike matters, he had to guide a Cabinet of rich and easy-going noblemen and country gentlemen—subject to every breath of parliamentary opinion—through the bewildering dilemmas of a world war. He had to bring them to prompt and clear-cut decisions on far-reaching issues. Above all he had to steel them to resist the constant temptation of the line of least resistance which gives initiative to the enemy.

In this task he could look for little help from his colleagues. His Foreign Minister and cousin, Lord Grenville, was even less fitted than he for the shocks of a revolutionary age. Proud, chilling and scholarly, he was more at home in a library than a Cabinet. He preferred to leave strategy alone and to concentrate on foreign policy. The chief Service member of the Government, Pitt's elder brother Chatham, the First Lord of the Admiralty, had been a soldier and was a man of good brains. But he found it more restful not to use them. Owing to his unpunctuality, he was known as the *late* Lord Chatham. The Master of the Ordnance, the Duke of Richmond, was a worthy country gentleman. The Secretary-at-War, Sir George Yonge, was not in the Cabinet at all.

For knowledge of men and affairs, Pitt had to rely on his Home Secretary, the 51-year-old Henry Dundas. This bustling, genial, irrepressible, ruddy-faced Scot looked after the worldly management of the Tory Party, and, while in office, of the country. He had, as Pitt liked to say of him, a turn for facilitating business. As befitted a master of honest jobbery—for the man, like all who surrounded Pitt, was a patriot—he was a great pluralist. As Home Secretary, he was also responsible for the Colonies. As First Commissioner for India, he controlled the political patronage and military operations of the East India Company. He was also Treasurer of the Navy and Groom of the Stole.

Dundas was Pitt's boon companion in his one human failing—the bottle. The confidences of these two over the port were the delight of the wits and cartoonists. The latter loved to portray them waxing maudlin over a bumper and a loyally emblematic chamber pot at Pitt's Wimbledon lodgings or swaying into the House of Commons after dinner.[1] With his Scottish accent, his commonplace, clubbable mind and his bluff, goodnatured "Wha' wants me?" Dundas was a great figure in the House of Commons and City. He was a first-rate politician: a past-master of jobs, compromises and arrangements, always thinking of the lobby and the next election. He knew nothing of the art of war, for which by training and temperament he was little fitted.

Unfortunately he supposed he was: for his self-confidence like his joviality was inexhaustible. His first act after the declaration of war was to draw up a Memorandum recommending that no change should be made in any of his many offices. Nor was it. Since the Secretary-at-War was outside the Cabinet and the First Lord of the Admiralty sunk in slothful good-living, Dundas, with his command of the Prime Minister's ear, his direction of Colonial and Indian operations and his footing in the Admiralty, became virtually Minister for Defence.

. . . .

Such were the men with whom Pitt faced the armed Jacobin. His mind was not trained to run in warlike grooves: it had just

[1] Among the 101 Bacchanalian Epigrams of the Opposition wits were:

"Pitt: 'I can't discern the Speaker, Hal, can you?'
"Dundas: 'Not see the Speaker! Damme, I see two!'"

and

"Pitt: 'Europe's true balance must not be overthrown:'
"Dundas: 'Damn Europe's balance: try to keep your own!'"

suffered a profound shock and disappointment. He was dazed by the unreasoning of this barbarous appeal to violence. Strategy, unlike finance, was an unfamiliar dimension to him.

Seeing France's naval weakness his first plan was to attack her only on the water. He would use his scanty military forces in conjunction with his fine fleet to strip her of her colonies. The wealth won in the West and East Indies would equip Allied armies to attack her by land. Increased customs receipts would pay for Austrian and Prussian subsidies. This was the "blue water" policy which his own father had made so glorious and profitable during the Seven Years War. Its principle of limited liability naturally appealed to a Minister whose main object had always been to balance national accounts and whose hatred of war was based at least partly on its expense. It commended itself, too, to the Navy, to the City whose treasure lay in Caribbean sugar islands, and to the politicians who reckoned that captured colonies would come in useful as bargaining counters at the peace conference.

Yet even this conception of war required men. And because of the country's pacific policy in the past men were lacking. There were not enough at first even to man the fleet. Nineteen, or nearly a quarter, of the eighty-one battalions which constituted the infantry strength of the British Army were already fully absorbed in garrisoning those West Indian islands from which the main attack on France's colonies was to be launched. Even these had had to be reinforced recently to cope with the unrest of the slave population. And so unhealthy were the islands that the normal annual wastage from disease was 25 per cent. To take the offensive an additional force of at least 20,000 was needed. To raise a fraction of it the Government was forced to take the "flank" or picked companies from every garrison battalion in Britain and commit them to a long sea voyage and a climate notoriously destructive to white troops.

But no sooner had promises of reinforcements been dispatched to the Governors of Jamaica and Barbados, than the Government's entire plan was unhinged by the course of events in Europe. Danger at her own front door at once deprived Britain of the initiative. On February 16th, Dumouriez invaded Holland. Prussia, treacherously husbanding her resources for aggression against Poland, failed to supply the army promised under its treaty obligations to its western neighbour. Beside themselves with terror the Dutch plutocrats appealed to Britain, unjustly reproaching her for their defenceless condition. The British Ambassador declared that they could scarcely ask more if their country were a part of Yorkshire. " But I incline to think," he added, "it should be considered as such for the present."

For if the Dutch and their coastline were not to fall to the Jacobins, Britain had no option. It was to prevent this that she had gone to war. There was only one hope. In the path of the French armies lay the Hollandsdiep—a broad estuary which British gunboats supported by a handful of resolute troops might be able to hold for a few weeks until the Prussian and Austrian armies arrived. The Cabinet promptly decided to send the only force available. On February 20th the seven battalions of the Foot Guards were drawn up on the Horse Guards' Parade. The King's soldier son, the Duke of York, told the men that it had been decided to dispatch the first battalion of each of the three regiments to Holland and asked for volunteers to bring them up to strength. True to its tradition, the entire Brigade stepped forward.

When the 2000 redcoats, narrowly missing shipwreck in their tiny, hastily-improvised transports, reached Helvoetsluys on March 1st, the situation appeared desperate. The Dutch were unable or unwilling to make the slightest effort to help themselves; a British Staff Officer complained that the unconcern with which the burghers listened to the French guns at Willemstad made his blood boil.[1] It looked as if nothing could stop the enemy. Yet on that very day the inherent weakness in the Revolution revealed itself. A hundred miles to the east the sluggish armies of Austria took the offensive and the Republican volunteer levies at once bolted. For their high spirits of the previous autumn had been sapped by the neglect and corruption of their political leaders. Their favourite demagogue, "Papa" Pache at the War Office, had swindled and starved them out of all confidence. Trusting no one, they took to their heels. But for the leisurely ways of the Prince of Coburg, the Austrian generalissimo, they might have been annihilated. As it was, Dumouriez's plan for the invasion of Holland was ruined. With his right flank exposed he fell back to Neerwinden, where he was again defeated on March 18th. A week later the Austrians were back in Brussels and the French inside their own frontiers.

Further Republican disasters followed. The trickery and greed of the Paris demagogues had destroyed whatever patriotism and patience the victor of Jemappes possessed. Furious at their knavery, the restless, scheming Dumouriez had formed the Cæsarian plan of marching at the head of his army on Paris as the saviour of a demoralised country. Defeated, he now decided to achieve his ambition with the help of the enemy. On the last day of the month he sent an aide-de-camp to the astonished Austrians and offered to evacuate the Netherlands and march against the Convention. Three

[1] "But the climate," he added, "is of a nature to keep us all tolerably cool."—*Calvert*, 25

days later he delivered up the French War Minister and three other politicians who had been visiting his headquarters. Failing to carry his troops with him, he followed himself on April 5th.

Within a fortnight the war had been transformed. The door was wide open to an Allied advance across the northern plains of France. The chance seemed too great to reject. Pitt and Dundas, strongly pressed by the King, consented to postpone their West Indian projects and throw their whole striking force into Flanders. To fill the place of the still missing Prussians they promised to put 40,000 British, Hanoverians and Hessians into the field. They thus committed themselves against their better judgment to a continental campaign of the costly kind dear to William III and Marlborough. Yet, reluctant to relinquish the more popular "blue water" strategy of their dreams, they insisted that the British contingent might be withdrawn whenever they chose. In this way they vainly imagined they could preserve their freedom of action.

Their Allies were equally anxious to preserve theirs. All of them had what seemed to them more urgent objectives than a common victory over the Republic they had once more ceased to fear. The Prussians wanted to extend their eastern frontiers. They were not prepared to waste men and money on another western campaign until this had been achieved. The Austrians wanted territorial accessions on the Danube to counterbalance the acquisitions of their Russian and Prussian neighbours. Without these they did not feel secure. They therefore put forward a plan for exchanging Belgium for Bavaria with the Bavarian Royal Family. Britain, whose historic barrier against French aggression in the Low Countries was the presence of Austria, hastily sought to prevent this by bribing the Imperial Government with a promise of French frontier fortresses.

All this chaffering lowered the tone of the war. The grand crusade of Burke's imagination was degenerating into a vulgar scramble for territorial aggrandisement. Even Holland put in a claim for compensatory fortresses. The Allies argued that they were the victims of French aggression—not for the first time in the past century—and that it was only fair that France should pay. But the evil did not end there. Though the road to Paris lay open, the Allied armies remained motionless on the French frontier for weeks while their politicians debated "indemnities." British unpreparedness as well as Allied greed contributed to the delay. For it was one thing for Pitt to promise an army: another to produce it. Hanoverians and Hessians bought with British gold might march in haste across the muddy lanes of north Germany; the Guards, joyously escaping from the boredom of Helvoetsluys, float down chilly

Dutch canals towards a kindlier Flanders, and the Government hurriedly replace every available regiment with home service "Fencible" corps raised for the duration. But the depleted ranks had to be filled with recruits, transformed overnight into soldiers by making them drunk with bounty money and bundling them, still dazed, into transports. A Staff Officer complained after they had landed that they were "totally unfit for service . . . being mostly either old men or quite boys, extremely weak and short." "How they are to be disposed of till they can be taught their business," wrote the apologetic Adjutant-General, "I am at a loss to imagine. I was not consulted on the subject until it was too late."[1]

The command of this polyglot army was entrusted to the 28-year-old Duke of York. Having been indentured by his father to Frederick the Great, he had acquired some reputation as a martinet if not as a soldier. The Government had little faith in the appointment. But it felt that the Duke as a prince of the blood might be able to hold his own with the Royalties at Coburg's headquarters. His Chief of Staff, Major-General Sir James Murray[2]—a brilliant but shy man—had as little confidence in himself as the Government in the Commander-in-Chief. The most experienced soldier in the expeditionary force was an old Scot, Major-General Ralph Abercromby.

. . . .

When on May 1st Coburg at last advanced, it was with the stately deliberation of eighteenth-century military science. He had more than 100,000 men, of whom over half were Austrians, many of them veterans of the Turkish wars. The diversity of their race, habits and uniforms much impressed their British comrades. "The drawings which Captain Cook brought back from the South Seas," wrote Major Calvert, "are nothing to some of our friends!" In the demoralised state of France there seemed little to stop a swift and resolute march on Paris. But the pedants of the Imperial Staff would do nothing contrary to the canons of their text-books. Every road by which a French raiding party might advance against rear or flank had to be guarded, every outpost laboriously driven in and even the smallest fortress stormed or blockaded. The army advanced with infinite slowness, spread out in an enormous cordon from Maubeuge to Ostend. As soon as it reached the frontier fortresses of Condé and Valenciennes, it stopped to besiege them in form. Nothing would induce Coburg to advance further till they had been reduced.

Here the Allied army remained for two months, trenching,

[1] *Calvert*, 52.
[2] In July, 1794, Murray assumed the additional name of Pulteney,

sapping and mining and suffering more from boredom than from the enemy, while the chances of ending the war in 1793 evaporated. Two hundred miles to the east 100,000 Prussians with like deliberation besieged the Rhineland city of Mainz. The British public watched these elaborate military exercises, at first with respectful interest and then with a growing sense of tedium. It thrilled with pride when it learnt how the Coldstream in a daring counter-attack had driven the enemy from a fortified wood near Vicogne. It listened with sympathy to tales of the trenches before Valenciennes. But by the time the town fell on July 28th, a feeling of weariness had set in. England was back where she had been before Chatham taught her to make war by striking across oceans: in the interminable labyrinth of Flemish barn and spire, march and counter-march, sap and parallel so familiar to the youth of Uncle Toby and Corporal Trim. Imperial Vienna's conception of a campaign was one of reducing places. To seek out and destroy the enemy's army in the field or spread dismay through his tottering system by a bold advance were operations alien to its measured pace. They were not provided for in the text-books.

The leisured country gentlemen who ruled *fin-de-siècle* England proved obedient pupils. They were the product of the salon, the palladian mansion, the stately periods of classic oratory and architecture. They also saw the war to crush the infant dynamic of armed Jacobinism as a campaign of capturing places. As soon as Valenciennes fell—with all the antique pageantry of paraded colours, massed bands and incongruously ragged *sansculottes* marching out with military honours to carry back death and desolation to their own insurgent countrymen[1]—the British Government staked out a claim of its own. Vigorously backed by the King, it claimed that the capture of Dunkirk on the Allied right was a prior British objective. For not only would its possession shorten the Expeditionary Force's communications but would provide a set-off to allied "indemnities" and a bargaining counter at the peace conference. It would also—and this was an important point for Ministers dependent on a parliamentary majority—deprive French privateers of their most dangerous base and compensate the City for the postponement of the West Indian campaign. As Dundas put it, such a diversion would help to "give a good impression of the war in England."

He failed to see that it would not help to win it. Instead of advancing southwards on Paris the Allied Army broke up, the Austrians investing Le Quesnoy and the British marching north to

[1] They were released on condition that they did not serve again against the Allies. They were promptly employed against the Royalists of La Vendée.

Dunkirk. Here they dug themselves in round the port pending the arrival of a squadron of gunboats and the plans which the Lord Chancellor had obligingly drafted to co-ordinate the combined operations.* Unfortunately the Cabinet's loquacity somewhat impaired the value of its deliberations, for its intentions quickly became public not only in London but in Paris.

. . . .

Yet though the Allies failed to strike the decisive blow, the door to victory remained open. Throughout the summer of 1793 the defeat of the Revolution seemed inevitable. The unreason and violence of the ruling demagogues in Paris had split France into factions. In La Vendée the peasants had taken up arms against the scum of the cities who had come to proscribe their priests and conscript their young men. That summer the country folk of the Bocage, the deep-wooded, patriarchal land south of the Loire, turned out in thousands to defend their hearths and altars. In Paris the Jacobins, installed in the new Committee of Public Safety, denounced the Girondins as traitors. Those of the latter who escaped the mob fled to the provinces, where they raised a revolt. Lyons, Marseilles, Avignon and Bordeaux all declared for a "Federal" Republic against the tyranny of Paris. By the end of June twenty-six out of the eighty-five Departments had repudiated the Commune. From Caen in Normandy, where the Federalists set up their headquarters, the Girondin heroine, Charlotte Corday, set out to assassinate the Jacobin journalist, Marat.

. . . .

Yet once again the Allies' selfishness and lack of constructive idealism healed France's divisions. When Valenciennes fell it was not the lilies of the native Bourbons that rose above the citadel but the hated bunting of the Hapsburgs. The Prussians spoke of Lorraine as an "indemnity," the Austrians of Alsace, the Spaniards, who had invaded France from the south, of Roussillon. As in the autumn of '92 the love of the peasant for the soil of his country turned such threats into a terrible boomerang.

The Allies were as selfish in action as in inaction. Even when the whole Rhône valley took up arms for the Federalists, the Austrians and Piedmontese refused to march. Pitt sent Lord Mulgrave to Turin to urge this obvious move. But the Court of Savoy mistrusted the Austrians, and the Austrians were too busy watching the Prussians in Poland to undertake another western offensive. They looked on at the suicidal struggle between the Jacobins and Girondins without stirring.

Alone among the Allies the British realised the opportunity.

Their strongest sympathies were naturally with the insurgents nearest their own coasts. The forest war of the Royalists of the West stirred the chivalrous Burke and Windham to white heat. But unfortunately the Government was in a difficulty. Pitt had always been careful to insist that Britain was not fighting to put back the Bourbons or to impose any particular form of rule on the French. The brothers of the murdered French King were not an inspiring rallying point for a liberating movement and commanded little general support. But the western rebels were their devoted adherents. To support them too unreservedly would be to commit Britain to a partisanship incompatible with her war aims.

But even greater impediments to effective British aid were lack of man-power and irresolution in using it. So serious had been the drain of the Flanders campaign that at one time there were only three regular infantry regiments left south of the Tweed. The main division of the Mediterranean Fleet, whose appearance in southern waters was urgently demanded by British diplomats at Vienna, Madrid, Naples, Turin and Lisbon, had been unable to sail from Spithead till the end of May and then only by drafting soldiers on board. And though a French squadron left Brest on June 4th to blockade the Royalists on the Brittany coast, the great ships of the British Channel Fleet were still in harbour a month later waiting to complete their crews. Before they sailed the insurgents had been repulsed from Nantes—the base designed for a British-Royalist advance on Paris.

For though the fates seemed determined to punish the moral delinquencies of the Revolutionary leaders, the human instruments through which Fate could alone work seemed equally determined to reject such chances. The British Government took each windfall from Providence as a matter of course and, when it had lost it, calmly awaited the next. Nothing could shake its astonishing complacency. When Fox moved that negotiations should be opened for peace, Pitt, pointing out that it would be strange to do at the start of a most successful war what could only be excused at the end of a disastrous one, claimed that British operations had been uniformly attended "with the most brilliant, rapid and unexpected success."[1] And the country on the whole agreed with him. Only Burke, watching from the prophetic shades of Beaconsfield, remained incredulous. "No," he declared, "it will be a long and a dangerous war—the most dangerous we were ever engaged in." But the general view was that with the Allies only 160 miles from Paris and all Christendom save Denmark, Switzerland and Venice leagued

[1] *War Speeches*, 93-6.

against the Republic, the southward march would soon be resumed and the dark menace of the Revolution ended.

. . . .

Had the French only remained quiescent it might have been. The British conception of war was a semi-static one: mildly active for themselves and wholly passive for the enemy. But passive was just what the Jacobins were not. During the summer and autumn of 1793 they were more active than anything seen on earth for a hundred years.

That July a young English girl living in Switzerland went to Stadt to gape at a party of Jacobin emissaries on their way to Venice. She and her *émigré* friends laughed heartily at the "foolish, poor, pale faces" of the despised and hated "*sansculottes.*" But had she known that for the next three years she and her family would be fugitives before their victorious armies and would be finally driven to take refuge on board an English man-of-war—the one unconquerable thing left in the world—she would more likely have cried.[2] For the French, having set up absolute liberty as their God and found it—as a God—a failure, had now set up another: human energy. Henceforward they worshipped only the red blood in their own veins: the ruthless will that knew no denial. Wherever freedom, in whose name they made such extravagant claims, impeded the triumph of their will, they crucified freedom. Because despotism and cruelty won their ends most swiftly, they glorified despotism and cruelty and called them liberty and justice.

Such a belief might be vile and, in the long run, false to eternal truth. But the French after a century of tepid faith and shams put their whole trust in it and—till it in turn failed them—gave themselves without reserve to its service. Those who talked with the ragged prisoners in Hampshire that summer were astonished at the intensity of their hatred of established religion: at Alresford four hundred Jacobin officers on parole openly boasted of their intention to massacre some neighbouring *émigré* priests at the first opportunity. A British naval officer who captured some French seamen described how one day he begged one of them who had a fiddle to oblige with the Revolutionary hymn. For some time the man refused, then struck up, accompanying himself by his voice. "When he came to that part 'Aux armes, Citoyens, formez vos bataillons,' he seemed inspired; he threw up his violin half-way up the formast, caught it again, pressed it to his breast and sung out 'Bon, Ça Ira,' in which he was joined by his comrades:

[2] *Wynne Diaries*, I, 206.

"'Fired with the song the French grew vain,
Fought all their battles o'er again,
And thrice they routed all their foes; and thrice they slew
the slain;'

and seemed ready and willing for any mischief."[1] Those who led such men—uncouth, imperfectly educated, perverted often by vile, sadistic passions and daemonic in their hatreds, ambitions and enthusiasms—were resolved to smash everything that stood in their path. And almost everything that the old world valued.

On the 24th of July—two days after the fall of Mainz—Robespierre, ousting Danton, joined the Committee of Public Safety. This man, mediocre in heart and intellect, possessed one almost superhuman talent: a single-minded belief in himself and his opinions. To them he was ready to sacrifice everything: liberty, justice, decency, his friends and, if need be, humanity itself. For he believed himself to be the embodiment of the General Will. For the moment the mob shared his belief. And as the triumph of his ideals necessitated the triumph of France, to destroy her enemies and his own, no sacrifice could be too great and no means too cruel.

Almost his earliest act was to send the general of the northern armies to the guillotine for the crime of being unsuccessful. Old Custine was the first of many who died for the same offence. The timely sacrifice electrified the survivors. Like the Long Parliament's Self-Denying Ordinance, it produced astonishing results.

So did the terror which Robespierre unloosed on the rebellious and the faint-hearted. "Better," cried one of his followers, "that twenty-five million beings should perish than the Republic one and indivisible!" On August 27th the Jacobins, routing the southern Federalists, stormed their way into Marseilles. In the wake of their armies came subhuman beings with unrestrained powers: men like the drunkard Collot d'Herbois; the little white-faced human ferret, Hebert; and the ex-priest Le Bon who sat all day in a fever of ecstasy watching the blood spouting from the guillotine. And when the guillotine proved too slow for their business, they tied men and women in droves together and mowed them down by chain-shot or threw them screaming into the rivers.

In the face of such terror resistance died. While the Queen, pale and listless, went amid jests to the scaffold, the Girondins who had dethroned her husband were hunted down like rats. Opposition became unthinkable. The slightest criticism of the Government was branded as treason. The thought of the Austrian flag waving

[1] Gardner, 159.

over French cities acted as an acid dissolvent to every malcontent cause.

Hatred of the foreigner and the foreigner's ally—the traitor—was forged that blood-stained autumn into a fearful weapon against the foes of France. "From this moment," cried Barère to the Convention on August 23rd, "until that in which every enemy shall be driven out of the territories of the Republic, every Frenchman is permanently under requisition for service with the armies. The young men will go out and fight: the married men will manufacture weapons and transport stores: the women will make tents and clothing and nurse in the hospitals: the children will make lint and dressings; the old men will cause themselves to be carried to the public squares, there to excite the courage of the warriors and preach the unity of the Republic and hatred against Kings."

Yet all this ruthless enthusiasm would not have availed but for the organising genius of a 40-year-old Burgundian captain of Engineers. Earlier in the summer Lazare Carnot, an obscure member of the Convention, had been sent to report on the fortifications of Dunkirk. His astonishing energy as well as his proved fidelity to the Revolution brought its reward. In the middle of August he was appointed—an utterly unknown man—to the Committee of Public Safety. He was told that his task was to organise victory. He set about it without wasting an hour.

Two days after his appointment a *levée en masse* was ordered for the entire manhood of France. It was a new conception of war, blending the modern nation with the embattled tribe of the remote past. It was Carnot who made it work. Austere, unsparing, a student of history and theology, with Roman virtues and Calvinistic ideals, the tall ungainly captain stretched out on the floor of his office among his maps and green portfolios unconsciously forged the weapon of the Cæsarian Napoleon. During the next twelve months he and his military colleagues worked as few men can ever have worked. They revolutionised the formation, discipline and training of every unit, chose the officers, set the armies in motion according to a single daring and methodical plan, organised the transport and commissariat and mobilised the intellect of the nation to devise weapons of war. Far away on the frontiers, and in the great confused camps of the interior, the ragged armies responded to their unseen touch, while, in the sun-drenched squares and narrow, evil-smelling streets of the cities, the gangs went about their business of terror and the guillotine rose and fell.

These were the "workers" of the great Committee that ruled France; Robespierre and his disciples, St. Just and Couthon, its civil administrators; Barère, Billaud Varennes and Collot d'Herbois the panders of the Terror. In the green room of the Pavillon de Flore at the end of the dark passage flanked by cannon—"the steps of the throne"—sat the dreaded "decemvirs" whose word was law, whose disapproval death. Outside Danton, banished by the intrigues of the jealous Robespierre from the Committee he had created, still went about his work of speech and inspiration. Between them these men, wielding a power undreamt of by Louis XIV, hammered France into a new shape for a particular purpose, centralised, hardened, despotic. Under their growing discipline, *ça ira* assumed a terrible meaning for the world.

. . . .

It was the Duke of York's forces, laboriously closing in on Dunkirk from marshy towns and villages figuring not for the last time in British history—Ypres, Furnes, Poperinghe—which first felt the tempo of Carnot's quickening hand. In mid-August, marching across the French front towards their new stations, the Guards had been in action at Linselles where, after a Dutch brigade had given way before a Republican attack, the big fellows from the English shires stormed a hill with the bayonet and, when their ammunition failed, cuffed and jostled the puny French like a London mob. Since then the British had been nibbling at the outer suburbs of Dunkirk, quartered in a great quadrilateral between the North Sea and the Bergues-Furnes canal amid morasses, ditches and sand-dunes, scanned in all their movements from the silent tower of Dunkirk Cathedral.

Here in the opening days of September Carnot struck. Using the interior lines which France's position gave her, he assailed Coburg's classic cordon—weak at every point and strong at none—with the shock of hammer blows concentrated against a single spot. The French came on in the new order that Carnot had prescribed for them: the picked men—the natural fighters—going before in fierce, impetuous waves of sharpshooters, the remainder massed in columns whose density made up for lack of training and whose superior numbers, launched in endless waves, enabled them to penetrate the defenders' lines. The covering force of Germans at Hondschoote, though fighting back with the stubborn hardihood of their race, were overwhelmed. Threatened with encirclement between the marshes and the sea, the Duke of York was forced to retire in haste, abandoning his siege guns and most of his stores.

The failure at Dunkirk was a grave disappointment for England. For a few days it endangered the Government. For Chatham at the Admiralty had not only failed to send the promised naval aid to the besiegers, but had not even protected them from bombardment by French gunboats. Pitt took it with his wonted courage. He wrote that it was a severe shock, but only, he trusted, a temporary one. "It ought to have the effect of increasing if possible our exertions."

His faith was rewarded. Hard on its tail came astonishing news from the Mediterranean. Since the arrival of Lord Hood's blockading fleet, the great naval arsenal of Toulon, isolated by the general anarchy of France, had been threatened with starvation. On August 27th, moderate elements in the town, terrified by the holocaust of massacre, rape and arson at Marseilles, ran up the white flag and invited Hood to take possession of the town in the name of Louis XVII. Thus it came about that the greatest arsenal in France and thirty ships of the line passed into the hands of a British fleet of only twelve. When eleven days later the news reached England people could scarcely believe their ears.

The Government was beside itself with joy. "I am much mistaken," wrote Grenville, "if the business at Toulon is not decisive of the war." Pitt thought it offered a better chance of victory than anything that had occurred, and even an experienced soldier like Calvert held that the town was worth more to Britain than the entire Flemish frontier. So it might have been had Hood had the troops to exploit it. But the only garrison available consisted of 1500 seamen and marines from the fleet and a few thousand ill-disciplined Spaniards hastily dispatched by sea from Rousillon and who, according to Captain Nelson, did nothing but cut their prisoners' throats. When Sir Charles Grey, the commander-elect of the intended West Indian expeditionary force, was asked how many men in his view would be needed to hold the fifteen-mile perimeter of the town, he replied 50,000: an expert opinion which Pitt preferred to ignore.

With Hood appealing for troops, there were four courses open to the Government. It could follow its first natural impulse and send its entire available force to Toulon, so laying the foundation of a great offensive to destroy the Jacobin power in the south. This would however necessitate not only withdrawing troops from Flanders but the abandoning of any idea of an expedition to either the West Indies or Brittany. Alternatively it could do as Burke and Windham were urging: send every man who could be raised to support a Royalist advance on Paris from the west. Or it could revert to the policy agreed in the spring and, by concentrating all its forces in Flanders, stake everything on an Allied invasion from the north. Or finally it could fall back on its original "blue water" strategy and, eschewing Continental adventures, dispatch an overwhelming force to the West Indies.

Any of these four courses offered some hope of success. But the Government failed to choose any of them. Instead it tried to achieve the impossible and carry out all four. It would not withdraw from Flanders because of the King's anxiety for his Hanoverian possessions and its own concern for the balance of European power. It would not abandon operations in the West Indies because the City would not let it. It would not renounce all idea of helping the western Royalists—for which it had begun in August to assemble a small force at Southampton under Lord Moira—because this would upset the Portland Whigs, a political body which it particularly wanted to mollify. And it would not relinquish its unexpected foothold at Toulon because the opportunity seemed too good to miss.

The result was as might have been expected. A partial withdrawal from Flanders led to a French break-through in October which had to be met by hurrying back other troops to Ostend. The delayed expedition sent to the West Indies in November was only half the size planned and was inadequate either to conquer the French colonies or hold them when taken. The scratch force assembled under Lord Moira waited for artillery and stores until December and then sailed without them to the Brittany coast only to find that the insurgents had already been driven from it and that the chance of a landing had passed. Meanwhile Toulon was starved of troops, not because the Government did not wish to send any but because it had not left any to send. Not until October 27th did the first British regulars reach the port and then only a small contingent of two battalions and a few guns from Gibraltar under General O'Hara. The latter almost immediately had the misfortune to be captured in a skirmish.

Pitt consoled himself by drawing up elaborate paper schemes for massing an international army at Toulon for a spring offensive. The treaties signed during the summer with the Mediterranean Powers had provided for the employment of Spanish, Piedmontese and Neapolitan contingents in British pay, and with his usual optimism the Prime Minister reckoned that by December, besides the parings of British garrisons, he could count on 9000 Piedmontese, 6000 Neapolitans, 4000 Spaniards, and at least 5000 Austrians. That this international army might be more difficult to command than a composite British force of equal size never even occurred to his unmilitary mind.

• • • • • • • •

No conceptions of war could have differed more than those of the British and French Governments. The former timidly based military action on public opinion. The latter brutally coerced public opinion to support military action. In Whitehall the first thought always was how "to give the war a good appearance." Ministers weighed rival interests, balanced one theatre of operations against another and doled out men and supplies to appease popular clamour. Invariably compromising, they fell between two stools. Shunning unpalatable decisions, they were never able to concentrate their forces and seize the initiative. Setting no tune themselves, they were compelled to dance to the enemy's. Seeking secondary objectives to conciliate the opinion of the hour, they would throw away next year's victory for to-morrow's announcement in the *Gazette* of the capture of a fortress or a sugar island.

While Pitt was gathering in imagination soldiers of every tongue to assail France from the furthest point of the compass, Carnot, relying on interior lines, was massing his forces to strike outwards. Unlike his enemies he perfectly understood the art of war. His first blow fell in the Rhône valley where, capturing Lyons from the Federalists, he removed all danger of Austrian infiltration across the Alps into the Midi. In October he struck again in Flanders, defeating the Austrians at Wattignies and a week later piercing the other end of Coburg's overstrained cordon in a two-days' drive through Menin, Ypres and Nieuport which all but cut the British off from their base at Ostend. The threat to Artois was thus lifted till the spring. A few weeks later both northern armies, floundering hopelessly in the Flemish mud, retired into winter cantonments.

With his vulnerable northern frontier safe, Carnot now concentrated his forces against the hapless Vendeans. Their gallantry and loyalty could not avail against the force and energy of the terrible Republic. By Christmas half the villages of the west were heaps of cinders and the fields strewn with thousands of corpses. As the blue-coated armies drove outward like some mighty force compressed and brought to boiling point, the bosses of the Jacobin machine followed them scotching dissension with terror. It was in part the expression of the nation's will to live, in part the foul vent of tortured and suppressed instincts after a century's misgovernment. Men of incredible evil pushed or wriggled their way to the broken surface of French life and wreaked their will on every one within their reach. Every life was at their mercy. The prisons were packed with the generous, the noble and the innocent. The guillotine worked ceaselessly. Samson, the executioner, was the high priest of the nation: Fouquier-Tinville, the pock-marked ex-financier and Public Prosecutor, the keeper of its conscience. "Let us go to the foot of the great altar," cried Amar in the Convention, "and attend the celebration of the Red Mass!"

The Terror served its purpose. The will of centralised authority became absolute. Every man not crippled by age or infirmity was pressed into the armies—a force purged by desperation of both fear and pity. Fanny Burney's husband, the amiable General D'Arblay, discovered to his amazement that the head of his family, a gentle, refined aristocrat devoted to the monarchical cause, had died fighting for the Republic on the Spanish frontier. The party tyrants accompanied the headquarters of every army, terrifying generals and soldiers alike into unquestioning obedience to the dictates of the great Committee in Paris.

By mid-December Carnot was ready for Toulon. Here he had gathered 35,000 men and had given command of the siege guns to a youthful Corsican artillery captain named Bonaparte. The defending force of Italians, Spaniards and French royalists with its sprinkling of British regulars and marines was weakened by international dissension and sickness. When the French attacked on the stormy night of December 17th a few thousand British and Piedmontese alone made any resistance: the rest became a rabble. By the morning the sulky Bonaparte, all unwonted fire, was running up batteries in the captured Fort Aiguillette to rake the harbour and roadsteads.

There was nothing for it but immediate evacuation. On the night of the 18th, with every gun firing on the blazing city from the surrounding heights and the criminals, released from the jails, putting man, woman and child to the sword, a young British captain, Sidney Smith, endeavoured to destroy the French fleet which it was now too late to remove. The Spanish sailors who shared his task were lacking in professional skill, or, as one disgusted naval officer put it, "the vilest set of lubbers that ever was seen." In the resulting confusion only thirteen of the battleships were accounted for. Eighteen others survived to fight another day.

A week later the British fleet, crowded with nearly 15,000 refugees—"fathers without families and families without fathers the picture of horror and despair"—was joined in Hyeres Bay by troops from Gibraltar intended for the defence of Toulon. Others lay idle in Moira's transports off the Isle of Wight while more were in mid-Atlantic, tossing up and down on their way to West Indian graveyards. And for a whole fortnight after its fall Downing Street relying on its mathematical calculations, continued to imagine that Toulon was defended by an ample army. "I think," wrote Pitt on Christmas Day, "there is still a very good chance of all proving right in that quarter."[1]

. . . .

The year, which had begun in cloud and storm and promised so brilliantly in the early summer, had ended again in cloud. In December the French had resumed the offensive in the east. Three days before Christmas Lazare Hoche stormed the lines of Froeschweiler. The Austrians and Prussians fell back towards the Rhine, abandoning the Palatinate and Alsace, while in the south Kellermann drove the Piedmontese once more beyond the Alps.

The British Government, however, remained soberly cheerful. "It is true," wrote the Foreign Secretary, "that the campaign has not answered all that one's wishes suggested nor even all that at one period of the year it seemed reasonable to hope. But surely to have begun by the defence of the Neerdyke and of Maestricht and to end with the establishment of our winter quarters close to the French frontier, and in some parts, well within their territories, would in January last have seemed worth compounding for." No enemy had set foot on British soil anywhere in the world. Pondicherry and Chandernagore had been captured in the East Indies and Tobago in the West. In Santo Domingo a British force from Jamaica had occupied several coastal points, including Mole St. Nicolas—the Gibraltar of the Caribbean. The enemy's flag had been swept from the seas and several of his finest frigates captured in engagements in which all the glory had rested with England.

Yet both in Parliament and the country there was a sense of frustration. Hopes had been pitched too high and too often had been dashed. There was criticism of the Government and even of the war. The campaign in Flanders had never been popular: the nation still retained its traditional horror of Continental commitments born of older "cruel wars in High Germany." Britons felt little enthusiasm for their Prussian and Austrian allies. Nor, much as they hated Jacobins, did they share Burke's sympathy for the French exiles. The more they saw of them, the less they liked them. When in December the guns in St. James's Park and the Tower fired salvos, public joy turned to dismay when it became known that they were celebrating no naval victory in the Channel but a landing in aid of Royalist planters in Santo Domingo.

What the country had wanted was a quick and glorious war at sea with plenty of prizes and few casualties: the kind of war that Chatham had given it. Instead there had been an uninspiring dribble of maimed and half-starved soldiers returning from

[1] *Rose*, I, 32.

Flanders, crowded between icy decks without even straw to sleep on and turned adrift in Kentish ports whose supine authorities had not even anticipated their reception. For this much blame was unfairly cast on the Duke of York, whose undisciplined officers, pining for the fleshpots of London, poured a stream of complaints into influential ears. Now in January came news of the loss of Toulon. The Government's attempt to dwell on the destruction done to the French fleet and arsenal was not a success. For the public felt that neither should have been lost.

The causes of failure were unperceived. They were partly the nation's reluctance to prepare for war, partly the Government's characteristic inability to follow any systematic plan. There had been no concentration of force: no persistence in policy. Instead Pitt and Dundas had improvised according to the needs of the hour, living from hand to mouth and allowing the enemy the initiative. Flabbiness of decision inevitably degenerated into a futile scramble to rush insufficient forces to whatever point of the Allied circumference the French chose to attack. "The misfortunes of our situation," wrote the shrewd old King, "is that we have too many objects to attend to, and our force consequently must be too weak at each place."[1]

But the Government seemed incapable of learning. It could not see that military operations were not static: that, once initiated, they grew of their own, making ever fresh demands on the nation's strength and manpower. Territorial magnates and lawyers had still to realise that the direction of a world-wide campaign called for at least as much forethought and precision as laying out a plantation or drafting a legal instrument. They let the war run itself—into tangles.

[1] When Fox argued in the House that, if the object of the campaign was to put an end to French tyranny, Toulon was the most important objective: if it was conquest, the West Indies, young Mr. Jenkinson of the India Board, replying for the Government, revealed the confusion in Pitt's mind: the country's war aim was to destroy the Jacobin menace to Europe but the defence of Toulon could obviously not be allowed to outweigh the importance of strengthening the Empire.

CHAPTER FIVE

The Enemy Strikes

1794-5

"We are in a war of a peculiar nature. It is not with an ordinary community. . . . We are at war with a system which by its essence is inimical to all other governments; and which makes peace or war as peace and war may best contribute to their subversion. It is with an armed doctrine that we are at war." *Burke.*

"I learnt what one ought not to do and that is always something."

Wellington.

THAT winter the fever of mass murder, atheism and reckless spending in Paris seemed to be approaching its climax. At Christmas the obscene and diseased journalist, Hebert, presided over the Feast of Reason in Notre Dame, where a whore was elevated at the high altar amid Rabelaisian rites. In the prisons thousands of innocent men and women, flung there by some Party sadist's whim, fed out of troughs on offal or were driven in droves chained like cattle through the streets.[1] To decent English minds it seemed unthinkable that men could survive who broke every law of God and man, who robbed and murdered and blasphemed, who denied justice, pity and humanity itself in their ruthless search for power. "From the nature of the mind of man and the necessary progress of human affairs," Pitt declared in Parliament, "it is impossible that such a system can be of long duration." "Surely," cried the high-minded Windham, "Heaven will presently put a whip into every honest hand to lash these villains naked through the world."[2]

The need to destroy the menace quickly before it could spread further was plain. "We are called in the present age," Pitt told the House, "to witness the political and moral phenomenon of a mighty and civilised people, formed into an artificial horde of banditti, throwing off all the restraints which have influenced men in social life. . . . We behold them uniting the utmost savageness and

[1] See the remarkable account of the sufferings of General O'Hara after his capture at Toulon described in *Farington*, I, 111-12.

[2] *Windham Papers*, I, 162.

ferocity of design with consummate contrivance and skill in execution, and seemingly engaged in no less than a conspiracy to exterminate from the face of the earth all honour, justice and religion." Because of the inequalities and corruptions of the past, they could count on allies in every country. They had the advantage of waging an ideological offensive. Already Revolutionary agents, with long purses and beguiling tongues, were undermining the resistance of Britain's allies. At Turin, Naples, Florence and Genoa even high officials had been involved in treasonable conspiracies. Spain, Holland, Switzerland, Sweden and Denmark were seething with subterranean Jacobinism.

It seemed vital to Pitt to keep the Grand Alliance in being. He was under no illusions about his allies and their selfish, divided aims. But so long as they could be induced to fight against the common enemy of mankind it was best to turn a blind eye to their faults. The human future depended on keeping a *cordon sanitaire* round France till the Jacobin fever had spent itself.

Pitt therefore welcomed a visit from Mack, the rising strategist of the Austrian Staff, and promised him additional troops for a renewed offensive in the spring. The army estimates presented to Parliament in February, 1794, after Mack's departure provided for 175,000 Regulars, 34,000 German Auxiliaries and 52,000 embodied Militia. But the bulk of the trained and mobile troops at the Government's disposal had already been committed far beyond recall through its failure to follow out a co-ordinated war plan. Tied to a major campaign on France's northern frontier, it had simultaneously encouraged its naval and military commanders to take the offensive in the Mediterranean and West Indies without a thought of how they could be reinforced and supplied. There were inducements for Britain in both these theatres of war. But in neither could operations be sustained from existing resources.

. . . .

It was Lord Hood and his political adviser, Sir Gilbert Elliot—the former Civil Commissioner for Toulon—who committed Britain to a war in Corsica. Sold to France a quarter of a century before by the banking Republic of Genoa, the turbulent island had only submitted to its new rulers after a desperate resistance led by Pascal Paoli. In the spring of 1793 a rebellion had broken out which drove the Republican garrisons into the coastal fortresses and sent Captain Bonaparte's "traitor" family flying to Marseilles for refuge. Though the Cabinet had toyed in the summer with the idea of a landing in the island, Paoli's appeals for British help had remained unanswered.

But in the New Year, with 1,400 troops crowded on board his transports, Hood saw Corsica as a heaven-sent opportunity. Having lost Toulon he needed a naval base from which to maintain its blockade. With a splendid anchorage the island was several hundred miles nearer the port than Gibraltar. Its forests supplied the masts and timber for the French Mediterranean Fleet. In February, therefore, Hood landed Major-General Dundas's troops and a contingent of sailors in San Fiorenzo Bay.

But neither the impetuous old seaman nor his adviser had considered the difficulties of conquering and garrisoning an island with four hundred miles of coastline. Though the brigands of the interior acclaimed the English, the strongholds of Bastia and Calvi were defended by 3,500 French regulars—more than double the original invading force. Their investment occupied a growing proportion of Britain's slender military resources for many months. Owing to the peremptory and sometimes almost contemptuous attitude of Lord Hood and his officers towards the Army, the operations led to a lamentable deterioration in relations between the Services. The general, who seemed "an old woman in a red ribbon" to impatient politicians and seamen, not without reason regarded the task demanded of him as beyond his professional powers. The admiral thereupon announced his intention of attacking without him.

"While General Dundas
And his eighteen manœuvres all sat on the grass,"

Nelson and the crew of the *Agammemnon* proceeded to invest Bastia on their own. The siege which followed, though successful, was conducted with grossly inadequate resources. Later, the army, reinforced from England, resumed its rightful place under the command of Major-General James Stuart, a younger son of Lord Bute, on whom the brilliant mantle of Peterborough seemed to have fallen. Largely owing to his and Nelson's efforts Calvi fell on August 10th, though it cost the eager little captain his right eye and all but his life. "Never," wrote Stuart's second-in-command, a still greater soldier named John Moore, "was so much work done by so few men."

. . . .

The West Indian campaign had even graver effects on the course of the war. In January, 1794, Lieutenant-General Sir Charles Grey's 7,000 troops, after a six week's voyage, reached Barbados. Despite their small numbers they at once attacked the French islands, and as a result of brilliant co-operation between Grey and Vice-Admiral Sir John Jervis overcame all resistance in Martinique, St. Lucia and Guadeloupe by the end of May. But the real campaign had scarcely begun. Almost at once the victors were simultaneously assailed by reinforcements from France and a negro and mulatto rising. For by denouncing slavery—the gap in Britain's moral front—the French had secured a formidable ally. With the help of the revolted slaves the force from Rochefort, which had evaded the loose British blockade, was able to reconquer Guadeloupe before the end of the year. Yet it was yellow fever more than any other cause which robbed Britain of her West Indian conquests. Within a few months the dreaded "black vomit" had destroyed 12,000 of her finest soldiers and reduced the survivors to trembling skeletons.

. . . .

In the conduct of these distant campaigns Pitt and Dundas were handicapped by the lapse of time between the dispatch of orders from England and the receipt of news from the theatres of war. They were still celebrating Grey's victories of the spring when his men were dying by thousands in the autumn. But their difficulties were increased a hundredfold by their failure to prepare for the inevitable consequences of their own actions. They undertook and promised more than they had any reasonable expectation of being able to perform. After initiating operations that called for a steady flow of reinforcements, they were forced to deflect them into other and more urgent channels.

The measures which the Government now took to remedy the shortage of trained troops and fulfil its promises to its Austrian allies lowered the discipline and dignity of the entire Service. Both senior and junior regimental rank were offered for sale in return for recruits. With every 450 men raised for an existing battalion, a lieutenant colonelcy was offered to the senior major for £600, and two majorities to the captains at from £550 to £700. Companies were sold to any bidder for £2,800. In the brisk competition that followed the price of a recruit rose to as much as £30 a head.

This degrading system, which appealed to an innate English snobbery, enabled the Government to raise 30,000 recruits by private bounty at little cost to the Treasury. It involved the passing over of the old professional soldier of modest means—the type from which generals like Abercromby and Dundas were sprung—in favour of upstart young plutocrats utterly ignorant of their profession. Minors found themselves commanding battalions while veteran subalterns, old enough to be their fathers, waited in vain for a company. Even children in the nursery received the King's commission: a contemporary print shows a minute officer of the Guards eating sugar plums at Kelsey's, the St. James' Street fruiterer.

As for the recruits raised under such a system, they were what might have been expected. They resembled Falstaff's men.

. . . .

Yet it is only fair to remember that Britain's principal contribution to the Allied cause was at sea. The Navy vote for 1794 provided for 85,000 men, or one per cent of the population of England and Wales. As the returning merchant fleets month by month dropped anchor in Thames and Avon, the press-gangs made up the complement of the King's ships. By the beginning of the year eighty sail of the line were in commission. On these depended not only the ring set round France but the subsidies which maintained the Allied armies.

During the first year of the war the Navy had driven the French flag off the seas, capturing for a loss of six of its own small craft fifty-two frigates and lesser ships-of-war and eighty-eight privateers. Had the state of France been normal this would not have yet had any decisive effect on the war, for only a fraction of her foreign trade was sea-borne. But owing to the anarchic dislocation of her social life, it threatened her with starvation. The harvest of 1793 had failed. By stretching the rights of blockade to include provisions, Pitt had recruited famine as an ally.

Had the aging men in control of the Navy shown the same understanding of blockade as their successors, the Republic could scarcely have survived the summer of 1794. Realising their danger the revolutionary leaders commissioned agents in America to buy grain and charter merchantmen. At the same time they made every effort to get their neglected Atlantic Fleet ready for sea. At Christmas they sent Rear-Admiral Vanstabel—a first-rate officer—with two ships of the line and three frigates from Brest to the United States to escort home the grain fleet that was to raise the siege of France.

Fortunately for the Jacobins the Admiral commanding the Channel Fleet did not believe in close blockade. Lord Howe was a gallant old man of 68—"undaunted as a rock and as silent"—and the first sea officer in the world. But like other elderly sailors he was obsessed with the supreme importance of safeguarding his ships. He refused to expose them to winter gales on the Brittany coast. In this he was strongly supported by the Treasury. In mid-December he accordingly withdrew the battle fleet to harbour, leaving only the frigates at sea. Thus it was that Vanstabel escaped, and others more important after him. For Brest could not be blockaded from Spithead nor even from Torbay.

Early in April five more ships of the line put out under Rear-

Admiral Nielly to meet the convoy which sailed on the 11th from Hampton Roads under Vanstabel's escort. No British warship was present to shadow either force. Vice-Admiral Jervis, who was later to prove how closely an enemy coast could be sealed, was engaged in military operations against Guadeloupe, while Captain Nelson, usurping the functions of a soldier, was wearing out his frail body in the trenches around Bastia. Had the qualities they showed five years later been employed at this time in bottling up the French Atlantic coastline, Europe might have been saved twenty years of bloodshed and tyranny.

. . . .

In April the Allies reopened the long-awaited campaign in Flanders. From the heights above Le Cateau, where on the 16th the young Emperor of Austria inspected 160,000 troops, they advanced with the steady leisure of the eighteenth century to besiege Landrecies. Their line stretched from the sea to the Sambre: the cordon of steel that was to strangle revolutionary France.

Carnot knew that France must break it or starve. All his hopes were pinned on the offensive—such an offensive as old Europe had never seen. He entrusted the command of his northern armies to a thirty-three year-old general, Charles Pichegru, the son of a Jura peasant. His orders were to attack at all costs and go on attacking till he had broken through.

On the 24th while the main Allied Army was grouped round Landrecies, Pichegru struck between the centre and the sea. Sweeping across the Lys valley, the French left under Souham—a thirty-four year-old ex-private—cut the Austrian cordon, drove past Menin and overwhelmed the astonished garrison of Courtrai. But there, though a salient was driven deep into the Allied line, the advance was halted. Confronted by the marshy ground between Scheldt and Lys and the stubborn resistance of the Austrian and Hanoverian regulars, Souham waited until the main force of his right could move forward.

But in the centre Pichegru's attack failed. Advancing to the relief of Landrecies, his imperfectly trained levies were taken in the flank at Beaumont by the Allied cavalry under the Duke of York and routed with a loss of 7000 dead and 41 guns. Landrecies thereupon surrendered.

Had Coburg followed up this brilliant exploit, Beaumont might have proved one of the decisive battlse of history. But the fleeting opportunity of those spring days of 1794 was not for the old man's grasping. Unable to think save in terms of defensive cordons, he made no attempt to break through Pichegru's demoralised centre or to send his magnificent cavalry sweeping forward to Paris—only ten days march away. Instead, he paused nervously to repair the rent in his right flank. The day after Landrecies fell the British Army was despatched north through rain and muddy lanes to Tournai to bar any further penetration into Flanders.

So, as in the previous summer after Neerwinden, the French were allowed a breathing space. It was not wasted by commanders who knew that the alternative to victory was the guillotine. To keep the enemy inactive till they were ready for a renewed general offensive, they launched a series of desperate assaults on the crossings of the Sambre.

With this battering on his left and a salient driven deep into his right, nothing would induce Coburg to risk an advance in the centre. His one concern was to restore the classical perfection of his line by driving back the French from Courtrai. But Mack and the Duke of York were able, after some argument, to persuade him to attempt a concerted movement to cut off Souham's 40,000 troops in the exposed salient from their base at Lille.

The scheme was worked out skilfully. But it relied too much on French passivity and Austrian punctuality. Three of the five Allied corps, on whose exact movements the operation depended, never reached the battlefield at all. Only the Duke of York carried out his part of the programme promptly. As a result 10,000 Britons, after taking all their objectives on May 17th, found themselves at nightfall in the heart of Souham's army.

Throughout the first four weeks of campaigning the British Army had enjoyed unbroken and deserved success.[1] It was now to enter upon a prolonged period of failure. At dawn on the 18th the French, grasping their opportunity, counter-attacked. Soon both the Guards Brigades under Abercromby at Mouvaix and Major-General Fox's Brigade near Tourcoing were encircled and cut off from each other. The Duke at his headquarters could make no contact with either. Everywhere on the misty, enclosed Flemish plain the enemy was swarming. Fortunately, the British soldier rose to the emergency. With superb calm the Guards, covered by the 7th and 15th Light Dragoons, fought their way back to Tournai. Fox's line battalions, defying the inevitable, struggled all day across country until, with a loss of nearly half of their strength, they regained the Allied lines. "No mobbed fox was ever more put

[1] Only a few days before its cavalry had ridden over three French squares in front of Tournai and taken 400 prisoners and thirteen guns. It was the last time for eighteen years —until a far day on the plains of Salamanca—that British horse were to break a French square.

to it to make his escape than we were," wrote Major Calvert. By superb effrontery the Duke of York also escaped capture, at one point galloping in front of his two escort squadrons of Dragoons in a dramatic chase over hedge and dyke with the Star of the Garter gleaming on his breast. Of twenty-eight British guns nineteen were lost. Throughout the day the British never set eyes on an Austrian. For, unlike the ragged French, the Emperor's white-coated columns did not march to the sound of the guns. Instead, they stayed and listened to them.

. . . .

While these events were happening on the Flanders plain the limelight of battle was shifting to billowing sails, waves and ocean clouds. On May 2nd a young Rhinelander, in the diplomatic service of Austria, watched from a hill near Cowes the Channel Fleet escorting two vast convoys of merchantmen to sea. Years later when he was the first statesman in Europe, Prince Metternich recalled it as the most beautiful sight he had ever seen. At a signal from the Admiral the merchantmen unfurled their sails, those bound for the East Indies passing to the east and those for the West Indies to the west of the island. Hundreds of vessels filled with spectators covered the roads, in the midst of which the great ships-of-war followed one another like columns on parade.

If this magnificent spectacle fired a foreigner, how much more so the thought of it inspired Englishmen! The Grand Fleet was at sea after its winter-rest, and the country rejoiced. Yet the significance of the event was better understood in hungry France. For on Lord Howe's ability to intercept the American grain convoy her whole future depended.

Had he taken his station off Ushant a few weeks earlier, no unit of the French Battle Fleet, now under orders to meet the convoy, could have left Brest. But a commercial country at war is not governed only by strategical considerations. The London merchants demanded protection for their own outgoing convoys, and not till these were ready could Howe sail. When at last he did so, he detailed a quarter of his fleet under Rear-Admiral Montagu to escort his precious charges far out into the Atlantic. Having thus divided his forces to secure secondary objectives the old man looked into Brest and then, seeing the masts of the main French Fleet still in the inner harbour, unaccountably sailed off into the blue to look for the grain ships.

But when, having found nothing in the wastes of the Atlantic, he returned to have another look at Brest on the 19th, his adversary had gone. Three days earlier Rear-Admiral Villaret Joyeuse had got to sea with twenty-six sail of the line. He carried with him a representative of the National Convention and a warning from Robespierre that failure to secure the safe arrival of the American grain would involve the loss of his head.

Not having watched the enemy's point of departure, Howe had no clue to his whereabouts or the oncoming course of the convoy. All he knew for certain was that five hundred miles out in the Atlantic Montagu, having set the British merchantmen on their way, was cruising over a two hundred mile stretch of water in the hope of intercepting the latter. In the event of his doing so, his six capital ships ran the risk of meeting not merely Vanstabel's two escorting battleships but Nielly's five and Villaret Joyeuse's twenty-six, all of which were sure to be shadowing the convoy's path.

For eight days Howe searched the Atlantic in vain. But on May 28th, 400 miles west of Ushant, his frigates sighted Villaret Joyeuse to windward sailing N.N.E. before the wind in three columns. Though there was a heavy swell and the French, ship for ship, were superior in tonnage and gun-power, Howe clung for two days to the enemy's tail, harassing his rear ships and battling for the weather gage. By the night of the 29th he had got the French to leeward and forced four of their ships out of the line for the loss of only one of his own. In forty hours of continuous fighting and manœuvring his skilful tactics had gone far to redress his earlier strategic error. He could look forward on the morrow to a fleet action with twenty-five battleships and an enemy on his lee with only twenty-two.

But during the brief summer night fog fell. For two days the fleets were hidden from one another. Occasionally, as narrow lanes of light parted the mist, the look-outs in the British frigates, clinging grimly to the French flanks, caught glimpses of shadowy giants gliding from darkness to darkness or saw aloft, caught in the sunshine, peaks of dazzling white canvas. Then the mists would close again. While they did so Nielly's squadron joined Villaret Joyeuse, bringing his strength up to twenty-six ships; and the great convoy, over a hundred vessels strong, passed within a few miles of the British Fleet sailing unscathed and unseen towards France. On the same day Montagu, despairing of finding either the convoy or his own admiral, put back to Plymouth.

By gradually leading Howe away from the convoy's track Villaret Joyeuse had saved France. But he could do no more. The English Admiral, confiding in his hard-wrought lifetime's craft of sailing ships and fleets, was not to be kept from his chosen prey. The dawn of Sunday, June 1st, rose on a clear horizon, a soft sea bathed in sunshine, and four miles to leeward the French Fleet.

At that glorious moment of his career, true to his country's tradition, Howe sent his men down to breakfast. At twenty minutes to nine, feeling his work done, he shut his signal book with the nearest he ever came to a gesture. For four days and nights the brave old man had been continuously on deck giving orders, snatching such sleep as he could upright in his chair. Now he was content. The rest he could leave to his captains and crews. They knew "Black Dick's" courage and devotion to duty and he had no doubt of theirs. Had he been aboard the *Prince*, he would have heard Captain Collingwood observing to his Rear-Admiral that it was about the time their wives were going to church, and that he trusted that the peal they were going to sound in the Frenchmen's ears would outring all the bells in England.[1]

As soon as the oncoming British ships were within range the French opened fire. But with a single exception, the British kept on their course in silence with their gunports closed. Between the long decks, where the brass-tipped cannon gleamed in double lines, the seamen, stripped to the waist, waited with the easy discipline of men perfectly trained to an art now about to be tested. In the *Brunswick* they sang to cheer themselves in the darkness, the lieutenant of the lower-deck reporting that till they got the word to fire they were all as happy as princes singing "Rule Britannia." It was about ten o'clock that Howe's flagship, the *Queen Charlotte*, breaking the French line, swept the giant *Montagne* with a single broadside, which killed three hundred of her crew and left a gap in her stern through which a coach could have been driven. "Such a fire," wrote Collingwood, "as would have done you good to have heard!"

There was little science in the actual fighting. It was a captain's not an admiral's battle. The French line, pierced in twenty places, dissolved into islands of smoke and thunder within which individual ships battered away at one another. The most famous of these duels was between the *Brunswick* and *Vengeur*. Unable to open the lower-deck ports, which were jammed against her opponent's sides, the guns' crews of the *Brunswick* fired through them at point-blank range, while her men dashed buckets of water over the flames. After losing her captain and a third of her company she forced *Vengeur* to strike, and almost simultaneously captured a French three-decker, which had attacked her on the other bow. Two hundred of the *Vengeur's* crew were rescued naked from the water, while others

[1] *Collingwood*, 21.

who had fortified their patriotism with liquor became a legend, and went down with her singing snatches of the "Marseillaise."

Everywhere the story was the same. The French had a slight numerical superiority in ships and a substantial one in guns and men: 20,000 to 17,000 sailors.[1] But though they fought bravely they were no match in seamanship and gunnery for their assailants. After some hours, Villaret Joyeuse, who, though recently only a lieutenant, handled his command with skill, withdrew his fleet and escaped to the north-west. Howe, almost carried by his officers from the quarter-deck, was too exhausted to pursue. Seven dismasted French battleships remained in his possession, one of which sank before she could be brought to port. "We have conquered the rascals!" wrote eleven year-old Midshipman Parker to his mother.

Nearly a fortnight after the battle the Admiral returned to Portsmouth with his prizes. Their decks were ploughed up with shot, and the wounded, many of them hob-nailed peasants, still lay in heaps where they had fallen. But the decks of the British men-of-war were scoured and spotless, the brass was shining and the crews alert at their stations. The aristocrats of the ocean had returned with their wonted glory. Their pleasure at their achievement was undimmed, for in the joy of the battle they had quite forgotten the object for which they had sailed: the French, Captain Collingwood told his friends, had been sent out with the express purpose of destroying them. The King went down to receive the victors, and every window in town was illuminated or smashed by the patriot mob. But Villaret Joyeuse brought back something more precious to his country than glory. On the day after Howe's return the grain fleet entered Brest. At the eleventh hour famine was averted.

Britain had lost her last chance of victory before the swelling military strength of France became too great to contain. While Howe was allowing the French battle fleet to lure him from the convoy's track the Emperor of Austria was leaving Flanders for Vienna. For far in the east the Poles, daring the impossible, had risen against their oppressors and driven them out of Warsaw. Once more the Prussians massed on their eastern frontiers, while the Austrian Chancellor, Thugut, mad with jealousy, became haunted by a single fear: that his country would be left out of the final partition of Poland. In comparison the retention of Belgium seemed to him of no consequence. He sought only to break off the western campaign and retire to the Rhine.

While Imperial headquarters meditated treachery and the Duke

[1] Among the British sailors was the 69th Regiment of Foot.

of York's forces avenged their losses in a stubborn stand before Tournai, the French continued their assaults on the Allied left. Relying on the inactivity of the Prussians, Carnot ordered Jourdan—the thirty-three year-old victor of Wattignies—to leave the Moselle undefended and march to the aid of the assailants. Early in June the reconstituted army of Sambre-et-Meuse crossed the Sambre, and after a series of desperate engagements invested Charleroi. When a fortnight later Coburg, with his main force, moved to the relief of the town it was too late. During an undecided action at Fleurus on the 26th the old German learnt that Charleroi had fallen. He called off the battle and retreated, leaving the Republicans masters of the field and, though no one knew it, of the next two decades of European history.

Carnot's purpose had been achieved. The speed and fury of his attack had triumphed: the persistence and numbers of his ragged peasant battalions had broken the overstrained cordon of the professional armies of the *Ancien Régime.* Its flank laid bare by the Austrian retreat, the British expeditionary force was compelled to abandon Tournai, Oudenarde and Ghent without a shot. On July 5th at an Allied Council on the future field of Waterloo the Duke of York pleaded with Coburg for a stand on the ridge of Mont St. Jean. But scarcely had the decision to fight been reached than the Austrians retreated again, this time eastwards towards their bases on the Rhine, leaving the road to Brussels open. By doing so they not only exposed York's flank but left him no alternative but to fall back in isolation northwards on his own base at Antwerp. All direct contact between the Allies was now severed. "The opinion which the British nation must have on the subject," the Duke of York wrote to Prince Coburg, "is that we are betrayed and sold to the enemy." A fresh force from England, which had been hastily landed at Ostend under Moira to save that indefensible port only escaped encirclement by a brilliant march across the French front to join its retreating comrades. Among its officers was the future victor of Waterloo, the 25-year-old Arthur Wellesley, who as Lieutenant-Colonel of the 33rd Regiment of Foot was seeing active service for the first time.

. . . .

During these fatal events Pitt was engaged in the political operation known to the eighteenth century as enlarging his bottom. For long the more sober of his former opponents had felt that the Party differences of the past were trifling compared with the Jacobin peril to civilisation. They took the view that support was due to any Government opposing it. "My determination," Windham had written, "is open, steady war against the whole Jacobin faction, and junction for that purpose with whomever it may be necessary to join."[1] The only thing which had prevented the main body of Whigs from entering a national Government had been the exaggerated scruples of their leader, the old Duke of Portland, about Fox.

At the beginning of July the importance of presenting the wavering Allies with the spectacle of a united Britain banished all remaining hesitations. Lord Fitzwilliam became President of the Council; Spencer, Lord Privy Seal; Windham, Secretary-at-War; and Portland Home and Colonial Secretary in place of Dundas, for whom a new Secretaryship of State was created, that of War. Soon afterwards Fitzwilliam took the Viceroyship of Ireland and Spencer succeeded Chatham as First Lord of the Admiralty. Burke, who had just retired from Parliament, gave the new Administration his blessing. Pitt offered a peerage to the old man who had done so much to bring about this national union but, broken by the fatal illness of his only son, he refused all honours.

These changes strengthened the Government internally as well as externally. Spencer might know little of the sea, but it was an advantage to have a First Lord who did not keep naval officers waiting every morning till he could bring himself to get up.[2] Dundas might not be the right man to wield its powers but a Secretaryship of State for War was an advance in the direction of administrative sanity. Though preferred only to a minor post, the chivalrous Windham brought to the administration a fanatic hatred of Jacobinism able to provide staying power in dark days.

Having reconstituted the Cabinet Pitt made another attempt to revive the spirit of his Allies. Feeling that it was better to defend the country on the Scheldt than on the Thames, he offered to add 30,000 troops to the payroll in return for a change in the Austrian high command and a more vigorous prosecution of the war. At the same time he instructed Malmesbury to press Prussia for the 62,000 men promised by that faithless kingdom in return for British subsidies.

But, true to their historic principle of taking everything and giving nothing, the Prussians remained motionless in the Palatinate. The Austrians, withdrawing their armies to the Rhine under a secret understanding with Robespierre, left the French to recapture their frontier fortresses unmolested. The Royalist volunteers in

[1] *Windham Papers*, I, 192.
[2] Lord Chatham said it did not signify, it was an indulgence. He could not give it up." —*Farington*, I, 54.

their garrisons were delivered over to their merciless countrymen. On the capitulation of Nieuport five hundred of them were driven into the fort ditch and mown down with grapeshot. The frenzied tyrants in Paris ordered even the British and Hanoverian prisoners to be massacred—an order which Pichegru, an honourable man, refused to carry out.

In its fear and selfishness the Austrian Court was now past caring for honour. It placed its hope in an end to the Revolution through the dictatorship of Robespierre: the strong man who that summer seemed to be liquidating all opposition. Everywhere in monarchical Europe the weaker brethren, appalled by the triumph of the "abominable spirit of liberty," sought to make their peace while they could: to buy at least a respite at the price of honour, gold and territory.

For France in July, 1794, was an intimidating spectacle. In Paris under the "lottery of Holy Guillotine" two or three thousand head were falling monthly, while in the provinces holocausts took place which made the blood of Christendom turn cold. At Nantes one monster massacred five hundred infants, having first offered their mothers the choice of prostitution or death. Another sadistic scoundrel put more than five thousand people to death at Arras.[1] Such men were as pitiless abroad as at home. Though Pichegru preserved a discipline which astonished those who recalled the plundering levies of a year before, his armies were followed by hordes of greedy agents who despoiled the Belgians of everything but the barest necessities.[2]

Conscious of these things, the majority of Englishmen, whatever the views of weaklings and malcontents, upheld the Government in its refusal to negotiate with Jacobins. When the Duke of Bedford moved a resolution in the Lords that his Majesty should be petitioned either to end the war or "be graciously pleased to state what the object of it was," and Fox echoed him in the Commons, Pitt asked what present prospect there was of an enduring agreement. Britain's war gain, he answered, was all that she would lose without it. "It is impossible to say what government we are to propose for France in the event of the Jacobins being overthrown, because that must depend on the circumstances of the times and the wishes of its inhabitants. But this much may be affirmed: that with the sanguinary faction which now rules its councils accommodation is impossible."

. . . .

[1] Among his victims were two English girls. Alison, III, 312.

[2] *Calvert*, 293. It should be remembered, however, that the Revolutionary armies imposed no creed of racial domination: no conquered foreigner was penalised for not being a Frenchman.

Only internal weakness arising from the moral failings of the Revolution saved the selfish and divided Allies from immediate destruction at the hands of the Republican armies. At the end of July the murderous fever in the French capital reached its peak. After suspending the last remaining forms of justice and virtually canonising himself on the Champ-de-Mars, Robespierre frightened the corrupt majority in the Convention into turning on him. On July 28th—the 9th Thermidor of the Revolutionary calendar—they drove him from the Assembly. Next day he and his terrible henchman, young St. Just, were sent to the guillotine before they could rouse the mob in their defence.

Power now passed to lesser men—jackals who for their own ends had obeyed the master terrorists. Tallien, Fouché, Barras were vile creatures but, unlike the grim idealists they had served and slain, they knew the advantages of moderation. They now became the leaders of a kind of revolutionary counter-revolution of profiteer regicides whose sole aim was to stabilise their own ill-gotten wealth and power. They were committed to the war because without it they could neither control the army nor stifle the popular reaction which might punish their past crimes. The sudden rise of these corrupt men brought a brief respite to Britain. For except for Carnot, who retained power for a few more years, they were not primarily concerned with winning the war. They were concerned only with its continuance.

But their enemies took no advantage of their respite. Britain's attempt to stiffen her allies failed dismally. The guarantee of an Austrian loan of £3,000,000 in September was promptly followed by the surrender of Valenciennes and further Austrian withdrawals. Meanwhile, Malmesbury wrote from Frankfurt that the conduct of the Prussians was becoming daily more shameful: "I lament every hour that I remain near them."[1]

Even Pitt now realised that German statesmen viewed England, as Grenville put it, merely as an inexhaustible milch cow. In an interview with the Prussian Ambassador he lost his temper and upbraided him for his country's breach of faith. But the only result was that King Frederick William gave orders that the campaign on the Rhine should cease altogether.

"Depend on it," wrote Major Calvert from the Duke of York's headquarters, "an English guinea is an article no German prince can withstand, and when a subsidy is in view it bewilders their senses and leaves them no inclination for exertion except for the attainment of it." Instead of relying any longer on them, this

[1] *H. M. C. Dropmore*, II, 636.

honest soldier hoped his countrymen would henceforward trust in nothing but God and themselves. Around him the Dutch, one of the bravest peoples in the world, now divided and ruled by plutocrats whose only law was profit, watched the British preparations to defend their native soil without stirring a hand to help them. Though Captain Sidney Smith, undeterred by his failure at Toulon, rushed in and out of their estuaries turning every vessel he saw into an imaginary gunboat, the stolid burghers remained indifferent. No preparations were made to destroy forts, magazines and ships against a French advance, and the most ordinary means of defence were neglected. "Anything so brutish, stupid and selfish," Windham wrote, "was never seen."

. . . .

Early in September, having replenished his supplies from the fortresses and harvests of the Low Countries, Pichegru resumed the offensive in overwhelming force. Crossing the Dommel, he drove the British on the 14th from the fortified post of Boxtel. A counter-attack under cover of darkness, in which Arthur Wellesley received his baptism of fire, failed disastrously, largely owing to the indiscipline and lack of training of the newly promoted and youthful regimental commanders from England. For where men mistrusted their officers no operation could succeed.

Sullenly the army retreated beyond the Waal. It was back where it had started eighteen months before. No wonder it swore terribly. "The rare old Duke of York," it sang:

"He had ten thousand men;
He marched 'em up a great high hill,
Then marched 'em down again."

Gone were the halcyon days when gentlemen of the Staff sat down to dine in shady Flemish gardens off food cooked by His Majesty's Hanoverian field-kitchen and served by laced footmen. Now they were lucky if they got anything to eat at all. Even the woollen gifts which the benevolent ladies of Great Britain had showered on their defenders in the first winter of the war had ceased to come. The army felt neglected and forgotten. Its boots were worn out and its uniforms stained and ragged; recruits arrived in thin, linen jackets and trousers without waistcoats, drawers or stockings. The Royal Waggon Corps, founded to supply its needs, had apparently been recruited from the thieves' kitchens of Blackfriars and Seven Dials, and was known as the Newgate Blues. The military hospitals were mere short cuts to the next world: a Dutch observer counted

42 bodies flung out of one barge of 500 sick who had been left untended on the open deck, without even straw. The surgeons' mates allowed the sick and wounded to starve, and spent the vast sums they claimed from the government in drinking and debauchery.[1]

From top to bottom the military administration, tested by adversity, was rotten. The best officers, like Moira, were recalled to England because under the Horse Guards' rigid rule of promotion for the higher ranks they lacked the seniority to be employed. Everything that could make an efficient fighting force was lacking except courage. "We want artillerymen," wrote Calvert, "we want a general officer at the head of the artillery, we want drivers and smiths; and we want three major-generals of infantry; we want a commanding engineer of rank and experience; we want a total reform in our hospitals; we want, at least, two out of the four brigades of mounted artillery with which his Grace of Richmond is amusing himself in England. We want a total stop put to that pernicious mode of bestowing rank on officers without even the form of recommendation, merely for raising (by means of crimps) a certain number of men, to restore to the Army those independent and disinterested feelings and those high principles which should actuate a soldier and form the basis of the military discipline of a free country."[2] The new Secretary at War, who, with his accustomed eagerness was on a personal visit to the front, commented bitterly on the shortage of artillery drivers. "One sits at home quietly and overlooks such particulars," he wrote, "but the fate of armies and of kingdoms is decided often by nothing else."[3]

With more than half its 21,000 infantry down with typhus, wounds and exposure, and with Dutch traitors and French agents swarming through its lines, the British Army had only one hope left—winter. The floods of November turned the Waal into an impassable barrier of desolate waters. Behind it a forlorn handful of redcoats preserved the last foothold of the *Ancien Régime* in the Low Countries. It alone stood between the Jacobins and the banks of Amsterdam and the Dutch Fleet and naval stores. To the east the French were already in Cologne, and the Austrian Army back beyond the Rhine. Prussia was secretly negotiating peace, and Spain, invaded and riddled with defeatism, preparing to do the same.

But in December, when the British Government, relying on winter, had withdrawn seven regiments for the West Indies and

[1] *Fortescue*, IV, 315; *Calvert*, 338.
[2] *Calvert*, 359-60.
[3] *Windham Papers*, I, 224.

recalled the Duke of York, an intense frost succeeded the rain. A week before Christmas the floating ice in the Waal began to pack. By the new year the frozen flood had ceased to be a barrier. Breaking every canon of eighteenth century war and trusting for supplies to a barren and ice-gripped countryside, Pichegru and Moreau crossed the river. To avoid annihilation the outnumbered British and Hanoverians fell back towards the Ysel.

The cold spell of that January was something which old men remembered fifty years afterwards. The birds fell dead from the trees, and morning after morning Parson Woodforde in Norfolk found the chamber-pot in his room frozen solid. The retreat of the British Army across the icy wastes of Gelderland had the quality of a nightmare. There was no shelter against the arctic wind. Discipline vanished, the Brigade of Guards and their traditional foes, the Hessians, engaging in pitched battle round the bread waggons. "Those of the Army that woke on the morning of the 17th of January," Sir John Fortescue has written, "saw about them such a sight as they never forgot. Far as the eye could reach over the whitened plain were scattered gun-limbers, waggons full of baggage stores or sick men, sutlers' carts and private carriages. Beside them lay the horses, dead; around them scores and hundreds of soldiers, dead; here a straggler who had staggered on to the bivouac and dropped to sleep in the arms of the frost; there a group of British and Germans round an empty rum cask; here forty English Guardsmen huddled together about a plundered waggon; there a pack-horse with a woman lying alongside it, and a baby swaddled in rags, peering out of the pack, with its mother's milk turned to ice upon its lips—one and all stark, frozen, dead. Had the retreat lasted but three or four days longer, not a man would have escaped."[1] As it was, more than six thousand—a third of the expeditionary force—perished in four days.

The retreat completed the disintegration of Holland. The Prince of Orange fled with his treasure in a fishing-boat to England, where his custom of drinking himself into a coma over his midday meal at Kew Palace put a severe strain on the hospitality of his allies. The great banking family of Hope did the same. Others, who had long been secretly treating with the enemy, openly acclaimed the conquerors: the mob rose, set up trees of Liberty and flaunted the tricolour. On January 20th the French entered Amsterdam and proclaimed a revolutionary Republic. There was not even time to remove the fleet. A few smaller vessels got away to England, but to the grief of the British Admiralty a flying body of French

[1] Fortescue, IV, 320/1.

horse and artillery galloped across the frozen Zuyder Zee and surprised the Dutch battleships ice-bound in the Texel. So sudden was the advance that Lord Malmesbury, returning to England from Brunswick with the future Princess of Wales, only narrowly escaped capture.

All hope of a stand inside Holland now vanished. The hungry and demoralised survivors of the British army fell back into North Germany, where they were insulted and neglected by the Prussians who, having no further hope of subsidies, treated them as a pack of contemptible and defeated tradesmen. Early in March the Government sent transports to the Weser to evacuate them. On April 13th, 1795, the infantry embarked at Bremen, the cavalry and a small force of artillery remaining behind to protect Hanover.

For northern Europe the war was over. Prussia had already made her peace with the Revolution. The French were in an arrogant mood, but the Ministers of Frederick William preferred to stomach it. For they saw in the ruthlessness of the new France—its centralisation, contempt for established morality and unabashed acquisitiveness—a temper akin on a grander scale to their own. Like the Jacobin Republic, the Kingdom of Prussia kept its eye on the main chance and its neighbours' territories.[1] If its rival, Austria, chose to weaken itself by continuing the war for ideological reasons, so much the better. On April 5th a treaty was signed at Basle by which France retained all German lands west of the Rhine until a general peace. If thereafter France still kept them, Prussia, with French connivance, was to compensate herself elsewhere: in other words at the expense of the Hapsburgs and the lesser Teuton states. The Republic was formally approved by a European Power which in return was left ruler of north Germany. "The treaty," wrote Malmesbury, "instead of one of a shameful and ignominious peace, may be considered as one of a predatory alliance; and such a league between two such Powers may have very serious consequences."[2]

It certainly shocked what remained of the conscience of Europe. King George when he heard the news could scarcely credit it.[3] But

[1] A valuable contemporary appreciation of Prussia is preserved among Lord Grenville's Foreign Office papers: "The character of this people, formed by a succession of rapacious Princes, is turned towards usurpation. The war with France was disagreeable to them because it melted down the accumulations of old Frederick, and did not present an immediate accession of territory. But the war with, or rather against, Poland was not unpopular, because the moral principles of a Prussian go to the possession of whatever he can acquire. And so little is he the slave of what he calls vulgar prejudice that, give him opportunity and means, he will spare you the trouble of finding a pretext. This liberality of sentiment greatly facilitates negotiation, for it is not necessary to clothe propositions in honest and decent form."—*H. M. C. Dropmore*, III, 232.

[2] *Malmesbury*, III, 250.

[3] *H. M. C. Dropmore*, III, 57.

countries within the Jacobins' reach took a more realistic view and followed Prussia's example. Tuscany even managed to make peace before her. In May the new Dutch or Batavian Republic concluded an alliance with France, granting her the use of its fleet against Britain, an annual tribute of four and a half millions and the permanent maintenance of a French army in Holland. Luxemburg surrendered in June, and Sweden made peace in the same month. In July Spain withdrew from the Coalition, ceding Hispaniola to the Republic and secretly promising to use her influence to turn Portugal against England. Only Austria, little Piedmont and the Two Sicilies remained languidly faithful to the Grand Alliance. All were far away from Britain. Between them and her lay victorious France with its dependent population swollen by conquest from twenty-six to thirty-five millions. "Dread and terrible times," noted Woodforde in his diary," appear to be near at hand."

CHAPTER SIX

The Home Front

1794-5

"It matters little whether the disasters which have arisen are to be ascribed to the weakness of Generals, the intrigues of camps or the jealousies of Cabinets; the fact is that they exist, and that we must anew commence the salvation of Europe." *Pitt.*

"Let us trust to nothing but God and ourselves, for I repeat it again and again, there is nothing else left on which we can rely with safety." *Major Calvert.*

THE collapse of Holland and the evacuation of the British army changed the character of the war. It gave the enemy the entire continental coastline facing England. It placed him on the flank of her trade-route with northern Europe and the Baltic—the life-line along which she imported naval stores and, in time of bad harvest, grain. It doubled the work of the Navy by extending the blockade. On the day that Amsterdam fell five ships of the line had to be withdrawn from the Channel fleet to watch the Dutch ports.

Britain was thus forced back on to her last line of defence. Simultaneously the Navy on which she had become more dependent than ever was crippled by the loss of her former allies' bases and ships. Holland's considerable fleet not only withdrew from the fight, but on May 16th, with the Batavian Republic's declaration of war, passed over to the enemy. Spain, with naval resources equal to France's own was an even greater loss. Only the unseaworthy and ill-disciplined squadrons of Sicily and Portugal remained to the Grand Alliance.

It seemed doubtful if the Navy could bear the strain. Many Continental observers thought not. Despite brilliant frigate exploits and the victory of the 1st of June, it had already shown signs of finding its world-wide burden too heavy. The American convoy had been allowed to reach Brest. Sierra Leone, on the West African coast, had been plundered by a Republican squadron in September, 1794,[1] and there had been moments in the summer when the King

[1] The acting Governor of the little station was young Zachary Macaulay, the father of the historian.

at Weymouth had seemed in some danger of being kidnapped by French smugglers who put nightly into the Dorset coves. During an alarm in September the frigates on guard in Portland Bay actually opened fire on one another.[1] In November, through Howe's policy of keeping his main fleet in harbour for the winter, a British battleship had been captured by a French division 200 miles off Ushant, and a fortnight later reinforcements for Guadeloupe had been allowed to sail from Brest. Nor was naval discipline satisfactory: a ship of the line, ordered to the West Indian station, had mutinied at Spithead, and had only been brought back to duty after the guns of the Fleet had been levelled against her.

Had it not been for the demoralisation of the French navy, Britain might easily have suffered disaster. But fortunately the French, though capable of inflicting damage, were not able to take the offensive. After Christmas Villaret Joyeuse's fleet, raiding in the Atlantic, lost no less than five ships of the line, three of them foundering in a tempest. Even this ill-fated voyage cost Britain seventy merchantmen, and enabled French naval reinforcements to reach the Mediterranean. Here also British convoys suffered, many hundreds of vessels being captured by French privateers for lack of proper protection.[2]

With the coastline of Europe to patrol from Hamburg to Genoa and convoys to protect in every part of the world the Navy needed leadership of genius. Instead it was commanded mostly by elderly men of routine. Lord Spencer, who had taken over the office of First Lord of the Admiralty from Chatham, was an upright and capable patrician who was later to show himself capable of bold decisions at a critical time. But for the present he was inexperienced and self-opinionated. Almost his first act was to quarrel with the best senior officer in the Service, Lord Hood, because the outspoken old man had given unpalatable advice. The Mediterranean command thus devolved on Lord Hotham, who was well described as a gentleman-like man but past the time of day for action.[3] As a result, when the French fleet put out from Toulon in March with untrained crews it was not annihilated as it deserved. Instead it was able, by good luck, to capture a crippled British seventy-four, and regain its base after an inconclusive engagement off Leghorn. The affair was only redeemed by Captain Nelson who, with a ship much inferior in size and gun-power, pursued and badly mauled the 80-gun *Ça Ira*. Hotham made no attempt to follow up his

[1] *H. M. C. Dropmore*, II, 634. See also 611-12.

[2] *Nicolas*, II, 32-3.

[3] "His soul has got down to his belly and never mounts higher now."—*Windham Papers*, I, 294.

brilliant subordinate's feat. "We must be contented," he told him, "we have done very well." Nelson afterwards confided to a friend that, had he taken ten sail and allowed the eleventh to escape, he would never have called it well done.

The Navy had not only to keep watch in European waters, it had to conduct operations in a pestilential climate thousands of miles away on the other side of the Atlantic. Here things, so bright seemingly in the spring of 1794, were going increasingly badly. Jervis and Grey had been driven into resignation in the autumn by an incredibly tactless letter of Dundas's, who, surrendering to the City, had backed false charges of corruption brought against them by West Indian merchants. The reinforcements promised to the fever-stricken garrisons never arrived, or when they did were far below the strength announced in the Secretary of State's letters. In March, 1795, Major Thomas Picton—many years later to become famous as the hardest-swearing general in the Peninsula—found 2600 raw boys, landed at Barbados instead of 10,000 men promised, riddled with typhus, too weak to hold arms, and without clothing for tropical campaigning. All the while French reinforcements kept slipping through the blockade: 6000 troops from Brest reached Guadeloupe in January. A few weeks later a negro rebellion broke out in the Windward Islands. In Grenada the governor and leading inhabitants were murdered; in St. Vincent the garrison was forced to take shelter in the coastal forts.

The rising was the price of Parliament's decision to postpone the abolition of the slave trade. The Jacobins, whose principles were truer in this to eternal law than those of their adversaries, reaped the benefit. The black man, with his numbers and immunity to the climate, fought on their side. The British Government, despite the entreaties of its commanders on the spot, even forbade the enlistment of loyal negroes lest military service should discontent them with their lot. The powerful West Indian Committee in London bitterly opposed every move towards a saner policy. Only General Vaughan's enrolment, in defiance of Dundas' instructions, of a small number of slaves with a promise of emancipation as a reward for good service, averted the total eclipse of British dominion in the islands.

• • • • • • • •

The Secretary of State for War deserved better of his country in the courage and promptitude with which he faced the threat to the eastern empire caused by the collapse of Holland. Dundas suffered from all the obvious failings of the parliamentary lobby-man in a rich country. But his zeal for the Imperial assets he administered was beyond doubt. The craven surrender of Amsterdam placed the Dutch East India Company's trading stations at Cape Town and Ceylon within the reach of France. Refusing to contemplate Jacobin domination of the sea route to the Orient, Dundas at once sent off duplicate dispatches to India instructing the Governor-General to take immediate steps to secure the Dutch possessions. Simultaneously he obtained from the lethargic Stadtholder an order to the Governor of the Cape to receive a friendly force. By the time the Batavian Republic declared war in May, the first of three British contingents was off the coast of South Africa. To forestall a Franco-Dutch expedition, the Government took great risks, sending out of the country a considerable part of its inadequate military force and dispatching it, in the spring gales, without convoy past an unblockaded Brest. But the stake was nothing less than the safety of India.

The Dutch surrender had a further embarrassing consequence. Amsterdam was the banking centre of the world and British trade was inextricably bound up with Dutch finance. Since the Revolution of 1688 the two countries, both libertarian and plutocratic, had been commercially interdependent. In the long run the flight of capital from Holland enriched Britain and enabled her by underground rivers of gold to sustain a long war. But for the moment it threatened the fabric of her monetary system and world-wide commerce. The French, contrasting her bagman's dominion with their own self-contained power, confidently awaited the downfall of *La nation boutique* of Barère's contemptuous phrase.

They reckoned without Pitt's obstinate courage or Britain's. "It has pleased inscrutable Providence," the former told the House of Commons, "that this power of France should triumph over everything that has been opposed to it. But let us not therefore fall without making any efforts to resist it. Let us not sink without measuring its strength."[1]

Yet Britain's resources both of men and money were put to a test never visualised when she went to war. When the Prussians and Dutch gave up the fight there were only 60,000 troops in the country including Militia and Fencibles. Even this force represented a 300 per cent increase on the pre-war establishment. The Coalition Government, grasping the magnitude of the crisis, now took immediate steps to augment the Army. In a single day it sanctioned the raising of fifteen additional Fencible battalions. Despite the heavy losses of the Flemish and West Indian campaigns it planned to have nearly 300,000 men under arms by the end of

[1] *War Speeches*, 119.

1795. Added to the 100,000 or more needed to man the Fleet the figure, though still far below the proportionate contribution demanded of France by the Jacobin exponents of total war, represented no insignificant part of the population.

These forces had to be raised by voluntary enlistment. Except for the use of press-gangs to man the fleet, legal compulsion was repugnant to the spirit and constitution of the country. The slightest attempt to apply it provoked a storm of opposition: jealousy of the Executive was strongly ingrained in all classes. The very word conscription was tainted with enemy origin.

Instead, in an age when the transmission of popular intelligence was slow and uncertain, the Government was reduced to such undignified shifts as touting at the prison gates and offering pardons to convicts and crown debtors in return for enlistment. But its chief resort was to the profit motive—the normal peace-time incentive of a free people. To any rogue capable of raising recruits ample reward was promised and no questions asked. In one case the War Office entered into a contract with a self-styled captain to supply 4000 Irish recruits at twenty guineas a head. Kidnapping became the profession of the hour. Every device from debauchery to downright trepanning was employed by the crimping houses to complete the contractors' quotas. As the poor and uneducated were the most affected the outcry against these abuses soon culminated in riots. In January, 1795 one in St. George's Fields led to the discovery of several young men in irons in a house near the Elephant and Castle, where they had been decoyed by prostitutes. A few weeks later indignation was aroused by the report that two famous pugilists, Mendoza and Ward, were employed by similar establishments in St. George's Fields. In the summer a crowd gutted a notorious house at Charing Cross and, after filling the roadway in front of Northumberland House with mattress feathers, marched to Downing Street to break Pitt's windows.

. . . .

The transformation of the least military country in Europe into an armed camp was carried out with all the formless improvisation dear to the national character. There was no logic in the pattern of the new army. Regulars, Militia, Fencibles, Yeomanry, Foreign Auxiliaries and every species of Volunteer corps competed with one another in a baffling mosaic of scarlet and blue. A visitor to Birmingham found twenty recruiting parties drumming and trumpeting away against one another on behalf of their rival units. Their terms of service were as variegated as their uniforms. Many, raised privately and loosely disciplined, were of the most unmilitary appearance: John Byng, passing the Cambridgeshire Militia on the march, noted that their order was that of a flock of sheep and that most of the officers followed in post-chaises.

Many out of patriotism, or to avoid the annual Militia ballot, joined the Volunteers. For members of this force were exempted from Militia service if they could produce a certificate showing they had attended exercises punctually during the six weeks before the hearing of the Militia list appeals. They were raised locally, generally in small independent companies for use in case of invasion or in aid of the civil power. They appealed mainly to the better-to-do classes: the Rutland Volunteers began with a meeting of a hundred and fifty noblemen, gentlemen and yeomen who bound themselves to attend when called upon under a £50 penalty, and chose a uniform of French grey and buff.[1]

In the yeomanry regiments there was always a great resort of farmers. The daughter of one recalled what a treat it was for the children when the day for exercise came round. "What polishing of sword and epaulette! What brushing of bearskin and broadcloth! With what admiration we used to walk round my father when he was fully equipped, and he affecting all the time to take it as a mere matter of course."[2]

Wherever one went one saw uniforms, their bright primary colours adding a new charm to the soft half-tones of the English background. The traveller at his inn found his landlord a local Fencible, eager to show off his arms and charger, or was woken at five in the morning to the sound of trumpets. High on the lonely fells, MacRitchie, the Clunie Minister, met Lord Darlington's Dragoons on their way to Penrith, mounted on bay horses and clad in scarlet cloaks with yellow facings: the Government moved its cavalry like shuttlecocks up and down the country.[3]

More than 40,000 recruits were raised in the spring and summer of 1794. The chaos produced by such rapid military expansion was indescribable. One immediate effect was an almost complete stoppage of naval recruitment. At Perth, early in 1795 as much as 25 guineas a man was offered without producing a single seaman.[4] The Government was forced to place an embargo on all merchant shipping for six weeks until 20,000 seamen had been impressed, and later had to suspend Army recruiting altogether. Before the Fleet could be manned, no less than fifteen regiments were drafted on board.

[1] *Times*, 21st April, 1794.
[2] Ham, MS.
[3] *Torrington*, IV, 59; *MacRitchie*, 19, 21.
[4] *MacRitchie*, 1.

Into this martial hodgepodge came in February, 1795, that erstwhile apprentice of Frederick the Great, the Duke of York. His appointment to the vacant office of Commander-in-Chief at the Horse Guards was made solely out of deference to Royal wishes to soften his recall from Flanders. But by a happy chance the Duke was a born administrator—a hard worker with an orderly mind, a royal memory and a mastery of detail, who had acquired a first-hand knowledge of the deficiencies and needs of the Army. Without a trace of genius, he was single-hearted in his devotion to the Service and—unlike his brothers—a gentleman. The Army never had a more useful patron.

It needed one. Beyond native courage and tenacity and a great regimental tradition the Army of 1795 possessed few assets. Its discipline was defective, its equipment inferior and inadequate, and its methods of supply and recruitment were anarchical. The Duke's work was to give it organisation: to do for Britain on a smaller and more leisurely scale what Carnot had done for France. During the next decade he forged the weapon which Moore and Wellington were to use. In the direction of the armies in the field he had no part: it was not his *métier*. That remained the business of the politicians, who, with Dundas in the Secretary of State's office, Windham in the old War Department and Huskisson as Under-Secretary-of-State, maintained a kind of all-party and sometimes mutually contradictory, direction of military operations. The Duke had merely to put the forces they misused into the field: to officer, train and equip them.

He wasted no time. Early in March, 1795, he issued a circular letter demanding a return of all captains under 12 and lieutenant-colonels under 20. The first need was to restore the vanished prestige and discipline of the commissioned ranks by ending the scandal of juvenile command which improvising statesmen had introduced to raise cheap recruits. Promotion by purchase the Duke could not abolish, for it was a long-established national institution—almost as much part of an Englishman's birthright as the devolution of landed property. But what he could and did do was to insist on fitness for command in the field. He initiated a system of returns and confidential reports that enabled his adviser, the Adjutant-General, to test the history and capacity of every officer in the Service. And by being readily accessible and appointing a Military Secretary as the official channel of communication between himself and all ranks, he put a check on the fatal habit of political interference in matters of discipline and promotion.

In the sphere of training his germinating work was equally

valuable. Detailed orders were issued for the exercise of troops in camp: Mondays and Fridays were allocated to battalion drill, Tuesdays and Thursdays to brigade training, Wednesdays to field-days. The Army was given system and direction. Time was necessary to attain results: conservatism was strong and the anomalies of the English administrative system were too many to be modified or removed quickly. The artillery still continued to be directed by the Ordnance Board—an independent body which, despite the removal of the Duke of Richmond and the substitution of the formidable Lord Cornwallis, remained a by-word for unpunctuality and inefficiency. But the Duke's steady hand brought a slow but solid improvement of method into every department of the Service. Without it the new Army would have been still-born.

. . . .

All this strengthening of the armed forces—essential now if Britain was to survive—made ever greater demands on the country's purse. By the modest standards of the eighteenth century the cost of the war was terrific. A ship of the line cost nearly £100,000 to build, and Britain had to keep at sea a force of more than a hundred of them as well as several thousand small craft. The yards were always full of vessels under construction, and shipwrights' wages under the stress of demand rose to more than twice those of agricultural labourers. With something approaching half a million men to pay, feed and equip in every part of the world, Pitt's capacity as a financier was sternly taxed.

The Prime Minister, educated in the new and, to an eighteenth century mind, enthralling principles of Adam Smith, and given supreme office while almost a boy to save a war-wracked country from financial ruin, remained unshakably convinced that the defeat of France would be achieved through the economic strength of Britain. In the short run he was tragically wrong: ultimately, in the course of a long war of attrition, he was proved right. He therefore husbanded the country's resources and placed the burden, whenever possible, not on the backs of his own over-strained generation but on those of a more peaceful posterity, believing that the foundations of the commercial wealth he had laid would ultimately make it seem light. In this also he was wrong in the short run, right in the long. His vast borrowings crippled the post-war generation and poisoned British social life for three decades with a sense of bitterness and frustration. Yet the nightmare of debt presently paled in the dawn of Victorian industrial expansion, and was forgotten.

At the time the taxes imposed to balance Pitt's war-budgets

seemed to our ancestors heavy enough. For they fell on almost every article of purchase or hire from playing cards to stage coaches. Imports, both of raw materials and manufactures, paid duties up to 30 or 40 per cent, and the price of foreign foods, some of them now common necessities, rose to almost prohibitive levels. A budget day cartoon portrayed John Bull giving up his breeches to save his bacon, while a peering Pitt cried, "More money! John: more money to defend you from the bloody and cannibal French! They're a-coming! Why they'll strip you to the very skin!" Yet the basis of taxation remained indirect: the freeman's right of choice to be taxed as he pleased survived. Even in the hour of national danger the individual was encouraged to earn as much as he could, spend the money in his own way and, if possible, grow rich. For it was Adam Smith's and therefore Pitt's belief that a nation of many rich men was a rich nation.

The price of passing on the burden was made heavier than it need have been. The science of raising money on public credit, though far ahead of that prevailing on the Continent, was still only partially developed: the money market a close one and in a few hands. The big bankers and loan-mongers exacted a grossly unfair toll on the nation for their services. Pitt's intention—a sound one—had been to float loans at par. But the bankers and their new rivals, the Jewish stock-jobbers, at first refused to touch anything but three per cents. These they absorbed at a huge discount which posterity was compelled to make good. In the opening year of war for every £100 borrowed, £138 of stock was created. In 1796, though the rate of interest had risen to 4 per cent, bonds of £100 had to be given to the money monopolists for every £60 advanced. Borrowing as no Minister in any country had ever borrowed before, Pitt in a few years doubled the national debt.

Had the nation in its hour of need assumed a direct control of its own credit instead of allowing it to become the monopoly of the professional moneylender, Britain's history in the next century might have been happier. But to have done so would have required a revolution in men's ideas and a resort to first principles alien to the pragmatic English mind. An Englishman in difficulties always went to the "Jews"—the ever improvident leader of the Opposition called his ante-chamber Jerusalem—and the nation did the same. The result was not only the rapid rise of a powerful moneyed class, which had as yet only imperfectly absorbed the national tradition, but a gradual disintegration of established standards, values and ways of life. Fox's criticism of Pitt's war finance that it turned a nation of sturdy peasants and squires into fundholders, industrialists and paupers was not wholly factious. It has been forgotten by posterity as much as it was by his own contemporaries that the great Whig in his seemingly treasonable opposition to the war was animated not so much by sympathy with French principles as by deep love of an abiding England which he felt was jeopardised by more than Jacobins. Like Cobbett after him he was haunted by a vague fear of the growth of something sinister: the indefinable "IT" of the radical yeoman's angry jargon.

Yet Pitt's England was so strong that it was little troubled by shadows. Its feet stood firmly and confidently on the solid ground. Freedom of money to move where it pleased was part of its tradition. If an ever larger proportion of its riches was going into fugitive and shifting forms of wealth, it did not seem less prosperous for the change but more so. Britain kept bank and shop as well as it kept farm: money-grubbing seemed to suit its hearty and vigorous people. Even a little town like Ripon had three private banks: silversmiths, grocers and cornfactors at the slightest encouragement would set up a banker's sign, purchase their customers bills and take money on deposit. In the north the industrial districts were full of thriving manufacturers whose grandfathers had been hammermen or weavers. Though they perpetually took great risks, they were making money hand over fist to spend and invest. Pitt is scarcely to be blamed that he refused to kill the men that laid the golden eggs. For he saw in the swelling industrial wealth of the country his trump card against the Jacobin.

. . . .

A Scottish visitor to England in the summer of 1795 saw little sign of the strain through which the nation was passing. On the surface he noted everywhere the symbols of wealth and long-established civilisation. He journeyed through clean market towns and broad, main streets with fine porticoed cloth-halls, elegant shops and inns, caught glimpses of thriving manufacturies in the hollows between the wild northern hills, and rejoiced in the smiling abundance of the countryside—the boundless Lancashire plain bright with corn, the rosy-faced girls in the fields with their petticoats of pink and blue tucked up as they tossed the hay, the universal good-breeding and courtly manners of the rustic population.[1] All things seemed to betoken a widespread culture and a people strong in the plentitude of their heritage: the Thames winding placidly by Eton's groves and spires with its musical picnic parties, its

[1] "In passing along the public roads in this country one cannot help remarking the good breeding of the people, displayed even in their children. You never meet a country person here, young or old, but salutes you with a bow or a curtsey, and a 'good morrow.'"—*MacRitchie*, 39.

coloured groups under the trees and classical temples on verdant slopes; the bells that sounded from every village tower; the fiddler on the roof of the stage-coach and the guard's horn; the rustic strings and hautboys of the church choirs; the painted signs over the ale-house doors with their rude, vigorous verses; the obelisks to Liberty and the "glorious Revolution" rising above the trees of stately parks.

At the top of Highgate Hill the traveller, first seeing London, paused for breath: a nearer view of that wonderful city, still enchanted by Wren's measuring rod, left him only the more amazed. The endless new streets and squares of Bloomsbury and Mary-le-Bone; the sight of Covent Garden in the morning with its profusion of roots, flowers and fruits, its barrows, wagons and rushing thousands; the coloured regattas on the Thames and the sparkling flow of fashion in Hyde Park; the forest of masts in the Pool, and the illuminated walks and murmuring arbours of Vauxhall were like so many transformations in an Arabian tale. No wonder that when the departing minister of Clunie mounted the northern stage-coach at the Green Dragon, Bishopsgate, he sat for long in a kind of maze, thinking with an indescribable mixture of feelings on all he had seen, suffered and enjoyed during his three weeks in the metropolis: its magnificence, extent, populousness, riches, poverty, dissipation, luxuries, vanities, vices.

. . . .

But this simple Scot, who on a bright July day followed the Horse Guards down the Mall behind an admirable band of music and gaped at them drawn-up in all their splendour before Whitehall, was seeing only one side of English life in 1795. There was a dark reverse, and had he stood on the other side of the Treasury windows he might have learnt something of it from Mr. Pitt. A few talks with the polite rustics he passed on his ride from Carlisle to London would have taught him even more: the shocking truth which John Byng discovered in the first autumn of war from a chance dialogue with a Staffordshire countryman: the rising price of every necessity and the growing misery of the poor. It was they whom war taxation on goods and services ruined, not the rich. For them there was no escaping its full force. One of the Bishops, defending the impartiality of Pitt's fiscal system, compared it to a building which, sinking equally in every part, suffered no structural injury. "True," replied Wakefield, the radical scholar, "and you, my Lord Bishop, who dwell in the upper apartments, might still enjoy the prospect from your window. But what would become of me and the good people who live on the ground floor?" [1]

[1] *Espriella* I, 41.

The autumn of 1794 saw the first of a succession of bad harvests: the new year was one of the severest winters ever known in England. While the army was retreating across the ice in Holland, the peasant and the artisan were shivering and tightening their belts. The London death roll of February, 1795, was the highest since the Great Plague. The undertakers' supply of black horses giving out, they were forced to "mow away brown." Coal sold in the City at 3½ guineas a chaldron, and so successful were the privateers on the east coast that during a whole month only a single collier entered the river. Throughout the summer—an exceptionally cold one which blighted sheep and crops—the rise in corn prices continued. By July the quartern loaf, the staple dietary of the poor, cost a shilling.

The remedies taken by the authorities only touched the fringe of the evil. Parish collections for the deserving poor, public kitchens —in Edinburgh during March 11,000 persons were fed by charity— royal proclamations advocating standard wheaten bread and discouraging the use of flour for powdering hair, softened but could not prevent acute national suffering. *The Times*, full of dieting advice, urged its comfortable readers to forgo foodstuffs essential to the poor. Fish was to be served as often as possible, the use of pastry to be forbidden, and "persons in affluent circumstances" were to sit down "with a determined resolution to eat only one kind of butcher's meat." The Middlesex magistrates forswore the consumption of puddings and pies, the East India Company abridged "the customary expense of their dinners," and the House of Lords and Privy Council put on solemn record the advantages of household bread. In all this the strength of libertarian tradition and the lack of any system of central organisation hampered the nation's war effort. Compulsion and uniformity were repugnant to the English mind. Remedial action was therefore voluntary, piecemeal and spasmodic.

According to its lights Parliament did what it could. Bounties were offered on imported wheat, and the manufacture of starch and distillation of spirit from grain were forbidden. The Army gave up the use of hairpowder and the Board of Agriculture—a semi-official, semi-voluntary institution of the indefinable kind peculiar to England—encouraged the digging of allotments in parks and offered a premium of a £1000 to the grower of the largest breadth of potatoes on virgin land. Prosecutions were also instituted against food speculators, forestallers and regrators and fraudulent bakers.

But as always in the eighteenth century, initiative in what was regarded as a domestic matter was left to the local powers—to the

Justices of the Peace. On May 6th, 1795, the Berkshire Magistrates assembled at Speenhamland took a step of momentous consequence. Their immediate concern was the unemployment of clothworkers in the Newbury district. They had met under the terms of an Elizabethan statute to fix a standard wage for day labourers. After the manner of their race they were seeking what seemed to them fair. But, influenced by the new economic doctrine of *laissez-faire*, and faced by the growing dependence of employers on uncontrollable world conditions, they chose to alleviate distress by subsidising wages out of rates. By fastening the price of relief to the price of the gallon loaf and the size of the recipient's family, they met a war-time emergency by a measure which in the course of the next generation pauperised the bulk of the rural population. For not only was the labourer's reward dissociated from his own industry, but the farmer was encouraged to pay low wages by the knowledge that the parish would make good the deficiency out of rates. The consequent rise in the latter—in one village they were to touch 18s. in the £—in turn drove the poorer ratepayers on to the parish.

The Berkshire magistrates were confronted with a grave social crisis which demanded an immediate solution. They tackled it, English-wise, without thinking about the future. Their brethren in other distressed counties followed their example. In the summer of 1795 there were serious riots: at Portsea the mob attacked bakers' shops and forced them to sell at popular prices, at Seaford the Militia broke out of barracks and seized all foodstuffs in the town. The authorities could not allow such a state of affairs to continue with the Jacobin at the gate. They took the first remedy at hand.

That it was temporary and cheapjack is easier to realise now than at the time. The evil had roots deeper than the war. The social machine was not standing up to the strain imposed by rapid economic change. The rigid parish system of poor relief and settlement, which had sufficed for a purely rural community, proved inadequate to the stresses of industrialism. The progress of enclosure, accelerated by the demand of the ever-growing towns, was reducing the formerly proud and contented smallholder into a landless peasant dependent on a wretched wage.

For with the elimination of the small landlord by the great went the destruction of the social balance of a thousand years. The process was as yet only gradual and partial and largely unperceived. The Government, absorbed in the war, saw the new rural poverty as a symptom of a purely ephemeral distress—something arising out of the struggle—instead of the first stage of a wasting disease. It mistook the resultant discontent with Church and State for abstract sympathy with the French Revolution. But the bitterness did not spring from any natural leaning to Jacobin ideology. It was merely the anger of men who compared their present lot with a happier past. It was the sorrowful and hopeless rebellion of the disinherited.

The sullen turbulence of the cottager deprived of the communal fallow and stubble pasture and his forefathers' right of cutting furze and turf on the common, seemed treason and defeatism to statesmen grappling with armed Jacobinism. Even a crowd at St. Neot's Fair, gaping at a peepshow of the King of France being guillotined, alarmed them. They could not differentiate between a factious partisan like the Duke of Bedford, who opposed the war and pretended to be a democrat while engrossing his neighbours' lands,[1] and a bewildered peasant robbed of his birthright who damned the King and "Billy Pitt" over a pot of ale or inveighed against the Game Laws which kept him from feeding his starving family. But such a malcontent had really little in common with the ambitious *frondeur* who sought to enlarge his political power through a National Convention or the youthful idealist whom the lofty declamations of the Girondins had made a Republican. What he wanted was not liberty or equality but justice—the eternal need of his race. Yet with horror piled on horror in Paris and a world at war, it was hard for the Government to distinguish.

Ever since the outbreak of war the Home Office had been tightening its measures against those suspected of revolutionary sympathies. In 1793 alone 200,000 cheap copies of Paine's *Rights of Man* had been sold. In Scotland, a third of whose parliamentary seats were controlled by 1300 electors, a powerful minority demanded reform; the weavers of Dundee, always a turbulent town, actually planted a Tree of Liberty. Dundas, who beneath his bonhomie shared the stark pugnacity of his race, gave the official word for strict repression. Among the victims was the poet Burns, who, to keep his appointment as exciseman, was constrained to make a humiliating recantation of the "democratic" expressions that had escaped him in his cups. The ringleaders of the "pro-Jacobin" faction were savagely punished by the Lord Justice Clerk, McQueen of Braxfield—an irascible old judge who made no disguise of his hatred for "traitors." Palmer, an old Etonian, was sentenced to five years transportation for an "Address to the People" telling them that they had been plunged into war by a wicked Ministry and compliant Parliament. A young advocate, Muir—Vice-President of the "Associated Friends of the Constitution and of the People"—suffered

[1] See *Torrington* III, 200.

even more severely on account of a suspicious visit to Paris and Ireland in the opening months of the war.

Agitation for parliamentary reform which had seemed innocent enough in peace time assumed a different aspect when it took the form of denunciation of a war for national existence. In January, 1794, the London Corresponding Society called a mass meeting to protest against the war and urged a Convention of the People. It did not soften the Government's asperity against such dissentients that their views found support in educated circles and even in Parliament, where Pitt was taunted by Fox's faction with having himself been a reformer a few years back. After further mass meetings in April at Chalk Farm and Sheffield it decided to act.

On May 12, Hardy, the shoemaker Secretary of the London Corresponding Society, was arrested at his shop in Piccadilly by Bow Street runners. This was followed by the discovery—such discoveries are easy in time of national panic—of treasonable conspiracies at Sheffield and in Ireland. A few days later Parliament suspended the Habeas Corpus Act. Among those detained were the secretary of the radical Earl Stanhope—Pitt's brother-in-law—John Thelwall, the fashionable lecturer, and the genial ex-parson, Horne Tooke, who over his cups at dinner at the Crown and Anchor tavern had declared that Parliament was a nest of scoundrels.[1]

As always in Britain in times of external danger, an overwhelming majority supported established authority. Even those who opposed the suspension of Habeas Corpus were outvoted by 261 votes to 42. As the Government spokesman put, it the country was driven to the necessity of imitating French violence in order to resist the contagion of French principles. Lenity could not be admitted when the constitution itself was at stake. For Jacobin sympathisers to hold seditious meetings under pretence of "parliamentary reform" could no more excuse their proceedings than the phrase "God save the King" at the foot of a seditious proclamation. But there is no doubt that the Government and its supporters went too far. Its theory of "constructive treason" disgusted even the King, never an enthusiast for freedom of opinion.[2]

The absurdity of a labourer being sentenced to five years imprisonment for calling out "No George!" "No war!" proved too much for the English sense of justice. In October 1794 the trials of

[1] In the course of the dinner, attended by about 300 persons, the company were said to have toasted success to the French and "sung the Marseillaise treasonable hymn and *Ça Ira*."—*Times*, 5th May, 1794. This to the contemporary English mind was like singing the *Horst Wessel* song to-day.

[2] "You have got into the wrong box, my Lord," the King told the Lord Chancellor, Loughborough, "you have got into the wrong box: constructive treason won't do, my Lord; constructive treason won't do."—Lord Campbell, *Lives of the Chancellors*, XI, 267.

Hardy, Tooke and Thelwall for high treason ended in acquittals, though sentences of imprisonment were awarded on lesser counts.

But the country as a whole wasted no sympathy on persecuted radicals. They were regarded at the best as misguided fools, at the worst as dangerous criminals. "If they are in truth acting upon principle," wrote the liberal Lord Spencer, "they would lead us, for all I know, to the horrors and miseries of France." The loathing felt at this time for Jacobin excesses transcended reason. Windham declared that the revolution was so diabolical that all who excused it were separated from him by an unbridgeable gulf. A leading Bristol merchant saw Fox as "a traitor with a firebrand at his tail" who was aiming at being "a second Oliver Cromwell."[1] The newspapers described the Jacobins as "baboons in the woods of Africa," with "the savage ferociousness of wild beasts." Even the gentle and pious Hannah More wrote fiercely of "the mad monkeys of the Convention!" and interrupted her work of reformation among the Somerset miners to write popular tracts against Paine and his fellow "atheists." Her dialogue, "Village Politics by Will Chip," ran into inumerable editions, and was hailed by patriots of the more conservative kind almost as though it were holy writ. Many of them had special editions printed at their own expense and distributed among their poorer neighbours.

Such feelings were not confined to the possessing classes. Hatred of Jacobinism ran like an angry streak through the nation. The fearful tales of escaped prisoners fatally discredited any one professing revolutionary sympathies. Merchant seamen captured by French commerce raiders were pelted by the rabble of Brest as they marched through the streets and tortured by their gaolers. In the filthy holes into which they were thrown there was often no room even to lie down. At Quimper typhus-infected Britons were reduced to eating raw rats and mice, and some were murdered by their guards for asking for water.[1] Long after the Terror in Paris ceased, the prisons and lesser public offices in France were staffed by the sadistic scum whom revolutions bring to the surface of national life; and simple Englishmen, engaged in a life-or-death struggle, are to be forgiven if they confounded their bestialities with the revolutionary philosophy, and even the entire French race. Nor can the latter in that hour of intoxication be acquitted of intolerable national arrogance: the universal triumph of the "Great Nation" excited a popular Chauvinism outstripping the pride of the Grand

[1] C. M. MacInnes, *A Gateway of Empire*, 324.

[2] Many owed their lives to the noble firmness of their interned compatriot, Lady Ann Fitzroy—sister of the future Duke of Wellington—whose force of character overcame even the stubborn inhumanity of the Commissary in charge. See *Long*, 172-91.

Monarque. For having discarded religion as an offence against reason, victorious France had fallen into the most perilous of all heresies: that of self-worship.

Despite their follies and obtuseness the British people never lost their feeling for common morality, their contempt for blasphemy, arrogance and destruction. To the progressive and beneficent theories behind the Revolution nine out of ten of them were blind. But ruined abbeys, desecrated churches[1] and murdered women and children aroused their unswerving sense of decency. In a crowded Greenwich stage waggon at the height of the treason trials a dispute arose between a recruiting sergeant, who maintained that Tom Paine was an atheist, and a Whig gentleman's coachman who denied it. The disputants stopped the coach and decided the matter, English fashion, on the greensward. The sergeant won, and there is little doubt that the verdict, though technically wrong, was England's.[2]

British anger at the Revolution was often brutal and crude. It struck out blindly at much that was good. A man of known democratic opinions could scarcely walk about his home-town without a demonstration of popular hatred.[3] Every liberal ideal came temporarily into disrepute: parliamentary reform, the movement against the slave trade, the infant Trade Unions, factory legislation. A Tory Bishop even accused the new evangelical Sunday schools of teaching atheism and blasphemy, while good Mr. MacRitchie, seeing a shepherd reading a newspaper on the Pentland hills, breathed a curse on the French politics that were ruining the country. Classicism itself came in for suspicion owing to the fondness of democratic orators for allusions to Roman tyrannicides. *Plutarch's Lives* was the most popular book in revolutionary France, while the radical Thelwall in his lectures was in the habit of taking Greek and Roman history as his subject, and by an ingenious twist making it reflect on living persons and present events.[4] Cockburn afterwards recalled how his old schoolmaster, Dr. Adam of Edinburgh, was spied on by his pupils and harried by the authorities for his innocent remarks about the Tarquins. To fools—and brave and honest fools were plentiful in Britain—the very liberty for which the country was fighting came to have a "Jacobinal sound." Like bulls in Borodale, as Coleridge recorded, they ran mad with the echo of their own bellowing.

For all this there was a heavy penalty to be paid in division and bitterness. For the fury of national patriotism in the hour of

[1] *Calvert*, 79; *Malmesbury*, III, 268, 272.
[2] *Times*, 5th Sept., 1794.
[3] *The Friend*, Section I, Essay V.
[4] *Crabb Robinson*, I, 66.

danger shut the door on many young and generous spirits who had early espoused the cause of the Revolution. "To hope too boldly of human nature," wrote the wisest Englishman of his generation, "is a fault which all good men have an interest in forgiving." In the frenzy of that time, it was not forgiven. Once a Jacobin always a Jacobin, was the general verdict. The youthful Wordsworths were harried by their neighbours from Alfoxden, and the two major conservative prophets of the coming era were dogged on lonely rambles over the Mendips by Dundas's spies.

Unhappily neither of the great men who led the forces of Government and Opposition in the first years of the war was temperamentally fitted to give the nation the flawless internal unity she needed. Pitt was reserved and impatient: his nerves overstrained by his inherent inability to relax. He treated criticism with cold contempt. Sir George Beaumont—Wordsworth's patron—told Farington in November, 1795, that Pitt's personal deportment had become "dry and rejecting. . . . This manner seems to grow upon him." The first duty of a wise advocate is to convince his opponents that he understands their arguments. Pitt and his supporters never tried to draw the Opposition into the national effort: to disarm criticism by entrusting it with a task.

Fox, on the other hand, with his generous sympathy with the rebel and under-dog, showed no sign of realising the overwhelming danger of the country and the magnitude of the Government's problems. In the delightful riverside retreat to which he had withdrawn after the excesses of his youth and the turmoil of Westminster, he seemed to lose touch with reality. He allowed his followers to indulge in irresponsible and unpatriotic faction that did their Party and the nobler causes for which they stood infinite harm. Instead of pleading for the poor and ignorant, the Foxites—as Coleridge said—pleaded to them. At the moment that their country, forsaken by false allies, was facing the greatest military force the world had seen, they never rose in the House without denouncing Ministers as tyrants and robbers. In their hatred of the Government their radical protégés even had inflammatory pamphlets piled on the backs of asses to be scattered about the highways, thrown into cottage windows and down the shafts of coalpits.

A crisis was reached in October, 1795. On the 27th the London Corresponding Society held a mass meeting in Copenhagen Fields, at which an Address was passed virtually calling for civil war. A hundred and fifty thousand persons were present, and though only a fraction of them were anything more than curious spectators, the violence of the speakers, the example of France and the known roughness and ignorance of the London mob were sufficient to occasion alarm in an unpoliced city. Two days later the King on his way to open Parliament was hooted by organised rowdies in the Mall. Parson Woodforde, on one of his rare visits to London, was in the crowd, the greater part of which was as loyal as himself. Just before the King reached Old Palace Yard, showers of stones were flung at the royal coach and a bullet from an air-gun broke one of the windows. "My Lords," announced the intrepid old man as he entered the Chamber, "I have been shot at."

The outrage provoked an outburst of passionate loyalty. When next night the King attended the theatre at Covent Garden the audience rose and sang the national anthem six times over. The Government, striking while the iron was hot, introduced Bills against Treasonable Practices and Seditious Meetings. Promoters of all political gatherings of more than fifty persons were to give notice to the magistrates, who were empowered to attend and arrest on the spot for seditious speech. Second offences could be punished with transportation. The passage of these measures—which however, left the freedom of the Press inviolate—was attended by bitter debates in the Commons and by efforts to arouse popular tumults. Three large meetings were held in Mary-le-bone Fields—the site of the present Regent's Park—and Burke, now a confirmed alarmist, hourly expected to see a guillotine set up on Tower Hill. But the Bill passed by an overwhelming majority, and when Wilberforce went down to his native Yorkshire to oppose a Whig appeal to the freeholders he was greeted by thousands of West Riding weavers calling themselves "Billymen" to mark their support of Pitt, and shouting, "Twenty King's men for one Jacobin!"

After the new Act became law open political agitation died away. The radical clubs confined their assemblies to forty-five members and their membership dropped quickly. Within a year even the London Corresponding Society was £185 in debt. Pitt was much amused by the report of one society whose members met in muzzles and conversed only by signs.[1] The parliamentary Opposition went still further in absurdity, for it presently withdrew for long periods from Westminster altogether, leaving its constituents unrepresented and the Government unopposed. Only beneath the surface the sullen discontent of a dissentient and embittered minority remained.

Yet the young Prime Minister, prematurely aged by his struggle against the revolutionary hydra, was no reactionary. Under the cold, chilling surface which he displayed to a world whose common

[1] *Farington* I, 137.

joys and sorrows he had never wholly shared, beat a heart boyish in simplicity, native tenderness and virtue. There was a side of Pitt's early-arrested nature which was unintelligible to contemporaries like Fox, who had been experienced men of the world before they had reached their 'twenties. About this time he began to display interest in Hannah More's tracts with their studies of humble life. Towards the end of 1795 he went down to stay with a friend in Essex and, after talking one evening of the good fortune which an industrious and virtuous labourer could enjoy in Britain, was taken by his host to view the dwellings of the poor in the town of Halstead. "The Minister," Lord Rosebery has written, "surveyed it in silent wonder, and declared he had no conception that any part of England could present a spectacle of such misery."[1]

It was perhaps because of this incident that Pitt, in a year dark with storm, gave so much of his thought to a far-reaching scheme of social reform which, had it been adopted by Parliament, might have changed the tenor of English history. He had already made partial attempts to adjust the social system to the new conditions of economic life, exempting dwellings with only one hearth from hearth tax and modifying the old harsh law of settlement which still gave parish authorities the right to expel newcomers who might become chargeable to the rates. Early in 1796 he took a more momentous step. At the end of the previous session, Samuel Whitbread—"the great fermentator"—had introduced a measure for fixing minimum wages, erroneously asserting that, while wages had risen threefold in the past two centuries, the price of food and clothing had multiplied seven and fifteenfold. Pitt, in demolishing these extravagant claims, took the wind out of Whitbread's sails by a plea for family allowances, compulsory national insurance, and a general system of technical education. He declined to consider a minimum wage as an infringement of economic law: "trade, industry and barter will always find their own level and will be impeded by regulations which violate their natural operation and derange their proper effect."[2] But to the chagrin of the Foxites he promised to introduce a Bill which should place the whole question of poor relief on a national basis.

The measure was delayed by the general election of the summer. But on November 12, 1796, Pitt laid it before the House. It provided that a father, unable to support his children, should receive a shilling a week for each child until it became self-supporting, and that poor and industrious persons whose wages fell below a certain level

[1] Lord Rosebery, *Pitt*, 1891, 169.
[2] J. H. Rose, *Pitt and Napoleon*, 1912, 82.

should have a legal claim on the rates for any deficiency. Up to this point the Bill did no more than give a national stamp to the provisions of Speenhamland. But in its remaining clauses it was revolutionary. By a bold use of national credit it empowered parish authorities to advance money for the purchase of a cow to any industrious man unable to support his family by his own unaided efforts. It established a Parochial Fund, to be raised by weekly subscriptions and rates, for contributory old-age pensions. And it created in every parish or union of parishes a School of Industry for training children in some craft or trade until they grew up. To feed them the uncultivated waste in every parish was to be enclosed by the Overseers. To meet the needs of agriculture boys over 14 and girls over 12 could be hired out at harvest time for a period of not more than six consecutive weeks. The work of the schools was to be supervised by the magistracy and the clergy. "With reform," the Prime Minister declared, defending a project far in advance of his time, "you disarm the Jacobins of their most dangerous weapon."

Pitt had copies of his Bill printed and circulated to experts. In their marginal comments a few approved whole-heartedly. But the general verdict of experience and authority was adverse. Indoor work for Schools of Industry, it was stated, would unfit boys for field labour; public morals would be ruined by allowing illegitimate children to qualify for relief; the labourer would sell or eat the cow advanced him by the parish. Most scathing of all was the great jurist, Jeremy Bentham, on whose chilling logic the next age was to rear the structure of Victorian utilitarianism. To him Pitt's remedies seemed wildly sentimental and dangerous. The Bill, it was felt, required more disinterested virtue than either the poor or the guardians possessed.

It was certainly far in advance of the prevailing level of British administrative science. The fury with which it was assailed by the magistrates of Mary-le-bone and St. Giles proved this. Their sole conception of their duty was to keep the rates down and their only use for pauper children sale to the north-country factories. Assailed by so much detailed criticism, the bill was withdrawn for amendment. Pitt never had another opportunity of introducing it. Few could see any reason for so costly a measure in a time of war and high taxation: in any case food prices had dropped with the better harvest of 1796, and the early part of the winter was exceptionally mild. The English mind could only envisage the immediate task of winning the war, and could not look beyond it. Within a few weeks the nation was in the throes of the worst financial crisis of its history, and any scheme for increasing the alarming burden of tax and ratepayers had ceased to be practical politics.

. . . .

With so much suffering and the chances of victory receding as Europe made her peace with the triumphing Jacobin, it was not surprising that there were patriots who sometimes despaired of the war. Even so close a friend of the Prime Minister as Wilberforce at one time brought forward a motion for peace. Noblemen like the Marquis of Buckingham, who had been among the first to panic at the Revolution, now talked of compromising with the sacrifice of a few colonial conquests, and argued that in its half-bankrupt state France was no longer to be feared. In the spring of 1795 a captain of the naval recruiting service told a traveller that, though Britain might beat France to loggerheads at sea, she would never be able to give laws to her. Even Nelson seemed to think peace inevitable and wrote home about buying a neat cottage in which to end his days.[1]

But Pitt, though more anxious for a genuine peace than any Englishman living, knew how hard it would be to obtain. Each successive Revolutionary government, he told the House, based its policy on "the same unqualified rights of man, the same principles of liberty and equality—principles by which they flatter the people with the possession of the theoretical rights of man, all of which they vitiate and violate in practice."[2] Adherence to pledged word had no place in their scheme of statecraft. A composition could only be followed by a few years of uneasy peace before the same storm broke in England. For Pitt saw in Jacobin France all that his father's training and his own frugal apprenticeship had taught him to dread: a "system of dividing the orders of the community," of representing property as "the easy prey of the indigent, the idle and the licentious," and religion and moral duty as useless superstitions. He knew how easily such doctrines might take hold of ignorant multitudes in the great cities if their rulers sought appeasement with those who championed them.

And the country, instinctively rather than intellectually, agreed with him. "How the storm gathers and blackens on the Continent," confided Miss Iremonger to a friend, "it really makes one tremble." She did not come of a trembling race. "My heart and my imagination are saddened," wrote Hannah More, "by the slaughter and devastation of my species with which every newspaper is full."

[1] ". . . As all Powers give up the contest, for what has England to fight? I wish most heartily we had peace, or that all our troops were drawn from the Continent and only a Naval war carried on, the war where England can alone make a figure."—*Nicolas* II, 8.

[2] *War Speeches*, 121.

But it never occurred to her to give in. The English view was expressed by Captain Harry Carter, the Cornish smuggler, who declared himself unafraid of all the lions in France. Gillray's comment on the peace proposals of the Opposition was to portray Britannia on her knees yielding crown, trident and Magna Charta to a flaming-headed, jack-booted monster while Fox and Sheridan, grovelling at her side, offered up the Fleet, the Church and the keys of the Bank. In another of his cartoons Pitt, over-running the lurking, traitor crew with their daggers and craven howls, drives godlike in his sun-chariot behind the Lion and Unicorn crying, "Inexorable peace or Eternal war!"

. . . .

So it was that instead of despairing of the Coalition, Britain, in the fatal summer of 1795, did her best to revive it. She offered an annual subsidy to Russia of a million sterling in return for a force of 50,000 men and to Austria a guarantee of a four and a half million loan for a renewed offensive on the Rhine. She sent a new ambassador to Spain, and tried, first by reason—and then, when it was too late, by bribery—to avert the final betrayal planned by her upstart Minister, Godoy. Such efforts were unavailing. Russia and Austria took Pitt's money but continued to make their main concern the final partition of Poland. Godoy—"a Birmingham Villiers" who had made himself indispensable to an amorous queen and a half-wit king—preferred Jacobin flattery and bribes to British and withdrew from the Coalition, ceding Spanish Santo Domingo to France. But the war went on.

CHAPTER SEVEN

Before the Storm

1795-6

"The plot seems to thicken as if the most serious part of the war were but beginning."

Capt. Collingwood to J. E. Blackett. 11*th May*, 1796.

WITH Austria confining her efforts in the campaign of 1795 to the Italian Riveria, Britain had four choices. She could concentrate her forces in Corsica for amphibious operations on the Austrian flank. She could open a new offensive in the West Indies. She could take the King's advice, renew the war in Hanover, where she still had 30,000 German auxiliaries and British cavalry on her pay-roll, and trust to Russian collaboration for a reconquest of Holland. Or she could aid the rising Royalist tide in France by a landing with all she had on the Brittany coast.

As usual the Government failed to make up its mind. It did bring itself to inform its Viceroy in Corsica—where a provisional government had been set up at the islanders' request under the British crown [1]—that the 5000 troops promised as a reinforcement could not be sent. But it allowed its cavalry to remain in Hanover, continued to prepare a West Indian expedition and drifted into becoming a party to operations in Brittany.

Such irresolution arose from the dual nature of the coalition Government. Carried away by the enthusiasm of Burke and Windham, the Portland Whigs had made themselves champions of the *émigrés*, in opposition to the King, who represented the typical John Bull distrust of all Frenchmen.[2] Against his judgment Pitt was gradually brought to a grudging recognition of their right to British support. Thousands of them had been released from the Allied armies by the end of the war in northern Europe. There was an opportunity to enrol them in British pay and in the growing royalism of Brittany a field for their services.

This policy was strengthened by the arrival in England of Count Puisaye, a giant Breton who had embraced the monarchical cause

[1] Thus technically making Napoleon Bonaparte a British subject.

[2] "My own inclination would tend to oblige every one of that perfidious nation here either to go on that service or, by the Aliens Act, be removed from this country." George III to Grenville, 2nd Aug., 1794. *H. M. C. Dropmore*, II, 609.

rather late in the day. He made up for it by the vehemence with which he now pressed it on his hosts. His idea was to band all the *émigrés* in Europe into a white army which, equipped by British money, should make a descent on Brittany during the summer. By its threat to Brest the landing would help the Navy—a consideration for an overstrained Admiralty—and, by carrying the war into the enemy's country, forestall any attempt to invade England.

Unfortunately—though Puisaye's enthusiasm obscured the fact—the Royalists were far from united. They suffered from the feuds common to political exiles in all ages. The aristocratic Court refugees who followed the murdered King's brothers, the Counts of Provence and Artois, regarded upstart rustics like Puisaye with contempt. In Paris the Royalist committee was jealous of the provincial leaders. In La Vendée, after the ravages of the Republican "infernal columns," the peasants had settled down to an uneasy truce confirmed by a mutually insincere pact between their chieftain Charette, and the Convention. The other Vendéan leader—the grim ex-gamekeeper, Stofflet—refused to recognise it and maintained a guerrilla war in the woods.

Yet the Royalist cause was undoubtedly gaining ground. Despite her victories the Republic was showing renewed signs of the spiritual and financial bankruptcy which Pitt had always foretold. The currency was discredited, the price of provisions soaring, and the peasants, trusting no one, were holding back their corn. The cities were full of bread queues and unemployed artisans. In the capital the Terror had been succeeded by a vicious reaction, directed by unprincipled profiteers and enforced by gangs of youthful *nouveaux riches* called Muscadins, who ran a counter-terror of their own in the streets and theatres. In May, 1795, a rising of the starving *faubourgs* was followed by a purge of the Popular Party: in this even Carnot, the organiser of victory, nearly lost his head. Thousands of decent and moderate folk began to think of a restoration as the only hope of justice, bread and peace. Several towns even elected Royalist mayors.

Seeking the establishment in France of a stable government with which an honourable peace could be made, Pitt could scarcely refuse the entreaties of Puisaye and his parliamentary backers. In May an official invitation was sent out to all the *émigrés* in Europe. An army of invasion was formed in Hampshire under the Bourbon flag. The Government provided money, arms and uniforms. It even—very unwisely—released a number of French prisoners who, wishing to return home, affected a Royalist conversion. It still hesitated to provide troops of its own. But it undertook to escort the expedition across the Channel and land it on the Quiberon peninsula.

On June 17th an advance guard of 4,000 with arms for 20,000 more sailed from Southampton. A British squadron under Commodore Sir John Borlase Warren accompanied it, while the Channel Fleet made a sweep under Hood's brother, Admiral Lord Bridport. On the 20th the latter encountered the French Fleet off Lorient and chased it back to port, taking three capital ships. A few days later the *émigrés* disembarked. They were greeted as saviours by thousands of Breton peasants. On July 3rd they captured the fort of Quiberon and some 600 Republican prisoners.

On hearing this the Government sent a fast frigate to Bremen for the Comte d'Artois who, through the death of his nephew in a Paris prison, had become Bourbon heir presumptive. It also decided to send a British force under Lord Moira to support Puisaye, who was now boasting that in a few weeks he would have 80,000 men in arms. Yet these hopes were offset by news of heavy Republican troop concentrations in the west. The liquidation of the Spanish war had released large new forces, and Hoche, the hero of France, was appointed to their command. The young giant's resolution contrasted ominously with the jealousies and delays in the Royalist camp. The aristocrats sneered at the clownish "Chouan" peasants and their fanatic, ignorant priests. The "converted" prisoners from England revealed their real sympathies. The Royalist commanders quarrelled among themselves, for the British Government with characteristic vagueness had failed to define their responsibilities.

The result was disaster. On the night of July 19th the Republicans entered the fort by treachery and destroyed or captured the entire Royalist force. Only Puisaye and a handful of fugitives escaped to the fleet. The prisoners, including the flower of the French aristocracy, were massacred, in spite of Hoche's safe conduct, by the orders of the Convention leaders who hoped in this way to cover their own treasonable correspondence.

This bloody fiasco, for which it was severely taken to task by the Opposition, placed the Government in a dilemma. It had committed itself to a campaign in support of the French Royalists and had invited Artois to England. But the Royalists had been defeated and their foothold in France lost. To make matters worse, the terms of the Peace of Basle on July 22nd revealed the treacherous cession of the Spanish half of Santo Domingo, turning what had hitherto been an allied base into hostile territory. This, combined with bad news from the Windward Isles, made the dispatch of reinforcements to the West Indies essential. Of the 20,000 British troops intended for Brittany, not more than 5000 could now be spared. Nor was Moira's comment on those that reached him at Southampton encouraging. "The foot want arms, the cavalry saddles; I hear that the 40th are a serviceable body of men, but they have never fired powder yet."

The proper course would have been to apologise to the French Princes and call off the expedition. But this would have injured the prestige of the Portland Whigs in the Cabinet. Sooner than endanger the coalition the Government decided to carry out its plan without either a landing-place on the mainland or an effective force to land. As Moira refused to undertake this, 4000 troops were sent off under General Doyle to occupy the island of Noirmoutier, off the mouth of the Loire, and use it as a base for renewed operations in La Vendée. The Comte d'Artois accompanied them with the ostensible hope of joining the heroic Charette. No one apparently asked how the expedition was to be maintained in the hurricane season on the most dangerous coast in Europe.

As a landing even on Noirmoutier proved impracticable, Doyle occupied his secondary objective, the small, barren island of Yeu. The hungry soldiers quickly ate the inhabitants out of hut and home. On the mainland the Vendéans, hearing that their prince was off the coast, rose in their thousands and acclaimed his coming. After some weeks of nervous hesitation, Artois declared his inability to land in person and sent Charette a sword of honour.

The rebellion fizzled out, and a few months later its betrayed leader died on the scaffold. A rising in Paris in October—the Thirteenth Vendemiaire—was suppressed by a timely "whiff of grapeshot." It marked a decisive step in the rise to fame of Brigadier Bonaparte, whom Barras had resurrected for the occasion, shabby and almost starving, from the discarded followers of Robespierre. Meanwhile, after several hundred men and horses had died from famine and exposure, Doyle's expedition was recalled to England. The evacuation evoked a superb piece of rescue work by the Navy in the Atlantic gales.

• • • • • • •

For the second time in six months Britain had been reminded that the gates of western Europe were shut to her inadequate armies. The invasion of the Continent was beyond her powers: she had too many responsibilities elsewhere. All through the summer of 1795 Dundas was on tenterhooks for news of the race to the Cape which he had set in motion in the spring. Not till November 23rd did the Park and Tower guns proclaim that the gateway to India was safely in British hands. Major-General Craig had reached False

Bay with the first contingent early in June, only to find that the Dutch Governor refused him leave to land. He had had to wait a month until reinforcements from home and St. Helena enabled him to gain a foothold at Simon's Town. Thence with 4000 troops and too little artillery he had fought his way through the pass of Muizenberg to Cape Town, which he had entered on September 16th. A Dutch naval expedition to regain the colony in the following year was destroyed by British warships in Saldanha Bay before it could land.

Elsewhere, too, Dundas's bold initiative against the Dutch colonies was rewarded. The bread he had cast upon the waters returned to him. Malacca, with its command of the vital highway to the Spice Islands and China seas, was captured on August 18th by a force from India. A week later Trincomalee, in the north of Ceylon, surrendered to Colonel James Stuart of the 72nd and 1100 Europeans and two Indian battalions. Colombo and the rest of the island were taken early in the following year, together with Dutch Amboina and Banka. The wealth of these places, thus denied to France, was deflected to swell the rising customs of Britain.

The new expedition to the West Indies was delayed by lack of men and equipment till the autumn. It sailed on November 16th under Sir Ralph Abercromby and Admiral Christian, and was at once overwhelmed by a terrific storm off the Chesil Beach. It sailed again early in December, only to be dispersed by a second storm.[1] Not till March 17th, 1796, did Abercromby reach Barbados, and not till the end of April could he assemble sufficient force to begin his work of putting down rebellion in the British islands. With only half the troops originally intended he succeeded in capturing St. Lucia, where he left the able John Moore—now a brigadier—in command and sent a detachment to seize Demerara, Berbice and Essequibo, the Dutch colonies on the South American mainland. These last brought Britain a rich return: during the next three years their exports to her of cotton, sugar and coffee multiplied tenfold. The story of these successes and the pains endured by Englishmen to achieve them—prickly heat, yellow fever, loathsome reptiles, salt pork and dry biscuits, no medicines or comforts and a barbarous "enemy determined to dispute every inch"—are epitomised in a survivor's proud if characteristically complacent phrase: "It was sometimes dubious how the affair would end; but British valour, perseverance and resolution, as it does on all occasions, triumphed at last."[2]

[1] Among those who suffered in the two storms was the future victor of Waterloo, who but for them might have perished of yellow fever in a West Indian swamp.

[2] *Dyott* I, 103.

The price was far too high. During the autumn disease reduced the British force in Santo Domingo from 9000 to 1600, and the garrisons of the other islands proportionately. Abercromby—a veteran of 61 with a love for his men—did his best by abolishing drills and parades in the heat, adapting stiff, stuffy uniforms to the tropics and improving camp sanitation. But nothing could have halted the wastage of the climate but the one measure which deference to vested interests forbade: the enrolment of a native West Indian army. Between 1794 and 1796, 40,000 British troops perished in these fatal islands.

. . . .

The drain on the country's man-power had serious repercussions on the continental campaigns of 1795 and 1796. After the defection of Prussia and the fall of Holland the Austrians had concentrated their forces against France's southern frontier. On June 13th, 1795, after the usual delays, they took the offensive, driving the French army of Italy southwards from the Apennines to the Genoese riviera. The capture of Vado with its fine anchorage opened a door to British amphibious operations on the enemy's flank.

The opportunity could not be taken because the reinforcements originally intended for Corsica had been deflected to La Vendée and the West Indies. Even without them the Navy might have seriously interfered with the French army's communications along the vulnerable Corniche Road. But Lord Hotham was incapable of initiative. In June he failed for the second time to destroy the Toulon fleet in a "miserable action" off the isles of Hyères. It is true that he sent Captain Nelson to Vado Bay to co-operate with Devins, the aged Austrian commander. But the force detached for the purpose was so weak that even Nelson's restless zeal could not make it effective. The latter at first was full of hope, expecting to see the Austrians in Nice by the autumn. But by September he was convinced that the only object of his allies was to touch another four millions of English money.

The opportunity of destroying the French army of Italy passed. Ragged and ill-disciplined though it was, it was not of the stuff that yields to a supine foe. In the autumn it received strong reinforcements from the Spanish frontier. Before the winter a plan of General Bonaparte's, now working in the Topographical Bureau of the Committee of Public Safety, was applied with startling results. On November 23rd General Schérer surprised the Imperial troops at Loano and drove them back beyond the Apennines.

But by a strange irony the failure of the campaign on which Austria had built her hopes for 1795 was offset by success in a theatre where she looked for none and had done her best to avoid fighting at all. On September 7th Jourdan and Pichegru with two French armies had crossed the Rhine to carry the war into Germany. The Jacobins anticipated that their offensive would complete the break-up of the ramshackle Reich, begun by the defection of Prussia in the spring. By an advance on Vienna down the Danube the French hegemony of Europe, so nearly achieved in 1704 under the Lilies, would be completed under the Tricolour in 1796. And this time, since the British had been driven from the Continent, there could be no Blenheim to save the Hapsburgs at the eleventh hour.

But though Pichegru seized Mannheim and every petty court in Germany echoed with the cry "the French are coming," the campaign did not go as the politicians in Paris planned. For they had not reckoned with the consequences of their own corruption. Under the cynical rule of profiteers, contractors and speculators the diaphanous robe of the *demi-monde* was now substituted for the bloodstained cap of liberty. The citoyenne Therezia, the wife of Tallien and mistress of Barras, drove in her scarlet coach through the unswept streets where half-naked wretches picked rubbish heaps for sustenance, her hair bright with jewels and her thighs encircled with diamonds. "The reign of the *san-culottes* was followed by that of the *sans-chemises*."[1]

The eternal laws which govern the operations of war are just. Men will not die for those whom they know to be unworthy of their sacrifice. Hungry and ragged, the armies of the Rhine lost heart, for they knew why supplies were failing and their families starving. When the Austrian generals, noting the change in Republican morale, counter-attacked, the invaders crumbled. On November 22nd the Imperialists recaptured Mannheim, and a few days later Mainz and Frankfurt. By Christmas they had regained the greater part of the Palatinate. The French, driven back across the Rhine, were reduced to pillaging their own countryside.

. . . .

Thus as 1795 drew to a close the war seemed to be approaching a stalemate. In France galloping inflation had set in. The value of the paper *assignat* fell to almost nothing: a bushel of haricot beans that had fetched 120 livres in the spring sold for twelve times as much by the autumn. Every one except the high livers in Paris was sad, disillusioned and hungry. The roads were breaking up, the hearths desolate, the hospitals deserted.

And the enemies of France after three years of war were as embarrassed. Austria, before her unexpected victories in the Palatinate,

[1] *Madelin*, 550.

had seemed at the end of her resources; Piedmont had already sued for an armistice; Spain, Holland and Prussia had given up the fight and entered the Jacobin camp. Britain was suffering from food shortage and unrest. In the autumn of 1795 she sustained serious losses at sea. Hotham allowed a French squadron to escape from Toulon into the Altantic, where it captured the entire Levant convoy of thirty-one vessels, together with one of the three escorting battleships. This grim disaster, which spread ruin through the City, was followed by a raid on the Jamaica convoy by French frigates. Another force from Toulon harried the Levant, and in the New Year squadrons from Rochefort and the Texel, evading Bridport's cruisers, threatened the East Indies and the Cape.

These calamities made the City think more kindly of peace. To idealists like Windham or to the old King it was still something unthinkable.[1] But shrewd men of business were growing concerned at the continued failure of British military enterprises and their rising cost. The tame dissolution of the terrible Convention in October and its succession by a board of five Directors—of a somewhat commercial complexion—seemed evidence of a more reasonable frame of mind. And now that the Republican armies, after all their victories, were shown to be as liable to defeat as the Austrian and British, might not some better basis be found for future security than eternal war? Even Pitt, never very far in his vantage point at the Treasury from the general feeling of the City, began to fancy so.

The first hint of the way his mind was moving came in a speech from the Throne at the opening of Parliament in October, 1795. Anarchy in France had at last led to a crisis: should it end in any order compatible with the tranquillity of other countries and the observance of international treaties, the Government would not be backward in readiness to negotiate a general peace. In the meantime the wisest course was to prosecute the war with vigour. A still clearer indication was contained in a royal message to Parliament a few weeks after the Directory assumed office.

The pursuit of such a peace became the Government's main concern in the new year. After a tussle with the King,[2] who foretold that any overtures would be met with a humiliating rejection, feelers were put out through the British agent in Switzerland. The King's prediction was exactly fulfilled. Britain was rudely reminded that the new Constitution had incorporated all France's conquests,

[1] *Windham Papers*, I, 302: II, 2-3; *H. M. C. Dropmore*, III, 149.

[2] The old gentleman had the last word, assuring Grenville: "I always choose to act on simple principles; Italian politics are too complicated paths for my understanding." King to Grenville, 9th Feb., 1796. *H. M. C. Dropmore*, III, 174.

and that return of the Netherlands to Austria or Savoy to Piedmont was out of the question. To crown the indignity the Directory, in defiance of diplomatic manners, published the correspondence.

What Pitt failed to see was that the new rulers of France no more wanted peace than the old. They were not high-minded patriots absorbed in the economic well-being of their country: they were only concerned with what happened to themselves. They were fraudulent contractors, debauchees, even murderers, who had stolen power and were now enjoying its fruits. They could not afford to let it go lest those they had wronged should avenge themselves. Peace was their nightmare; as Sieyès put it: "We shall all be destroyed if peace is made." The slightest turn of the roulette of terror which had brought them to the top would sink them.

Even had they been altruistic patriots, longing to give their countrymen peace, it is hard to see how they could have done so. The two inescapable facts in French life in 1796 were bankruptcy and the army. The latter's pay was years in arrears: it could only exist by living on a civilian population. No Frenchman wanted it to live on that of France. To disband it would mean chaos. Its only future was conquest, which also seemed the one way to lighten the Republic's burden of debt. The only alternative to a vista of drab poverty was victory.

In all ages statesmen have found it hard to understand the psychology of revolutionary governments bound to the wheel of armaments and debts. For it is a cycle that cannot be reversed. It can only be broken or its pace accelerated. Pitt, in his touching belief in the inevitable triumph of financial integrity, could never realise the explosive force of the evil thing against which he was contending. That guest of Wilberforce was wiser who, hearing how the Prime Minister said he would calculate to a day the coming collapse of France, asked if any one could tell him who was Chancellor of the Exchequer to Attila?

For to Pitt's hopes of quietly strangling the Republic with the strings of a money bag, the Directors' answer was conquest. Belgium and Holland, with their treasuries, had already been swallowed and exhausted. There remained Italy—with its fertile plains, fabulously rich cities, its corrupt governments and effete peoples. It was, as Nelson said, a gold mine that, once entered, was without the means of resistance. So far French attempts to invade it had been stopped by the immense barriers of the Alps and Apennines. But the victory of Loano had given the Republic possession of the Ligurian Passes. And in Paris the young General who had saved the Directorate from the mob of Thermidor was ceaselessly pointing out how that possession might be used.

Carnot resolved to give him his chance. "Behind the door lies abundance," he wrote to Bonaparte, "it is for you to break it down." The all-powerful Barras was agreeable. His cynical price for the appointment—a job, as it seemed to him—was that the Commander-in-Chief elect of the Army of Italy should marry his cast-off mistress, the widow-by-the-guillotine, Josephine de Beauharnais. As Bonaparte—distinguished in that dissolute society by his absurd austerity—had fallen head over heels in love with the fascinating Creole, there was no difficulty. On March 11th, at the age of 26, the Corsican, with his commission in his pocket and his great forehead bulging with plans, set out for the south through a listless and down-at-heels France.

. . . .

It was Bonaparte's belief that to daring everything was possible. "He who stays in his entrenchments is beaten," was one of his sayings. He had immense will power, inexhaustible energy, lightning perception, unbounded ambition. There was genius in every inch of his Tom Thumb frame. He arrived at Nice on March 26th, 1796, to find the army starving, despondent and in rags. Within a few days he had inspired it with something of his own dazzling faith and vitality. Then on April 10th, while far away in England farmers grumbled at the "cold, barren, growless weather," the young eagle struck. For just under a fortnight the struggle in the mountain passes continued, Bonaparte making untold demands on his men and taking enormous risks. Had the British been able, as Nelson urged, to land even a small force on the Corniche Road in his rear, his army might have been annihilated, for his tenuous communications were the Achilles heel of his plan. But though he broke all the rules, in six battles against divided forces of twice his strength he drove a wedge between the Austrians and Piedmontese. On the 23rd, with the Alps turned and Turin threatened, the terrified House of Savoy sought an armistice. The victor gave them a few hours to accept terms which reduced Piedmont to a cipher for a generation. Then, with his flank secured, he poured into Lombardy.

The war had suddenly come to life. While Nelson's letter, describing the stalemate between the struggling armies in the snow-clad hills above Ceva, was still on its way to his friend Collingwood, Bonaparte's men were marching at unprecedented speed eastwards along the south bank of the Po, seeking for a crossing to cut old Beaulieu off from his bases. On May 6th, having covered 44 miles in 36 hours, they found it in the small neutral town of Piacenza. Without formality they held its rulers to ransom and crossed the river. Three days later they flung back a bewildered Austrian army from the bridge of Lodi and drove on to Milan. On the 15th the conqueror entered the Lombard capital, the inhabitants, feminine in their worship of success, strewing flowers in his path. "People of Italy!," they were told, "the Army of France has broken your chains: the People of France is the friend of all other Peoples! Come to greet it!"

Their joy vanished when the young hero presented them with his bill. An immediate contribution of twenty million francs, vast stores of provisions and thousands of horses were demanded as the price of French protection. A hundred of the finest carriage horses in the province were despatched across the Alps to grace the coaches of the Directors. The Grand Duke of Parma, who had been slower to acclaim the liberator than the fickle Milanese, had to yield twenty of the best pictures in his gallery and a crushing tribute. And when the people of Pavia contested Bonaparte's requisitions, they were quickly enlightened as to the conditions of Italian emancipation. The magistrates and leading inhabitants were shot, the city sacked and all who resisted massacred. A few weeks later a village near Bologna was burnt to the ground and the entire population murdered to strike fear through Italy. For Bonaparte, once a follower of Robespierre, did not believe in terror for its own sake but only as an instrument of policy.

Before the end of May he had resumed his eastward march across the richest plain in Europe. On the 30th he forced the Mincio and laid siege to Mantua. Around this great marsh fortress the failing fortunes of the old Europe turned during the next few months, while the Austrians from the Alpine passes to the north made attempt after attempt to relieve it and regain control of their lost province. Meanwhile the rest of the peninsula lay at the conqueror's mercy. As the fame of the French triumphs flashed down its mountain spine to its corrupt courts and cities, prince after prince sought to make his peace with the terrible Republic.

Within a few weeks the Mediterranean situation had been transformed. At the end of June, having sworn eternal peace to its Grand Duke, Bonaparte sent his most brilliant cavalry officer, Joachim Murat—the 29-year-old son of a Gascon innkeeper—on a flying raid into Tuscany to seize Leghorn and the goods of its British merchants. For one English girl the sudden scamper of the British colony to Nelson's waiting frigates brought romance; the clean, beautiful ship, the attentive officers who gave up their cabins, the calm, efficient assurance and friendliness of it all set Betsey Wynne's heart in a whirl of love for its fiery dark-eyed captain.[1]

The unconscious Captain Fremantle and his Commodore—"old" Nelson, as 17-year-old Betsey called him—had preoccupations which they courteously did not betray to their guests. For their position had suddenly become intensely grave. The whole of Italy had turned stony and hostile, and with "the flesh kettles" of Leghorn cut off and Gibraltar nearly a thousand miles away, only barren Corsica remained open to their ships. It did not look as though even Corsica would do so long. For not only was the island inhabited, in Admiral Jervis's words by "infernal miscreants" seething with unrest, but the garrison was quite inadequate to protect its coastline from French landings. Appeals for reinforcements had met with little response from England: the Secretary of State, raising his ducal spectacles with infinite slowness from his nose to his forehead, had written to remind the Viceroy that his countrymen were not foreign politicians and had no interest in their expensive Mediterranean possession.[2] And it was only too plain from Bonaparte's preparations at Leghorn and Genoa that he was contemplating invasion.

Fortunately the new Commander-in-Chief was a very different man from Hotham. Sir John Jervis, who had taken over the Mediterranean fleet at the end of the previous year, was worthy in his own element to cross swords with Bonaparte. "Old Jack," as the seamen called him, was a naval strategist of the first order. As a young officer he had piloted Wolfe on his last journey to the Heights of Abraham; in the present war he had won fame as the sailor who had helped Grey to reduce Martinique, Guadeloupe and St. Lucia in thirteen weeks. His arrival in the Mediterranean had been delayed by a scandalous vote of censure moved on him by West Indian financiers in the House of Commons for having levied a contribution on merchandise in Martinique: but for this, he always believed he could have prevented the Austrian defeat at Loano and so have saved Italy from Bonaparte.[3] He was now 61. The child of poor parents, he had evolved through a stern, impecunious youth into a man of iron: a devotee of duty in its grimmest and most unyielding aspects. He had long steeled himself out of both moral and physical fear: none of the ordinary failings of men affected his cool judgment. With his long nose, heavy brows and thoughtful

[1] She subsequently married him, accompanied him on his voyages, nursed him and Nelson after their wounds at Tenerife, and, first seeing her native land in their company, became the ancestress of a line of English Admirals.—*Wynne Diaries.*

[2] See also *Collingwood*, 27.

[3] *Spencer Papers*, II, 400-1.

eyes, he was the picture of a disciplinarian. Yet he had unexpected streaks of warmth in his rock-like composition: a saturnine humour,[1] great generosity to those who merited it and, when he could escape the effects of ill-health and a harsh dictatorial temper, a taste for unbending in congenial company. Betsey Wynne and her sisters when he entertained them on board the *Victory* found him a kind, gallant, friendly old man, without anything stiff or formal, who made them sing duets after dinner and thanked them for their trouble by a chaste embrace. "The old gentleman is very partial to kisses; he abuses all who do not salute the ladies and always obliges all the gentlemen that are present to kiss us." To Nelson he always showed the softer side of his character: the ardent, sensitive, affectionate captain was happier under his command than he had been since Hood left the Mediterranean. For he felt that Jervis appreciated him.

The issue which the Admiral had to face called for all his powers of judgment and fortitude. They were equal to the occasion. "Strong nerves and manly sense," he told the Admiralty, were superior in treating with barbarians to the finesse of the Corps Diplomatique. He applied them to the affairs of southern Europe. In consultation with the Viceroy he ordered the blockade of Leghorn and the occupation of Elba—a small Tuscan island between the mainland and Corsica. On July 9th Nelson accordingly appeared off the capital, Porto Ferrajo, and landed troops without opposition from the authorities. Indeed, they seemed to welcome this unorthodox but masculine diplomacy.

But the security of Corsica was the least of Jervis's worries. Expelled from the Italian mainland, cut off from all sources of fresh food and dangerously short of frigates and corvettes, the British fleet was now faced with a new danger. Ever since his craven surrender Godoy—since raised to almost royal dignity by the doting Queen under the fantastic title of Prince of the Peace—had been playing with the idea of reviving the hundred-year-old family alliance between France and Spain. Many motives prompted him: personal vanity, hatred of the stiff-necked island ally he had betrayed, a natural sympathy towards those who like himself had overcome the disadvantages of mean birth. Though the old blood-link between the Bourbon Courts of Versailles and Madrid had been snapped, that between the peoples remained. Gallic victories on land might be matched by Iberian triumphs at sea, and the two great Latin nations of the west might together re-establish their

[1] It was a pleasantry of his when the weather was rough to summon the chaplains of the fleet for a conclave.

ancient ascendancy over Saxons and Teutons. Spain had many old scores to settle with England: Gibraltar, the West Indies and two centuries of interloping by heretic freebooters. A great naval and imperial power with seventy-six ships of the line in her harbours and half the Americas as her private property, she had the strength to enforce her just pretensions.

So Godoy argued, seeing himself as a second Alberoni, and wily Jacobin agents encouraged him in his dreams. Needing the Spanish fleet and harbours for use against Britain, they represented the presence of British troops in Corsica and Santo Domingo as an affront to Spain's dignity. Against such arguments, the British Ambassador, Lord Bute, pleaded in vain. The ramshackle Power, which a year before had withdrawn from alliance into neutrality now sank from alliance to non-belligerency. Early in 1796 the French squadron which had captured the British Levant convoy put into Cadiz with its prizes and began openly to refit in the royal dockyards. Nor could all Bute's representations remove them. French privateers used Spanish harbours to attack British shipping, and Spanish naval arsenals hummed with unwonted activity. "Spain," Nelson wrote in May, "is certainly going to war with somebody." There could be little doubt with whom.

The Government, however, feeling that it had its hands full, did its best to ignore these provocations. It instructed an appeasing ambassador to do all in his power to preserve peace. Nor was Godoy in a hurry to bring matters to a head. He needed time to man his fleet and to see how the campaign in Italy went before finally committing himself. Even his ignorance and presumption could not blind him to the fact that past wars with England had proved expensive for his country.

. . . .

For these, as for reasons of even greater purport, the eyes of Spain and Britain became focused on the struggle in the Lombardy plain. Here Bonaparte was trying to reduce Mantua with a siege train of only half the gun-power of the fortress, while preventing the Austrian veteran, Wurmser, from relieving it through the Alpine passes. The struggle seemed uneven, for the Directors, now jealous of his fame, were secretly starving their youthful general of men and guns. With 40,000 men Bonaparte had simultaneously to contain 11,000 Austrians in Mantua and beat off 60,000 more from the north. Nelson, writing from his station off Leghorn, felt full of confidence again: the French army had suffered terrible losses, the outraged Italian states were combining against the aggressor, Wurmser would soon be in Mantua, Naples would stand firm in her alliance.[1]

At the end of July, 1796, Wurmser began to emerge from the mountain defiles, moving southwards along either shore of Lake Garda and driving Massena's covering troops before him. Hardly had he done so when the whirlwind struck him. With almost incredible speed Bonaparte abandoned the siege of Mantua and every other inessential and hurled his entire force on the Austrian columns before they had time to assemble south of the lake. In the first five days of August, in operations around Castiglione he defeated both halves of Wurmser's army in turn and flung him back north-eastwards into the passes. "All our expected hopes," wrote Nelson to Jervis, "are blasted. . . . Austria, I suppose, must make peace, and we shall, as usual, be left to fight it out." Britain would have to give up Corsica and withdraw from the Mediterranean. As for the Dons, they would pay for it, if they were fools enough to involve themselves in war.[2]

. . . .

On August 4th, the French raiders, refitted after their long stay at Cadiz, were escorted into the Atlantic by the Spanish fleet, Admiral Man's small observation squadron discreetly withdrawing. The news of Castiglione removed Godoy's last doubts. On August 19th he signed at San Ildefonso a full offensive alliance with the Directory. By a secret clause Spain was later to cede Louisiana to France, while France was to assist Spain to conquer Gibraltar and Portugal. War was to be declared on Britain within a month, the King of Spain was to become Grand Admiral of the Republic, and the two Latin Powers, sinking ideological differences, were to advance together inexorably to the final overthrow of "the province of England." In view of French victories on land, Spanish geography and the joint naval strength of France, Spain and Holland—together nearly double that of Britain—it looked a safe gamble.

A week later the Spanish Ambassador, making a flimsy excuse, left London. Already Pitt, seeing the writing on the wall, was buying naval stores for a long siege: ship timber from the Adriatic, masts and hemp from North America, corn, tallow, hides, hemp and iron from the Baltic.[3] On the 31st the Cabinet, anticipating an early surrender by Austria, reached the momentous decision to abandon Corsica and withdraw the fleet from the Mediterranean. Orders were at once dispatched to Jervis and Elliot. To defend her

[1] *Nicolas*, II, 212, 219.
[2] Nelson to Jervis, 20th Aug., 1796 : *Nicolas* II, 248-9.
[3] *Mahan, Sea Power* I, 74.

scattered possessions a concentration of Britain's effort had become essential. She could not longer contain the power of France from the circumference.

Yet just when Austria, reeling under Bonaparte's blows, seemed at her last gasp, the clouds for a moment lifted. A second attempt of Wurmser to relieve Mantua had ended in the discomfited old man being forced to take refuge with a remnant of his army in the fortress he had come to deliver. But in Germany, where both French and Austrians had planned their main campaign, the tide of war turned unexpectedly in Austria's favour. At the end of May the French armies had crossed the Rhine and pressed into the heart of Germany, laying waste Suabia, Franconia and Bavaria and threatening Vienna itself. An urgent application to Pitt for aid was promptly met with an advance of £1,200,000 on the Prime Minister's personal responsibility.[1]

This help enabled Austria to make a last effort. Her new commander-in-chief, the Archduke Charles—a man no older than Bonaparte—having shown patient stoicism in retreat, now successively defeated Bernadotte at Neumark on August 16th, and Jourdan at Wurzburg on September 3rd. Had it not been for Austrian fears of Prussia, which kept 80,000 troops watching the Silesian frontier, the French retreat to the Rhine might have become a rout. As it was, for the third time the Empress of Russia unwittingly aided the Republic by concentrating an army on her western borders. For it was the weakness of the German powers that, facing both ways, they could never decide in which direction to act or consistently pursue any policy without becoming distracted.

The autumn of 1796 in Germany had consequences even more important than the military. For it first crystallised the real as opposed to the idealistic issue between Revolutionary France and Europe. Hitherto the Jacobins in all countries had been able to represent the war as an ideological one: a crusade to liberate the peoples from the despotism of selfish rulers and outworn laws. As a result the poorer and to a large extent the middle-classes had been lukewarm in their support of their governments, and many had openly sympathised with the French and welcomed their coming. Only in Britain had patriotism proved a stronger force than horizontal discontent, though even here a minority had displayed Jacobin leanings.

But after the invasion of southern and central Germany these illusions began to fade. For the invaders, carrying fire and sword,

[1] Fox subsequently tried to impeach Pitt, but the House condoned the Premier's brave action by 285 votes to 81.

inflicted immense suffering. It fell, as always, most heavily on the poor. The plundered hen-roost, the emptied granary, the burning cottage represented the entire wealth of the peasant: not only his income but his capital. The Jacobin doctrine of making the conquered countryside maintain the victor's army awoke in its victims feelings of patriotism and national unity that had scarcely existed in the medieval medley of the older Europe. By making Germans aware that they hated Frenchmen, it made them conscious that they were Germans.[1]

The growth of this feeling was slow. For the moment its effects were confined to acts of revenge against French stragglers. Nor did the spirit of patriotism touch the governments, which continued in Germany as in Italy to be actuated by dynastic and personal motives. The Franconian and Suabian States bought a selfish peace with the invader who was fighting the titular Emperor of Germany. Prussia, on news of Bonaparte's victories, sought a closer understanding with France and encouraged the larger north German states to enlarge their territories at the expense of their smaller neighbours. In its jealousy of the Hapsburgs, the House of Hohenzollern exploited the Revolution to destroy what was left of the old Christian Reich and the fabric of European civilisation. By a secret pact signed in early August it agreed to recognise France's right to the Rhine frontier in return for compensation at the expense of the German ecclesiastical princes.

. . . .

It was the Prussian attempt to form a northern federation—friendly to France and non-belligerent towards Britain—which, even more than the lowering aspect of Spain and Bonaparte's victories, made the British Government again contemplate peace. A threat to Hamburg and the Baltic ports—the chief source of naval stores and of surplus grain for the growing industrial towns—touched Pitt's most sensitive spot. It had been the Armed Neutrality of Prussia and the Baltic States that had tipped the scale against his country when he stood at the threshold of public life in the dark hours of the American war. A friendly Prussia and the trade of the North had always been corner stones of his foreign policy. At the end of June, 1796, he wrote to Grenville that since Austria would almost certainly be unable to continue the struggle after the end of the year, it would be inexcusable not to try "honourably and

[1] "Have you seen," wrote an English lady a few years later, "a German Hymn for the Emperor Francis in the manner of our God Save the King? and set by Haydn; the words are translated by Dr. Burney into English—the music is very fine." (*Bamford*, 201.) The hymn, expressing the Austrian peasant's love for his fatherland, was *Deutschland uber Alles.*

safely to set on foot some decent plan of pacification." For either now or in a few months Britain would find herself "left to sustain alone the conflict with France and Holland, probably joined by Spain and favoured more or less openly by the Northern Powers."[1]

But the road to peace was not easy. The King was still against any concession and, like Burke, looked on a "Jacobin peace" as a deal with Satan.[2] And though every report showed that the French people were heartily sick of war, their rulers gave no sign of readiness to meet Britain half-way. A feeler through the Danish Chargé d'Affaires was met by an insolent demand for a direct application. "If such a communication," wrote the King, "will not rouse the British lion, he must have lost his wonted energy!" Yet peace was so needful that even pride was worth sacrificing to obtain it. In July there was a financial crisis during which Consols fell below 60: the City said openly that unless Pitt made peace before Christmas the Bank would force him to resign.[3]

The Government, therefore, decided to swallow its scruples and to apply to the Directory for a passport for a Minister Plenipotentiary. With Pitt's approval a pamphlet of Lord Auckland's was published to prepare the public mind. The King was assured that the internal state of the country required it and that only when the opponents of war had been convinced of its necessity by a French refusal to conclude even the most reasonable peace, would the nation be united enough to face a world in arms.[4] "As Lord Grenville and Mr. Pitt think a further step of humiliation necessary to call forth the spirit which used to be characteristic of this island," the old man wrote, "I will not object." The first diplomat in Britain, Lord Malmesbury, was selected for the mission. The embodiment of English tact, good nature and common sense, "the white lion," as his friends called him, was the perfect appeaser.

It had been hoped to bring Austria into the negotiations. But by the time Malmesbury set out for Calais on October 16th the Court of Vienna was veering once more. Bonaparte's Italian victories had been offset by the Archduke Charles' German campaign, and the old imperial hauteur had revived. Thugut had hopes of inducing Russia to join in stemming a French advance to the Adriatic—a sea in which the scheming Empress Catherine was interested as protector of the Orthodox Christians. The scene was thus set for a counter-offensive in Italy and a new attempt to relieve Mantua. For this reason, three days after Malmesbury left

[1] Pitt to Grenville, 23rd June, 1796.—*H. M. C. Dropmore*, III, 214.
[2] King to Grenville, 30th July, 1796.—*H. M. C. Dropmore*, III, 227.
[3] *Farington*, I, 158.
[4] *H. M. C. Dropmore*, III, 242.

London the Cabinet countermanded its earlier orders to abandon Corsica. For, forgetting both its defencelessness and the promise made to its inhabitants, the politicians supposed that the island might be useful as a bribe to bring Russia into the war.

Therefore when Malmesbury reached Paris—travelling, wrote the infuriated Burke, "the whole way on his knees"—his proposal for a European pacification was met by an inquiry whether the Court of Vienna concurred. How, the French Foreign Minister asked, could a general peace be expected when every day brought new accounts of the Emperor's determination to carry on the war? The truth was that both sides were temporising until an issue had been reached elsewhere. The Austrians were waiting for Russia's decision, for further victories on the Rhine and the relief of Mantua; the French for an end to the Lombardy campaign and a Spanish move at sea. Malmesbury therefore remained in Paris, recording only such minor triumphs and set-backs as the civility shown to his diplomatic uniform and the necessity—repugnant to an English nobleman—of having to wear the tricolour in the streets.

Meanwhile Spain had declared war. Godoy handed Lord Bute the official declaration on October 5th, accompanied by a long list of imaginary Spanish grievances. Four days earlier Admiral Man, sailing to Gibraltar with seven ships of the line, was attacked without warning by nineteen Spanish battleships, losing two of the merchantmen he was convoying. Further up the Mediterranean Jervis and Nelson were putting into execution the Government's orders of August 31st—received in the last week of September—to evacuate Corsica. Here, despite the odds, the feeling was one of confidence: it was a tradition in the Navy to despise Spain. "The Dons may make fine ships," Nelson had written when they were allies, "but they cannot make men." A Spanish war was sure to bring in prize-money, and though few sailors quarrelled with the decision to leave Corsica, the desertion of the Mediterranean was regarded as unnecessary. Eight months of Jervis's discipline had given his command an astonishing assurance. "They at home," wrote Nelson to his wife, "do not know what this fleet is capable of performing; anything and everything . . . I lament our present orders in sackcloth and ashes, so dishonourable to the dignity of England, whose fleets are equal to meet the world in arms."[1]

Yet it was probably as well that the Government's countermanding orders did not reach Jervis in time. For on putting into Gibraltar after his rough handling by the Spanish fleet, Admiral

[1] *Nicolas*, II, 290.

Man, his anxious mind obsessed by thoughts of being "hemmed in by superiority of numbers," decided to return to England instead of rejoining his chief in San Fiorenzo Bay. This breach of orders deprived Jervis at a critical moment of a third of his fleet. With only fourteen ships of the line against a Franco-Spanish combination of thirty-eight he waited for the errant Man until November 2nd, when he sailed in desperation for Gibraltar. Before he left the Corsican coast, the French had already landed in the island.

. . . .

On the same day the Austrian Alvinzi crossed the Piave with a force nearly twice as large as that with which Bonaparte was besieging Mantua. On November 11th he drove back the French at Caldiero. For forty-eight hours it looked as though the relief of the fortress was certain. Then on the night of the 14th Bonaparte gave orders for one of the most daring marches in history. It ended three days later in the victory of Arcola. The third attempt to relieve Mantua had failed.

The same day also brought news of the death of the Empress Catherine. A fortnight earlier she had been found in an apoplectic fit on the floor of her writing closet. Her successor, the Tsar Paul, was mad, and reputed to be opposed to Russian intervention in a western war. The French at once began to raise their terms. Malmesbury's temperate and inflexibly honest restatements of Britain's position—her readiness to surrender conquered sugar islands in return for adjustments in Europe and a vindication of the outraged law of nations—grew ever more remote from the realities of Parisian extravagance. Every time he met Delacroix, who like all revolutionary diplomats was apt to shout when excited, the French Minister became more unreasonable, insisting that all France's acquisitions were sacred and "indivisible," whereas Britain's colonial conquests were mere robbery and must be immediately restored. After the news of Arcola only a glimmer of hope remained.

There was another reason for France's increasing obduracy. On November 13th Malmesbury, keeping his ears open for rumours, dispatched a courier to London with information that eleven ships of the line and fifteen thousand troops were at Brest preparing for sea. It was certain, he reported, that they were intended for Ireland. Had he been able to see the letters which since the summer had been passing between Carnot, Hoche and Wolfe Tone, the founder of the United Irishmen, then in Paris, he might have been even more alarmed. "I am practically certain the English Government is at its wits' end," Hoche had written; "the kind of war I propose to wage on our rivals is a terrible one." On Tone's assurance that half a million men would rise the day the French landed, Ireland had been selected as the first objective of Carnot's favourite project—a direct attack on the British Isles.

Until the expedition was ready to start the French Foreign Minister continued to keep Malmesbury amused. Two days before the end of November he gave him a long interview, in the course of which he tried to prove that while Britain's ambitions were commercial and colonial, those of France were purely continental.[1]

He did not mention that a few weeks before his Government had passed a decree confiscating every neutral ship carrying British goods. In a later and more impassioned meeting Delacroix declared that with the Rhine as the natural boundary of France the tranquillity of Europe would be assured for two centuries. At last on December 18th Malmesbury received peremptory orders from his hosts to leave Paris within forty-eight hours. For on that day it became known that Hoche had sailed for Ireland.

Meanwhile Britain was preparing for the storm. Ever since the summer the Adjutant-General's office had been drawing up detailed plans for defending the southern counties against an invader. On October 18th Pitt met Parliament with proposals for doubling the Militia and adding 15,000 seamen to the fleet by a compulsory quota on all parishes. The House voted supplies for over 400,000 men. These included a new force of Provisional Cavalry, to be raised by compulsion, the owner or owners of every ten horses being responsible for one fully equipped horseman; and another of sportsmen and gamekeepers to be used as riflemen and skirmishers. To meet the increase in expenditure the Prime Minister not only trebled the assessed taxes but adopted a revolutionary procedure. Instead of resorting to professional financiers he applied direct to the nation. Early in December a Loyalty Loan of eighteen millions, issued at £112 10s. per £100 of stock, and bearing interest at 5 per cent, was offered to the public. Though a more expensive purchase than other existing stock, the entire loan was subscribed in less than sixteen hours. "The Constitution," Pitt proudly announced, "inspires the steady affection of the people and is worth defending with every drop of our blood."[2]

[1] "Commerce is your empire. It is to be founded in the Indies and in your colonies. But as for France, I should be better pleased with an addition of four villages on the frontiers of the Republic than by the acquisition of the richest island among the Antilles, and should be even sorry to see Pondicherry and Chandenagore again belong to France."—*Malmesbury*, III, 334.

[2] *War Speeches*, 172.

CHAPTER EIGHT

Her Darkest Hour

1796-7

"Be assured I will omit no opportunity of chastising the Spaniards, and if I have the good fortune to fall in with them the stuff I have in this fleet will tell."

Sir John Jervis to Lord Spencer. 2nd Oct., 1796.

"And Jack the tawny whiskers singed
Of the astonished Don."

Dibdin, "*A Dose for the Dons*," 1797.

On the evening of December 15th, 1796, the French armada for Ireland, having stood through the narrow Goulet out of Brest, anchored in the Camaret Roads. There was no sign of the British Fleet save for three frigates cruising on the Atlantic horizon. The French had seventeen ships of the line, twenty-six smaller warships and transports, most of the 15,000 troops being crowded on board the battleships.

For nearly six weeks the wind had been in the east. It had blown the British blockading fleet far out into the Atlantic and opened the gateway to Ireland. Wolfe Tone, the rebel Irish leader, had cursed the delays of the Directory and its chaotic Navy. "Damn them! damn them! sempiternally damn them!" There was no discipline in the Fleet and dockyards, nobody obeyed or respected anybody, nobody worked.

But the Republican army—its wonderful enthusiasm, its ardour, its pride—had impressed the excitable Irishman as much as the navy depressed him. In the Festival of Youth in the church of a provincial town he had seen hundreds of young recruits, bareheaded before the statue of Liberty, receiving their arms from veterans to the strains of the "Marseillaise." Here, he felt, was true Liberty and Patriotism: a moving contrast to the depressed, drunken drafts he had seen shambling off to the colours in his own downtrodden land. And this army was led by men who shared its aspirations and passionate youth: still in their twenties and early thirties, unfettered by the caste prejudices and follies of the elderly aristocrats who misdirected their enemies.

Now at last the great liberating expedition was at sea, led by the splendid young giant, Lazare Hoche—himself agog with zeal to drive the odious English usurpers back to their own doomed island —and the gallant old Admiral, Morard de Galles, whom Hoche had substituted for the timid Villaret Joyeuse. As Hoche and Carnot had planned it, it was to be the first stage in eliminating the islanders from their own watery element. Controlling Ireland the Republic would not only be able to invade England and deny her those valiant Hibernian fighters who, according to Tone, constituted the greater part of her Navy and Army, but could strangle her commerce. Straddling the western approaches from Ireland to Finisterre, the combined French and Spanish fleets would cut the trade routes through which the City money spiders sucked the blood of Asia, Africa and America.

Already a grand Latin fleet of more than thirty Spanish and French battleships had left Toulon: its advance-guard under Villeneuve was expected daily at Brest. The remnant of Britain's former Mediterranean Fleet cowered at Gibraltar. The storm that had blown the British squadron from its station off Brest, had driven three of Jervis's battleships from their anchors in Gibraltar Bay, wrecking one of them on the coast of Morocco. Britannia, it seemed, no longer ruled the waves.

Perhaps she no longer deserved to. For though Admiral Colpoys' winter guard off Brest had been doubled to meet the invasion threat, the lax habit of keeping station eight leagues west of Ushant to save wear and tear had caused him to be driven so far into the Atlantic that he had even lost touch with his own frigates. The remainder of the Channel fleet, according to its winter custom, was in harbour two hundred miles away.

But Hoche and Morard de Galles, taking counsel together in the soft sunshine of December 16th, did not know this. To the west at the mouth of the Iroise Channel they could see the English frigates beating up and down, and it was reasonable to assume that the blockading battleships were not far away. Sooner than encounter them with his crowded ships the Admiral, instead of making straight for the open sea, decided to steer south through the rocky Raz de Sein. But during the afternoon the wind got up and, fearing the shoals, de Galles countermanded his orders. In the gathering winter evening many of the captains did not see his signals. Some returned to the main Iroise channel and sailed westwards, others continued south into the Raz. But that stout Cornishman, Captain Sir Edward Pellew, of the *Indefatigable*, seeing his opportunity, stood boldly into their midst and, remaining with them all night, fired off so many rockets and minute guns from his single frigate that the labouring battleships and transports imagined that they were being attacked by the entire British Fleet. In the confusion and panic one ship of the line struck a rock and foundered, and two others collided. When morning broke the French fleet was dispersed into three widely separated bodies, Worst of all, the frigate *Fraternité*, carrying the Admiral and General Hoche, had vanished altogether.

Thus the expedition was crippled at the outset by the inherent weakness which vitiated all Revolutionary France's efforts at sea. Indiscipline and lack of the essential training, patience and precision requisite to success in naval affairs made Frenchmen the slaves and not the masters of the elements. Had it not been for sins in their adversaries of a different kind—complacency, elderly indolence and Treasury pedantry about exposing expensive ships to storms—the French fleet might have been destroyed off its own coast. As it was, divine retribution for its shortcomings was represented only by the human agency of Pellew's solitary frigate. Its scattered divisions, though ignorant of one another's whereabouts, were able to proceed on their way. Colpoys with his fifteen battleships, lost in the ocean solitudes fifty miles to the west of Ushant, never learnt of their sailing till a week after they left Brest. Having no advice from the Admiralty as to their probable destination—Ireland, the Mediterranean, the West Indies or Portugal—he made no attempt to follow them. Instead he returned home for orders, reaching Spithead on the last day of the year. The first news of the French escape was brought to Falmouth on December 20th by Pellew. Only on the 21st did the Commander-in-Chief of the Channel Fleet, still in his house at Portsmouth, learn that the enemy he was theoretically blockading had been at sea for nearly a week.

Meanwhile the French, more by accident than design, reassembled in the longitude of Mizen Head. With only eight ships missing, including, however, the frigate *Fraternité*, they sighted the Munster coast at dawn on the 21st in calm, sunny weather. Next day they entered the long reach of Bantry Bay. There was still no sign of the General and Admiral and none of the dreaded British Navy.

Up to this point fortune had favoured the would-be invaders. But on that day the wind freshened. In order to land at the head of the bay they had to beat up through thirty miles of angry, narrow sea in the teeth of a rising easterly gale. The task was too much for their seamanship: the over-crowded ships, manned by landsmen, were continuously forced to give way as they crossed each other's paths. For three days the struggle continued. "We have made 300 tacks and not gained 100 yards in a straight line," wrote the infuriated Tone. By Christmas Day the storm had reached gale pitch; it was bitterly cold and the air full of driving snow.[1] A landing was out of the question, for no boat could have lived in those icy waters. In the evening, to Tone's unspeakable chagrin, Admiral Bouvet ordered his ships to cut their cables and run with the wind to the open sea. A few vessels, failing to see the order, hung on for a few days in the bay: then, lacking guns, horses and equipment, followed their consorts back to France. The last to reach port—on January 14th, 1797—was the *Fraternité*, carrying Hoche and the Admiral. Their only sight of their command in four despairing weeks had been on December 29th when, beating back from the Atlantic against the gale, they encountered off the Irish coast two battleships, one sinking and the other engaged in rescuing her crew.

In these operations the Channel Fleet took no part. On learning that the French were at sea, Lord Bridport on December 21st had announced that he would sail in four days. But in attempting on Christmas Day to reach St. Helens in the teeth of a south-easterly gale, four of his battleships fouled one another and a fifth went aground. It was not till January 3rd, just as the last French ship was leaving the Irish coast, that the British Fleet began to sail majestically down the Channel. It might as well have stayed in harbour. When after a month's cruising it returned to Portsmouth it had not so much as sighted an enemy. The only serious encounter of the campaign took place on the stormy night of January 13th when Pellew with two frigates came up with the 80-gun battleship, *Droits de l'Homme*, off the Brittany coast. Though heavily outgunned, the frigates by brilliant manœuvring kept raking the big ship till she and one of her assailants had run aground in Audierne Bay. Here more than a thousand French sailors and soldiers perished on the rocks.

Such might have been the fate of the entire expedition had the British command been in more vigorous hands. Had Colpoys been at his station off Brest instead of allowing himself to be blown into the Atlantic, the French could never have left their own coast. Had the main Channel Fleet been at Falmouth or even Torbay, it would have had time after receiving Pellew's tidings to annihilate them in Bantry Bay. But the Government, though it had given Colpoys strength to deal with any force emerging from Brest, had failed to galvanise the Admiralty out of prescriptive habit. The inertia of eighteenth century decorum and Service seniority was too strong.

As it was, England owed her deliverance solely to divine intervention, or more accurately to her enemies' failure to observe the

[1] In Norfolk Woodforde recorded it as a day of intense cold, and at night so bitter as to prevent him from sleeping. At other places in England the barometer fell as much as 35 degrees below freezing point.—*Times*, 28th Dec., 1796.

hard laws on which success at sea depends. She ought to have lost Ireland. There were only 2000 troops and two field guns at Cork to protect naval stores worth a million and a half sterling. Apart from some highly unreliable Militia the total force in Ireland barely numbered 12,000, mostly newly-raised Dragoons and Fencibles. Hoche's 15,000 veterans should have made short work of these.

. . . .

Moral strength and weakness are rewarded or punished in war more swiftly than in any other human activity. Cause and consequence follow each other in inescapable succession, though owing to the judgment which attends both combatants simultaneously these are not always easily discernible at the time. England lacked troops to defend Ireland—the joint in her moral armour—because her politicians had preferred wishful to logical thinking about their military resources and, in deference to vested interests, had squandered 80,000 white troops in trying to conquer sugar islands climatically unsuited for operations by Europeans. By allowing private profit precedence over national necessities, they had followed the line—always fatal in war—of least resistance. Had their enemy's hands been substantially cleaner than their own, they might have suffered an overwhelming reverse, and their country with them.

Even at this hour, with doom hanging over the land they loved, Pitt and Dundas could not bring themselves to clear thinking. Before Christmas, though aware of the French preparations at Brest and the growing menace of Spain, Dundas had tried to waste two precious battalions on an insane project to seize the Helder and precipitate an imaginary counter-revolution in Holland. Fortunately Duncan, the shrewd Scottish Admiral blockading the Texel, had promptly sent them home again. About the same time the Goverment ordered Abercromby—half of whose earlier West Indian expeditionary force had perished of yellow fever—to seize the rich island of Trinidad, though it could neither supply him with information about the strength of the Spanish garrison nor send him any reinforcements. As usual it gambled on hopes, staking the national security for a windfall that would "give a good impression of the war in England." It remained incorrigibly, and at moments criminally, optimistic. Yet even in its most fatuous complacency there was something about it almost noble. While the French Directors broke Bouvet for his unavoidable failure in Bantry Bay, the British Cabinet defended Bridport against all attacks and even refused a parliamentary inquiry as implying an unmerited censure on the old Admiral.

As a matter of fact Abercromby succeeded beyond all reasonable expectation. In February, taking 4,000 of his 9,000 surviving effectives from the Windward Islands, he boldly landed in Trinidad. The Spaniards, sunk in sloth and corruption, made no defence and surrendered a ship of the line and a hundred pieces of artillery intact. But instead of being satisfied with its undeserved fortune, the Government merely doubled its stakes and ordered Abercromby to take Puerto Rico, which with his inadequate resources he naturally failed to do. Meanwhile, stimulated by the spectacle of an administrative and military incompetence even greater than his own, Dundas pursued the wildest projects for expeditions and revolutions in Spanish South America. These quixotic visions were encouraged not only by a specious Venezuelan adventurer and ex-Revolutionary General named Miranda but by the prosaic young Under-Secretary for War, William Huskisson.[1] Happily no troops were available; had they been, they would probably have been sent off into the malarial blue to conquer an unknown continent. As it was, Dundas even canvassed the possibilities of using the garrison of the Cape and the police force of the convict settlement of New South Wales before he was recalled from his dreams by more pressing dangers at home.

Of the magnitude of these the Government received a reminder early in February. On the day that the last French ship limped back into Brest, Bonaparte won his final and greatest victory of the Lombardy campaign at Rivoli. A fortnight later Mantua fell and the French were virtual masters of Italy. The last ports in the peninsula were closed to British ships and the Pope—the "old priest" of Bonaparte's contemptuous phrase—only averted a sacrilegious march on Rome "to extinguish the torch of fanaticism" by a colossal indemnity and the cession of Bologna and Ferrara to a puppet republic which the young general was creating out of his conquests. The elimination of Austria from the struggle was now only a question of weeks.

Britain would henceforward have to stand alone against the greatest military power yet seen on earth and the combined fleets of France, Spain and Holland. If Austria fell only Portugal would remain by her side, and with its vulnerable Spanish frontier Portugal was more of an encumbrance than a help. There were few in Europe who thought much of Britain's chance of survival. Amid the snows of Tulczyn that February the hero of Russia cried out across his dinner table to an English traveller: "Tweddell!"—for old Marshal Suvorof, after the manner of his countrymen, despised prefixes—"the

[1] To meet his fate, after a lifetime of fiscal administration, under the wheels of a train at the opening of the Manchester and Liverpool Railway.

French have taken Portsmouth. I have just received a courier from England. The King is in the Tower and Sheridan Protector."

Meanwhile the French were undismayed by their failure off the Irish coast. Pending the arrival of the Spanish fleet and the sailing of a vaster armada against the doomed British Isles, the Directory was collecting galley slaves and jailbirds for a nuisance raid to stir up trouble in England. The command was entrusted to an American adventurer of blood-curdling reputation named Colonel Tate. He was to land in the Bristol Channel, burn Bristol, "the second city in England for riches and commerce," and cause as much damage and panic as possible, by destroying bridges, magazines, docks, warehouses and factories. He was then to sail to Wales and, marching swiftly across the mountains, threaten Chester and Liverpool. His men, equipped with ample "combustible matter," were promised pardon for their crimes, a free rein to their passions and all the booty they could get.

On February 17th, 1797, this fearsome force—designated the Black Legion—sailed from Brest in a lugger and a corvette escorted by two frigates. It proved scarcely worthy of its instructions. On the 19th at the mouth of the Bristol Channel it missed a chance of capturing the Dublin packet boat, which it mistook for a man-of-war. Next day it came to anchor off Ilfracombe, where a small party landed and burnt a farmhouse. But on hearing that the North Devon Volunteers were on the march, the expedition hastily weighed anchor and, abandoning all ideas of Bristol, made for the Welsh coast. Here on the 22nd it landed near the lonely village of Fishguard. But even this secluded spot proved too exposed for its courage. The local aristocrat, Lord Cawdor, instead of running away or waiting to be roasted by his peasants, called them out in their respective corps—the Castle Martin Yeomanry, the Cardigan Militia and the Fishguard Volunteers—and, though outnumbered, boldly advanced against the invaders. Colonel Tate thereupon surrendered, "upon principles of humanity," he explained. It was all his captors could do to prevent the Welsh women along the London road from cutting his throat.

The only lasting effect of the expedition was to convince the common people of Britain that the Government cartoonists were right and that the French from Bonaparte downwards were a collection of ragged, plundering, cowardly scarecrows who burnt barns, stole chickens and raped servant girls. But the immediate consequence threatened to be more serious. For Tate had sailed on his filibustering raid just when the delicate mechanism on whose destruction the French had so long counted was on the verge of breaking down. Pitt's policy of financing war out of loans and the drain of bullion to keep the Allies in the field had strained the credit of the country to breaking point. After Bonaparte's Italian victories and the naval withdrawal from the Mediterranean, Consols had fallen to 53—a level as yet only equalled during the most disastrous year of the American War.

The Irish Government's despairing appeal for funds to equip the Army after the Hoche scare reduced the depleted reserve of specie in the Bank to little more than a million and a quarter.[1] With invasion fears causing farmers and traders to withdraw their bank balances for more primitive forms of hoarding, a run began in the middle of February on the north country banks. The news of Tate's landing on the evening of February 23rd precipitated a financial panic. By the time the Government was able to announce the sequel on the 25th, the country was within a few hours of bankruptcy. Queues of clients besieged the doors of every bank and general repudiation seemed certain.

Pitt acted promptly. On Saturday the 26th the Cabinet agreed to authorise the suspension of cash payments. The King came up from Windsor and the Privy Council met to issue a Proclamation pending parliamentary sanction. The Bank of England was empowered to issue £1 and £2 paper notes as legal tender. For two days it was touch and go: then on the 27th a reassuring statement showed that, after meeting all liabilities, the Bank had legal assets amounting to nearly ten millions. The sound sense of the country did the rest, and by the time Parliament had passed the necessary legislation, the worst was over. "The French do not know this wonderful people," wrote Southey afterwards. "It was supposed that the existence of the English Government depended upon the Bank and that the Bank would be ruined by an invasion: the thing was tried, men were landed in Wales, away ran the Londoners to the Bank to exchange their bills for cash, and the stock of cash was presently exhausted. What was the consequence: Why, when the Londoners found there was no cash to be had, they began to consider whether they could not do without it, mutually agreed to be content with paper and have been contented ever since. The Bank is infinitely obliged to France for the experiment."[2] Once again the adaptability of the national character proved Britain's greatest asset.

Yet for a few weeks, until the City and the provinces had adjusted themselves to the situation, the position of Pitt's Government was

[1] It had stood at £8,000,000 two years before.—*Pitt and the Great War*, 308.

[2] *Espriella*, III, 137-8. The Bank had reason to be, for being enabled to increase its note issue at its own discretion without fear of bankruptcy, it freely lent its own paper money at 5 per cent. of its face value—a very profitable transaction. Between 1797 and 1800 the note circulation rose from £8,500,000 to £16,000,000. Cash payments were not resumed till 1821.

seriously shaken. Restoration of national credit had been his peculiar achievement, and with it the great finance Minister stood or fell. For some time his strength had mainly lain in the lack of any one to replace him: he had many bitter enemies and few friends. In November his coach was stoned and hooted by a mob, and he seriously confided to Wilberforce that were he to resign his head would be off in six weeks.

For Pitt was showing signs of strain. He was now just on thirty-eight and had been Prime Minister continuously for thirteen years, the last four in time of war and national peril. He felt acutely the solitude of his place, was often impatient, particularly with his critics in Parliament, and was much troubled by headaches. Early in the New Year—though only a few knew it—he had deliberately turned his back on what seemed his greatest hope of happiness. During his occasional visits to his Kentish home, Holwood, he fell in love with the eldest daughter of his neighbour, Lord Auckland. A lovely, vivacious girl of twenty, Eleanor Eden, naturally flattered, returned his attentions, and the Edens and Pitt's few close friends looked forward to a new and serener era in his life.

But on January 20th Pitt wrote a letter to Auckland renouncing all hope of claiming his daughter's hand. He gave no reasons, but the shocking state of his finances was the probable cause. Absorbed in public work, he had long left all private business to servants who made the housekeeping bills at Downing Street and Holwood a bottomless pit of debt. Recently his mother and brother had made heavy drafts on his limited purse. A poor man, almost entirely dependent on his official salary, he refused like his father to use his official position to enrich himself. He even refused a modest place to his prospective father-in-law which would have provided a portion for his bride. In an age in which a certain display was regarded as an essential part of a public man's equipment, he chose to remain a bachelor because marriage with the woman he loved would have compelled him either to retire or to stoop to a form of theft from his country which all the world but he practised.

But the act of repudiation seemed to shrivel his frail body. Thereafter he became even more solitary than before. At council meetings in February it was noted that his face looked swollen and unhealthy. His foes rejoiced and even his friends complained at his want of energy.[1] The Bank crisis was made the occasion of a full-dress attack on him in the House: two days after the suspension of cash payments the Opposition carried eighty-six members into the lobbies. "We have too long had a confiding House of Commons,"

[1] *Farington*, I, 194.

Fox declared, "I want now an inquiring House of Commons." The City Common Hall even passed a resolution to address the King to remove his Ministers. There was talk of a new Government under Lord Moira, excluding "all persons on either side who had made themselves obnoxious to the public."

From this trough of depression Pitt was raised by great tidings. On the evening of March 3rd news reached London of a naval victory against Spain. For a moment the clouds of that terrible winter parted. Through them men saw the gleam of something swift and glorious, and of a new name—Nelson.

. . . .

The victory which had come so unexpectedly was owing in the first place to Sir John Jervis. After a visit to Portugal to re-animate its despairing government and re-fit his storm-battered fleet, he had left Lisbon on January 18th, 1797, with eleven ships of the line. He had refused to remain there a day longer than necessary: "inaction in the Tagus," he wrote, "will make us all cowards." The bad luck which had dogged the tough old man for the past two months still held, for as he left the estuary one of his only two three-deckers went aground. This, his fifth casualty since the great gale of December 10th, reduced his fleet to ten. Nevertheless, though he knew that close on thirty Spanish ships of the line were expected off Cadiz on their way from the Mediterranean to Brest, he never faltered. After escorting a Brazil-bound convoy into the Atlantic, he beat back through winter storms to his chosen station off Cape St. Vincent. Here he waited for the enemy and for the battle which he was resolved should determine the fate of Britain.

Meanwhile the man of destiny who was fated to be England's answer to Napoleon was almost boyishly challenging danger in the abandoned Mediterranean. On December 15th, 1796, Commodore Nelson had sailed from Gibraltar with two frigates to evacuate troops and stores from Elba. Off Cartagena, the main Spanish base, he fell in with two enemy frigates and at once engaged them, capturing one. He reached Porto Ferrajo on the evening of Christmas Day, just in time to escort the erstwhile Betsey Wynne, now united to his friend Captain Fremantle, to a ball where he was received by the delighted British colony—who were feeling a little isolated—to the strains of "Rule Britannia." On January 29th, 1797 he sailed again to rejoin Jervis.

Two days later the Spanish fleet, twenty-seven battleships and twelve large frigates, left Cartagena for the Atlantic. Their orders were to join the French at Brest and, sweeping the Channel and North Sea with their joint forces—greater than anything Britain could assemble—escort an army of invasion from Holland to Ireland. They passed the Straits on February 5th, and Nelson, who reached Gibraltar four days later, was forced to sail right through them as they battled with the unwonted Atlantic gales. While closely pursued by two Spanish battleships, one of his men fell overboard and his First Lieutenant, Hardy, lowered a boat and went to the rescue. To save him, Nelson, checking the course of his ship, risked almost certain destruction. But the Spaniards, bewildered by their tiny prey's unaccountable conduct, checked too, and Nelson got away. Next day he rejoined Jervis off Cape St. Vincent, and hoisted his Commodore's pennant in the *Captain*, 74.

That night the two fleets drew near. The Spaniards were ignorant of Jervis's presence, but he, shadowing them with his frigates, was well aware of theirs. The night was misty and the Spanish ships, strung out over many miles of sea, fell into confusion, puncturing the silence with minute guns. At 5 o'clock on February 14th—St. Valentine's Day—they were sighted fifteen miles to the south-west: "thumpers," as the signal lieutenant of the *Barfleur* reported, "looming like Beachy Head in a fog!" Jervis had been reinforced a week before by five ships from England, but he was outnumbered by nearly two to one. Of his fifteen capital ships only two carried 100 guns, while of the Spanish twenty-seven, seven were three-deckers with 112 guns or more, one of them—the four-decker *Santisima Trinidad*—the largest fighting ship in the world. Yet Jervis was determined to force a battle. For he knew that a victory at that moment was essential to his country.

But Jervis was no gambler. He had reckoned the odds carefully: he knew the strength of the Spanish fleet but he also knew its fighting capacity. He possessed in a supreme degree that comprehensive common sense and balance which, with clarity of decision and endurance, are the chief attributes of a master of war. Defeat would spell disaster to England but so would failure to engage. As the mist lifted and the flag-lieutenant called out the odds, he remained grimly unperturbed. "There are eighteen sail of the line, Sir John." "Very well, sir."—"There are twenty sail of the line, Sir John." "Very well, sir."—"There are twenty-five sail of the line, Sir John." "Very well, sir."—"There are twenty-seven sail of the line, Sir John; near double our own."—"If there are fifty sail of the line, I will go through them." "That's right, Sir John," cried the giant Canadian, Captain Hallowell, in his enthusiasm actually slapping his Admiral on the back, "and a damned good licking we'll give them!"

In two columns, imperceptibly merging into an impenetrable line with sterns and bowsprits almost touching, the British fleet bore down on the enemy, making straight for a gap—nearly three miles wide—between the main force and a straggling division to leeward. It was like the inexorable thrust of a sword into a lanky giant's careless guard. The Spanish Admiral made a gallant effort to close it, but too late. The *Principe de Asturias*—a three-decker of 112 guns—tried to break through to join the severed squadron only to encounter the *Victory's* broadside and drift out of the fight with tattered sails and splintered topmasts. Then with the *Culloden* leading, Jervis turned into the wind, his ships tacking in turn and meeting the Spanish line on a parallel course. "Look at Troubridge," he remarked with triumph suffusing his stern countenance as the *Culloden* went into action, "he handles his ship as if the eyes of all England were upon him!"

Down in the dark of the gun decks and in the "slaughter houses" near the mainmasts, the men waited with the precision born of long practice. As each enemy drew alongside and all was ready—the ports open, matches lighted, the guns run out—they broke into three tremendous cheers more daunting to their foes even than the thunder of their broadsides. "We gave them their Valentines in style," wrote one of the gunners of the *Goliath*; "not that we loved fighting, but we all wished to be free to return to our homes and follow our own pursuits. We knew there was no other way of obtaining this than by defeating the enemy. 'The hotter war, the sooner peace,' was a saying with us."[1]

The climax of the battle came at about one o'clock. At that moment the head of the Spanish line was nearing the tail of the British. Nelson, flying his flag in the thirteenth ship in the British line, saw with the instinct of genius that only one thing could prevent the main Spanish division, which had suddenly turned to leeward, from rejoining its isolated ships and so confronting Jervis with a reunited fleet before he could alter course. The Spaniards were battered but they were still intact: another few minutes and the chance of the decisive victory that England needed would have passed.

Without hesitation, disregarding the letter of the orders he had received and anticipating those there was no time to transmit, Nelson bore out of the line and placed the *Captain*—the smallest two-decker in the British fleet—straight in the course of the giant *Santissima Trinidad* and four other ships. For ten minutes it looked as though the *Captain*, her foremast shot away and her wheelpost broken in a tornado of fire, would be blown out of the water. But when the smoke cleared she was still there, and the *Excellent* under

[1] Long, 193.

Captain Collingwood was coming to her aid. The Spaniards' line was in inextricable confusion, all hope of a junction between their sundered divisions at an end and Jervis beating back into the fight with the remainder of his fleet.

But before the victory was complete, Nelson had done a very remarkable thing. Crippled though she was from her duel with the *Santissima Trinidad*, he placed the *Captain* alongside the 80-gun *San Nicolas* and prepared to board. Helped by a soldier of the 69th, the one-eyed Commodore climbed through the quarter-gallery window in her stern and led his boarders in person through the officers' cabins to the quarterdeck. Here he found Captain Berry, who had jumped into the enemy's mizen chains, already in possession of the poop and hauling down the Spanish Ensign. At that moment fire was opened on the boarding party from the stern-gallery of the three-decker, *San Josef*, which in the confusion of the fight had drifted against the *San Nicolas*. Placing sentries at the tops of the ladders of his still scarcely vanquished prize, Nelson directed his boarding party up the side of the *San Josef*. There, as his friend Collingwood described it, on the quarter-deck of a Spanish first-rate he received the swords of the officers of the two ships, "while one of his sailors bundled them up with as much composure as he would have made a faggot, though twenty-two of their line were still within gunshot."[1] Presently the *Victory*, now in the thick of the fight again, passed that triumphant group on the *San Josef's* quarter-deck, saluting with three cheers. The cool daring of the thing tickled the imagination of the Fleet: "Nelson's patent bridge for boarding first-rates" was for long the admiring joke of the lower-deck. In the English mode, it rivalled Bonaparte's feat at the Bridge of Arcola.

Four battleships, two of them first-rates, remained in the victors' hands. The Spanish fleet, still superior in numbers, withdrew under cover of night to Cadiz, bearing wounds that freed Britain from serious danger in that quarter for many months. Imperial Spain had been proved the insubstantial wraith the Navy had always believed it to be: the dreaded junction between the French and Spanish fleets a dream. The nation when it heard the news felt a quickening of its pulse: it was reminded what British courage and resolution could do. The Government, saved at the eleventh hour, showered rewards on the principal commanders; Jervis became Earl St. Vincent with a parliamentary pension of £3000 a year, the Vice- and Rear-admirals were made Baronets and another subordinate Admiral soon afterwards became an Irish peer. But the real hero of the day was the

[1] *Collingwood*, 39.

till then unknown Commodore who was created a Knight of the Bath: his sudden exploit caught England's imagination. Fretful in inaction and querulous under neglect, Nelson was happier than he had ever been, "rich in the praises of every man from the highest to the lowest in the fleet."[1] For all men knew him now for what he was. That knowledge was the measure of his opportunity. The years of testing and obscurity were over, the sunrise gates of fulfilment opening before him.

[1] *Nicolas*, II, 359.

CHAPTER NINE

The Fleet in Mutiny

1797

"The able seamen of the fleet . . . are the only description of men now serving his Majesty whose situation by common exercise of their trade could be bettered fourfold if they were released from the service of their country."

Captain Pakenham to Earl Spencer, 11th Dec., 1796.

"If there is, indeed, a rot in the wooden walls of old England, our decay cannot be very distant . . ."

R. B. Sheridan.

NELSON had appeared on the horizon at the very moment that the corporate force he embodied was contending with powers which almost seemed too great for it. That force was the Navy, which had made its entry on the world stage under Drake and the great Elizabethans, had sunk into insignificance under the early Stuarts, revived under Cromwell and the second Charles to wrest the imperial sceptre of commerce from Holland and, given administrative discipline by the life-long labours of Pepys, had remained throughout the eighteenth century the principal arbiter of human affairs at sea. Yet its ascendancy had never been undisputed. For over a hundred years monarchical France, with its greater population and resources, had contended with Britain for the command of the sea and on more than one occasion had all but attained it. Britain's danger had been greatest when France and the Atlantic empire of Spain had joined hands against her: then, as during the American War and now in 1797, her fleets had been outnumbered and she had had to fight for her very existence.

But Britain had always triumphed because in the last resort the sea was her whole being, whereas with her Continental rivals it was only a secondary consideration. "The thing which lies nearest the heart of this nation," Charles II had written a century before, "is trade and all that belongs to it." Being an island her commerce was maritime and its protection an essential interest of an ever-growing number of her people. They were ready to make sacrifices for the Navy which they would never have done for the Army or any other service of the Crown. For it was on the Navy, as the Articles of War put it, that under the Providence of God the safety, honour, and welfare of the realm depended.

Because of these things the Navy touched mystic chords in the English heart which went deeper than reason. The far sails of a frigate at sea, the sight of a sailor with tarry breeches and rolling gait in any inland town, and that chief of all the symbolic spectacles of England, the Grand Fleet lying at anchor in one of her white-fringed roadsteads, had for her people the power of a trumpet call. So little Byam Martin, seeing for the first time the triple-tiered ships of the line lying in Portsmouth harbour, remained "riveted to the spot, perfectly motionless, so absorbed in wonder" that he would have stayed there all day had not his hosts sent a boat's crew to fetch him away. From that hour his mind was "inflamed with the wildest desire to be afloat."[1] Bobby Shafto going to sea with silver buckles on his knee was an eternal theme of eighteenth century England: of such stuff were Admirals made.

They had a hard schooling. Flung like Nelson at twelve into an unfamiliar world of kicks and cuffs, crowded hammocks and icy hardships, or after a few months under "Black Pudding," the omnipresent horsewhip of the Naval Academy, Gosport, apprenticed as midshipmen to the cockpit of a man-of-war, they learnt while still children to be Spartans, dined off scrubbed boards on salt beef, sauerkraut and black-strap, and became complete masters before they were men of a wonderful technical skill in all that appertained to the sailing and fighting of ships.

They were as inured to roughness and salt water as gulls to wind. Boys in their teens would spend days afloat in the maintop, ready at any moment to clamber to the masthead when topgallant or studding sail needed setting or taking in. They grew up like bull-dogs, delighting to cuff and fight: in some ships it was the practice while the officers were dining in the wardroom for the midshipmen to engage regularly in pitched battles on the quarterdeck, Romans against Trojans, for the possession of the poop, banging away, "all in good part," with broomsticks, handswabs, boarding pikes and even muskets. Midshipman Gardner of the *Edgar*, being pinked in the thigh by a comrade with a fixed bayonet in the course of one of these friendly scraps, retaliated by putting a small quantity of powder into a musket and firing at his assailant, marking "his phiz" for life.[2] So toughened, they faced the world on their toes ready for anything and everyone. Such were the high-spirited midshipmen who pelted the British Ambassador with plums at the Carnival at Pisa and, as

[1] *Martin*, I, 4.
[2] *Gardner*, 83.

he looked angry, hove another volley at his lady, observing that she seemed better tempered than his Excellency.[1] So also the officers of the wardroom, dining at the best inn in Leghorn and growing somewhat merry, rolled the waiter among the dishes in the table-cloth and pelted the passers-by with loaves and chicken legs.[2]

These were the permanent cadre of the Navy; the officers of the Establishment, "born in the surf of the sea," who, unlike the lower deck, coming and going as occasion demanded, lived in the Service and died in it. They were bound together by the closest ties of professional honour, etiquette and experience. Socially they were of all sorts: one high-born captain filled his frigate with so many sprigs of aristocracy that his first lieutenant—no respecter of persons—was wont to call out in mockery to the young noblemen and honourables at the different ropes, "My lords and gentlemen, shiver the mizen topsail!" The majority were of humbler origin, occasioning Sir Walter Elliot's remark that, though the profession had its utility, he would be sorry to see any friend of his belonging to it. Few had much of this world's goods nor, unless exceptionally lucky over prize money, could hope for much. Some were scholars—for it was a literary age—and read their Shakespeare or discoursed learnedly on the classical associations of the foreign ports they visited: more often they were simple souls "better acquainted with rope-yarns and bilge water than with Homer or Virgil." But one and all were masters of their profession, proud in their obedience to King and country and ready to give their lives and all they had whenever the Service demanded. "A bloody war and a sickly season!" was the closing toast of many a jovial evening in the wardroom: it was so that men rose in their calling.[3]

Such men not only officered the fleet: they gave it their own tone and spirit. They were often rough teachers, full of fearful oaths like the master's mate of the *Edgar* who ended every sentence with a "Damn your whistle," and too fond of enforcing their commands with the lash. But the men they commanded were rough too; hard-bitten merchant seamen and fishermen, brought into the Service for the duration by the pressgangs, with always a sediment in every ship of jailbirds and incorrigibles whose only chance of freedom was the hard life of the sea. The unresting, automatic discipline which the handling of wind-propelled warships in northern waters demanded

[1] Gardner, 140.
[2] *Ibid.*, 142.
[3] So Nelson wrote to his father: "I wish I could congratulate you upon a rectory instead of a vicarage; it is rather awkward wishing the poor man dead, but we all rise by deaths. I got my rank by a shot killing a post-captain, and I most sincerely hope I shall, when I go, go out of the world the same way; then we all go in the line of our profession—a parson praying and a captain fighting."

could not have been enforced by gentler souls: it was that which gave Britain command of the waves and kept the Royal Navy from the slovenly, helpless degradation which befell that of revolutionary France. From the admiral, piped on board, to the boatswain's mate with his colt ready to "start" the lower deck to action, strictly ordered subordination and readiness to obey were the hallmarks of the Service.

The life of the seamen was a life apart; something that was of England and yet remote from it. A King's ship was a little wooden world of its own, with its peculiar customs and gradations unguessed at by landsmen; its proud foretopmen, the aristocrats of the sea, and far down out of sight its humble waisters: pumpers and sewer-men, scavengers and pigsty keepers. In such a community, often years together away from a home port, men learnt to know each other as they seldom can on shore: to love and trust, to fear and hate one another. There were ships that became floating hells, ruled by some sadistic tyrant, with drunken, flogging officers "crabbed as fiends," and savage, murderous crews such as that which flung Bligh of the *Bounty* to perish in an open boat in a remote sea. There were others commanded by captains like Nelson, Pellew and Duncan, where the men looked on their officers as fathers and were eager to dare and do anything for them. Here something of the unspoken sympathy between experienced rider and horse entered into the relationship between quarter and lower deck.

The nation honoured its rough, simple seamen, as it had cause to, though it usually saw them at their worst: ashore on their brief spells of leave, with discipline relaxed and their hard-earned money riotously dissipated on brandy and the coarse Megs and Dolls of the seaports. But it saw too, as we also can glimpse from the prints of the old masters, the fine manly faces, the earnest gaze, the careless attitudes so full of strength and grace for all the gnarls and distortions of weather, accident and disease: symbols of rugged-headed courage, manly devotion and simple-hearted patriotism. They were children—generous, suspicious, forgiving, with the fortitude and patience of men: rough Britons tempered by the unresting sea into virtue of a rare and peculiar kind. The sight of a Monsieur's sails roused in them all the unconquerable pugnacity of their race: the whine of Johnny Crapaud's shot whipped their quick tempers to savagery. Though chivalrous and generous victors, they were not good losers like the courtly Spaniards and the aristocrats of the old French navy; they had to beat their adversary or die. As they waited at quarters before a fight, "their black silk handkerchiefs tied round their heads, their shirt-sleeves tucked up, the crows and handspikes in their hands and the boarders all ready with their cutlasses and tomahawks," they reminded an eye-witness of so many devils.[1]

Yet from such scenes the British sailor could pass in a few hours to the buffoonery and practical jokes dear to the lower deck, the fiddler's lively air, the droll or pathetic ballads with their rhythm of the waves, while the seas broke over the forecastle and the ship pitched and rolled; and to those tenderer moments when, homeward bound, hearts panted with the anticipated happiness of meeting wives and sweethearts and the headwind's moping contrariness was lulled by the chorus of "Grieving's a folly, Boys!"

> "And now arrived that jovial night
> When every true bred tar carouses,
> When, o'er the grog, all hands delight
> To toast their sweethearts and their spouses."

History loves to linger over the good-humoured jollity between decks when port was reached: the girls on the seamen's knees with sturdy, buxom arms around their necks; the reels and gigs as Susan's bright eyes promised her Tom Tough his long-awaited reward; the grog and flip that passed about under the light of the flickering lanterns. And judging by the popularity of Dibdin's songs, the nation liked to think of such scenes too and took deep comfort in the thought of the hearts of oak and jolly tars that kept its foes at bay.[2]

. . . .

It was because of these things that the news, whispered round London on the morning of April 17th, 1797, came as a knock-out blow to England. The fleet was in mutiny. Surprise, terror, grief appeared in every face. The Navy, which three months before had saved the country from invasion, was now ready to betray it to its enemies. The hour of this parricidal stab could not have been more fatal. The Austrians had asked Bonaparte for a truce, Ireland was defenceless and a new army of invasion was embarking under cover of a Dutch battle squadron at the Texel. And now the Channel Fleet—the buckler on which everything depended—had refused orders to sail and mutinied for an increase in pay. Britain had never known anything like it.

Naval pay, fixed by ancient enactment, had stood for nearly a century and a half at 19s. a month for an ordinary seamen and 24s. for an A.B. But the price of the commodities on which the sailor's

[1] *Gardner*, 130.
[2] "I never sit down to dinner," wrote one lady, "but I wish them a share."

family depended had not remained constant. To the normal rising trend of prices had been added war inflation now aggravated by the bank crisis. In the merchant service the laws of supply and demand had raised the seaman's pay to four times the naval rate. Prevented by the pressgang from selling their highly skilled services in the open market and forced to let their wives and children starve while they served their country, the men were conscious of a grave injustice of which their rulers—ill-served by statistics—were blissfully unaware. Even the despised soldiers had been given a small rise since the war.[1] But the sailors—the pride and defence of the nation—had had nothing done for them, though certain of their officers had recently had increases. So strong was their feeling that at the beginning of March before sailing for the spring cruise the men of the Channel Fleet combined to send round-robins to old Lord Howe, their nominal commander-in-chief. In these they respectfully pointed out that the cost of living had doubled and that their pay was insufficient to support their families. And since it was only paid in the port of commission, whence in war-time a ship might be absent for months and even years, it was frequently in arrears.[2]

As Howe was an invalid at Bath and about to hand over his command finally to his deputy, Lord Bridport, he merely forwarded the petitions to the Admiralty. Here they were ignored. For in the critical state of the country's finances, application to Parliament for a rise in naval pay seemed out of the question, and discussion of the matter would thus obviously be undesirable. As the petitions were anonymous no reply was made. When the Fleet returned to Spithead at the end of March the men found their request met by silence. They were very angry and took steps to prepare a petition to Parliament and to support it by joint action. "They had better," the *Queen Charlotte*'s men wrote of the Government, "go to war with the whole globe than with their own subjects."[3]

Of all this Lord Bridport was unaware. For through an administrative oversight the Admiralty had failed to inform him of the petitions. But on April 12th he accidentally learnt of a plot to seize the ships and hold them as pledges for redress of grievances. He was naturally profoundly shocked and, hearing at second hand of the petitions to Howe, became exceedingly indignant with the Admiralty.[4] In his heart he sympathised with the men's demands. But when he

[1] Thanks to the Duke of York. It was an additional grievance that whereas a Chelsea pensioner received £13 a year, a Greenwich pension only brought in £7.

[2] Admiral Duncan thought this the greatest of all the sailor's grievances.—*Spencer Papers*, II, 122.

[3] Bonner Smith, *Mariner's Mirror*, XXI, 447.

[4] Bridport to the Admiralty, 15th April, 1797, Bonner Smith, *Mariner's Mirror*, XXI, 439.

raised the matter with Whitehall, he was merely told to take the Fleet to sea. For the Admiralty was determined to sidetrack the matter.

On the morning, therefore, of April 16th—Easter Sunday—Bridport reluctantly ordered the Fleet to weigh anchor. His signal was ignored. In the *Queen Charlotte*, Howe's former flagship, the men, seeing an attempt to forestall the mutiny, manned the shrouds and gave three cheers—the pre-arranged signal for revolt. At once the leaders put off in boats and rowed round the fleet, ordering the crew of every vessel to send two delegates that night to the *Queen Charlotte*. Bridport, who like all the Hoods was a shrewd and sensible man, forbade his captains to resist. Instead he ordered them to muster their men and ask them to state their grievances.

That evening the delegates of sixteen battleships assembled in the *Queen Charlotte*'s state-room to draw up rules for the regulation of the fleet. They ordered watches to be kept, drunkenness to be punished by flogging and ducking, and yard-ropes to be rove at every fore-yard arm to enforce their authority. Women were to be allowed aboard as usual in harbour, but to prevent tittle-tattle were not to go ashore till the matter was settled. Respect was to be paid to the rank of officers, but, until the desires of the men were satisfied, not an anchor was to be raised. To symbolise their unanimity the shrouds were to be manned morning and night and three cheers given.

It was a strange position. The Fleet was in indubitable mutiny. Yet the men did not regard themselves as mutineers and persisted in trying to behave as though ordinary discipline prevailed. The country was at war with an ideological creed which glorified revolution: it was hourly expecting invasion. Yet in the rebellious ships there was no sign of sympathy with that revolution: on the contrary the delegates declared that the Fleet would sail at once if the French put to sea. They even stopped the frigates and small craft from taking part in the mutiny lest the country's trade should suffer. Nervous folk on shore, imagining "secret Jacobin springs," looked for foreign agents and agitators. But if there were any such, they were unsuccessful in impressing their principles on their old foes of the Channel fleet. In its good order, common sense and almost pathetic legalism the start of the English revolution contrasted strangely with the French.

Meanwhile Admiral Pole, despatched post-haste with news of the mutiny, had reached the Admiralty at midnight on the 16th. In the small hours of Tuesday morning he told his horrifying story to the First Lord. Earl Spencer was the best type of patrician—an athlete still in early middle age, a scholar with liberal leanings, red-haired, and handsome. He acted with promptitude and vigour. As soon as it was light he hurried to the Prime Minister and after a day of interviews set out for Portsmouth with two junior Lords and the Secretary of the Admiralty.

Here on the 18th the Board, formally sitting in the Fountain Inn, opened its proceedings. Refusing to compromise its dignity by meeting the seamen personally, it used the flag officers of the Fleet as go-betweens. It might have been wiser for Spencer, who was over-persuaded by his Service colleagues, to have settled the matter directly with the delegates, whose real weakness was not Jacobinism but excessive suspicion. As it was, in the delays and second thoughts born of too much coming and going, the seamen's conditions tended to rise. A new petition on the 18th added demands that rations—on paper a pound of meat, a pound of biscuits and half a pint of rum a day—should no longer be subjected to the purser's customary deduction of an eighth, that fresh vegetables should be provided in port, that the sick should be properly cared for, that pay should be continued to the wounded until discharged, and that in harbour men should have leave to go ashore instead of remaining aboard like prisoners. The unknown hand who framed this document asked that the sailors should be looked upon as a number of men standing in the defence of their country, and that they might in some wise "have the grant of those sweets of Liberty on shore when in harbour." He ended by assuring the Admiralty that the men would suffer double the hardships they complained of sooner than allow the Crown to be imposed on by a foreign Power.[1]

The new requests were in themselves reasonable: they were all in the end granted without doing the country the least injury. Pursers who "took care of their eighths" were far too common: the meat was often uneatable, the biscuits weevilly, the butter rancid and the cheese full of long red worms.[2] Many ship's surgeons were drunken wastrels who had gone to sea as the last resort in a life of professional failure. And considering that the seamen had been torn away from their homes and callings to indescribable hardships and tedium, it seemed monstrously unjust to keep them on board in harbour.

But however reasonable, the ultimatum was presented at a time when the country was in graver danger than any since the Spanish

[1] *Bonner Smith*, *Mariner's Mirror*, XXII, 74.

[2] It was an old saying in the Service that Judas Iscariot was the first Purser. But Boatswains often ran them fine in the art of peculation. It was Johnny Bone, the Boatswain of the *Edgar*, to whom the great Adam Duncan observed: "Whatever you do, Mr. Bone, I hope and trust you will not take the anchors from the bows."—*Gardner*, 71.

Armada appeared off Plymouth. To yield unconditionally at the pistol's mouth might undermine the whole fabric of naval discipline and precipitate the same tragic train of events which had brought monarchical France to massacre and ruin. To aristocrats like Spencer the very discipline of the mutineers seemed ominous: it argued, as Lady Spencer wrote to "weathercock" Windham, a steadiness which overpowered her with terror.[1] Therefore, though the Board prudently eschewed violent counsels, it determined to make some sort of a stand: to keep the seamen at a distance and, while granting the substance of their demands, to make as many minor abatements as possible. In fact it tried to avoid paying the full price for its own former and very English failure—through complacency, inertia and reluctance to inquire too closely into uncomfortable facts—to reform abuses while it had time to do so with dignity.

The results of this obstinacy were not happy. On the 20th the Prince of Wurtemberg, who had come to Portsmouth to marry the Princess Royal, had been cheered and saluted as though nothing unusual was happening while being escorted by Spencer round the mutinous Fleet. This singularly English episode encouraged the Lords of the Admiralty in their firm resolve. But next day, while Admiral Gardner was arguing with the delegates in the *Queen Charlotte's* stateroom, the men—after seeming agreement had been reached—grew suspicious and declared that a final settlement must wait till a pardon had been received under the King's hand. At this the Admiral, who thought it high time the Fleet was at sea, lost his temper and denounced the delegates as "a damned, mutinous, blackguard set" of "skulking fellows" who were afraid of meeting the French. In his fury he even shook one of them and threatened to have him hanged. At this there was a riot which ended in the apoplectic old man's being hustled out of the flagship and the red flag being hoisted in all ships. The officers were placed under confinement or—in the case of the unpopular ones—sent ashore.

Once more, faced by urgent crisis, Spencer acted promptly. That night he set out for London to obtain the royal pardon, secured next morning an immediate Cabinet council and by midnight had obtained the King's signature at Windsor and had had copies printed for circulation in the fleet. But by the time that these, galloped through the night, reached Portsmouth, the good temper of the Navy was already re-asserting itself. The astonishing delegates, while still insisting on the redress of grievances, had apologised gracefully to Bridport for the flag-striking incident and begged him as "father

[1] *Windham Papers*, II, 48.

of the Fleet" to resume command. This the admiral did on the morning of the 24th, reading the Royal proclamation to the crew of the flagship and making a speech in which he promised general satisfaction of all demands. The mutiny thereupon ended. Next morning the greater part of the Fleet dropped down to St. Helens to await an easterly wind to carry it to Brest.

But though the country congratulated itself that a dreadful week had been attended by no worse consequences, suspicion and unrest remained. The men were not sure that the Government meant to honour its promises. The inexplicable delays attendant on parliamentary processes[1] increased their distrust. During the next fortnight while the fleet waited for the wind, the ferment continued to work. The seamen had tasted power and learnt their strength. Moreover the recognition of their principal grievances had reminded them of others.

On several occasions in the recent past abuses in particular ships had been so serious that they had provoked isolated mutinies. Over-rapidity of war-time expansion and the difficulty of raising men and keeping them from desertion had aggravated the severity of discipline. With the jails emptied to supply the pressgangs, it is not surprising that some officers could only enforce order at the cat's tail. Such a regimen could be accompanied by a horrible brutality. "The ill-usage we have on board this ship," the crew of the *Winchelsea* wrote to the Admiralty early in the war, "forced us to fly to your Lordships the same as a child to its father." Another ship's company referred to its treatment "from the tirant of a captain" as more than the spirits and hearts of Englishmen could bear, "for we are born free but now we are slaves." These things were against the Regulations, but, with each ship a world of its own and often far from port, the Regulations were hard to enforce. In certain ships the officers, as Collingwood said, beat the men into a state of insubordination.

Grievances apart, the Fleet was ripe for trouble. The dilution of the better elements with the worse had left a dangerous sediment at the bottom of every crew. In four years of war naval personnel had swollen from 16,000 to 120,000. Many of the latest joined were "quota men" raised under the Act of 1795 which had imposed on every parish the obligation of supplying the Service. Among these were inevitably some of superior station—broken-down tradesmen, fraudulent attorneys and the like, who were disgruntled with their lot. Ten per cent of the seamen were foreigners. Another ten per cent were Irish, some of them under sentence for political offences

[1] The King with his usual common sense complained of these.—*Spencer Papers*, II, 124.

and illegally smuggled into the Fleet by high-handed officials. Recently an increasing number had been United Irishmen and sympathisers with the principles proclaimed by France.[1]

The agitation and struggle of those seven breathless days at Spithead stirred all this perilous matter into a ferment. This was no ordinary mutiny, for it had succeeded. Suspicion that its fruits were going to be filched by parliamentary chicanery was now aroused by two circumstances. On the 3rd the Duke of Bedford, making party capital out of a national misfortune, contrived by an awkward question in the Lords to convey to uninitiated seamen poring over their newspapers the false idea that the Government was going to drop the bill for supplementary naval pay. Simultaneously the Admiralty circulated a foolish document forbidding captains to temporise with mutiny, and directing the marines to be kept in constant readiness for action. This was no more than a childish attempt of official pride to recover official face. But by accident or design its contents became known to the Fleet. On Sunday, May 7th, when on a change of wind Bridport hoisted the signal to sail, the seamen at St. Helens once more manned the shrouds and broke into defiant cheers.

This time mutiny wore a graver aspect. The seamen of the *Royal George*, swearing their officers had deceived them, seized the arms and ammunition. A broil in Admiral Colpoys' flagship at Spithead, in which a seaman lost his life while rushing the quarterdeck, nearly ended in the Admiral and the officer who had fired the shot being summarily hanged. In other ships unpopular officers were bundled ashore and left with their belongings on the quayside. Some of the marines, the traditional keypins of naval discipline, joined the rest. The people of Portsmouth, confronted with the spectacle of the fleet flying the red flag and of shaken captains and admirals dumped on the sea front like *émigrés*, hourly expected the arrival of the French and the guillotine. As a Civil Lord of the Admiralty wrote to Spencer, the situation formed "the most awful crisis" the country had ever known.

Meanwhile the conflagration had spread. At Plymouth the crews of Sir Roger Curtis's squadron had mutinied on April 26th and turned most of their captains ashore. Four days later ominous cheering signalled an outbreak of revolt in the flagship of the North Sea Fleet waiting at Yarmouth for a wind to blockade the Dutch invasion fleet in the Texel. But in this case the Admiral in command was equal to the occasion. Towering with rage, the giant Scot, Adam Duncan,

[1]Wolfe Tone himself was nearly pressed while sailing in 1795 from Ireland to America. —Lecky, III, 496.

called his men out of the foreshrouds and rated them like a father. The affair ended—for they adored the fine old man—in their promising to go to any part of the world with him and writing a letter thanking the Lords of the Admiralty for their compliance with the request of the Channel Fleet.

For underneath the suspicion, the smouldering grievances and agitation ran the English individual sense of humanity. A worthy officer remained in the seamen's eyes a worthy man, however much he might theoretically embody the forces of despotism. All the generalisations of French ideology or Irish logic could never persuade them otherwise.

It was this deep-rooted manliness of the British sailor that saved the day. The authorities, at last abandoning false pride, behaved with equal good sense. The supplementary estimates providing for the increase in pay were hurried through their remaining stages, and the one line of approach to the disgruntled seamen which was certain of success—the simple human one—was chosen. Someone with a flash of the inspiration which always seems to come to the salvation of England in the last ditch suggested the victor of the First of June as a *deus ex machina*. Armed with full powers to redress grievances on behalf of the Admiralty and to grant pardon on that of the Crown, Lord Howe, overcoming gout and infirmities, set off for Portsmouth. Without wasting a minute he had himself rowed across the Solent to St. Helens where, visiting every ship in turn, he set to work to restore the confidence of the seamen in their rulers.

By May 13th, six days after the renewed mutiny had begun, the old hero had achieved his purpose of quietening what he described as "the most suspicious but most generous minds" he had ever met. The demand of the men to dismiss the more unpopular officers was tactfully turned by getting the latter to petition the Admiralty for transfer to other ships. There only remained to celebrate the reconciliation of Fleet and nation. On May 15th, after twelve hours of rowing round the cheering fleet amid the strains of "Rule Britannia," "Black Dick"—as exhausted as after the battle of the First of June—was carried by the sailors shoulder high to the port governor's house. Here in a perfect delirium of patriotic emotion he and his lady entertained the delegates to a grand dinner and jollification. At Plymouth, where a similar happy ending occurred, Captain Boger, after being kept a prisoner in the *Cambridge* guardship, was paraded with his fellow captains in open carriages round the town on a broiling summer day, amid tumultuous cheering. Dressed in full uniform, with a face scarlet from the heat, he repeatedly asked for a glass of water but his men, who were extremely fond of him, horrified at the request, told him that "his Honour might have any sort of grog, but that as for water, they would not suffer his Honour to drink it."[1]

Two days later the Channel Fleet put to sea to seek the enemy. But the country had no time for relief. During the second Spithead mutiny the news reached London that Austria, brought to her knees by Bonaparte's advance on Vienna, had signed an armistice at Leoben and that France was free to concentrate her entire force against England. Already a Dutch army was waiting at the Texel. Every day brought new alarms. On May 12th, while Howe was completing his work of pacification, a brilliant young Tory M.P., George Canning, penned some mock verses congratulating his friend Windham, who had made a comforting ministerial reference in a recent speech to "negative successes," on a "day of no disaster."[2] He was too soon. For on that very day, while rumours percolated through London that the Household troops had revolted, the men of the flagship at Sheerness defied their officers and turned the forecastle guns on the quarterdeck. The rest of the battleships lying in the mouth of the river at the Great and Little Nore followed their example.

The good humour and sense which had characterised proceedings at Spithead were lacking at the Nore. The chief ringleader was an ex-schoolmaster who had recently taken the Government's quota money to get himself out of a debtor's prison. The son of an Exeter tradesman, Richard Parker, now thirty years of age, had been three times to sea, had served as a midshipman and had been court-martialed for insubordination. He marked his return to the Navy by helping to stir up trouble in the port flag and depot ship, the *Sandwich*, already rife with discontent through her foul and overcrowded condition. Like many other famous talkers he was full of good intentions, on which later apologists have dwelt at length. But he was without moral ballast. He was ambitious, vain, untruthful, weak and so excitable as to seem at times mentally deranged.

[1] C. N. Robinson, *The British Tar in Fact and Fiction* (1909), 129.

[2] "Oh tell me! does to-day's event
Serve to illustrate what you meant?
—Or will the soldiers riot?
Oh! if the Guards have not rebell'd,
And if the naval fray is quell'd,
If Portsmouth yet is quiet;

"Come, Windham! celebrate with me
This day of joy and jubilee,
This day of *no* disaster!
Our Government is *not* o'erturned—
Huzza!—Our Fleet has *not* been burned;
Our Army's *not* our master."

In his hands the smouldering grievances and resentment of rough and ignorant men became a terrible menace.

The mutineers at the Nore formulated no specific demands. It was mutiny without an objective. It disregarded the general settlement reached at Spithead. Like the French Revolution in miniature, it proceeded on its own momentum and degenerated into rebellion for the sake of rebellion. Parker, who styled himself President and kept up an Admiral's state, never stirred without the accompaniment of musical honours and banners. He told the men that the act for the increase of their pay was only a temporary Order in Council and, when shown to be wrong, declared that it had no validity beyond the end of the year. Only after repeated requests for the men's grievances did he present Admiral Buckner—in whose presence he remained contemptuously covered—with an ultimatum of eight articles. One of these affirmed the right of seamen to dismiss their officers. But he refused to discuss matters with any one but the Lords of the Admiralty, insisting that they should wait on the delegates.

Meanwhile his followers ceaselessly paraded the streets of Sheerness or rowed in procession round the port, armed with pistols and cutlasses and accompanied by brass bands playing "Rule Britannia" and "Britons, Strike Home!" For the men, though greatly enjoying their holiday and unwonted power, Englishwise refused to admit any disloyalty in their attitude. When the Government marched two regiments of militia into the place, Parker wrote to Admiral Buckner protesting at the "insult to the peaceable behaviour of the seamen." He added that the Lords of the Admiralty were themselves remiss in their duty in failing to attend where their appearance would give satisfaction.

As the Admiralty declined to obey, the mutineers proceeded to more vigorous measures. On May 23rd they seized eight gunboats lying in Sheerness harbour and carried them off in triumph to the Nore. Next day they despatched delegates to Yarmouth to urge the men of the North Sea Fleet to join them. Here Admiral Duncan, having received news that the Dutch fleet was embarking troops at the Texel, was about to sail for Ireland. Though the fatal infection was at work in his ships, he trusted to his personal popularity to overcome it. Only a week before he had dealt with a further outbreak in the *Adamant* by hoisting his flag in her and asking the turbulent crew whether any man dared to dispute his authority. When one of the ringleaders said he did, the giant Admiral had picked him up by the collar with one hand and, bearing him to the side of the vessel, had cried out, "My lads, look at this fellow who dares to deprive me of the command of the Fleet!" After which incipient mutiny in that ship at least dissolved in laughter.

But on the 29th, while standing out for the Dutch coast, one after another of Duncan's ships left him and sailed home to the Nore. Only his flagship, the *Venerable*, and the now faithful *Adamant* kept their course. "I am sorry," wrote the gallant old man, "that I have lived to see the pride of Britain disgrace the very name of it." Not since an enemy sailed up the Medway had such shame befallen the Navy.

Meanwhile on the evening of the 27th the Cabinet, faced by the gravity of the situation, resolved that the Admiralty must swallow its pride and go down to Sheerness. A new Royal Pardon was made out specifically covering the post-Spithead mutinies. That night Spencer, accompanied by two colleagues and the Secretary of the Board, set off again on his travels. But on reaching Sheerness on the 28th, he found what he had already suspected, that the Fleet's attitude was not unanimous and that many of the men were already sickening of Parker's presumption. He therefore refused to receive the delegates and, remaining in the Dockyard Commissioner's house, used old Admiral Buckner as an intermediary. And as Parker refused to abate anything from his demands, the First Lord presently returned to London with his mission unaccomplished. With Parker to deal with, it is doubtful if any other course was ever possible.

It was now war to the knife. Neither side would admit of compromise. While the mutineers were enthusiastically welcoming Duncan's absconding battleships, the Government was giving orders to cut their communications with the shore. All fraternisation between the Fleet and the Army was stopped and the sailors were to be resisted by force if they attempted to land. A Bill was hurried through Parliament extending the death penalty to persons having intercourse with rebellious seamen. Finally the provisions of the Fleet at the Nore were stopped. These measures, which passed both Houses with only one dissentient vote, were stern in the extreme. But they reflected the mood of the nation. They were an instance of the English method of grappling with a problem only when it became unmistakably dangerous but then doing so without second thoughts or hesitation. For the rulers of England weakness was a thing of the past.

Nor did they stand on pride. The Army, whose loyalty was so vital in that hour, was treated with a new consideration. Increases in pay long asked for in vain by the military authorities were immediately granted by Parliament. The soldiers responded cheerfully: having been so often sneered at by the seamen for their inefficiency and defeats, it was a pleasant change to become the heroes of the nation and be set to police the proud favourites. Under the command of Sir Charles Grey, the most popular officer in the Army, the troops kept close watch along the Kent and Essex shores and scarcely allowed a man to pass.[1]

Behind them was the nation. Its patriotism and sense of danger were alike aroused: fear of the invader waiting at the Texel and the intangible bogy of revolution that had grown up during the horrors of the Terror and the unreasoning years of war propaganda. To simple Britons Fox and his gang of traitors and defeatists lurked under the delegates' table in the stateroom of the *Queen Charlotte.* To frustrate their vile tricks and save the nation, thousands of middle-class citizens enrolled as "peace officers" or volunteered to serve in the flotilla of gunboats which Commodore Gower was organising in Long Reach to defend London from the mutineers. The East India Company placed all its ships at the Government's disposal: hundreds of private merchants followed its example.

The stoppage of the Fleet's victuals placed the delegates in a quandary. Since they would not go back, they had to go forward. On May 31st they decided to "show the country that they had it in their power to stop the trade of the river." But when on June 2nd they did so, seizing every ship entering or leaving the Thames, they merely united the country more vigorously than before. The trading community, attacked at its most sensitive point, was appalled and, because it was appalled, furious. So were the good people of the Thames-side towns who found tarred and feathered officers dumped by piratical crews on their waterfronts. This was plainly the prelude

[1] The kind of treatment to which the despised "lobsters" were subjected in the seaports is illustrated by an extract from Commander Gardner's *Recollections* (16), describing an incident on Gosport beach when a party of soldiers was marching some French prisoners to Forton Jail: "A *posse* of women rushed out of Rime's noted alley, and, pointing to the soldiers, sang the following beautiful ditty:

"Don't you see the ships a-coming?
Don't you see them in full sail?
Don't you see the ships a-coming
With the prizes at their tail?
Oh! my little rolling sailor,
Oh! my little rolling he;
I do love a jolly sailor,
Blithe and merry might he be.

"Sailors they get all the money,
Soldiers they get none but brass;
I do love a jolly sailor,
Soldiers they may kiss . . .
Oh! my little rolling sailor,
Oh! my little rolling he;
I do love a jolly sailor,
Soldiers may be damned for me!"

to the orgy of massacre, rape and arson which the anti-Jacobin cartoonists had taught them to fear. When the Government retaliated against the blockade by removing the buoys and beacons at the mouth of the Thames, there was not a dissentient voice from a seafaring people.

As the rest of the nation became more unanimous, the seamen became less so. The mutiny was popular so long as it remained a holiday demonstration with plenty of triumphal processions ashore, patriotic songs and brass bands and an unwonted freedom for airing grievances and slighting tyrannical officers. It became another thing altogether when it meant being cooped in idle ships, denied the liberty of the shore and its taverns and kept to short commons. But what really sapped the spirit of mutiny was the realisation that the nation, which however sparing it might be in other things had always lavished unstinted praise on its sailors, now regarded them as traitors and French dupes. Even their brethren of Spithead and Plymouth, now returned to their allegiance, wrote to the men of the Nore expressing horror at their proceedings. This imputation was more than the sailors could bear. The sense of community and playing for one's side so strong in Englishmen kept them a little while longer loyal to the mutiny, but they became moody, suspicious of one another and openly critical of their leaders. "Dam my eyes," wrote one of them in desperation to a silent, unrelenting Admiralty, "if I understand your lingo or long Proclimations but in short give us our Due at Once and no more at it, till we go in search of the Rascals the Eneymes of our Country."[1] In such a mood their attempts to celebrate Oakapple Day and the King's Birthday on June 5th,[2] which struck their compatriots as an impertinence, assumed a pathetic significance.

On June 6th the Government formally declared the mutineers rebels, though still extending its offer of pardon to all who should submit except the ringleaders. About the same time it became known in the Fleet that Parker had been keeping back the terms of this offer from his followers. Discontent at his admiral's airs and peremptory ways had been growing for some time: it now turned to open murmuring. The more popular officers detained aboard the ships were quick to take advantage of the change of temperature: and the sober seamen who had never approved of the mutiny began to come into their own.

The first sign of collapse came on the morning of the 9th when Parker, sensing the altered mood of the men and desperately re-

[1] *Manwaring and Dobrée*, 201.
[2] It actually fell on the 4th, a Sunday.

solving to take the hungry Fleet over to the Texel, gave the order to put to sea. Not a vessel stirred. The mutiny had come full circle. On the same day the officers of the *Leopard* seized control of the ship from the divided and disillusioned crew and set sail for the Lower Hope. The example was at once followed by the *Repulse* and, despite a desultory fire from the rest of the Fleet, both ships made good their escape.

For the next few days the Fleet presented a curious spectacle to watchers from the shore as red, blue and white flags fluttered up and down the mastheads while the ships' companies contended whether they should return unconditionally to their allegiance, make new attempts to parley with a stony-hearted Admiralty or sail for America or Ireland. But all the while the sands of mutiny were running out. The Admiralty refused to consider any proposition short of unqualified submission, and the men knew they had no alternative but to submit. By the 12th only two out of the twenty-two ships still at the Nore flew the red flag of defiance. Every day more of them slipped their cables and made their way up river to surrender to the authorities.

On the 15th the crew of the *Sandwich* repudiated Parker's authority and sailed under the guns of Sheerness. The mutiny was over. A few of the ringleaders made their escape to Calais. Parker, handed over to the military by his comrades, was taken to Maidstone jail under an escort of the West Yorks Militia. Here he was tried by court-martial and spent the remaining hours of his life writing an apologia for his actions and a long tirade against the men he had helped to mislead.[1] He was hanged on the last day of June from the yardarm of the *Sandwich*. Fifty-eight others were condemned to death, of whom twenty-eight were executed. Others were flogged or sentenced to terms of imprisonment. Of the 412 ringleaders found guilty, 300 were pardoned.

No other end to the affair was possible, for any other would have spelt the loss of naval discipline at a moment when its preservation was vital to the country and the future of human liberty. When Parker demanded the submission of the Admiralty to a seamen's council and held the nation's trade up to ransom, he threatened to smash the edge of a sharp and delicate instrument which in Nelson's hand was to establish the Pax Britannica and keep free the sea routes

[1] "May heaven grant that I may be the last victim offered up in the cause of a treacherous and debased commonalty. . . . Remember, never to make yourself the busybody of the lower classes, for they are cowardly, selfish and ungrateful; the least trifle will intimidate them, and him whom they have exalted one moment as their Demagogue, the next they will not scruple to exalt upon the gallows."—*The Dying Declaration of Richard Parker*, *P.R.O.* (Ad. 1/5339) cit. *Manwaring and Dobrée*, 274-5.

of the world for a century. Only undeviating firmness on the part of Admiralty and Parliament and an undivided endorsement by the nation could have saved the Navy from the fate of that of Republican France. Mutiny at the Nore had arisen from the same causes as at Spithead and Plymouth. But with Howe's redress of wellnigh insupportable grievances, naval rebellion in the Thames lost its justification. Its continuance exposed the country to dangers greater than any in her history. In acting as they did, the Government and Country showed the soundness of their instincts. So did the seamen in repudiating their leaders.

Yet the mutinies, terrible as they had seemed at the time, had served a purpose. They had brought home to the Government and country the abuses which were impairing the discipline and spirit of the Fleet and which, persisted in, must have proved fatal. Though at first they shook, they helped in the end to restore confidence between ruler and ruled: to re-establish the conditions in which alone officers like Nelson could operate. They began a slow but steady improvement in seagoing conditions: a kind of practical English revolution based not on abstract theories but on concrete needs. Before the Spithead mutiny the men of the Royal Navy, though praised and fêted, were not treated as human beings but as automata: after it their right to decent living and feeding conditions and proper care in sickness, disablement and retirement became gradually recognised. It was something for Englishmen to have initiated such a revolution in time of war and national crisis, and to have done so without disaster.

CHAPTER TEN

The Firmness of Ancient Rome

1797-8

"Torn as we are by faction, without an Army, without trusting entirely to a Navy whom we may not be able to pay, and on whose reliance no firm loyalty can be placed, how are we to get out of this cursed war without a revolution?"

Lord Cornwallis.

"Fifteen sail were the Dutchmen bold,
Duncan he had but two;
But he anchored them fast where the Texel shoaled,
And his colours aloft he flew.
'I've taken the depths to a fathom,' he cried,
And I'll sink with a right good will:
For I know when we're all of us under the tide,
My flag will be fluttering still.'" *Newbolt.*

During these events the Government had shown superb courage. By its neglect, lack of foresight and subservience to vested interest, it had been largely responsible for the country's agonising peril. Yet it had gone far to atone for all its faults. For, faced by stark disaster, it had known what to do and had not hesitated to do it.

How catastrophic the situation had been is illustrated by a simple entry in Windham's diary recording a council meeting to discuss an imminent mutiny of the Guards: "There does not seem anything to prevent their being masters of the Tower, the Mint, the Palace and the Cabinet." At that moment the entire reserve armament of the country was in the Tower and both the Spithead and Nore Fleets were in revolt. Under the universal foreboding of disaster three per cent Consols fell to 48, the lowest in their history. Even the revolution-hardened hero of Poland, General Kosciusko, could not conceal his agitation, and spoke of leaving London for America.

But Pitt showed no sign of perturbation. The First Lord, having reported to him at midnight that the marines were marching on London from the Nore, found him on his return a few hours later sound asleep. Whatever Ministers lacked, they did not want healthy nerves and strong wills. Prince Hardenberg, the Prussian statesman, noted with wonder that during the mutinies England did not withdraw a single ship from the blockade of Brest and Cadiz; it seemed to him like the firmness of ancient Rome. In the House on June 2nd,

Pitt in a magnificent appeal for national unity asked the Commons to show the world that there was no difficulty they would not meet with firmness and resolution as "the representatives of a great, a brave, a powerful and a free people."[1] For national unanimity, he declared, he would sacrifice everything. Even the tiny Opposition, shamed by the patriotism of Sheridan, voted in the Government lobby.

Yet courage and resolution could not alter the gravity of the situation. Even with the collapse of the mutinies it remained almost as menacing as before. The peace preliminaries at Leoben, which the Austrians attributed to the British withdrawal from the Mediterranean and the consequent domination of the Adriatic by French cruisers, were followed by the announcement of the Emperor's readiness to sign a definite peace. This was accompanied by news of a treacherous attack by Bonaparte on the territories of the Venetian Republic. It began with a carefully engineered anti-French riot in Verona, which gave him the excuse to overturn the constitution in favour of the Jacobin minority who were ready to yield the country and its fleet to France. The young conqueror would take no apology from the abject Senate but, describing the fracas at Verona as the "most atrocious affair of the century," insisted on the suppression of the constitution by a puppet gang of traitors who, guarded by French soldiers, burnt the insignia of the Doge and the golden Book of the Republic in the square of St. Mark.

For Bonaparte was preparing to remodel and militarise Italy as his predecessors had Holland, in order to use her against England. Austria, renouncing all her Italian possessions west of the Oglio, was to be indemnified by the Venetian mainland, while France was to annex the Adriatic possessions of the Republic and the Ionian islands for further operations against British commerce. A sham Jacobin revolution in Genoa simultaneously placed England's other principal customer in the peninsula under French rule. The Papal States were carved up to form with Lombardy and the former petty Dukedoms of the north a puppet French "Cisalpine" Republic.[2] Britain's former supremacy in the Mediterranean was as though it had never been: she had no longer trade or place in that sea.

[1] *War Speeches*, 192.

[2] Bonaparte, like Mussolini, boasted that he had fostered the growth of a new Italian spirit. "From this moment," he wrote, "the habits of the Italians were altered. In place of the cassock, which hitherto had been the fashionable dress for young men, came the military tunic. Instead of frittering their lives away at the feet of women, the young Italians sought out the riding-school, the fencing-floor and the parade-ground. Children began to play games of mimic warfare with regiments of tin-soldiers. . . . The national spirit was formed. Italy had its patriotic songs, its military marches. The women repelled with disgust the approaches of men who, to make themselves pleasing, adopted a feminine demeanour."—Frischauer, 46.

Meanwhile Spain was preparing to invade Portugal—Britain's only remaining ally. Two thousand British troops evacuated from Elba and some shockingly ill-disciplined French *émigré* regiments were all that the Government could spare to guard Lisbon. On its defence depended the victualling of the fleet blockading Cadiz, where twenty-three crippled Spanish ships of the line were held by fifteen British. Thirty-four French battleships had to be watched at Brest, where a new French army of invasion was gathering. Two more were at Lorient and one at Rochefort, while another eleven were in the Mediterranean. But the gravest menace of all came from the Texel, where 30,000 Dutch troops under General Daendels and a powerful fleet were waiting an opportunity to sail for England, Scotland or Ireland, no man knew which.

Here from June 1st to the 4th, while an east wind blew fair for an invasion, Duncan with two ships of the line, both presumably on the verge of mutiny, blockaded fifteen Dutch battleships, eight frigates and seventy smaller craft and transports. But the enemy was allowed no inkling of his plight, for the stout Admiral signalled perpetually to an imaginary fleet on the horizon. He told his men that by his reckonings his flag would remain flying at high tide if the Dutch should succeed in sinking him. His ships were still at their station when the wind changed. A few days later they were heartened by the appearance of a small Russian squadron which, through the good offices of Ambassador Vorontzoff, lent its moral support until one after another the defaulting battleships returned to their duty. The Dutch had lost their chance.

. . . .

Had they taken it, the appearance of General Daendels' army in Ireland might have proved fatal to England. For here in the spring and summer of 1797 a situation developed that threatened the Empire at its heart. A third of the population of the British Isles was ready to repudiate its allegiance to the Crown.

It was the culmination of more than a century of injustice and racial and religious persecution. Ireland was the black page in the English record. Recently there had been a growing desire on the part of English statesmen to make amends. During the American War Ireland had been given her own parliament, and since his rise to power Pitt had striven to place her commerce and constitution on a juster basis.

But to all such attempts there had been three obstacles: religious bigotry, the violence of the Irish character and the selfishness of the Dublin Castle bureaucracy. Intolerance towards Papists had been a main inspiration of the great Anglo-Saxon libertarian movement of the seventeenth century: the dispossession of the Catholic peasantry by Protestant landlords and clergy the coping-stone of the Revolution Settlement. And though a century of doctrinal security and rational culture had made the English aristocracy the most tolerant in the world, the common people and middle class still retained the old insensate fear of Rome. Their prejudice was shared by their Sovereign, who held that the retention of the constitutional barriers against Catholic participation in government had been enjoined on him by his coronation oath. When at the outbreak of war Pitt had extended the franchise to Catholic two-pound freeholders, the King had vetoed the attempt to admit Catholics to Parliament.

Membership of the Irish parliament was therefore confined to the communicants of a minority creed. The ignorant Catholic freeholder was given the vote but his educated and wealthier co-religionist was denied any active share in the government of the country. This suited the Dublin Castle bureaucracy, whose conception of rule was of the narrowest and most illiberal kind. It was to govern by dividing: to oppose everything that might make Ireland a nation and foster everything, however unjust, that prolonged her tutelage, ignorance and misery. The Irish Parliament was a mere tool of the Administration: at least two-thirds of its members were pensioners and place-holders, while only a dozen boroughs in all Ireland enjoyed a free vote. Corruption was universal.

Deprived of political responsibility, the Irish gentry, both Catholic and Protestant, shirked or evaded the social duties of their station. They were indolent, irresponsible and—in the face of popular unrest—cowardly. Many were absentees and more rack-renters. They pursued their pleasures and squeezed their tenants to pay for them. The parallel with the pre-Revolution aristocrats of France was alarming. It was almost impossible for a patriot to think of Ireland without trembling.

The Whig nobles who had repudiated Fox's leadership in order to join the Government were acutely conscious of this. They were closely associated with a little group of liberal-minded Irish aristocrats who, led by the great patriot Grattan, opposed the corruption and exclusiveness of Dublin Castle. Their mentor was Burke, himself an Irishman, who wrote at the beginning of the war that though he knew of no solid security against Jacobinism—the "grand and dreadful evil of the times"—he was certain that what came nearest it was to interest as many as possible in the present order of things; "to interest them religiously, civilly, politically by all the ties and principles by which men are held."[1]

[1] Lecky, IV, 69.

It was a condition of the Portland Whigs' junction with Pitt that a new spirit should be infused into the Irish administration. The Lord Lieutenancy was expressly promised them. Unfortunately the great nobleman chosen to hold it acted with a lack of rudimentary prudence and tact which brought all their liberal plans and those of Pitt to naught. Before he had even landed in Ireland in 1795, Lord Fitzwilliam had made sweeping promises of immediate Catholic emancipation and announced a wholesale purge of officials. Every outraged vested interest and prejudice was at once mobilised against him. The alarm of the King and of Protestant opinion generally compelled the Cabinet first to repudiate, then to recall, the imprudent Viceroy. Only pressing danger and the entreaties of Burke and Windham prevented the collapse of the Coalition.

The Whig attempt at Irish reform thus resulted in nothing but an acute consciousness of Irish grievances. It left the country sad and disappointed. On the day of Fitzwilliam's departure, all shops and businesses were shut and the better-to-do citizens wore mourning. He was succeeded by Lord Camden, a narrow if worthy Protestant who endorsed every obscurantist prejudice of Dublin Castle. But, though the public humiliation of the Catholic under British rule was advertised to the whole world, for the moment there was little Catholic feeling. For by a curious paradox the Irish dissentients of the time were not Catholic but Protestant. It was the radical Dissenters of the north who had embraced the heady republican gospel of Revolutionary France. The illiterate Catholic peasantry, taking the lead from its priests, was too shocked by Jacobin atheism and blasphemy to be seduced.

Thus it was that the appearance of a French armada in Bantry Bay in the Christmastide of 1796 made no impression on the pious south. But in Ulster it had caused the wildest excitement. Everybody except a few terrified gentry appeared to be engaged in making or stealing arms and drilling in anticipation of a French landing. The very garrisons had their arms filched while they slept. Woods were cut down to make pike handles, nocturnal bands broke into houses, burnt barns and destroyed corn only to disappear in the morning as though they had never been, while attempts to arrest were followed by rescue and murder. Mysterious beacons blazed, shots sounded from bog and mountain, and multitudes paraded the fields carrying white banners and singing republican songs. The Irish genius for disorder, for combining to destroy, blew like a gale over the green hills of Ulster.

Early in March, 1797, Camden placed the province under martial law and ordered General Lake to disarm the people. In the next fortnight nearly 6000 guns were seized and a great quantity of other arms. But as so often in Ireland, the cure only aggravated the evil. Civil disorder begat military. The imperfect discipline of the Militia and Yeomanry broke down under the strain of house-to-house visitations in a hostile countryside. Small bands of soldiers unaccompanied by their officers—of whom there were too few to go round—broke at night into lonely farmhouses and cabins and subjected their occupants to search. Drink was the besetting sin of the British Army and under its influence horrible outrages were committed. A Welsh regiment of Fencible cavalry stationed at Newry won a particularly unenviable reputation. An officer who visited a mountain village it had beaten up found burning houses, piled-up corpses and cowering prisoners.

When the better type of landlord and magistrate protested, the government at Dublin—after the manner of privileged bureaucracies—turned on the objectors. Its venom against the liberal element of the Irish aristocracy grew more bitter than ever. It stigmatised the demand for parliamentary reform and emancipation as treason. Loyal Irish patriots like Grattan, Curran and the Ponsonbys were almost hounded from public life. When Portland asked on behalf of the English Cabinet whether something might not be done for the Catholics who had proved loyal during Hoche's expedition, Camden replied that concession would only be made an excuse for rebellion, and that, so long as Ireland remained useful to England, she must be governed by an English party.[1] From its policy of narrow exclusion Dublin Castle now reverted to one even narrower; the black intolerance of Limerick and the Boyne. It deliberately appeased the Protestant minority by whipping up fanaticism against the Catholic majority. By so doing it unloosed forces beyond its control.

To the zealots of the north the right to persecute religious enemies appealed far more than any republic. Irish nationalism became a poor, shabby thing in their eyes when it became identified, as of old, with the cause of the priest-ridden "croppies." After the Orange Club boys had been out for a few nights on the war-path, they forgot all about their love for abstract Liberty and Equality. They only remembered their forbears' hatred of Popery and wooden shoes. Before long they were surpassing the military in their savage persecution of every symbol of Irishry. By mid-summer, 1797, Republicanism was already dead in the north.

But as it died Irish hatred of the Saxon heretic and usurper revived. With Catholic chapels and cabins blazing in half the

[1] Camden to Portland, 3rd April, 1797. *Lecky*, IV, 66.

villages of the north, there began an exodus unparalleled since the bad old days of the seventeenth century. A stream of refugees carried the tale of unmerited woes and wrongs into the rest of Ireland. It lost nothing in the telling, and struck bitter chords in Irish memory. The rumour of the coming of a French army which had scarcely stirred the lazy surface of peasant consciousness at Christmas now assumed an apocalyptic significance. For the French revolutionaries, atheists and blasphemers though they might be, had suddenly become what their forerunners were in the days of James II and Louis XIV: avengers and liberators. Ancient prophecies, long forgotten, were recalled: bards sang how the ancient race and Faith would win back lost lands and the usurpers be expelled for ever:

> "O! the French are on the sea!
> Says the Shan van Vocht,
> And it's where they ought to be,
> Says the Shan van Vocht!
> For ould Ireland shall be free
> From the Shannon to the sea . . ."

Ulster ceased to be the mainstay of United Ireland: Catholic, peasant Ireland took its place. Hundreds of thousands swore the fatal oath and dedicated themselves to the dark, treasonable designs of Wolfe Tone and Napper Tandy. As immediate assassination was the punishment for even the suspicion of betrayal, and the flame of rebellion spread unchecked. Its leaders fanned it by evoking the two most enduring hates of the Irish peasant: for the alien landlord and the heretic tithe-owner.

• • • • • • •

The repercussions of Irish unrest beyond the borders of Ireland were serious. In their panic the Irish authorities illegally sent hundreds of arrested suspects to the fleet. These carried the infection of United Irishry to their countrymen serving in the King's ships. Coupled with the news of successful mutiny in England it constituted a major problem for the Navy in every part of the world.

Nowhere was it so dangerous as in the fleet off Cadiz. Here Jervis, now Lord St. Vincent, tossing with his crowded ships off the Spanish port, grappled for a whole year with an ugly hydra. The news of the seamen's triumph at Spithead, which reached the Fleet in the second half of May, cast his officers into deep gloom. With so many of the crews miscreants capable of any crime, it was hard to see how they could escape the prevailing infection.

But St. Vincent no more feared mutiny than he did the Spaniard.

He dealt with the least sign of it without hesitation or mercy. Asked to pardon an offender because he was of good character, the grim old man replied that he was glad of it, for till now he had only hanged scoundrels but henceforward men would know that no virtue could atone for mutiny. For more than a year he sat on the lid of a powder barrel, until in May, 1798, the captain of the *Marlborough* reported that his crew would not permit a shipmate condemned for mutiny to be hanged. St. Vincent received the captain on the quarter-deck of his flagship. He listened in silence to the request that the execution should be carried out on another ship. "Do you mean to tell me, Captain Ellison," he asked, "that you cannot command His Majesty's ship *Marlborough*? If that is the case, sir, I will immediately send on board an officer who can. That man shall be hanged at 8 o'clock to-morrow morning and by his own ship's company, for not a hand from any other ship in the Fleet shall touch the rope." Next morning armed launches from every ship surrounded the *Marlborough* with orders to fire into her on the slightest sign of resistance. As her unwilling crew hauled up the victim, every man in the Fleet knew whose will was master.[1]

It was not only its chief's resolution that preserved discipline in the former Mediterranean Fleet, but the humane spirit of its captains. Such officers would not countenance the petty tyranny and corruption that had driven ships like the *Sandwich* to mutiny. They cared for their men, and their men repaid their care. One day early in June, 1797, a paper was found on the quarter-deck of the *Theseus*:

> "Success attend Admiral Nelson! God bless Captain Miller! We thank them for the officers they have placed over us. We are happy and comfortable, and will shed every drop of blood in our veins to support them."[2]

In Collingwood's ship the discipline of the lash was largely superseded by such minor punishments as exclusion from mess and watering the grog. The seamen's recreations and the proper treatment of the sick were their captain's constant care. But on less fortunate stations years elapsed before the Navy was free from the menace of mutiny. In September, 1797, the crew of the *Hermione*, cruising off Puerto Rico in the West Indies, murdered her officers

[1] Mahan, *Sea Power*, I, 238-9.

[2] Only a month earlier St. Vincent had written: "The *Theseus* is an abomination. . . . If I can prevail on Captain Aylmer to go into the *Captain*, Rear-Admiral Nelson and Captain Miller will soon put *Theseus* to rights." (*Spencer*, II, 403.) Nelson's view of the Spithead mutinies was expressed in a letter on June 30th. "I am entirely with the seamen in their first complaint. We are a neglected set and, when peace comes, are shamefully treated; but, for the Nore scoundrels, I should be happy to command a ship against them."—*Nicolas*, II, 402.

and delivered the frigate—one of the finest in the Service—to the Spaniards. In July Duncan, blockading the Texel, reported that few of his ships could be depended upon. Later in the year there was serious trouble at the Cape.

. . . .

It was with such considerations and the knowledge that all Europe had yielded to the aggressor that Pitt in the summer of 1797 again explored the possibilities of peace. "I feel it my duty as an English Minister and a Christian," he wrote to his Foreign Secretary, who did not share his views, "to use every effort to stop so bloody and wasting a war." Despite the opposition of the King, as well as of the powerful faction that followed Burke and Windham, he carried the Cabinet.

For with Camden writing urgent warnings from Ireland entreating him to make terms before it was too late, with the fleets still simmering with suppressed mutiny, with three great naval powers at her throat and two armies of invasion preparing to assail her, Britain seemed to have no alternative. "If peace is to be had, we must have it," wrote Canning. "When Windham says we must not, I ask him, 'Can we have war?' It is out of the question, we have not the means; we have not what is of all means the most essential, the *mind*."[1]

For the country was at last losing faith in its power to achieve its war aims. It was no longer prepared to fight for them. It would make further sacrifices only for bare existence. "We can break off upon nothing but what will rouse us from sleep and stupidity into a new life and action." Canning continued, "We are now soulless and spineless." The desperate unity engendered by the menace of the Nore mutiny had been succeeded by a feeling of exhaustion; the sacrifices of the past four years appeared in vain, victory farther off then ever. Men had momentarily lost confidence in their leaders and the organs of public opinion; a naval officer who that summer captured a French privateer commented bitterly on the lying newspapers that gave out that the French were starving, whereas in reality their ships were loaded with luxuries.[2] A cartoon of Gillray portrayed Pitt as a sleepwalker descending, with guttering candle and fixed staring eyes, the gaping stairway of a tottering ruin. Nelson, writing from Cadiz at the end of June, heard that he was

[1] "For my part I adjourn my objects of honour and happiness for this country beyond the grave of our military and political consequence which you are now digging at Lille. I believe in our resurrection and find my only comfort in it."—*Malmesbury*, III, 398.

[2] "Barrels of meat of every description—alamode beef, ham, fowls, and tongues, casks filled with eggs, coffee, tea and sugar, all kinds of cordial, with plenty of brandy and different wines; so that instead of starvation, there appeared the luxury of Lucullus."—Gardner, 200.

out; "it is measures must be changed and not men," he commented. The general feeling in the Fleet was that peace was now inevitable.[1] Even St. Vincent sent Spencer suggestions for demobilisation.

Accordingly at the beginning of July Malmesbury set out for Lille where Republican plenipotentiaries had been appointed to meet him. The recent French elections had clearly shown the popular desire for peace. Though three of the five Directors wanted the war to continue at all costs, an open rejection of the British overtures was more than they dared. They had therefore decided to play for time.

At first the "white lion's" reports were hopeful; he had been treated with courtesy, even old-world ceremony: the French plenipotentiaries were very different from those of the previous year; everywhere the weary, disillusioned country people wanted peace. Britain was no longer under any obligation to press for the return of Austrian territories: she was prepared to abandon the old conception of the balance of power and her claim to control the fate of Holland and Belgium. And, as she was also ready to restore unconditionally all her colonial conquests except Spanish Trinidad and Dutch Ceylon and the Cape, there seemed little to dispute. But soon the old doubts arose: the Directory was making difficulties, demanding unconditional compensation for the ships destroyed at Toulon four years before and the repudiation of the King of England's historic French title as indispensable preliminaries to negotiation. Before long it was asking still more: that before any discussion Britain should surrender every colonial possession she had taken not only from France but from Spain and the Batavian Republic.

In this doubtful season and while the Dutch invasion fleet with its transports waited for westerly winds to veer to the east, Burke died. For long he had been in despair: "If I live much longer," he had written, "I shall see an end of all that is worth living for in this world." The departure of Malmesbury on yet another abject mission had been the final blow to the angry, vehement old man: he could not survive it. But as he lay dying in his home at Beaconsfield and his anguished disciples stood around him, a flash of the old prophetic power returned. "Never," he whispered, "succumb to these difficulties. It is a struggle for your existence as a nation, and, if you must die, die with the sword in your hand."

. . . .

Far away off Cadiz, Nelson was preparing with three ships of the line and four frigates to storm the great Spanish island fortress of Tenerife and capture the Mexican treasure fleet which was

[1] *Wynne Diaries*, II, 183.

believed to be sheltering there. On July 15th, 1797, he parted from St. Vincent and five days later sighted the snow-capped peak and frowning cliffs under which he proposed to take his ships. A more desperate enterprise was never attempted: the fortress of Santa Cruz bristled with guns and was defended by 8000 Spanish troops. Against them Nelson could oppose a bare 1000 sailors and marines. On the night of the 24th, he brought his landing boats to within half a gunshot of the shore before the church bells sounded the alarm and a hurricane of grapeshot swept the harbour. With his right arm shattered to the bone Nelson was borne back half-unconscious to his flagship, while a forlorn hope of four hundred men under Troubridge carried the mole and, driving through the deserted streets, actually reached the great square before their ammunition ran out. Here from a convent into which they retired they prepared fireballs and torches to storm their way into the citadel until the governor—a kindly and sensible man—admiring the extravagance of these mad Englishmen, made propositions so generous that they yielded. Providing them with boats to depart—for their own had been dashed to pieces—he gave to each man a loaf and a pint of wine and sent them back to their ships.[1]

. . . .

At Lille the prospects of peace depended on the moderates in the Legislative Councils prevailing over the corrupt Directors. A secret approach to Malmesbury by one of the plenipotentiaries, urging him to await the triumph of the peace party, prolonged negotiations for many weeks after rational hope of a successful issue had faded. The British Government, needing it so much and assured by Malmesbury that peace would sap the failing strength of the Revolution, abased itself and went on exchanging notes about the return of Dutch and Spanish colonies. It subsequently transpired that the new French Foreign Minister, Talleyrand, was using these delays to speculate in British Funds.

With the expiry of Carnot's term as President of the Directory on August 24th, 1797, his colleagues completed their plans for an appeal to the sword. Behind them were the power and prestige of the young hero to whom their leader, Barras, had given his first chance. General Bonaparte did not love Barras, but he loved the peace party and the Royalists of the Club de Clichy even less. At the moment he was

[1] He entertained Captain Troubridge and Captain Hood to dinner and, with the chivalry of his proud race, showed them every kindness. The courtesy was returned by Nelson, who carried the Spaniard's official report of his successful defence to Cadiz. Earl Spencer, on hearing of the episode, wrote to his colleague, the Foreign Secretary: "Being on the subject of compliments, I really think that some notice should be taken (but I don't exactly know the proper mode) of the Spanish Governor of Santa Cruz who behaved so well to our people after the treaty they made for retreating to their ships."—*H. M. C. Dropmore*, III, 375.

negotiating the final formalities of the Treaty of Campo Formio, which was to set the seal on the preliminary peace of Leoben and substitute France for Austria as the dominant power in Italy and the Adriatic. His bloodless conquest of Venice and the Ionian Islands had fired his imagination: he saw himself as the successor of the Doges, holding the golden East in fee, using the Venetian fleet to seize Malta from the Knights of St. John and striking through Egypt to found a new empire in the Levant and India. Such a policy was utterly incompatible with peace with England: now, when that greedy, soulless power was decaying at the centre, was the moment to strike off her eastern tentacles. Her subsidised allies were all gone and she could do nothing without them.

With these thoughts the young conqueror addressed a flamboyant proclamation to his troops. "France," he told them, "is separated from us by the mountains; but should it be necessary you will traverse them with the speed of an eagle to maintain the Constitution, to defend Liberty and to protect the Government and Republic." This document he had circulated through France, where it made a great impression. For though the war-weary, faction-torn country longed for peace, it longed for a saviour even more, and the romantic hero of Lodi and Rivoli seemed the one man who could rescue it from a swarm of thieving, inglorious politicians. "The deputies ought to be put in a wood," was a popular saying of the time, "and the wood set on fire." The General was the obvious man to light it.

As Bonaparte—heir of the Revolution—knew better than any man, nothing could be achieved without force. Realist that he was, he sent the rough Augereau from his camp to Paris to command the troops who were to take the place of the Jacobin mob and keep the Revolution in being. The *coup d'état* of Fructidor on September 3rd was a repetition of a familiar theme, with soldiers playing the part of the roughs of the "glorious Faubourg." Barras, defying the majority in the Council because he was secure of the armed majority without, screamed across the Chamber to Carnot, once the organiser of victory, " There is not a louse on your body but has the right to spit in your face!" The Triumvirate of "Jacobin" Directors called in the military to disperse the Councils and by a savage proscription sentenced several hundred of their chief opponents—deputies, newspaper proprietors, editors, priests—to perpetual banishment in the swamps of Guiana and Cayenne. Carnot and a few others contrived to escape: the rest perished as miserably of fever under the "dry guillotine" as their predecessors had done under its bloodier counterpart.

. . . .

This was the end of the peace negotiations. "This cursed revolution," wrote Canning, "has baffled our good intentions." The Jacobins had triumphed again, and there was no peace to be had with Jacobins. New French negotiators who arrived at Lille in place of the old at once requested that all former French, Spanish and Dutch possessions should be restored without demur as a preliminary to further conversations. The final terms, according to French Foreign Office archives, were to include the surrender of the Channel Islands, Canada, Newfoundland, Gibraltar and British India.[1] On refusing Malmesbury was ordered to leave within twenty-four hours. He was pursued by dark hints as to the possibility of bribing the new Directors. For a sum of £1,200,000 to be privately divided between Barras and Rewbell Britain would be allowed to keep Dutch Ceylon, and for another £800,000 the Cape. So desperate was the state of affairs—"Europe abandoned," as Grenville wrote, "without defence of any kind to these monsters"—that Pitt even played with the idea of effecting something by these dubious means. But they came to nothing and appeared to be inspired only by French politicians trying to speculate in British stocks and shares.

"If this country could but be brought to think so it would be ten thousand times safer to face the storm than to shrink from it."[2] So wrote the Foreign Secretary on October 8th. Two days later Windham echoed him: "What are called prudent counsels are the most replete with danger."[3] The French had overstepped themselves. By the treaty of Campo Formio with Austria they gained Belgium, the Rhine boundary, Savoy, Corfu and the Ionian islands and unchallenged control of Holland and Italy. The "natural frontiers" of France had been achieved and the war on the Continent liquidated. And Britain after pouring out her blood and treasure for four and a half years had offered to return Martinique, St. Lucia, Tobago, the French part of Santo Domingo, the islands of St. Pierre and Miquelon, Pondicherry, Chandernagore and all the French trading factories in the East. In all her history, even in the days of the Grand Monarch, France had never been able to command such terms. And she had spurned them.

That refusal opened the country's eyes. It was not only victory the Republic wanted: it was the domination of the world and the elimination of Britain as a nation. Peace, however much desired, was not to be had with such adversaries. Collingwood when he heard the news summed up the real issue. "The question is not

[1] Lecky IV, 162.
[2] *H. M. C. Dropmore*, III, 379.
[3] J. W. Fortescue, *Statesmen of the Great War* (1911), 125.

merely who shall be conqueror with the acquisition of some island or colony ceded by a treaty . . . but whether we shall any longer be a people—whether Britain is still to be enrolled among the list of European nations—whether the name of Englishman is to continue an appellation of honour, conveying the idea of every quality which makes human nature respectable or a term of reproach and infamy, the designation of beggars and of slaves."[1]

As for the claim that the Republic was fighting for liberty, that pretence was exposed for the nauseating hypocrisy it was by the bloodstained clique in power. In the spirit of their own General Bonaparte's cynical "I have shot the municipality of Pavia," they had brutally seized all who dared to oppose them and huddled them off to die in tropical concentration camps. Here, Pitt told the House, "was a system of tyranny the most galling, the most horrible, the most undisguised in all its parts and attributes that has stained the page of history or disgraced the annals of the world."[2] Set against it, and stigmatised as an anachronistic despotism by sordid tyrants who had just annulled the elections in forty-nine Departments and sent two thousand political opponents to the galleys, was a mild constitutional monarchy whose worst offence against civil liberty during a year in which the very foundations of its existence had been threatened was the sentencing of a Lincolnshire blacksmith to a few months' solitary confinement for damning the King.

. . . .

A fortnight after Malmesbury's hasty departure from Lille the Directory launched its attack. Throughout the summer Duncan had been holding grimly to his station off the Texel where Daendels' army was waiting to embark for Ireland. At one period in July the troops had actually boarded the transports, only to be driven ashore again by the prolonged spell of westerly winds which marked the critical summer of 1797. For six weeks, while Wolfe Tone blotted his diary with expletives, it blew steadily from the same quarter, as though Heaven were fighting for England. Meanwhile Brigadier John Moore, invalided from the West Indies, inspected the defences of Clacton beach, and young Walter Scott, Quartermaster of the Royal Edinburgh Volunteer Light Dragoons, rose at five each summer morning to charge imaginary Frenchmen on Musselburgh Sands before going to his legal labours in the Parliament House. And far away in Ireland Lake's dragoons went about their grim business of disarming the populace.

In mid-August, the favourable season for invasion nearing its

[1] Collingwood, 63-4.
[2] *War Speeches*, 204.

close, the Dutch abandoned the idea of a large-scale attack on Ireland for a raid on Scotland. A month later, on September 19th, Hoche, the one disinterested champion of Ireland's cause in France, died prematurely of consumption. Irish emancipation fell into the background at the very moment that Irish wrongs had made it the most deadly of all explosives with which to destroy the Republic's last enemy. The feeling was growing in Paris that, with Austria making her formal surrender at Campo Formio and the entire resources of France and her allies available for a direct assault on England, an attempt on starving Ireland was no longer necessary. The victorious liberators of the Great Nation could not be expected to be bothered with a "levée-en-masse of potatoes."

Early in October, 1797, the Dutch fleet at the Texel received orders to put to sea to disable the British North Sea squadron and so prepare the way for a raid on the English or Scottish coast. Equinoctial gales had driven Duncan back to Yarmouth to refit: the old man, who had long been anxious to retire with an Irish peerage, had recently complained that his flagship, the *Venerable*, was so unseaworthy that even his cabin was not dry when it rained. "When she has much motion she cracks as if she would go to pieces," he told Spencer.[1] He was lying in Yarmouth Roads on the morning of the 9th when the sound of a lugger firing at the back of the sands gave the signal that the enemy were at sea. Leaving many of his officers still ashore, he weighed anchor at once and was on his way back to the Dutch coast before noon. Early on the 11th he sighted the enemy.

The battle that followed showed the world that the resistance of Britain, which appeared to have been crumbling during the naval mutinies and the peace negotiations at Lille, was still a factor to be reckoned with. The memory of Camperdown was soon eclipsed by Nelson's more famous victories but at the time it seemed—and was—a crowning deliverance. The two fleets were well matched—sixteen battleships against sixteen with a Dutch superiority in gun power—but the British were in an invincible mood. The men, who four months before had refused to follow their Admiral and hoisted the red flag, were on their mettle: resolved to re-establish their patriotism and worth in the eyes of their countrymen. And they knew that they were fighting literally for their country's existence; a defeat at that hour would have sealed her doom.

Duncan, having the weather gauge, boldly endeavoured to put his fleet between the enemy and the shore to prevent their escape. Then flying the signal for close action, and not waiting to form

[1] 7th Aug., 1797, *Spencer Papers*, II, 188.

line of battle, the stately old giant went in like a boxer set on victory. The spirit of the day was epitomised by the captain of the *Belliqueux* who, puzzled by the Admiral's signals, flung down the signal book with a "Damn it! up wi' the hellum and gang into the middle o't!" The Dutch fought with traditional stubbornness and skill: unlike the ill-disciplined French and Spaniards, firing low and doing great execution to the British hulls. The carnage in Duncan's flagship was so great that at one moment he and the pilot were the only men unwounded on the quarterdeck. But the British gunnery was transcendent. When after a three-hour duel Admiral de Winter struck his flag, he surrendered not so much a ship as a mortuary.

Only seven Dutch vessels escaped. Ten others were taken, including seven ships of the line. They were too battered to be of much use to the victors. But their eclipse meant the end of the North Sea menace. Henceforward Britain could concentrate her main force against Brest and the Atlantic ports: the Dutch navy as a striking force was out of the war. For this, and still more for the needed fillip his victory gave to British spirits, his countrymen hailed Duncan as a saviour.[1] Pitt, over his dinner at Walmer Castle, heard the news from a smuggler and broke into a boyish ecstasy: Dundas wrote joyously that an Irish peerage would no longer do for the brave old man now. Bonfires blazed in every city and village, and a public subscription in London for the families of fallen sailors reached £5000 in a day. Later a solemn thanksgiving for the victory was held in St. Paul's: in the centre of the royal procession through the City were three wagons guarded by seamen with cutlasses and adorned with captured French, Spanish and Dutch flags. Nor was it in Britain only that Camperdown was acclaimed. The Russian Ambassador wrote that all over the universe honest men rejoiced with the good people of England. For it was a portent that nations could still command their own destiny.

It was some such thought that must have been passing through Pitt's mind when his old tutor, the Bishop of Lincoln, consulted him about the thanksgiving sermon. The Prime Minister agreed with the proposed text: "Except these abide in the ship, ye cannot be saved," but went on to suggest its application. "Your sermon would be to prove that God who governs the world by his providence never interposes for the preservation of men or nations without their own exertions." After a pause, he added, "I really think with that text, it will be the best sermon ever preached."

He preached it himself when he met the Commons on November

[1] "One of the greatest objects is raising people's spirits."—Grenville to Spencer, 13th Oct., 1797.—*Spencer Papers*, II, 196.

10th to recount the breakdown of the peace negotiations at Lille. He described his inextinguishable wish for peace even with a Revolutionary government if it could be had on terms which did not rob the nation of its security or honour. But since it could not, there was no extremity which was not preferable to a base surrender. Upon such an alternative, he declared, no Englishman would hesitate. Once more he asked for unity, with which the country could accomplish anything, and for a cessation of the defeatist jeremiads of the Opposition Press which seemed to know "no other use of English liberty but servilely to retail and transcribe French opinions." He appealed instead for the virtues which a reverse of fortune had never failed to evoke from England: "the virtues of adversity endured and adversity resisted, of adversity encountered and adversity surmounted."

The Prime Minister's speech ended with a great peroration. "There is one great resource which I trust will never abandon us. It has shone forth in the English character, by which we have preserved our existence and fame as a nation, which I trust we shall be determined never to abandon under any extremity, but shall join hand and heart in the solemn pledge that is proposed to us, and declare to His Majesty that we know great exertions are wanting, that we are prepared to make them and at all events determined to stand or fall by the laws, liberties and religion of our country."[1] When Pitt sat down Sir John Sinclair withdrew his hostile amendment and the whole House rose spontaneously to sing "Britons, Strike Home!"

Rider and steed were worthy of one another. All through the autumn, under the surface of depression and the cross-currents of defeatism, the tide of popular resolve had been rising. The victory of Camperdown and the Prime Minister's great appeal heralded an epoch of national revival and glory. The long years of apathy and retreat were over: rising from the last ditch of disaster and peril, the country prepared to wrestle with destiny. That November, under the shadow of defeat and invasion, a curious electric current ran through the land. Wilberforce's *Practical View*, with its scorching contempt for moral complacency and unprofitable respectability, enjoyed for a religious book an almost sensational sale: forced by the all-pervading threat to existence to examine their consciences and the roots of belief, men found a new quickening of faith. Early in December a notice was given in at the fashionable church of St. George's, Hanover Square, that an officer wished to return thanks to Almighty God for his recovery from a severe

[1] *War Speeches* 228-9.

wound and the mercies bestowed on him. It was the one-armed, one-eyed Nelson.

Duncan's guns and Pitt's words marked the beginning of the English counter-attack against the French Revolution. It began, characteristically, when "that ungovernable, intolerable, destroying spirit" had broken down all other resistance and was threatening to engulf the island itself.[1] Though men of the older generation, oppressed by continuous difficulties and defeats, could not yet feel the turn of the tide, Pitt's young disciple, Canning, recovering from the gloom of the autumn, had already published the first number of his *Anti-Jacobin.* The new paper was nothing if not aggressive: during its brief existence "Pitt's Kindergarten" in one brilliant squib after another took the offensive against the cherished idols of revolutionary ideology, contrasting them in scathing verse and satire with the sorry performances—murders, perjuries and outrages—of the French "friends of humanity" and the vanity and ignorance of their English sympathisers:

"Come, little drummer boy, lay down your knapsack here,
I am the soldier's friend, here are some books for you,
Nice clever books by Tom Paine the philanthropist."

Against these it contrasted the virtues of old England—the "little body with a mighty heart"—which the Jacobins despised but which would yet prove too strong for them.

. . . .

It was to harness the resurgent forces of the nation to the war effort that Pitt laid his plans at the close of 1797 for the biggest Budget in its history. He had to face a deficit of nineteen millions. Reckoning the taxable income of the country at just over a hundred millions, he proposed to raise a quarter of it for national purposes during the coming year, besides demanding a further loan of fifteen millions to support the war. To do so he trebled and in cases quadrupled the assessed taxes, an impost which, levied on larger inhabited houses and windows, on male servants, horses, carriages and similar luxuries, fell almost entirely on the propertied classes. This augmentation of what was virtually a direct tax on wealth threatened to undermine the whole basis of the British fiscal system.

[1] Across the Atlantic the young Anglo-Saxon Republic had just realised that the political convulsion in France was not a new birth of freedom akin to its own but a despotism which only the resistance of stubborn, stupid England could prevent from enslaving the earth. Farington has a note in his diary for 31st January, 1798: "Eyes of America now opened—did favour France—but now see nothing permanent, no integrity—though do not approve all in England, yet see it a country which can be depended on." A few months later Britain modified a Convoy Bill before Parliament to please the U.S.A.—See *Rose*, I, 209.

At the first shock this revolutionary proposal was almost too much for the patriotism of the possessing classes: it outraged both their native conservatism and their sense of liberty. The Opposition argued that its result would be universal starvation, for, though the poor would escape its direct effect, it would dry up the wealth which employed them. Fox, making one of his rare appearances in the House, declared it would annihilate trade and property. When Pitt drove to the City to attend the thanksgiving service for Camperdown his coach was hooted by a hired mob. "The chief and almost only topic of conversation," wrote one society lady, "is the new taxes; how people are to live if the Bill is passed I know not." Even Fanny Burney, established with her refugee husband in Camilla Cottage on the proceeds of her latest novel, felt that the increased assessment, though just and necessary, would spell ruin to herself and her father. "We have, this very morning," she wrote at Christmas, "decided upon parting with four of our new windows."

Yet the Finance Bill passed the Commons—on January 5th, 1798—by 196 votes to 71, and the Lords by 75 votes to 6. For it expressed, if not the wishes of all taxpayers, the will of the country. Down in Somerset, Hannah More reported that the poor villagers of Blagdon, fired by the glories of Camperdown, went in a body to their parson and stated their readiness to be taxed double. And after a little reflection and a good deal of characteristic grumbling, their betters proved worthy of them. By a happy suggestion of the Speaker, the pill of compulsion was sweetened by the addition of a self-imposed or voluntary contribution towards the cost of defending the country. And this, illogically enough, was subscribed with enthusiasm. Pitt, a poor man heavily in debt, headed the list with £2000: every member of the Government gave a fifth of his official salary, the King £20,000 a year—a third of his Privy Purse income—the Bank of England £200,000. A rough Lancashire calico maker named Robert Peel, whose son was one day to lead Pitt's party, subscribed £10,000 and was rebuked by his partner on his return to Bury for not having given double. The manager of Covent Garden, with the habitual loyalty of the theatre, devoted the profits of a special performance to the patriotic contribution. At the Royal Exchange, where a platform was erected in the piazza for the receipt of donations, subscriptions came in at the rate of £400 a minute, and when the Lord Mayor left the hustings on the first day a merchant called out, "Gentlemen, let us give a cheer for old England." In all, nearly two and a half millions was received in sums ranging from the £100,000 of the Duke of Bedford—hitherto a strong opponent of the war—to the 10s. subscribed by every seaman of H.M.S. *Argonaut* "to drive into the sea all French scoundrels and other blackguards."[1]

Danger alone could not explain the national revival, for Britain had long been on the verge of disaster. But danger there was, and as 1797 drew to a close it grew more urgent. On October 17th, a few days after Camperdown, the formal treaty between Austria and France was signed at Campo Formio. It was accompanied by the cynical elimination of an ancient sovereign state—for many centuries the bulwark of Europe against eastern barbarism—and most ominously for England, a commercial oligarchy. A week later the Directory appointed "Citizen General" Bonaparte Commander-in-Chief of the Army of England.

There could be no doubt what that army was for. "Either our government," its chief wrote to Talleyrand, "must destroy the English monarchy or must expect to be destroyed by the corruption and intrigue of those active islanders. The present moment offers us a fair game. Let us concentrate all our activity upon the navy and destroy England. That done, Europe is at our feet." After a brief stay at Rastadt, where he attended the Imperial Conference which was arranging the new French orientation of Germany, Bonaparte set out for Paris. "Conquest," he declared, "has made me what I am, and conquest can alone maintain me."

He was received with wild enthusiasm. But he saw with the perception of genius that the corrupt, pleasure-loving capital was not ready for his sway. With Madame Tallien enthroned at the Luxembourg by her keeper, Barras, with society a huge demi-monde, and the only conversation of fashions and balls, theatres and restaurants, terror-purged Paris could not yet brook the yoke of the Cæsars. Hungry, desolate France—the embittered peasants and ragged provincials who cheered the young conqueror so deliriously in every town and village on the road—would have to wait a little longer. So would Bonaparte. "After all," he remarked to his aide-de-camp, Junot, "we are only twenty-nine."

So, back in Paris, he bided his time and left the politicians to weave their own ruin. With his slender form, pale face and ascetic ways and his talk of "peace for men's consciences" and "unity for the common good," he seemed more of a Cincinnatus than a Cæsar. He simulated an almost embarrassing modesty, wore in the midst of gilded receptions his old shabby uniform, and ostentatiously affected

[1] Nelson, now recovered from the loss of his arm and waiting at Bath for orders, wrote on January 29th, "I hope all the Nation will subscribe liberally. You will believe that I do not urge others to give and to withhold myself; but my mode of subscribing will be novel in its manner, and by doing it I mean to debar myself of many comforts to serve my country, and I expect great consolation every time I cut a slice of salt beef instead of mutton."—*Nicolas*, III, 5.

the society of artists, bookworms and savants. All the while he busied himself with preparations for the downfall of England. He spent much time in conversations with naval and port officials, attended secret midnight rendezvous with smugglers and privateers familiar with the English coasts, and even gave three interviews to Wolfe Tone, for whom, however, and his country he quickly conceived an immense contempt. Over all he met he exercised his usual extraordinary ascendancy: his lightning mind and dominant will seemed to evoke all the latent energy of men. Even the sleepy French naval authorities began to stir.

All this was attended with much publicity: it was part of the Revolutionary technique. It was meant not only to inspire France but to frighten England. Tales were circulated of huge armoured rafts that the great mathematician, Monge, was constructing, which, 2000 feet long and 1500 broad, guarded by hundreds of cannon and propelled by giant windmills, were each capable of carrying two divisions complete with artillery and cavalry. They were taken quite seriously by English journalists and cartoonists until an ingenious *émigré*, writing in the *Gentleman's Magazine*, pointed out that such a raft would absorb 216,000 trees and weigh 44,000 tons.[1] Fishing smacks were requisitioned in Holland and in the French Atlantic and Channel Ports, the naval dockyards hummed with unwonted activity, canals and rivers far inland were reported to be full of strange, flat-bottomed barges moving towards a single destination. "Go," cried Barras at a reception to Bonaparte at the Luxembourg, "capture the giant corsair that infests the seas; go, punish in London outrages that have been too long unpunished. . . . Let the conquerors of the Po, the Rhine and the Tiber march under your banners. The ocean will be proud to bear you."

More immediate measures were taken against England's commerce. Neutrals, especially those of the Baltic, were warned that every ship carrying British goods or goods of British origin would be seized, and that persistence in trading with the contumacious islanders would mean war. Immense dispositions of men and ships were ordered to be completed by the end of February, 1798, and at the beginning of the month Bonaparte himself left Paris for the northern ports. He was at Dunkirk on the 11th—a tornado of energy, issuing orders, rebukes and exhortations, and leaving again for Ostend on the 13th to arrange for the building of flat-bottomed boats in the Belgian ports. One of Pitt's spies met him on the road to Furnes. The same authority reported that Lille, Douai, Cambrai, Peronne, Evreux and Rouen were full of troops moving oceanwards. He

[1] *Gentleman's Magazine*, Vol. LXVIII, Part I, 1798, 315, cit. Wheeler & Broadley, I, 81.

estimated—a little wildly—that there were 275,000 of them within twenty-four hours of the coast.

The British Regular Army in the United Kingdom at that moment did not number 32,000 men, with some 25,000 temporary Fencibles serving for the war only. A further 40,000 troops were in Ireland. By an act passed in January the embodied Militia was increased from 45,000 to 100,000 men, and the Commander-in-Chief was empowered to enrol up to 10,000 existing Militiamen in the Regular Army to bring its depleted regiments up to strength. Since the evacuation of the Continent the quality of the army had been much improved by the Duke of York's administration. But owing to its premature and reckless use in the West Indies it had not been given a chance to mature. New brigades had been sent overseas before their officers had had time to train them—a politician's pennywise economy that nullified every reform. 40,000 of them had died, mostly of fever, and a further 40,000 had been discharged as unfit through the ravages of that atrocious climate.

For the moment therefore, as in every previous stage in the war, Britain was short of trained troops when she most needed them. But this, though it concerned her rulers, gave little anxiety to her people, for they had now passed far beyond anxiety. Instead of worrying they enrolled in tens of thousands as Volunteers and, lacking arms and training, confidently awaited the attack of the victors of Rivoli and Arcola. In London alone, where the City Fathers called on all male inhabitants to rally to the banner of their wards, 40,000 associated volunteers enrolled. The Government, ignoring memories of mutinies, incitements to riot and treasonable Corresponding Societies, called the population to arms. "This crisis which is approaching," Dundas declared in the House, "must determine whether we are any longer to be ranked as an independent nation. . . . We must fortify the menaced ports, accumulate forces round the capital, affix to the church doors the names of those who come forward as Volunteers and authorise members of Parliament to hold commissions without vacating their seats. I am well aware of the danger of entrusting arms to the whole population without distinction. . . . But, serious as is the danger, it is nothing to the risk we should run if, when invaded by the enemy, we were unprepared with any adequate means of defence."[1]

For the malcontents of three years before had suddenly become insignificant. Most of them had long been swept into the main tide of national consciousness and, like the erstwhile republican exciseman, Robert Burns, had donned the scarlet or blue coat and white

[1] Wheeler and Broadley, I, 126.

nankeen breeches of the local volunteers. In Scotland they were still singing the dead bard's repudiation of his former doubts:

> "The kettle o' the kirk and state,
> Perhaps a claut may fail in't;
> But deil a foreign tinker loon
> Shall ever ca' a nail in't;
> Our fathers' bluid the kettle bought,
> And wha wad dare to spoil it;—
> By heaven, the sacrilegious dog
> Shall fuel be to boil it."[1]

In England the song of the hour was "The Snug Little Island" from Thomas Dibdin's patriotic play, *The British Raft*. First sung at Sadler's Wells on Easter Monday, 1797, it had quickly acquired an immense popularity:

> "Since Freedom and Neptune have hitherto kept tune,
> In each saying, 'this shall be my land';
> Should the army of *England*, or all they could bring land,
> We'd show 'em some play for the island.
> We'll fight for our right to the island,
> We'll give them enough of the island,
> Invaders should just bite at the dust,
> But not a bit more of the island!"

The organisation of the Volunteer forces remained haphazard. The Prince of Wales enrolled his servants *en masse* in a corps attached to the parish of St. James'; the Duke of Northumberland provided clothing and equipment and service pay at a shilling a day for all his tenants and labourers; the Phœnix Insurance office turned its firemen into gunners; and the Bank of England raised eight companies from its clerks to defend its buildings. Every type of uniform and headgear was worn, for every corps chose its own; bearskins, helmets with feathers or hair cockades, facings of red, blue, black, yellow or white.[2] The only feature common to all was a small breastplate bearing the regimental name or initial. Some places

[1] Burns' last days were troubled by a bill for £7 4s. for his volunteer uniform. His comrades of the Dumfries Volunteers—"the awkward squad"—gave him a soldier's burial, little guessing whom they were honouring.

[2] "The first Company of the Bath Volunteers met this day and elected for their Captain, Mr. Bossier; First Lieutenant, Captain Young; Second Lieutenant, Mr. Redwood. They likewise chose at the same time for their uniform, a scarlet jacket with black collar and lappels, white waistcoat, and blue pantaloons edged with red."—*Bath Chronicle*, 3rd May, 1798, cit. Wheeler and Broadley, I, 132.

even formed juvenile corps for training boys in "military manners." Every morning the King was up before dawn signing commissions for all these martial bodies: he indeed was in the heyday of glory. Gillray portrayed him—"*medio tutissimus ibis*"—grinning happily in the midst of a crowd of his devoted people, stout, curtseying matrons, adoring damsels and cadaverous, pigtailed army officers.

"I did not enjoy much of poor Mr. Hoare's company," wrote Hannah More after a visit to town, "so occupied was he in arming and exercising. He rises at half-past four at Mitcham, trots off to town to be ready to meet at six the Fleet Street Corps, performing their evolutions in the area of Bridewell, the only place where they can find sufficient space; then comes back to a late dinner, and as soon as it is over, goes to his committees, after which he has a sergeant to drill himself and his three sons on the lawn till it is dark."[1] For the country in its sober way never doubted that the French ruffians would attempt to land any more than it doubted—provided every Briton did his utmost—that they would meet a bloody end. The venture might be a desperate one, but after five years of war every one knew that the French Jacobins were ruthless monsters who would stop at nothing. Pitt himself, writing in January, felt sure that an invasion would be attempted before the end of the year. The print shops were full of drawings of French rafts and of blood-curdling invasion posters for display on town walls and church doors predicting murders, rapes and robberies. Bonaparte's name had at last begun to circulate among a people notoriously late in their apprehension of Continental events;[2] not as the romantic young genius of patriotic French imagination but as a perverted little monster, slightly comic and wholly horrible, who ground soldiers' bones beneath his carriage wheels, doted on the groans of the dying and perpetuated ghastly massacres, not for policy but for pleasure.

Assured of such a satanic visitation even the clergy could hardly be restrained from flying to arms. In April, 1798, the Archbishops were forced to issue a circular enjoining them not to abandon their sacred calling for a soldier's, in which their service could be but very limited and might not even be wanted at all. "But," it added, "if the danger should be realised and the enemy set foot upon our shores, our hand with that of every man must in every way be against those who come for purposes of rapine and desolation, the

[1] 7th May, 1798, *Hannah More*, II, 12. It was, however, much the same in her Somerset home. "Our quiet village begins to wear a very military aspect . . . Our most respectable neighbours were forming Volunteer corps at their own expense; and the coast just below being one of the places which lie most open to invasion, gun-boats are stationed and fortifications erected."

[2] Despite his astonishing Italian victories, there is no mention of him in the *Annual Register* for 1797.

vowed champions of anarchy and irreligion, defying the living God." A month later the Bishop of London was forced to suspend his Pastoral journey, his Essex diocesans being too full of the prospect of an invasion to pay any attention to ecclesiastical orders.

In spite of all this martial activity and the complete confidence of the average Briton in his power to deal with an invader, there were some misgivings. For one thing there was so grave a shortage of arms that in many districts balls had to be issued for use with fowling pieces. Even from first-line positions like the Isle of Wight came complaints that, though the Militia had been instructed in the use of cannon, these had never arrived.[1] "Associations are forming rapidly and of a real useful kind," a local enthusiast wrote to Whitehall, "but we shall be able to do nothing without arms. . . . We must have the number required from some quarter. We must not suffer again this spirit to cool." In a commercial country much given to individual self-help and little to national planning, there was an inevitable tendency to leave such matters to chance and the laws of supply and demand. An advertisement in the *Bath Chronicle* shows how much:

> "*The Members* of the *Bath Armed Association* may be supplied with *Warranted Firelocks* at £2 each at *Stothert & Co.'s* warehouse, No. 15 Northgate Street.
>
> "Likewise *Pistols* and *Swords* from the first manufactory *Belts* and *Cartouch Boxes*."

It was not only the Volunteers who raised misgivings in the few people in England who knew something of the new continental warfare and the technique of the Revolutionary armies. That fine old soldier, Lord Cornwallis, wrote on February 23rd to a brother of the future Duke of Wellington: "I have no doubt of the courage and fidelity of our Militia, but the system of David Dundas and the total want of light infantry sit heavy on my mind."[2] The new Regular Army had had too little training in European fields to cope on equal terms in enclosed country with a supremely active enemy fresh from triumphs over the most powerful and warlike nations in Europe. Even a politician like Windham was full of apprehension at the deficiency in equipment, the endless muddle and delays, the vague indecisiveness of the dispositions which the Cabinet was perpetually discussing and amending.[3]

[1] *Wheeler and Broadley*, I, 112.
[2] *Cornwallis*, II, 333-4.
[3] *The Diary of the Rt. Hon. William Windham* (ed. Baring), 395.

Not that the Cabinet was without a plan. It had many. "I hope," Pitt wrote in January, 1798, "we shall have to make the option between burning their ships before they set out, or sinking them either on their passage or before their troops can land, or destroying them as soon as they have landed, or starving them and taking them prisoners afterwards." Innumerable suggestions were canvassed, ranging from an antiquarian's report on the measures used against the Armada to an ingenious Pimlico machinist's new war chariot, "in which two persons, advancing or retreating, can manage two pieces of ordnance (three-pounders) with alacrity and in safety, so as to do execution at the distance of two furlongs."[1] Directors were appointed to evacuate cattle and vehicles and waste the countryside in the enemy's path and elaborate instructions issued to the public for the house to house defence of London. Blockhouses were to be built in every square, barricades erected in the principal streets with bells to summon the inhabitants to their stations, hand-grenades served out to corner-houses, night cellars searched for aliens, underground tunnels blocked, fire engines mobilised, guards posted at water works and on bridges, and all boats moved to the north bank of the Thames.

But these preparations would probably have availed little had the country's first line of defence not been the sea. The Channel Fleet with its advance division of great ships off Brest, the light squadrons of frigates and gunboats in the Downs, St. Helens, Portland Road, Cawsand Bay and the Western Approaches, were the real bulwark against the invader. The Admiralty was full of vigour and new-found confidence that spring. It even abandoned its professional conservatism to enrol from the hardy smugglers and fishermen of the south coast an amateur force of Sea Fencibles, to serve in flotillas, gather intelligence and guard the lesser creeks and coves. Gillray came out in February with a cartoon, "The Storm Rising," portraying Fox and his traitor crew vainly hauling over the embattled raft of "Liberty" with its bloody banners of Slavery, Murder, Atheism, Plunder, Blasphemy, while Pitt to repel it blew out of the clouds giant waves labelled with the names of Howe, Duncan, St. Vincent, Gardner and Curtis.

The naval authorities did not however guarantee that the French would be unable to land. In the view of Admiral Sir Charles Middleton, expressed in a letter to Dundas of January 28th, 1798, invasion would be quite a feasible operation. "The truth is," he wrote, "that there are very few things impracticable to active minds with sound judgments, and, if the French will venture to sacrifice

[1] Wheeler and Broadley, I, 119.

50,000 men, of which there cannot be much doubt considering what has already passed, I see no insuperable difficulties in landing 30,000."[1] At the end of February there was an alarm when a report of unidentified ships south of Portland was flashed to London over the new semaphore telegraph which, with its giant arms and shutters and chain of towers stretching from the naval ports to the roof of Westminster Abbey, brought news to the Admiralty from the coasts in a few minutes. Only after a special Cabinet meeting had been called was it learnt that the strange sails belonged to a fleet of homecoming West Indiamen. A few days later there was another alarm when guns were heard firing out at sea at Eastbourne and mysterious lights seen at Brighton.

But the Admirals who advised the Government were not relying on defensive measures. Like Drake, they advocated carrying the war into the enemy's country. They envisaged a number of small, highly-trained, joint naval and military units capable of striking sudden blows at every opportunity.[2] These were to attack the flat-bottomed invasion boats in shallow waters, pounce on their ports, shipping and arsenals and generally keep the French in a constant state of tension and confusion. In the event of a landing they were to transport picked troops by sea and to harass the enemy's rear. General Sir Charles Grey, commanding the south-eastern District, issued from his headquarters at Barham Court, Canterbury, special instructions to all troops in danger zones to train men for such operations. They were to carry only blankets, haversacks and canteens: "not one woman," it was added, "must on this occasion accompany the soldiers. . . . The General is sure that every thinking good soldier will readily see the convenience to themselves and propriety of this order and cheerfully submit to a short separation."[3]

These vigorous offensive measures commended themselves to Secretary Dundas, who was indeed their principal patron and pro-

[1] *Spencer Papers*, II, 269.

[2] "Nothing appears better calculated on the one hand to keep this country in a state of security, and on the other the enemy in a constant state of awe and apprehension, than a sufficient movable sea-and-land force, calculated to act with celerity, and to seize every favourable occasion of destroying their preparations and attacking them on their own coast. Considered as a plan of humbling and distressing the enemy, creating a conviction in France that all their projects of invasion are fraught with disgrace and ruin, and thereby to increase the clamour for peace and against the present government, it is the best that can be undertaken with our present means.

"It is also the best in another view, not less essential to the support of the war at home, namely, as affording the most effectual means of counteracting the manœuvres of the disaffected and the alarms of the desponding, of showing the energy of the nation, and above all of keeping alive the *spirit of enterprise* by which alone our *public spirit* (now fortunately raised by the late conduct of the enemy) can be maintained in a disposition suitable to the difficulties of our situation."—*Anonymous Memorandum* (possibly by Dundas), *Spencer Papers*, II, 235.

[3] *Annual Register*, 1798. Appendix to Chronicle, 189.

tagonist. First nurtured in the school of Chatham he was a strong believer in the principle that the worst defence is to sit still and let the enemy attack. "Our Army is a very small one," he told his colleague of the Admiralty, whom he was constantly favouring with his projects, "but we must make the best use we can of it with a view to the *joint* defence of Great Britain and Ireland, comprehending under that view some mode of at least alarming our enemies along the coast." His mind was full of projects for sinking old ships in the mouth of enemy ports, landing small raiding parties and testing, in his own words, how far Calais or Boulogne or Gravelines might be proper subjects for a few bombs or fireships.[1] "We cannot so effectually annoy the enemy," he wrote, "or keep alive the spirits of our country as by constant unremitting offensive operations during the whole summer."[2] But the weakness of Dundas's method of waging war was that its technical execution never came up to its strategic conception. Incurably a politician, he never grasped the overriding necessity for flawless accuracy of detail that even the simplest operation of war requires. Any expedient or compromise which promised to avoid or turn a difficulty satisfied his mind, and he left the rest to hope.

In April, encouraged by a successful bombardment of Havre, where a small French invasion force was waiting to attack the British island of St. Marcou, Dundas persuaded his colleagues to embark on an ambitious venture against Ostend. The scheme originated in the mind of that clever but incurably plausible naval officer, Captain Home Popham. His idea was to blow up the Saas lock of the new Bruges-Ostend canal, along which the French were expected to move great masses of invasion barges from Holland. Secondary objectives were to destroy the port installations and carry out a raid on transport concentrations at Flushing. Popham, who had the supreme merit to a politician of being always "very sanguine," succeeded in arousing the enthusiasm of General Sir Charles Grey. Together the General and Dundas, who was enthusiastically backed by the Under-Secretary-for-War, Huskisson, so bombarded Spencer that the latter compelled the Admiralty to appoint Popham to the naval command of the expedition. The result was that his superiors in the Service, who regarded Popham with some justice as a young man with more bounce than experience, gave the venture as little support as they could and by needless delays possibly contributed to its failure. 1400 troops, including 600 Guards wrung from a reluctant King, were embarked in flat-

[1] *Spencer Papers*, II, 317.
[2] *Ibid.*, 351-2.

bottomed gunboats and landed under cover of Popham's frigates at Ostend during the night of May 19th. At first all went well: the French were taken by surprise and the sluice gates destroyed with only a few casualties. Then the wind backed into the wrong quarter and, as more experienced sailors than Popham had from the first foreseen, the rising surf made it impossible to re-embark the troops. After several hours of useless resistance, in which sixty men lost their lives, the remainder laid down their arms.

Yet the raid at the moment when all Europe was expecting the invasion of England showed men the dauntless character of the islanders. "The spirit and courage of the country," wrote Pitt, "has risen so as to be fairly equal to this crisis. . . . The French go on, I believe in earnest, but the effect here is only to produce all the efforts and all the spirit we can wish."[1] A distinguished foreign writer, Mallet du Pan, visiting England that May, paid a striking testimony to the national temper. "Here we are in the full tide of war, crushed by taxation, and exposed to the fury of the most desperate of enemies, but nevertheless security, abundance, and energy reign supreme, alike in cottage and Palace. I have not met with a single instance of nervousness or apprehension. The spectacle presented by public opinion has far surpassed my expectation. The nation had not yet learnt to know its own strength or its resources. The government has taught it the secret and inspired it with an unbounded confidence almost amounting to presumption."

[1] Lord Rosebery, *Pitt* (1891), 208.

CHAPTER ELEVEN

Britain Strikes Back

1798

"I trust my name will stand on record when the money-makers will be forgot." *Nelson.*

"Britannia needs no bulwarks,
No towers along the steep;
Her march is o'er the mountain waves:
Her home is on the deep." *Campbell.*

ON Thursday, April 12th, 1798, Parson Woodforde dined on a neck of pork roasted. "By the public papers," he noted, "everything appears most alarming not only respecting Great Britain but every state in Europe and beyond it. *O Tempora O Mores!*" England was expecting invasion, Ireland on the verge of rebellion and the Continent lost. With Austria's surrender the last barriers to French aggression had gone. In February, in flagrant defiance of their own promises, the French marched into Rome, emptied the Papal treasury and sacked the city. In March, on a trumped-up pretext, they invaded Switzerland, seized sixteen million gold francs, annexed Geneva and Mulhausen and proclaimed an "indivisible" Helvetic Republic. Here as in Italy their liberating march was marked by demolished houses, profaned churches, outrage, hatred and fear.[1]

Yet running through all this cruelty and destruction was a thread of policy. The Republic was refilling its coffers before its next pounce. And it was doing so at the instance of General Bonaparte. It was one of his confidential officers, Commandant Berthier, who robbed the Pope. "In sending me to Rome," he wrote, "you appoint me Treasurer to the English expedition: I will endeavour to fill the chest."

But it was no longer a direct leap at the throat of England nor even an assault on Ireland that Bonaparte was planning. His inspections of the ports had convinced him that even temporary command of the narrow seas was at present beyond the reach of France. In a report on his return to Paris on February 23rd he declared that a seaborne invasion without it would be "the boldest

[1] See *Wynne Diaries*, II, 213, 217.

and most difficult operation ever attempted." It was idle to underestimate one's opponent. She was still a great Power, and the Republic must never threaten in vain.

So Bonaparte assured the Directory. Yet it was not of the Republic nor of France that the little Corsican was thinking. He had no fear of British shopkeepers playing at soldiers: the veteran army of Italy, even if only a third of it reached the Kentish shore, would soon make short work of these. As for Ireland the country was already nine-tenths conquered: a few French cannon rumbling over the Cork or Dublin cobble stones that angry spring, and every British throat in the island would be cut. But the chances of tide and wind were too great to stake a world conqueror's course on. There were surer and richer prizes to be won first. After all it would profit Bonaparte little to revolutionise Ireland and overturn Pitt's England only to lose his life or mar his bright star in some sordid, watery skirmish with a chance cruiser. He was not going to waste his incomparable genius to make the world—his oyster—safe for Barras and the plutocrats of the Luxembourg.

For Bonaparte believed that Britain, with her antiquated feudalism, corroding commercial habits and loosening colonial ties, was already doomed. There was no need to strike prematurely at her heart when she was dying at the extremities. Her trade with Europe was at an end, for the greater part of the Continent had entered the Revolutionary order. If her commerce with Asia could be cut also, her bankers and oligarchs would face ruin. Without the colonial produce with which they paid for the grain of the Baltic and supported their unreal structure of usury and broking, their Navy would rot for lack of money. Invasion would become unnecessary.

So Bonaparte told his political masters. The best way to injure England was by an expedition to the Levant and a threat to India where France could avenge herself for lost colonies. The selfish, greedy Directors believed him or pretended to. He wished to be gone. "I can no longer obey," he told a confidant, "I have tasted command and I cannot give it up. Since I cannot be master I shall leave France." There was nothing the Directors more ardently desired. If Bonaparte chose to take himself, his ambitions and his Caesarian army to Egypt he should be enabled to do so.

But had the Directors been able to penetrate his disguise, they would have thought him even more dangerous than they supposed. To the few to whom he dared confide his dreams, he declared that he was about to conquer an eastern empire surpassing the fables of antiquity. He would not only destroy England's sordid hegemony in the Orient but found another, far vaster, in its place. In the East he told his brother Lucien, there were six hundred million men. Compared with Asia, Europe was "a mere molehill." He would not only become its dictator but its prophet. He would found a new religion. His genius and passionate will would mould not only the present but the remote future.[1] "We shall change the fate of the world," he told Talleyrand.

The road to the East was open. By his Italian conquests he had driven the English battleships from the Mediterranean and secured a line of stepping-stones stretching along the Dalmatian and Ionian coasts towards Egypt. It would be child's play to seize that sandy, fabulous land in the name of its remote Turkish Sultan and "free" its effete people from the despotism of its Mameluke "aristocrats." It would only be another repetition of the familiar Revolutionary technique of conquest.

Even before he had completed his inspection of the Flemish ports, Bonaparte had requested the naval authorities at Toulon to hold up the warships ordered for Brest and assemble transports. Three weeks later on March 5th he drew up detailed plans for an Egyptian expedition. Thereafter events, as always when he directed, moved swiftly. On April 12th engineers, openly wearing French uniforms, landed at Alexandria and began to prepare for the reception of military forces and to collect information about the desert roads to Suez, the navigation of the Red Sea and British dispositions in the Indian Ocean. Already French agents were stirring up trouble in the great Indian state of Mysore, and its ruler, Tippoo Sahib, had sent ambassadors to the Jacobin governor of Mauritius to invite a Franco-Arab army to India.

Rumours of these preparations, which had been secretly going forward ever since Bonaparte's rape of Venice, had been slowly filtering through to England. In January Captain Sidney Smith, who was much employed by Grenville in confidential missions, smuggled a message out of Paris, where he was imprisoned, reporting that France had designs on Egypt and the Levant trade, But in its preoccupation with invasion and Ireland, the government paid little attention to such warnings. It had more urgent dangers to consider. With every available ship concentrated in the Channel and off the Irish coast and with St. Vincent blockading a superior force in Cadiz, nothing could be spared for the Mediterranean. A Britain expecting invasion in Sussex could not police the Levant. Since the

[1] "In Egypt," he told Madame de Remusat, "I found myself free from the weariness and restraints of civilisation. I created a religion with a turban on my head and in my hand a new Koran which I should compose according to my own ideas." It is interesting to compare the crazy dreams of Hitler as outlined in Dr. Rauschning's *Hitler Speaks.*

Mediterranean was now a French lake, information from that quarter was in any case notoriously unreliable and took many months of perilous travel to reach England.

Yet by a strange combination of coincidence and daring, the British Government in the crucial spring of 1798 weakened its naval defences at home and sent a fleet into the Mediterranean. It did so without much thought of defeating Bonaparte's grandiose eastern designs, of which it was either ignorant or wholly sceptical. Its object was rather to prompt the European powers to revolt against the Jacobin yoke. For Pitt, knowing that his country could not contend for ever alone against the armed Revolution, was again endeavouring to build up a Coalition. It seemed the surest way of saving Britain.

Already there were signs that this was no empty hope. Prussia still refused to rouse herself from selfish sloth; Russia under her half-mad Emperor Paul remained a remote and inscrutable factor. But Austria, jockeyed at the council table at Rastadt from her ancient leadership of Germany and insulted by upstart Jacobins, was growing restive. In March Chancellor Thugut instructed his ambassador Starhemberg to ask if Britain would aid his country against "a fierce nation irrevocably determined on the total subversion of Europe." And he suggested the return of a British Fleet to the Mediterranean.

At the beginning of April Pitt therefore raised the question in Cabinet. Lord Spencer and the naval authorities were wholly unfavourable. With thirty Spanish battleships at Cadiz and thirty French—in whatever state of readiness—at Brest, with the seven Dutch survivors from Camperdown still at the Helder, Britain would need at least seventy capital ships to justify the risk of detaching even the smallest force to the south. At the moment, though several new ships were nearing completion, she could only dispose of fifty-eight, twenty-four off Cadiz and the remaining thirty-four in home and Irish waters. The dispatch of a battle squadron to the Mediterranean, the Junior Sea Lord reported, might be attended by the most dreadful consequences.[1]

These professional counsels failed to dispirit Pitt. His instinct, which was in accord with that of his country, told him that the moment had come to change to the offensive and that the only real security lay in so doing. Something of his father's spirit and genius for war seemed to have entered into him that spring. He saw clearly that St. Vincent's position off Cadiz would soon be untenable

[1] Observations of Rear-Admiral William Young, wrongly dated February, 1797, in *Spencer Papers*, II, 231. For Spencer's opinion see *ibid.*, 322.

unless the European situation was radically changed in England's favour. Ever since the autumn the feeble Portuguese Court, terrified by the threatening preparations of Spain, had been plotting to free itself from its British treaty commitments and close the Tagus to St. Vincent's provision ships. The intimidating presence of the old Admiral at Lisbon and the masterly handling by General Stuart of a small British force from Elba, which had landed for the defence of Portugal, had so far staved off surrender. But it was ultimately inevitable, for though reports from Cadiz showed that the Spaniards, who had nothing to gain and everything to lose by further Gallic triumphs, were heartily sick of the war, the Directory's contemptuous hold over the dictator Godoy was far too strong to be shaken so long as the French were masters of the Continent.[1]

Pitt, as always when his mind was resolved, carried the Cabinet with him. The increased risk of invasion was not too high a price to pay to bring Austria and her satellite Naples back into the war, and he felt sufficient confidence in the newly-revived spirit of Britain to take it. He was strongly supported by Dundas whose mind, true to the Chatham tradition in which it had been cradled, always ran on the offensive.[2] For all his ignorant and wasteful blunders, the sturdy Scot never lost confidence. "If we can be alive in our offensive movements at home and can strike some great stroke in the Mediterranean," he wrote to the First Lord, "the game must be up with the French government."[3] Grenville and the Foreign Office, with their eyes on the wider interests of Europe, also backed the Prime Minister. So did the chivalrous Windham.[4]

Accordingly on May 2nd, 1798, Cabinet instructions were sent to St. Vincent to detach part of his fleet for a sweep in the Mediterranean. They were accompanied by a private letter from Spencer. "When you are apprised," he wrote, "that the appearance of a British squadron in the Mediterranean is a condition on which the fate

[1] Captain Collingwood wrote on January 26th, 1798, that Spain was no longer an independent nation. Five months later he added: "The Spaniards are well disposed to peace and the interest of their country requires it; but God knows whether their French friends will allow that . . . . Nothing is more certain than that the continuance of the war is disastrous to Spain."—*Collingwood*, 62, 67-8. British and Spanish naval officers corresponded on the friendliest terms, exchanged presents of wine and food and even on occasion entertained one another, while Spanish peasants sold supplies to British sailors. It is interesting to compare this enforced Franco-Spanish alliance with the present relations between Germany and Italy.

[2] See *Spencer Papers*, II, 317.

[3] See *Spencer Papers*, II, 353.

[4] "An English fleet," he had written at an earlier juncture, should be . . . in the Mediterranean to give that succour and protection which I conceive all the countries upon those shores are looking for at our hands and which it would be a proud distinction in us to grant. I long to think that Rome, our common mother, should owe her safety . . . to the protecting justice of Great Britain."—*Windham Papers*, I, 119-20.

of Europe may at this moment be said to depend, you will not be surprised that we are disposed to strain every nerve and incur considerable hazard in effecting it." And the First Lord went on to suggest that in the event of St. Vincent not commanding it in person, it should be entrusted to the junior flag officer on the station, Sir Horatio Nelson.

By a strange coincidence, on the day that this letter was written Nelson left St. Vincent's fleet for the Mediterranean. Only a month before he had sailed from England after a long and painful convalescence. "The wind is fair," he had written to his father from Portsmouth, "in two hours I shall be on board and with the lark I shall be off to-morrow morning." He reached the blockading fleet on April 30th, a little depressed at the prospect of an uneventful summer off Cadiz. Within two days he had been ordered by St. Vincent to proceed with three battleships and five small craft to Toulon to report on the preparations and destination of a powerful French fleet. His mission was not to fight but to obtain information.

For, despite French attempts at secrecy and Bonaparte's studied delay at Paris, news of immense concentrations in Provençal and Italian ports had reached St. Vincent. At Toulon and Marseilles, at Genoa, Civita Vecchia and in Corsica hundreds of transports were assembling, troops embarking and battleships, frigates and corvettes moving into position for some great venture. As early as April 24th, only twelve days after the Directors in Paris had signed the formal order for the Egyptian expedition, *The Times* printed circumstantial details of the force. Three days later the same paper reported its destination to be either Ireland or Portugal. Collingwood wrote on May 1st that the French had announced the objective to be Naples and Sicily—a view strongly held by the terrified Court of Naples—but that the Americans who had brought the intelligence to Cadiz were convinced that it was England.

The possibility of Egypt does not appear to have been seriously canvassed in London. This was the more curious because during April Dundas received warning from a spy of a scheme for sending 400 French officers via Egypt and Suez to India to offer their services to Tippoo Sahib and the Mahratta chiefs and stir up war in Hindustan.[1] And India was always the apple of Dundas's eye. Only a few days earlier in a letter to Spencer he had stated his belief that any European Power gaining control of Egypt would acquire the master key of the world's commerce.

But for the moment the obvious danger to the Empire was not

[1] News of the landing of French engineers at Alexandria on April 20th, 1798, did not reach the British Government till July 5th.

to its circumference but its heart. It never seems to have seriously occurred to the Cabinet that France's impending blow could fall elsewhere. If the new armada in the south was not, like that at Brest, Cadiz and the Texel, intended for the British Isles, it must be bound for Naples and Sicily to forestall any new Coalition and so safeguard the French rear during the hazards of an invasion. By far its most likely destination was Ireland. This was the firm conviction both of the Irish government and of Pitt. The dispatch of part of St. Vincent's fleet to the Mediterranean seemed an anticipation of an encounter which must otherwise be fought off the Irish coast.

. . . .

For here in the island which she had conquered, misgoverned and never understood, proud England was faced with disaster and defeat. Four million Irish were united in a sudden resolve to fling off the yoke of ten million English, Scots and Welsh, themselves engaged in a life and death struggle with more than forty million Frenchmen, Spaniards and Dutchmen. To crush the republicans of United Ireland, Dublin Castle had played its time-honoured trump card of Protestant ascendancy. But instead of crushing republicanism the Protestant ascendancy was itself threatened by a fanatic Catholic insurgence. Holy Ireland had been transformed by the bureaucracy into a Jacobin province.

Dublin Castle had been repeatedly warned of its folly. It had paid no heed. In November, 1797, that fine soldier, Lord Moira—himself an Irish landlord—had declared in the English House of Lords that he had witnessed in Ireland "the most absurd as well as the most disgusting tyranny that any nation ever groaned under." Three months later another soldier made an appeal for a wiser policy. At the end of 1797 Sir Ralph Abercromby, back from the West Indies, was appointed Commander-in-Chief of the Army in Ireland. He found its demoralisation a greater menace to English rule than any invader. At the end of February, 1798, appalled by the outrages that followed the Lord Lieutenant's illegal license to the military to aid the civil power without magisterial authority—in Irish to act as agents of partisan warfare—the old soldier took the grave step of issuing a general order in which he described his army as being in a state of licentiousness that made it "formidable to every one but the enemy."

The only effect of this bombshell was a clamour by the Irish bureaucracy for Abercromby's recall: a demand to which Pitt and Portland gave way.[1] Nothing could shake the obstinacy of Dublin

[1] The King, whose narrowness in religious matters did not extend to questions of Army discipline, refused to countenance his Ministers' betrayal of this brave old soldier and showed him marked attention at the next Levee.

Castle: at every moderating suggestion it pointed to the very real horror of Irish atrocities as a reason for increasing its own oppressions. It was even accused by the Opposition of deliberately inciting a rebellion in order to discredit its opponents. Nothing could have been farther from the truth. Yet nothing could have seemed more like it. For in its intemperate fear of Papist risings, massacres and French landings, it invited all three.

By the spring of 1798 the British garrisons in Ireland outside the Protestant pale were barely holding down the native population. Everywhere little islands of red were receding before a rising tide of sullen green. "The lower ranks," Abercromby wrote in January, "heartily hate the gentlemen because they oppress them and the gentlemen hate the peasants because they know they deserve to be hated."[1] Every one was waiting for the French. A discovery at the end of February revealed the existence of an elaborate channel of communication between Ireland and the Continent. A round of arrests in London was followed on May 19th by the seizure of Lord Edward Fitzgerald in a Dublin slum. Mortally wounded in the encounter the brilliant young Irish aristocrat died a fortnight later.

His arrest threw the Irish leaders into confusion, for he was the pivot on which rebellion turned. It had been planned for the night of May 23rd. But that day the authorities, acting on information, seized thousands of arms. Only a discouraged handful of rebels, assembling in the suburbs of the capital, obeyed the orders of the Irish Rebel Directory. Farther afield in Kildare and Wicklow bands of insurgents attempted to seize strong points on the roads into Dublin but were everywhere repelled.

But on the 26th the revolt broke out in a more serious form and where it was least expected. Led by Father Murphy, a Catholic priest, more than 30,000 armed peasants rose in the thriving countryside of Wexford. Believing their leader to be under the special protection of Heaven they seized the hill of Oulart, annihilated a force of Militia and, advancing on Ferns, burnt the episcopal palace.

Whitsunday, May 27th, was a day of terror. In England it was marked by intense heat and by a strange encounter in a lonely dell of gorse and silver birches on Putney Common. For two days before, during a debate on manning the Navy, Pitt, maddened by the obstructive tactics of the Opposition, had accused Tierney of deliberately sabotaging the country's defence and had been ruled out of order by the Speaker. Refusing to withdraw his words, he had been challenged by the stout irascible Irishman and, before either the

[1] *William Pitt and the Great War*, 352.

King or public opinion could intervene to prevent the scandal, the two statesmen had met and fired off pistols at one another—fortunately without effect. The public alarm was immense.[1] That night London learnt of the rising in Wexford.

Next day the rebels captured Enniscorthy, celebrating their triumph by a night of massacre and arson. Scarcely a Protestant escaped. On the 30th Camden, beside himself with terror, believed the situation to be beyond repair. To crown his fears he had heard three days earlier from Portland: that nine battleships had been sent from the Irish station to reinforce St. Vincent's fleet off Cadiz. He wrote to Pitt on the 29th telling him that Ireland was irretrievably lost without reinforcements from England: it was useless to send cavalry as they were powerless against the pikes of the fanatic peasantry. Pitt replied on June 2nd with the calm habitual to him in time of crisis: the troops, including Guards, had already been dispatched but should be returned as soon as possible so as not to dislocate the general conduct of the war. About the same time he received intelligence that the French fleet had left Toulon, bound, as he believed, for Ireland.

But it was not for Ireland, where on Vinegar Hill 30,000 victorious rebels awaited their long-promised coming, that the French had sailed. Instead of seizing the greatest chance he was ever to know for striking England to the heart, Bonaparte was receding into the Orient for his own personal glory. A moral flaw in her rule of a subject people had placed England at her foe's mercy. A still greater flaw in her foe caused the chance to be neglected. Had the logic of Jacobin philosophy resulted in the rule of a selfless patriot like Carnot such a blunder could never have been made. But it had led inevitably—as Burke had always foretold—to the dictatorship of a scoundrel like Barras and a military adventurer like Bonaparte. For their failings France had to pay dear.

. . . .

The opportunity which the Corsican missed now passed to another. In his public actions Nelson was swayed by only one thought—love of country. "In my mind's eye," he told Hardy, "I ever saw a radiant orb suspended which beckoned me onwards to renown." But by renown he meant not glory for its own sake but for the good of his country. For all the failings of an ardent nature, he was essentially a moral man. Born in a Norfolk parsonage, he was a child of the Church of England. From the influence of its homely piety, he had passed at the age of twelve to the rough life of the Navy. Its leading principle—that of unquestioning duty—had

[1] *Hannah More*, II, 14-15.

been transformed in the crucible of his imagination into a source of passionate inspiration.

Without influence he had risen by sheer merit to the rank of post-captain before he was twenty-one. He impressed every one with whom he came into contact professionally with the sense that he was no common being. But his greatest success was with those under his command. He was a man who led by love and example. There was nothing he would not do for those who served under him. There was nothing they would not dare for Nelson.

The exigencies of peace after the American war and what seemed to his superiors in that mediocre time the inconvenient excess of his zeal for the Service had deprived him in 1787 of employment. For five years he led the life of a poor half-pay officer, eating out his heart ashore, farming his father's glebe and fretting under the tedium of a respectable but ill-assorted marriage. They were years in which his career seemed finished and in which he and his friend Collingwood in like retirement told each other that they despaired of chance ever drawing them back to the seashore.

The outbreak of war found Nelson bombarding the Admiralty with requests for a ship, though it were only a cockle boat. They gave him a sixty-four, and since then—save for a winter's sick leave after the loss of his arm—he had been on continuous service in the Mediterranean, cheerfully fulfilling every mission entrusted to him and by his anxiety to excel in the execution of duty winning a reputation for almost foolhardy gallantry. For four years he had toiled and waited for his hour until the discernment of Jervis and the chance of battle at St. Vincent brought him on to a wider stage. Then in his first independent command as a flag officer he had tasted defeat—albeit glorious defeat—at Tenerife. He had returned to England physically shattered, with the hope of ever serving again almost vanished.

Now, nearing his fortieth year, he was again in command, with his reputation a little uncertain as of a man too reckless for his age. His countrymen, slow to recognise intellect, knew his courage and ardour but had little conception of the quality of his mind. They had yet to realise its infinite capacity for taking pains, its knife-like penetration, its brilliant clarity. Its very lucidity, reducing every scheme and command to elemental terms such as a child could understand, tended to deceive them. They thought of him as a simple sailorman. They never conceived of him, till his miraculous deeds enlightened them, as the supreme embodiment of the genius of their country.

After many years of apprenticeship, he was now to be pitted

against the most dazzling genius of his age—himself the embodiment of that great and terrifying explosion of human energy which patient England was struggling to hold in bounds. Nelson's success or failure was to depend on his ability to guess and anticipate the thought of his adversary. To that test he brought qualities of an almost unique order: immense professional knowledge and experience, the fruits of life-long application and discipline, selfless devotion to duty, inspired courage, a great heart and the imagination which can mobilise the evidence of the present and past to predict the future. His was that strange combination of brooding patience, study and intense concentration with a mercurial temperament that rose like lightning out of storm and in the hour chosen of destiny lighted the path to victory. Above all his power was based, like his country's, on adherence to moral law: once he was convinced that a course was right, nothing could shake his constancy to it and the burning tenacity of his purpose. The strength of his will was equal to Napoleon's. And because it derived more consistently from enduring principles it prevailed. Nelson's career of fame rose from victory to ever greater victory. Napoleon's rose and then fell.

. . . .

On the 8th of May, 1798, Nelson left Gibraltar with three ships of the line and five frigates, sailing at dusk to conceal his eastward course from watching eyes. Nine days later, cruising in the Gulf of Lyons, one of his frigates captured a French corvette from Toulon whose crew under examination disclosed that the famous General Bonaparte had arrived in the port from Paris, that thousands of troops were embarking and that fifteen battleships of the line were waiting to sail.

Had it not been for the usual confusion and corruption of the Revolutionary ports they would have sailed already. Nearly 40,000 picked troops, more than three hundred transports and fifty warships had been assembled. This huge armada was laden not only with horse, foot, artillery and stores of war but with engineers, architects and professors of every science and art, "from astronomers down to washerwomen."[1] It was equipped for colonisation as well as for conquest. It was commanded by a brilliant galaxy of talent, for under Bonaparte's triumphant banner sailed Kléber, Desaix, Davout, Lannes, Murat, Bessieres, Marmont and Junot, while Brueys, with Ganteaume, Decrès and Villeneuve, directed the fleet.

On the 19th, the day of Lord Edward Fitzgerald's arrest, the main division of the expedition with Bonaparte aboard weighed from Toulon, coasting north-eastwards along the Riviera shore in

[1] *Collingwood*, 69.

the direction of Genoa to gather its consorts. Nelson did not see it sail for he was still some way from the port. On the following night his flagship, the *Vanguard*, suffered disaster, her newly commissioned crew losing main and mizen topmasts and foremast in a sudden gale. For two days she was battered by the waves off the Sardinian coast and was only saved from total wreck by the cool daring of Captain Ball of the *Alexander*, who took her in tow and persisted in spite of intense danger to his own ship in bringing her under the lee of San Pietro Island.

Here on May 24th, while British sailors and Irish patriots were fighting in the village streets of Meath and Kildare, Nelson wrote to his wife to tell her of his setback. "I firmly believe that it was the Almighty's goodness to check my consummate vanity." In four days of herculean labour, the *Vanguard* was rigged with jury-masts and made fit for sea. Then with his three battleships Nelson sailed for the secret rendezvous where his frigates, scattered by the storm, were to have awaited him. But when he reached it on June 4th the frigates were not there. Next day, still waiting, he received momentous tidings. For Hardy in the dispatch brig *Mutine* arriving from Cadiz brought news not only of the errant frigates which, despairing of the *Vanguard's* plight, had gone to Gibraltar, but of Nelson's appointment to the command of a fleet. The opportunity for which he had waited so long had arrived.

It had come at a strange moment. Bonaparte had sailed a fortnight before and had gone no one knew where. A few days after Nelson had left Cadiz St. Vincent had received Spencer's instructions about sending a fleet into the Mediterranean. Though the Spaniards, under orders from Paris, made as if about to put out of Cadiz, and though a concerted movement of United Irishmen threatened a new outbreak of mutiny in the Fleet, the old Admiral never hesitated. On May 19th he despatched Hardy with Nelson's commission. On the 21st, without even waiting for the arrival of the promised reinforcements from England, he sent his ten finest battleships and captains —the élite of the Fleet—under Troubridge to join Nelson.

On June 6th Troubridge found his new commander. It was characteristic of Nelson that he refused to transfer his flag from the storm-battered *Vanguard*. His other two battleships were beyond the horizon searching for the newcomers. He did not wait for them but left the fifty-gun *Leander* to bid them follow. His orders were couched in the broadest terms. He was to pursue the Toulon fleet and attack it wherever found. Since Britain had no base in the Mediterranean and necessity dictated, he was not to stand on ceremony with neutrals. Should they out of terror of the French refuse to grant him supplies he was to compel them at the cannon's mouth.

His instructions gave him little clue as to Bonaparte's destination. They mentioned Naples, Sicily, Portugal and Ireland, but made no reference to Egypt. He had no reliable information as to the strength of the French battle fleet though he believed it to consist of fifteen or sixteen ships of the line. He knew even less of its whereabouts. Having no frigates he could not comb the seas for intelligence. He had only the light of his intellect to follow and the strength of his will. "Be they bound to the Antipodes," he assured Spencer, "your Lordship may rely that I will not lose a moment in bringing them to action."[1]

Following the course of the French he skirted the Genoese Riviera and Italian coast. The seas were strangely empty, for the French control of the Mediterranean had banished most of its former commerce. Day after day no sail appeared on the blue horizon. Once a convoy of distant Spanish merchantmen was sighted—plunder that might have made his captains rich with prize money and bought him some fine estate in England with white Jane Austen house and trim lawns and deer park. But his mind was set on his purpose and he let them pass unmolested. He dared not lose an hour.

On June 14th, while far away the fate of Ireland trembled in the balance and the rebel leaders in the green-bannered camp on Vinegar Hill waited for the tidings of French sails, Nelson obtained second-hand news from a passing ship that ten days earlier a great fleet had been seen to the west of Sicily. He accordingly sent the *Mutine* ahead to Naples with a letter begging Sir William Hamilton, the British Ambassador, to urge the king and his English-born Prime Minister, Acton, to shake off their subservience to the dreaded Jacobins and strike while the iron was hot. On the 17th he arrived off the port to learn what he had already suspected: that the French had gone to Malta and were either about to attack or had already attacked that island stronghold.

In a fever of excitement he wrote again to Hamilton. The Neapolitan king, who hated the French, whose sister-in-law had died on the scaffold in Paris, who had secretly implored British aid, had a unique opportunity to strike a blow which should save his throne, liberate Italy and shatter the dark clouds that hung over Europe. The most formidable of French generals and the flower of the French army were at his mercy. For though Nelson had with him a matchless instrument, it could only do the work of a battle fleet. To destroy the enemy, if at Malta, he needed fireships, gunboats and bomb vessels; to annihilate their transports, if at sea, he must

[1] Mahan, *Nelson*, I, 327.

have frigates. The Court of the Two Sicilies, if it would take its courage in its hands, could supply both. "The King of Naples may now have part of the glory in destroying these pests of the human race; and the opportunity, once lost, may never be regained."

But though the timorous Italians sent good wishes and a secret promise of supplies, they would dare no more. Nelson must beat the French before they would stir, even though their craven inertness robbed him of all chance of victory and themselves of survival. Without wasting time, though still bombarding Hamilton with letters, he pressed through the Straits of Messina and, crowding on all sail, hurried southward down the coast of Sicily heading for Malta where he hoped to catch the enemy at anchor. On the 22nd at the southern point of Sicily off Cape Passaro the *Mutine* fell in with a Genoese brig and learnt from her master that the French had captured Malta from the Knights of St. John—which was true—and—which was not true—had sailed again on the 16th eastward bound.

With the instinct of genius, though his instructions had given him no inkling of it, Nelson had already divined Bonaparte's intention. A few days earlier he had written to Spencer, "If they pass Sicily, I shall believe they are going on their scheme of possessing Alexandria and getting troops to India—a plan, concerted with Tippoo Sahib, by no means so difficult as might at first view be imagined."[1] His instructions cautioned him against allowing the French to get to the west of him lest they should slip through the Straits of Gibraltar. But he reckoned that with the prevailing westerly winds Bonaparte's vast and unwieldy armada had little chance of beating back to the Atlantic. Egypt on the other hand would be an easy run for it. If it left Malta on the 16th, it must be already nearly at Alexandria.

Nelson therefore decided to act. He called a council of his captains, but the result was a foregone conclusion. Men like himself in the prime of life—their average age was under forty—they were little given to hesitation. They endorsed his opinion that all the probabilities—the seizure of Malta, the reported equipment of the expedition, the direction of the wind and the enemy's point of sailing—pointed to Bonaparte's having gone to Egypt. The safe course was for the British to await events where they were: guarding the two Sicilies, keeping the weather gauge and making sure that the enemy could not get to westward. A lesser man than Nelson,

[1] Mahan, *Nelson*, I, 328. "If they have concerted a plan with Tippoo Sahib to have vessels at Suez, three weeks at this season is a common passage to the Malabar coast, where our India possessions would be in great danger.—*Ibid*, I, 334.

playing for his professional career and safety from official censure, would have taken it. But to have done so would have been to abandon that for which he had set out: the annihilation of the French fleet and transports. With the stake nothing less than the future of the world, he at once set course for Alexandria.

. . . .

But the French had not sailed from Malta on June 16th. They had appeared off the island on the 9th and summoned its international custodians, the Knights of St. John, to surrender. The scene had been carefully set: the Maltese had no stomach for their rich and obese masters' cause, the island was swarming with French agents and traitors, and the Knights, comfortably set in their ways and undermined by subtle propaganda, were divided as to the advisability of resistance. After three days discussion they surrendered, and Bonaparte, whose besieging armada would otherwise have fallen an easy prey for Nelson on the 22nd, took possession of Valetta—"the strongest place in Europe." Here he remained for nearly a week, helping himself to the accumulations of seven centuries of luxurious and cultured living. Then, leaving a strong garrison behind him to hold the strategic half-way house to France, he sailed on the 19th for Alexandria after making arrangements to dispose of the booty.

So it came about that Nelson's look-outs on June 22nd saw the sails of French frigates on the far horizon. But Nelson did not stop to investigate them for he guessed that they could not belong to Bonaparte's main fleet which, according to his own information, had left Malta six days before. Had he possessed any frigates of his own, he would soon have discovered his error. But to have pursued the French with his battle fleet alone would have led him nowhere for they would inevitably have lured him away from his real quarry, the great ships and transports. So instead he kept on his course. Shortly afterwards darkness fell, and during the night, which was hazy, the British line of battle, swift, compact and intent, passed unknowing through the converging track of the French expedition. The sound of the British minute guns firing through the mist caused the French Admiral to sheer away to the northward in the direction of Crete. Had dawn come half an hour earlier it would have revealed him and his helpless transports *flagrante delicto*. But by sunrise on the 23rd the last French sails were just below the horizon.

That was one of the decisive moments of the world's history. A long train of events had brought the two fleets to that place at that hour, of which the most important were Bonaparte's dynamic ambition and Nelson's zeal for duty. Had they clashed the result would have been certain: the élite and cadre of the Grande Armée would have found a watery grave seventeen years before Waterloo and its terrible chieftain would either have shared it or become a prisoner of the English. For superior though they were on paper—in size and gun power though not in numbers—the French battleships would have been no match on the open sea for the British. Old and shamefully neglected during their long-enforced sojourn in port, destitute of marine stores and crowded with useless soldiers, they could never have withstood those lean, stripped, storm-tested dogs of war from St. Vincent's fleet. Their crews, drawn from the lawless dregs of the Revolutionary ports, had had little training in gunnery or manœuvre. Nelson's knew exactly what to do. Thanks to the Cabinet's bold resolution, to St. Vincent's discipline and self-abnegation, above all to Nelson's inspired fixity of purpose, the blundering, persistent patience of Pitt's England seemed on the afternoon of June 22nd, 1798, about to be rewarded. Bonaparte, epitomising the Revolutionary weakness for desperate gambling, had staked everything on Britain's not being able to send a fleet to the Mediterranean. And now at the moment that he was reaching out to grasp the prize of the Orient, the British Fleet crossed his path. . . .

Crossed it and vanished. The Corsican's star had proved too strong and bright for the clumsy purpose of England. But Bonaparte's fortune did not only lie in his star. With all his genius, he could not understand why his Admirals trembled so at the thought of encountering a British fleet in mid-ocean. He had 40,000 soldiers with him: he had only to close and let them board the English corsairs. With England's many dangers nearer home there could not be many of them. He had never seen the destructive power of a British man-of-war in action: could not, battle-scarred though he was, conceive it. Not destiny—which had still to obliterate his bright name—but an error of Britain had saved him. Lack of frigates alone robbed Nelson of a victory that should have been Trafalgar and Waterloo in one. Again and again St. Vincent had pleaded with the Admiralty for more frigates: pleaded in vain. He had had to send his brilliant subordinate into the Mediterranean with too few and these—now vainly seeking him—had failed him. Treasury parsimony, the unpreparedness of a peace-loving people, above all the needs of restless, ill-treated Ireland had all contributed to this fatal flaw. It was to cost Britain and the civilised world seventeen more years of war, waste and destruction.

. . . .

So it came about that on the 23rd the two fleets, having converged, passed out of reach of one another, Brueys with his momentous freight edging cumbrously northwards towards the greater security of Crete, Nelson with every inch of canvas spread direct for Alexandria hoping to catch Bonaparte before he could disembark. "We are proceeding," wrote Captain Saumarez of the *Orion*, "upon the merest conjecture only, and not on any positive information. Some days must now elapse before we can be relieved from our cruel suspense."[1] On the sixth day Nelson reached Alexandria and to his unspeakable chagrin found the roads empty. No one had seen anything of Bonaparte's armada, though the sleepy Turkish authorities were making languid preparations to repel it and threatening to decapitate any belligerent who dared to land in their country.[2] Still believing in his false information that the French had left Malta on the 16th, it never occurred to Nelson that they had not yet covered the distance. Without waiting he at once put to sea again, steering for the Syrian coast in hope of news of a landing at Aleppo or an attack on the Dardanelles.

As early on June 29th the British sails dropped over the eastern horizon, watchers at Alexandria saw the French rise over the western. Hampered by its lack of skill, vast size and triangular course, Bonaparte's expedition, averaging only fifty miles a day, had taken just double the time of its pursuer. Once more, cruelly crippled by his lack of frigates, Nelson had missed an epoch-making victory by a few hours. With nearly four hundred vessels the French had crossed the Mediterranean and had not lost a ship. With the superb arrogance of their race and revolutionary creed they boasted that the British had not dared to measure their strength against them. But, though he had still no idea how narrow had been his escape, Bonaparte wasted no time before disembarking. On the 1st of July he landed and issued a grandiloquent proclamation in the style of Mahomet calling on the Faithful to rise against the Mamelukes. On the 5th he stormed Alexandria, putting all who resisted to the sword. A fortnight later, advancing at his habitual speed across the desert, he routed the main Egyptian army under the shadow of the Pyramids. On the 22nd he entered Cairo. Another nation had been overwhelmed.

Meanwhile Nelson, fretting with impatience and full of remorse "for the kingdom of the Two Sicilies," had sought in vain for his elusive quarry in the Gulf of Alexandretta. Thence, skirting the shores of Crete, he beat back against westerly winds to Syracuse. Years later he told Troubridge that in his mortification he believed

[1] Mahan, *Nelson*, I, 336.

[2] *Lloyd's Evening Post*, 19th-21st Sept., 1798.

he had almost died through swelling of the vessels of the heart. To St. Vincent, to whom he wrote to ease his mind, he declared that the only valid objection he could conceive against the course he had taken was that he should not have gone such a long voyage without more certain information. "My answer is ready—'Who was I to get it from?' . . . Was I to wait patiently till I heard certain accounts? If Egypt was their object, before I could hear of them they would have been in India. To do nothing, I felt, was disgraceful: therefore I made use of my understanding and by it I ought to stand or fall. I am before your Lordship's judgment (which in the present case I feel is the tribunal of my country) and if under all the circumstances it is decided that I am wrong, I ought, for the sake of the country, to be superseded."

Already in England men who knew nothing of the circumstances were saying that he should be. The news of his appointment had been greeted with a clamour of tongues: Collingwood wrote from Cadiz that the resignation of two senior Admirals, furious at being passed over, had interrupted all intercourse of friendship in St. Vincent's fleet, which was in consequence in a most unpleasant state.[1] Their friends and many others naturally said that Nelson had blundered. A man not yet forty was not fit to command a fleet on so important a service. Tempers were short in England in the summer of 1798: the long suspense of the spring and the reaction when no invasion came were beginning to fray men's nerves. The Irish rebellion, suppressed after four anxious weeks by Lake's victory at Vinegar Hill, was still simmering. It was known that Bonaparte was at large and that Nelson had failed to find him. He might by now be in Naples or he might be sailing towards Ireland. All that was certain was that Nelson had missed him: had bungled his mission. There were demands for his recall and for the resignation of the Ministers who had appointed him.

On July 19th, with his water nearly exhausted, Nelson reached Syracuse, having in his own words gone a round of six hundred leagues with an expedition incredible and being at the end of it as ignorant of the enemy's situation as at the beginning. "The Devil's children," he wrote, "have the Devil's luck!" His only thought was to be off again. He suffered agonies when the governor of the port, standing on his neutrality, refused to admit more than four ships at a time for revictualling. "Our treatment is scandalous for a great nation to put up with," he wrote to Lady Hamilton, "and the King's flag is insulted. . . . If we are to be kicked in every port of the Sicilian dominions, the sooner we are gone the better. . . . I have

[1] *Collingwood*, 70. See *Farington* I, 236, 244.

only to pray I may find the French and throw all my vengeance on them."[1]

But when the tactful offices of the Hamiltons at the Neapolitan Court had secured an open welcome and ample supplies for the fleet, the essential magnanimity of the man returned. He reproached nobody but himself. "Your Lordship," he wrote to St. Vincent, "deprived yourself of frigates to make mine the first squadron in the world.... But if they are above water, I will find them out and if possible bring them to battle. You have done your part in giving me so fine a fleet, and I hope to do mine in making use of them."[2]

On the 25th he was ready for sea. Disregarding the protests of the Neapolitan Prime Minister, who wished him to stand sentinel over the Sicilies, he sailed again, this time—since all intelligence showed that the French were not to the west of him—towards the Morea. With all canvas spread the great ships sped on their search—*Culloden*, *Theseus*, *Alexander* and *Swiftsure; Vanguard*, *Minotaur*, *Defence*, *Audacious*, *Zealous; Orion*, *Goliath*, *Majestic*, *Bellerophon*. The sea was empty, for their journeying had filled the French authorities in every port of southern Europe with dread.[3] They sailed in order of battle, in three compact divisions in case the French should be encountered at sea: two to tackle Brueys' battle fleet and the other to do the work of the missing frigates and destroy the transports.

Every day throughout the long chase the men were exercised at their guns and small arms. Whenever the weather permitted the captains went aboard the *Vanguard* to discuss with the Admiral the precise function which each was to fulfil in battle. In the "school for captains" on Nelson's quarterdeck they unconsciously entered into his mind till each of his ideas—lucid, precise and devised against every eventuality—became as natural to them as to him. Long linked by the comradeship of sea and Service, these rough, weather-beaten men, with their wonderful professional skill were distilled into a single instinctive instrument of war in the alembic of Nelson's mind and spirit. They became what in his love he called them—a band of brothers.

The keynote of the fleet's readiness for battle was a minute imaginative attention to detail: the sure hall-mark of a great leader. "No man," Mahan has written, "was ever better served than Nelson by the inspiration of the hour; no man ever counted less

[1] Mahan, *Nelson*, I, 340-1.

[2] Mahan, *Nelson*, I, 341.

[3] A convoy of twenty-six large supply ships, urgently needed by Bonaparte, lay in Toulon harbour all the summer for fear of Nelson.—Mahan, *Sea Power*, I, 291.

on it." Every ship was ready day and night for action: every man schooled in an exact part. Five thousand wills and bodies moved to a single purpose infinitely diversified in individual function. It was a living discipline that wasted nothing: of muscle, mind or matter. Everything was prepared because everything was foreseen. Thus in the *Alexander* Captain Ball had every spare shroud and sail constantly soaked in water and rolled tight into hard non-inflammable cylinders.

On the 28th, three days after leaving Syracuse, Nelson obtained news of the French from some Greek fishermen in the Gulf of Koron. A month before a great fleet had been seen spread far over the seas sailing south-eastwards from Crete. With the wind in the west for the past month it was evidence enough. Bonaparte must have gone to Egypt after all. Once more all sail was set for Alexandria.

A little before noon on August 1st, 1798, the Pharos of Alexandria became visible and soon after the minarets of the city and the masts of merchantmen in the port. But of the French fleet there was no sign. Sending the *Swiftsure* and *Alexander* in to investigate more closely, Nelson sadly turned eastwards along the coast as he had done a month before. Dinner was a meal of gloom on every ship: "I do not recollect," wrote Captain Saumarez of the *Orion*, "ever to have felt so utterly hopeless as when we sat down. Judge what a change took place when, as the cloth was being removed, the officer of the watch came running in saying, 'Sir, a signal is just now made that the enemy is in Aboukir Bay and moored in a line of battle.'" In an instant every one was on his feet and every glass charged. As Saumarez came out of his cabin on to the quarterdeck, the crew broke into exultant cheers.

At the masthead of the *Goliath*, leading the fleet with the *Zealous*, the straining eyes of Midshipman Elliot scanning the low Egyptian shore in the hot haze had caught the first sight of those heavenly masts. Fearing to hail the quarterdeck, lest keen ears in *Zealous* should hear and gain the credit, the exultant boy slid quickly down a backstay and ran to Captain Foley with his tidings. But before the fluttering signal, "Enemy in sight," could reach the masthead, *Zealous* had guessed the meaning of the scurry and cluster of flags on the deck of her sister ship and had been before her. As the signal reached each crowded ship, a "wave of joy" ran through the fleet. Nelson, whose inflexible will had equalled Bonaparte's, had run his quarry to earth at last. "If we succeed," cried Berry voicing his unspoken thought, "what will the world say?" "There is no *if* in the case," replied Nelson, "that we shall succeed is certain; who will live to tell the story is a very different question."

Fifteen miles east of Alexandria the French battle fleet lay at anchor in a great bay guarded by shoals to eastward and by the batteries of Aboukir Castle at its western end. There were sixteen ships in all, thirteen of the line with the *Orient*, Brueys' giant flagship, in the centre of the line. They lay as close inshore as the sandbanks allowed, forming for nearly two miles a line of thousands of guns with 160 yards between each ship. At the head of the line, guarding it from approach from the west, lay Aboukir island crowned with mortars.

At half-past two, about the same time as the English sighted their prey, the French look-outs saw the English sails. As his van was so strongly protected and as to attack his centre or rear his assailants would have to face the concentrated fire of his whole line, Brueys felt convinced that there would be no battle that day. It was to his advantage that it should be postponed. His ships were bigger than the British and more heavily gunned, but many of his men were ashore, discipline was lax and the decks were cumbered with stores and booty. Only the most reckless of foes would be likely to attack him in so strong a position with equal or inferior force. By the time they could reach the bay and negotiate the sandbanks it would be almost dark. It would be insanity for them to attack at night. Brueys was, like most ordinary commanders, a static man and he imagined that he had to do with static men like himself.

But the British squadron never paused. It came on out of the west with all sails set. For Nelson at his journey's end was as eager to do that for which he had come as Bonaparte had been to land and take possession of Egypt. His sufferings and anxiety were over at last. He viewed the obstacles, his flag-captain noted, with the eye of a seaman determined on attack. He saw the strength of the French centre, where Brueys had concentrated his greatest ships and of its rear where the next strongest were gathered. But he also saw the weakness of the van if he could bring his fleet round inside the island and pass between it and the leading ships. And though he had no chart of the shoals except a rough plan taken from a prize, "it instantly struck his eager and penetrating mind that where there was room for an enemy's ship to swing, there was room for one of his to anchor."[1]

It had always been Nelson's plan, discussed on innumerable occasions with his captains, should he find the enemy at anchor to throw the whole weight of his strength on a part of their line and crush it before the rest could come to their aid. Only by doing so

[1] Capt. Berry's account.—*Nicolas*, III, 50.

could he win the annihilating victory which it was his purpose to achieve: the ding-dong battles of the past two centuries, in which every Englishman laid himself alongside a Frenchman and battered away till one side tired and drew off, could not give it him. There was only just time to work round the island and the shoals before night fell: three of his thirteen capital ships—the *Swiftsure* and *Alexander* reconnoitring Alexandria and the *Culloden* towing a prize—were some miles away and could not reach the scene of battle before darkness. There was no opportunity for consultation or elaborate signals; but there was no need for them. Every captain knew what was in his Admiral's mind. At five-thirty he flew the signal to form line of battle in order of sailing, and silently and imperceptibly without slackening their majestic advance the great ships slid into their appointed places. The *Goliath*, whose look-out midshipman had revenged himself on his rival in the *Zealous* by anticipating Nelson's signal while it was still fluttering to the masthead, took the lead. The flagship dropped back to the sixth place where the Admiral could exercise tactical control of the battle, seeing how his leading ships fared and using his position to vary the disposition of the remaining five.

In the hour of suspense Nelson made two other orders. In order to guide the latecomers and avoid the danger of Briton firing on Briton, every ship was directed to hoist four lights at the mizen peak. And on reaching her allotted station she was to anchor by the stern instead of by the head and so place herself in immediate fighting posture. By this simple precaution the enemy was denied the opportunity of raking each British ship as her bows swung round into the wind.

Having rounded the island and "hauled well round all dangers," the ships, avoiding the direct approach, shortened sail and hugging the coast worked their way to windward of the van—the weakest, because in his belief the securest, part of Brueys' position. The sun was just setting—"and a red and fiery sun it was"—as they went into the bay. Down below the men were stripping to their trousers, opening the ports and clearing for action: an officer commanding at the guns jotted down the following conversation:

Jack: "There are thirteen sail of the line, and a whacking lot of frigates and small craft. I think we'll hammer the rust off ten of them, if not the whole boiling."

Tom: "We took but four on the first of June, and I got seven pounds of prize-money. Now, if we knock up a dozen of these fellows (and why shouldn't we?) d—n my eyes, messmates, we will have a bread-bag full of money to receive."

Jack: "Aye, I'm glad we have twigged 'em at last. I want some new rigging d-bly for Sundays and mustering days."

Tom: "So do I. I hope we'll touch enough for that, and a d—d good cruise among the girls besides."[1]

It had been Nelson's plan to anchor one of his ships alternately on the bow and quarter of each of the leading Frenchmen. But whether by an eleventh hour suggestion of the Admiral or by his own inspiration Captain Foley of the *Goliath*, who was the only officer in the fleet with a French chart, rounded the head of the enemy lines and, sounding as he went through the shallow waters, attacked it from the shoreward side. It was a feat of superb seamanship. Relying on the proximity of the sandbanks the French had never conceived such a thing possible and, feeling themselves safe, had not even taken the trouble to clear the port batteries, which were carelessly cluttered up with stores. *Zealous*, *Orion*, *Theseus* and *Audacious* followed *Goliath*. As each leviathan swept past the undefended flank of the leading French ships she swept them in turn with a fire that left them helpless and broken. Within ten minutes all the *Guerrier's* masts were gone, and within ten minutes more the *Conquerant's* and *Spartiate's*.

Meanwhile Nelson led the *Vanguard* and the remaining ships against the other side of the French line. By seven o'clock, within half an hour of the commencement of the action, the five leading seventy-fours were being raked by eight English ships of similar size and greatly superior to them in gunnery while their consorts to leeward watched helpless and inactive. Two British ships, the *Majestic* and *Bellerophon*, over-shooting their mark in the growing darkness, engaged the French centre, the first losing her captain in a swift interchange of broadsides with the *Heureuse* and then passing on to engage the *Mercure*, while the second audaciously placed herself alongside Brueys' flagship, *Orient*—a vessel of nearly twice her size.

Wrought to the highest tension by their long, tenacious pursuit, the British fought, as Berry put it, with an ardour and vigour impossible to describe. The French also fought with great gallantry. Captain Dupetit Thouars of the *Tonnant*, after losing both arms and a leg, had his dying trunk placed in a tub on the quarterdeck where he refused to strike his colours though every mast was gone and every gun disabled. But the British were fighting with the certain

[1] Long, 201.

conviction of victory and, every man knowing what to do in all emergencies, with an order and freedom from confusion absent in the Republican ships. Early in the engagement, when the issue was already a foregone conclusion, Nelson was struck on the forehead by a piece of flying iron from the *Spartiate's* langridge. Flung to the deck and blinded by the strip of bleeding flesh that fell over his solitary eye, he was carried below thinking himself a dying man. Here in the crowded cockpit he lay in intense pain, insisting on taking his turn at the surgeon with the other wounded men and constantly calling with what he believed to be his dying breath for news of the battle. Once he bade Berry hail the *Minotaur*, anchored ahead of the *Vanguard*, that he might thank Captain Louis for his conduct before he died. Already three enemy ships had struck and three more were disabled, and with his brain wandering a little he endeavoured to dictate a dispatch to the Admiralty. His secretary was too overwrought to write, so the blinded man took the pen himself and with trembling hand traced the words: "Almighty God has blessed His Majesty's arms . . ."

By now the British reserve was entering the fight. The *Culloden*, the finest ship in the fleet, had met with disaster, her brave Captain Troubridge, in his anxiety to arrive in time, having taken the island too close and struck on the tail of the shoal. Here he remained all night in full view of the battle and in a state of agitation impossible to conceive, suffering the pounding of the sea and struggling to clear his vessel. But he served as a beacon for the *Swiftsure* and *Alexander* hurrying up from the west. The two great ships, furiously fired at by the battery on the island, rounded the reef safely in the haze and darkness and swept down on the centre of the French line, guided by the flashes of the guns and the lanterns gleaming through the British gun ports. In both vessels absolute silence was preserved, no sound being heard but the helmsman's orders and the shout of the leadsman calling the depths.

At one moment a dark shape loomed up in front of the *Swiftsure*. It was the *Bellerophon*, dismasted after her duel with the *Orient*, drifting out of the fight with a third of her crew dead or disabled. Only Captain Hallowell's flawless discipline prevented her from being swept by the *Swiftsure's* guns before her identity was revealed. But, despite the suspense and the spasmodic fire of the French, not a shot was fired. At 8.3 p.m. precisely the *Swiftsure* dropped into the *Bellerophon's* vacant berth two hundred yards from the French flagship. At 8.5, anchored and with her sails clewed up, she opened out with a tremendous broadside. A few minutes later Captain Ball in the *Alexander* followed suit.

It was about nine o'clock that Hallowell, still fresh to the fight, noticed flames pouring out of one of the cabins of the *Orient*. He at once directed every available gun on the spot. The fire spread quickly owing to the way that oil, paint and other combustibles had been left about the French flagship. As the great vessel, the finest in the Republican navy, blazed more fiercely, every British ship in the neighbourhood trained her guns on her. Down in the hold of the British flagship Nelson heard of the impending fatality and insisted on being led up on deck to watch: as soon as he saw her imminence of doom he ordered the *Vanguard's* only undamaged boat to be lowered to rescue the survivors. With the fire racing downwards towards the *Orient's* magazine, the ships about her closed their hatches or drifted away to avoid the explosion. Only *Swiftsure* and *Alexander* remained firing grimly up to the last moment, with long lines of men with buckets stationed to extinguish the outburst when it came.

At a quarter to ten the *Orient* blew up with a terrifying detonation. The shock could be felt by French watchers at Rosetta ten miles away, and down in the magazine of the *Goliath* the boys and women[1] at their blind, monotonous task of passing up the powder thought that the after-part of their own vessel had exploded. The whole bay was lit as brightly as day by the expiring flame of the great ship as she rose into the air. After she vanished silence fell on the combatants: then after some minutes the guns opened out again. As they did so the moon rose dazzling in her Egyptian beauty over the wreckage and slaughter.

Yet though the night was still young the battle was losing momentum. With the great Admiral who had conceived it dazed and disabled by his wound, the soul was gone out of it. Five of the French ships had already struck: another, the 80-gun *Franklin*, was failing fast. But the victors after sailing and fighting all day were exhausted. They would fire for a time and then desist: all night the battle flared up and then died away. "My people was so extremely jaded," reported Captain Miller of the *Theseus*, "that as soon as they had hove our sheet anchor up they dropped under the capstan bars and were asleep in a moment in every sort of posture."[2] After the surrender of the *Franklin* the second lieutenant of *Alexander* approached Ball to tell him that, though the hearts of his men were as good as ever, they could do no more and begged him to let them sleep for half an hour by their guns. Nelson's slightly disjointed messages speeding through the night were received rather than

[1] One Scottish woman bore a son in the heat of the action—Long, 198.
[2] Mahan, *Nelson*, I, 355.

obeyed: in that confused interminable nightmare of weariness nothing was ever quite carried through to an end.

As it began to grow light the magnitude of the victory became apparent. At 5.27 a.m. Captain Hallowell noted that six enemy battleships had struck their colours; on board his own ship "carpenters were busy stopping the shot holes . . . , people employed knotting and splicing the rigging." At six he heard the minute guns of the *Majestic* firing as she buried her captain. The whole bay was floating with charred wreckage and dead bodies, mangled and scorched. By this time it was light enough to see that three other battleships were at the victors' mercy: dismasted hulks aground or drifting. Only Villeneuve's three spectators in the rear remained uninjured. Presently these slipped their anchors and began to bear out to sea. But one of them, the *Timoleon*, in her haste to be gone ran on to the sandbanks. Her crew swam ashore and made off inland, a cloud of smoke revealing that her captain had fired her. Alone of the thirteen French ships of the line the *Guillaume Tell* and the *Généreux* with two frigates, escaped into the blue of the Mediterranean. For a while *Theseus*, the only British ship sufficiently undamaged to carry sail, pursued them till a signal from the Admiral recalled her.

In the first aftermath of battle Nelson and his men could scarcely conceive the fullness of what they had done. All day on August 2nd they were engaged in fishing naked prisoners from rafts and floating wreckage—sullen, downcast fellows very different from the merry Frenchmen some of the older sailors remembered capturing in the American war before the Tricolour had supplanted the Lilies.[1] More than two thousand unwounded prisoners were taken and nearly fifteen hundred wounded: that night Nelson dined half a dozen wounded French captains in his cabin. Brueys, the first Admiral in France, had been cut in half by a British cannon ball before the *Orient* blew up. Two thousand more of his men had been killed or drowned, nine of his thirteen battleships captured, two more destroyed. Nothing like it had been known since the day when the Duke of Marlborough had entertained a French Marshal and two Generals in his coach after Blenheim.

For it was not so much defeat that the French had suffered as annihilation. Though superior to their assailants by thirty per cent in men and twenty per cent. in weight of broadside, and fighting in a chosen position in a dangerous bay with the head of their line protected by shore batteries, they had been overwhelmed by the skill and ferocity of the attack. In a few hours they had literally been

[1] Long, 199.

blown out of the water. And the price paid by the victors had been scarcely 200 men killed and 700 wounded. It was an astonishing testimony to the intensity and accuracy of British gunfire, to Nelson's leadership and to the new school of close fighting he had initiated. Above all it revealed, in the hands of an inspired commander, the quality of British discipline. In his general order thanking his men Nelson, recalling the mutinies of the previous summer, emphasised this point. "It must strike forcibly every British seaman how superior their conduct is, when in discipline and good order, to the riotous behaviour of lawless Frenchmen."[1] Nothing so deeply impressed the same lawless Frenchmen, many of them professed atheists, as the religious service which was held on the morrow of the battle on the splintered, bloodstained decks of the British flagship. It struck them as an extraordinary thing that six hundred men—the roughest of the rough—could be assembled for such a purpose amid the scene of so much carnage and profess their mild faith with such order and quietness.

The battle was evidence also of the inadequacy of Revolutionary France's administration and the selfishness of her General. Because of the corruption prevailing everywhere after nine years of social scramble, the great ships—triumphs of the marine builder's art—were neglected and rotten, short of essential stores and their crews ill-fed and discontented at the long arrears in their pay. These handicaps to French courage and *élan* had been increased by Bonaparte's conscienceless theft of skilled gunners and seamen for his land operations and by his utter disregard of the needs of the fleet since his landing. Only a week before the battle Brueys had urged that its security depended on an immediate return to Toulon to refit. This, though he afterwards endeavoured to conceal the fact, Bonaparte had forbidden. Wishing to retain the fleet for his private purposes, he ignored expert advice and jeopardised the existence of the force on which French mastery of the Mediterranean depended. For so long as the Republican battle fleet was in being, the incursion of the British into that, to them baseless, sea could be only temporary and precarious.

With its destruction the whole position had changed in a night. On August 1st the French, as masters of Egypt, Corfu and Malta and—save for Naples—of the entire southern shore of Europe from Cadiz to the Turkish frontier, held the Mediterranean in their grip. On August 2nd they were themselves immobilised in all the lands and islands they had crossed its waters to conquer.

[1] Mahan, *Nelson*, I, 359.

The full consequence of this only dawned on men gradually. The transformation wrought by the battle of the Nile was too sudden to be realised in a night. The first assessment came from the ignorant Arabs of the Egyptian shore, who promptly cut the throats of every Frenchman within reach and, lighting bonfires on the dunes, illuminated the coastline for three nights. Only the courage and energy of Bonaparte saved the victorious French army from immediate disaster. "Ah well," he observed when the news was brought him, "we must either remain in this country or quit it as great as the ancients. . . . These English will compel us to do greater things than we meant." But though he rallied his men and by ruthless terrorism suppressed an Arab revolt, the fact remained that he and his army were virtually prisoners in a remote land, encircled by sea and desert, with no possibility of either receiving supplies from, or returning to, France. Five months after the battle he wrote that no news of any kind had been received from the Directory since July 6th. Even his communications between Rosetta and Alexandria were cut by the British warships.

• • • • • • • •

Through weaknesses inherent in the early conduct of the war the Navy had failed to blockade the enemy in his own ports and so keep an unbroken ring of water round his swelling power. It had failed through a shortage of frigates to destroy the enemy's offensive while at sea. But in the third resort, through the splendour of Nelson's offensive, it had succeeded gloriously. By destroying the enemy's communications it had paralysed his movements. By depriving him of stores, reinforcements and sea-borne transports it had stopped Bonaparte from advancing on either India or Asia Minor. It had re-established British control over two thousand miles of vital sea highway, making possible the expulsion of the French from Malta, Corfu and the Adriatic islands, the defence of Naples and Sicily, the capture of bases in the Balearics and the resurrection of all the dormant forces of Europe against the overgrown power of France.

For months past the cowed nations of the Continent had been showing signs of revolt against the greed and overbearing tyranny of their conquerors. In April a Viennese mob had torn the Tricolour, insolently flaunted in the populace's face, from the French embassy, and, though the Imperial authorities had subsequently made an abject apology, the underswell of national feeling remained. In May the Neapolitan Crown, terrified by the presence of "the merciless French robbers" in the States of the Pope, had secretly concluded a defensive alliance with Austria. Three months later the Emperor

Paul of Russia, enraged by the French seizure of Malta, signed a military convention with Austria.

Yet so long as the French controlled the sea lanes of the Mediterranean, these indications of the reviving spirit of European independence were confined to the street corner and the secret archives of the Chancelleries. It was the news of Nelson's astonishing victory, spreading outwards in ever larger ripples, that woke the closet courage of the continent. Five weeks after the battle, the Sultan of Turkey—first of the European rulers to hear the tidings—resolved to resent the intrusion of the French into his territories and, rejecting Talleyrand's insinuating diplomacy, declared a Holy War against the infidel invaders of Egypt.

But because of Nelson's lack of frigates and the very depth of his penetration into the French position, the news of his achievement travelled slowly. Its effect was not an instantaneous explosion but the spluttering of a charge of powder. For many days after the battle the victors remained in Egyptian waters, remote from a world which had lost trace of them. It took Nelson a fortnight before he could make his dismasted prizes fit for sea. Three he was forced to burn: the other six he sent off to Gibraltar under escort of seven of his battleships on August 14th. Their progress up the Mediterranean was painfully slow.

Want of frigates, Nelson wrote, would be found stamped on his heart. The first vessel available to carry the report of the victory to St. Vincent, the 50-gun *Leander*, did not leave Aboukir Bay until nearly a week after the battle. As ill-luck would have it, she and Captain Berry—the bearer of the official dispatches—were captured twelve days later in a calm by one of the two fugitive survivors of Brueys' line of battle.

So it came about that no intelligence of the victory reached western Europe till September 4th, when it was brought to Naples by the *Mutine* sloop, which Nelson on the arrival of his long-lost frigates had sent off with duplicate dispatches on August 14th. Before they arrived Nelson himself was on his way to Europe. On August 14th he had received a summons from St. Vincent to return to save Naples from the threat of sea-borne invasion and co-operate in the capture of a British Mediterranean base in the Balearics. Accordingly, leaving three battleships and three frigates under Captain Hood to blockade Egypt, Nelson reluctantly set out on the 19th for Neapolitan waters. He was still suffering from the effects of his head wound and from perpetual headaches and vomitings. The voyage, prolonged by the derelict state of his flagship, acted as an enforced holiday.

On September 22nd, towed ironically by a frigate, the *Vanguard* anchored off Naples. "I hope," Nelson wrote to Sir William Hamilton, "to be no more than four or five days at Naples, for these are not times for idleness."[1] He had reckoned without the Ambassador's lady. Accompanied by the King and Queen of Naples, this large, fascinating, vulgar, dynamic woman of thirty-three bore down on the Admiral with the same spirit that he himself had borne down on the French. She had only set eyes on him once before when, five years earlier during the siege of Toulon, he had borne dispatches to Naples. But she was resolved to conquer him as he had conquered Brueys. Acknowledged as a mistress of dramatic effect—her "attitudes" were the talk of the less exacting *salons* of Europe—she positively boarded the unsophisticated sailor on his own quarterdeck. Still bemused from that astonishing encounter he described it in a letter three days later to his wife. "Up flew her ladyship and exclaiming 'O God, is it possible?' she fell into my arm more dead than alive." She was followed by the King who, seizing the Admiral by the hand, hailed him as his deliverer and preserver.

It was all too much for Nelson and his poor dazed head. The loveliest city of southern Europe was in summer gala to receive him, the most voluptuous of women at his feet. After the strain and intense excitement of the summer and the dreary reaction of the voyage west, he could not refrain from yielding to all this overflow of tenderness and adulation. It seemed a sailor's due, after the hardships and deprivations of the sea. He had known little of luxury and nothing of Courts. He found himself when he was least able to withstand its fatal charm the adored hero of the most luxurious and enervating society in existence. He struggled for a little while: wrote to St. Vincent a week after his arrival that he was in a country of fiddlers and puppets, whores and scoundrels: that it was a dangerous place for a simple sailor and he must keep clear of it. A fortnight later he sailed for Malta, where the islanders had risen against the French garrison at the first news of the Nile to organise a blockade of Valetta. But he left his heart behind in Naples and early in November, at the first stirrings of Continental war, he returned there to be the counsellor of an admiring King and Queen and the hero of a lovely and designing woman, and to waste his genius in an element alien to it.

. . . .

While Nelson was driving in triumph under the Neapolitan sunshine England was still waiting for news. Throughout the summer the country remained in suspense. During the agony of his

[1] Mahan, *Nelson*, I, 368-9.

long chase, criticism of the young Rear-Admiral had been widespread and even his friend, Collingwood, who never doubted his skill and courage, began to have fears that his good fortune had forsaken him. About the time that he reached Alexandria the second time it became known in London that he had sailed for the first time to seek the enemy in the Levant and that Bonaparte had left Malta on June 19th. For a few days expectation, therefore, ran high. "The grand event," wrote *Lloyd's Evening Post* on Saturday, August 4th, "which has in all probability taken place in the Mediterranean between the English and French fleets, nearly occupies the entire attention of the public as if, on the fate of the expedition entrusted to Bonaparte, depended that of the existing war." Lady Spencer, catching the confidence of old St. Vincent, even speculated as to how she should treat Bonaparte when he dined, a prisoner, at her side: should she do it, she asked, "in a sincere and a brutal style? or in a false and a generous one."[1]

But by the second week in August nothing had come in but vague reports from French sources that Bonaparte had landed in Egypt and—though nobody would admit this—that he had met Nelson at sea and been victorious.[2] The country, still drilling against an increasingly dubious invasion, began to grow despondent. "At no period of the war," wrote a leading Daily on August 8th, "have public affairs been more critically situated than they are at the present moment. But we are sorry to say, that to whatever point we direct our attention, there is much to lament and little to console us!" The only hopeful sign was in Ireland, where, since the arrival of Lord Cornwallis as Viceroy in the middle of the rebellion, a wise combination of firmness and clemency had been producing steadying results.

On August 22nd an overland courier from Constantinople brought authentic news that the French had landed at Alexandria at the beginning of July. It caused a sudden drop in the Funds. It was offset by exciting though unreliable accounts from German newspapers of a great sea fight off Crete in which Nelson had sunk many transports and blockaded the *Orient* with Bonaparte aboard or, according to another version, driven her on to a rock.

At the height of the tension caused by these reports news arrived that a small French force had landed in the west of Ireland on August 22nd. It turned out to be only a single brigade from Brest—too small to be a menace to the British and too late to be of any aid to the Irish. But though the first thing that greeted its commander,

[1] *Windham Papers*, II, 108.
[2] Pitt to Rose, 10th Aug., 1798.—*Rose*, I, 216.

General Humbert, on his landing at Killala Bay was the sight of a French agent hanging on a tree, and though the disarmed and dispirited peasants of the west gave him little support, he boldly brushed aside the local Fencibles who attempted to oppose him. Three days later at Castlebar he plunged the whole country into alarm by routing, with a quarter of their force, 4,000 Militia and Dragoons: a disgraceful exhibition of British incompetence which justified all that experienced soldiers like Abercromby and Cornwallis had said about the discipline of the Irish Army. But the ultimate defeat of Humbert's little force of veterans was a foregone conclusion. After covering a hundred and fifty miles in seventeen days in a series of swift, fox-like movements, it surrendered to Cornwallis at Ballinamuck on September 8th. A week later that noted Irish patriot, Napper Tandy, appeared in a Dunkirk brig off the lonely Donegal coast and on hearing what had happened returned at once to France.

By this time advices from Italy had made it plain not only that the French had successfully landed at Alexandria but that Nelson had missed them there and returned to Syracuse. All hope now vanished: seldom had public opinion been so depressed.[1] Travellers' tales of French defeats at the hands of the Arabs could not dispel the gloom. The British people (save for Pitt who continued hopeful[2]) were coming to believe with their enemies that Bonaparte could not be defeated.

On September 18th the Admiralty received official news of Nelson's departure from Syracuse on July 26th to search the Levant for the second time. Three days later certain London newspapers drew attention to a vague reference in the supplement of the Paris *Redacteur* of the 14th to an attack on Admiral Brueys' squadron by a superior British force off Beguieres in which the French flagship and several other vessels of both navies had been burnt or driven ashore. The public regarded it with sceptism, especially as no such place as Beguieres could be found on any atlas. None the less it seemed hard to explain why such unfavourable news, if not true, should have appeared in the official journal of the French Directory. During the following week no confirmation came from any source, though an ingenious person pointed out that Beguieres might be a French translation of the Arab Al-Bekir or Aboukir, mid-way between Alexandria and Rosetta.

The expectation of the people of England had been raised to the highest pitch. It had been repeatedly disappointed. It was now to be exceeded beyond all rational hope. At two o'clock on Monday,

[1] *British Chronicle*, 10th Sept., 1798.
[2] Stanhope, III, 139.

October 1st, exactly two months after the battle, the postscript of *Lloyd's Evening Post* announced that the Hamburg mail had arrived with news of a glorious victory in which Admiral Nelson had destroyed or captured all but two of the French battleships. Next morning Captain Capel of the *Mutine* delivered Nelson's dispatches to the Admiralty. Within a few minutes the Park and Tower guns began to fire and all the church bells to peal. And as the steeples started to rock, the wife of the First Lord sat down to write to the hero of England. "Joy, joy, joy to you, brave, gallant, immortal Nelson! May the great God whose cause you so valiantly support, protect and bless you to the end of your brilliant career. . . . My heart is absolutely bursting with different sensations of joy, of gratitude, of pride, of every emotion that ever warmed the bosom of a British woman on hearing of her country's glory."[1]

There was scarcely anybody in England who did not realise the magnitude of the victory. The *Annual Register* described it as "the most signal that had graced the British Navy since the days of the Spanish Armada." The old king, when the despatch reached him at Weymouth, read Nelson's opening words, then stopped and, standing silent for a minute, turned his eyes to heaven. It seemed to promise not only a lasting salvation for England, but preservation from anarchy, distress and misery for the still free countries of Europe, liberation for the enslaved, and in the fullness of time, peace.

For that October, as illuminations lit the streets, and cities and tithe barns reeked with celebration beef, plum puddings and punch and echoed with jubilant "Rule Britannias," the confidence of the country in the certainty of victory came flooding back. Within a fortnight the news of the Nile was followed by that of Admiral Sir John Borlace Warren intercepting a squadron of French warships and transports on their way to Lough Swilly and capturing all but two of them, including a ship of the line, three frigates and the redoubtable Wolfe Tone. The fears of the previous winter vanished in a swelling crescendo of British triumph: Gillray in one of his grandest cartoons drew the one-eyed Nelson slaying the Revolutionary crocodiles of the Nile and in another John Bull taking his luncheon of naval victories and crying out to the Frenchmen: "What, more fricassés! why you sons of bitches you, where do you think I shall find room to stow it all?" And *The Times*, in a report that the French Government had ordered the building of sixteen new battleships and eighteen frigates, added the comment, "Good news this for old England! It saves us the trouble and expense of

[1] *Nicolas*, III, 74.

building them ourselves, for they are sure to find their way into our ports!"[1]

A great nation had received the first fruits of its own endeavours. That autumn it emerged from a long dark valley of tribulation into the sunshine. Even the weather smiled and gave the country a bumper harvest. Despite the stringencies of prolonged war, trade was reviving and revenue expanding: imports for 1798 showed an increase of nearly seven millions and exports of four millions. It was with a full and proud consciousness of these things that Pitt in his Budget speech of December 3rd called on the country to bear new burdens that it might help not itself alone but others. Rather than burden posterity with war debts and impair its inheritance, he proposed the unprecedented step of a direct tax on all incomes of more than £60, rising in the case of all those exceeding £200 to two shillings in the pound.

"Let us do justice to ourselves," he declared, "We have been enabled to stand forth the saviours of mankind. . . . We have presented a phenomenon in the character of nations." Already the peoples of Europe were rising in their wrath against the spoiler and oppressor. Turkey had already declared war on France, Russia was marching, Naples and Austria arming. A second Coalition was forming to reduce France within its ancient limits. "A general war," wrote Farington in his diary on November 13th, "is looked upon as certain."

[1] *Times*, 26th Nov., 1798.

CHAPTER TWELVE

The Lost Chance

1798-1800

"Experience shows that nothing is to be reckoned an obstacle which is not found to be so on trial; that in war something must be allowed to chance and fortune, seeing that it is in its nature hazardous and an option of difficulties; that the greatness of an object should come under consideration as opposed to the impediments that lie in the way."
General Wolfe.

"Failure will always be the lot of maritime expeditions when, instead of pushing the invasion rapidly, one limits oneself to acting pusillanimously, leaving time to the enemy to manœuvre."
Jomini.

It was the fiery Nelson who began the offensive. Reflecting the new belief of his country that aggression was justified where it anticipated a ruthless foe,[1] he persuaded the Neapolitan Court to strike at the French in the despoiled territories of the Pope to the north. Thirty thousand troops in their glittering Italian uniforms marched past the saluting base in the camp of St. Germaines and were pronounced by the famous General Mack, lent by Austria to its little ally, as the most beautiful army in Europe. On November 24th, 1798, they crossed the border while Nelson, who now saw himself as the saviour of Italy, landed a force in the enemy's rear at Leghorn.

But the nerve of the Aulic Council failed at the eleventh hour. It was not yet ready for war. As soon as the French realised that Austria was not going to march, they struck back. In the north they forced the hapless King of Piedmont to abdicate. In the Campagna, having withdrawn from Rome, they turned on Mack's pedantically scattered forces. The gleaming, scented Italian officers took to their heels at the first shot and their men followed. "The Neapolitans," wrote Nelson, "have not lost much honour, for God knows they have but little to lose; but they lost all they had." A few weeks later, while the King fled in Nelson's flagship to Sicily, the French entered Naples after liquidating a brief resistance by

[1] "To avert by anticipation a meditated blow where destruction would follow its infliction is surely justifiable."—*Lloyds' Evening Post*, August, 1798.

the mob. Here they set up a Parthenopean Republic of middle-class traitors under cover of which they proceeded to plunder the country.

. . . .

Yet the Neapolitan affair was only an incident. The Mediterranean conflagration was spreading. In October the Turkish and Russian fleets, emerging in unwonted amity from the Dardanelles, attacked the French in the Ionian islands. At Malta a Portuguese squadron took its place beside the British fleet and the insurgent Maltese in a common front against the despoilers of Valetta.

Farther down the Mediterranean Britain had struck at the Balearics. Since Spain's entry into the war Dundas had been waiting the chance to seize Minorca and its great naval base, Port Mahon. Even before the news of the Nile he had ordered British and *émigré* regiments in Portugal to be sent under secret cover of St. Vincent's ships to attack the island. At the Admiral's entreaty the operation was entrusted to their former commander, now Lieutenant-General Charles Stuart. "No one," he wrote to the Secretary of State, "can manage Frenchmen as him, and the English will go to hell for him." [1] It says something for Dundas's magnanimity that he consented, for Stuart—a true son of the proud, erratic House of Bute—was in the habit of treating politicians with contempt. He frequently disobeyed their orders and never failed to point out their absurdities. "I am determined," he had written to Dundas at the outset of his defensive campaign in Portugal, "to be guided by your instructions so long as they are within the reach of my comprehension."[2] Whenever—as often happened—they were not, he disregarded them.

Stuart's Minorca campaign was as successful as Nelson's Neapolitan essay was inglorious. Unlike his great contemporary, the soldier was operating in his own element, and he was complete master of his business. He was fortunate in having as second-in-command a fellow Scot who, five years his senior, had until as many years before known nothing of war or soldiering. Thomas Graham of Balgowan was forty-five when he first served as a volunteer on Lord Mulgrave's staff at the siege of Toulon. But though impelled to arms mainly as a distraction for the loss of a beloved wife and out of a political fury roused by a Jacobin mob's insults to her coffin,[3] he was as natural a soldier as Cromwell. After displaying the cool courage of his race in mountain fighting round the doomed port, he had returned to England, where having raised

[1] *Fortescue*, IV, 606.
[2] *Ibid*, IV, 604.
[3] He was bringing her body home in 1792 from the Riviera where she had died. His bereavement was to make him, in the fullness of time, perhaps the greatest of Wellington's Peninsula commanders.

a regiment at his own expense—to-day the Second Scottish Rifles—he had been gazetted a temporary Lieutenant-Colonel. Since then he had served under General Doyle in the expedition to the Isle d'Yeu and later, as British Military Commissioner with the Austrian Army in Italy, had distinguished himself by carrying dispatches for the starving garrison of Mantua through Bonaparte's lines.

On landing in Minorca on November 7th—an operation facilitated by complete British command of the sea—this gallant soldier was sent by Stuart with 600 troops to capture the Meradal Pass in the centre of the island. This he accomplished without loss, cutting all communication between Port Mahon and Ciudadella. The last stronghold with 3,600 defenders surrendered a week later to a British force of 3,000 which, owing to a blunder in the Ordnance Department, had been sent without field guns. But Stuart, by exquisite economy of means and a mixture of shrewdness and bluff, conquered the entire island in just over a week without losing a man. It is hard to escape Sir John Fortescue's conclusion that, had he lived longer or been given a fair field for his gifts, this brilliant soldier might have won as great a name as Marlborough or Wellington. After the capture of Minorca he increased his claim on his country by disregarding all Dundas's entreaties for raids on the Spanish coast and the great fortress of Cartagena. "Let no persuasion of the Navy," he told him, "lead you to conceive its reduction could be accomplished by a handful of men."[1] Instead he husbanded his slender forces and prepared for the day when Minorca might have to defend itself by making every landing place an impregnable maze of earthworks. His power of making British soldiers dig was remarkable.

To Stuart came early in 1799 an urgent summons from Nelson to save Sicily from invasion. In the midst of a craven, panic-stricken Court and a wild, barbarous peasantry, the great sailor wrote on February 16th to beg for a thousand British infantry from Minorca to hold Messina against the rising Jacobin tide. He did not appeal in vain. For the clear-headed soldier was profoundly aware of the strategic importance of Sicily and its possibilities as a base for those amphibious operations against the southern flank of the French armies which he was at that very moment urging on the British Government. Though short of troops, he at once sailed with the 30th and 89th Regiments of Foot, arriving at Palermo on March 10th. Within five hours of landing he was on the road to Messina where his fiery energy and magnetism and astonishing understanding of peasant mentality turned the resentful suspicions of

[1] *Fortescue*, IV, 620.

the native husbandmen into an enthusiastic patriotism. During his brief stay he drafted a masterly plan for the defence of the island in which he anticipated the events of the next decade by showing how a brave peasantry might be armed and used to break the heart of disciplined armies. "Essential military operations," he wrote, with a genius that still burns through his stilted eighteenth-century phrases, "are too often avoided, neglected and misarranged from the false idea that they can only be effected by disciplined troops, whereas in many cases, in many countries and particularly in Sicily, the joint efforts and exertions of armed peasants are more likely to prove effectual."[1] Then, his work done and leaving Colonel Graham behind him, he hurried back to Minorca. A few weeks later, worn out by his own restless energy, he was forced to return, a sick man, to England.

. . . .

While these events were taking place in the Mediterranean, Pitt was putting forth all his powers to align Europe against the aggressor. On November 16th, 1798, in a dispatch to the Russian, Austrian and Prussian Governments, he defined his aim as a grand alliance "to reduce France within her ancient limits . . . to which every other Power should be ready to accede." It was to them as much as to his countrymen that he addressed his Budget Speech of December 3rd, which Mallet du Pan thought the greatest survey of a nation's financial strength ever made.

For the Income Tax was imposed not so much to save Britain as to free Europe by putting the armies of the Continent once more into the field. In the closing days of 1798 a formal alliance was signed with Russia by the British Ambassador in St. Petersburg: in return for an advance of £225,000 for Russia and monthly subsidies of £75,000, the Tsar promised 45,000 men for action with British and, it was hoped, Prussian and Swedish troops against the French invaders of Holland. Already he had sent to Galicia 20,000 of the 60,000 soldiers guaranteed to Austria by the military convention of the summer. A French declaration of war on Russia followed immediately.

For these reasons, Nelson, despite his Neapolitan disappointment, wrote on New Year's Day that he hoped before the year's end to see the French crushed and peace restored to the world. The inherent weakness of the dreaded Republic had suddenly become apparent. Corruption and materialism had rotted France's giant strength. The country swarmed with deserters and robbers, the bridges, roads and canals were perishing from neglect, the public finances

[1] *Fortescue*, IV, 625.

were in indescribable confusion. In a land in which morals and religion had long been discarded as antiquated superstitions, every man thought only of himself and how to defraud the commonwealth. France was racked by senseless feuds: in Brittany the ministers of religion were hunted down like wild beasts. The only people who seemed happy were government contractors.

The extent of the Republic's conquests increased its danger. For throughout Germany, Italy, Holland and Switzerland the greed of the Directory's agents aroused the common people against the French and the rootless bourgeois who collaborated with them. Their anger kept the Republican armies scattered in a thousand garrisons. Nobody trusted France: every one loathed and feared her. Even the infant American Republic, bound to her by old ties of gratitude, broke off relations with her in the summer of 1798, George Washington in a Presidential message to the Senate voicing his countrymen's abhorrence of the French Directory's "disregard of solemn Treaties and the Laws of Nations."

Yet the shortcomings of Revolutionary France were once more matched by those of the legitimist rulers of Europe. Austria, though she had reorganised her armies, had failed to cast off the petty selfishness of her Court and Council. The Emperor and his Minister, Thugut, nursed not only ancient jealousies of Prussia and Russia, but more recent grudges against Britain. For it is the nature of defaulting allies to feel resentment towards those they have injured. Austrian statesmen could not readily overlook the loans which Britain had advanced to them and which they were unwilling to repay, or their own betrayal of her at the Peace of Campo Formio.

Yet the logic of events was too strong for such cross-currents of selfishness to do more than check the tide which had set in against France with Nelson's victory. Pitt's purpose was delayed but not prevented. Throughout the winter—the coldest in human memory—the armies of Europe were rumbling towards the coming battle line. Even the Tsar Paul of Russia—a petulant maniac—scouted the French suggestion that he should be allowed to partition Turkey as his mother had Poland, for his vanity, stronger than his ambition, had been mortally affronted by Bonaparte's seizure of Malta, of which he had had himself declared Protector. The Aulic Council of Austria might refuse to be hustled into war, but it knew that war was its only alternative to extinction at the hands of the insatiable Jacobins. And though the frosts and snows of that awful winter held up mails for many weeks, keeping Pitt's envoy three months on the road to Berlin, no frost lasts for ever. On January 31st, 1799, the Directory, exalted by its entry into Naples and its easy conquest of yet another European monarchy, informed Vienna that, unless the Russian corps in Galicia was withdrawn within fifteen days, war would immediately follow. No reply was made. Passively rather than actively the Hapsburg State aligned itself with Russia, Britain, Turkey, Portugal and the Two Sicilies in a second Coalition against the overgrown power of France.

. . . .

Before the Directory's armies poured across the Rhine, their General in Egypt had taken the offensive against Turkey. Undeterred by his isolation, Bonaparte had spent the autumn with his usual indomitable activity. Nor, for all the seas of salt and desert around him, were his plans in the least defensive. In October he was reported to be trying to buy over the wild Abyssinians and obtain a port on the Red Sea eight hundred miles to the south. When he found this too visionary, he prepared for an advance across the two hundred miles of desert between Egypt and Palestine to seize the Levantine corridor into Asia Minor. From Damascus he reckoned that he would be able either to drive to Constantinople and found a new Byzantine Empire on the ruins of the Sultan's crumbling power, or strike eastwards along the caravan routes into Mesopotamia towards the Persian Gulf. For, true to the Revolutionary creed of energy of which he was the embodiment, Bonaparte believed that to men of will all things were possible.

On January 15th, 1799, when his arrangements for a desert march were almost complete, he wrote to Tippoo Sahib announcing his arrival with an invincible army and asking him to send envoys to Suez to concert plans for the overthrow of the British in India. Ten days later he learnt from a long delayed dispatch from France—the first to reach him since September—that Turkey had been at war with the Directory for several months and that the Sultan was concentrating armies in Syria and Rhodes for an invasion of Egypt.

It was never Bonaparte's way to wait to be attacked. Early in February, when the snow in England lay so deep that Parson Woodforde could not reach that place of use at the end of his garden which he called Jericho, the Army of Egypt set out across the eastern desert. On the 20th, after a brief siege, it captured El Arish from the Pasha of Syria who had occupied it a month before with the Turkish advance guard. Thence it drove up the coast through Gaza to Jaffa, which it stormed on March 5th; finding the 3000 Turks of the garrison an embarrassment to his commissariat, Bonaparte had them massacred. It would be a useful warning, he reflected, to their countrymen of the unwisdom of resisting the French. Then, without wasting time, he resumed his march for Acre—a little town poorly fortified, some sixty miles to the north, barring the coastal road into Syria.

But here his fate was awaiting him in the now familiar shape of the British Navy. On March 3rd, to the disgust of many of his professional superiors, Captain Sidney Smith had taken over the command of the small squadron which had remained after the Nile in Egyptian waters. This erratic and plausible officer had recently escaped from the Temple prison in Paris and, having returned to England with a great deal of information, reliable and otherwise, about French ambitions in the Orient, had prevailed on Lord Spencer to send him out to the Levant with a roving commission. His command consisted of two battleships and three small frigates. On hearing that Bonaparte had captured Jaffa he sent a brilliant young *émigré* engineer, Colonel Phélypeaux, to assist the Turkish Governor of Acre. A few days later Smith followed in person.

On March 17th, Bonaparte, driving northwards from Haifa, saw in his path the white walls of Acre jutting out into the Mediterranean blue. Beyond them lay Aleppo and Damascus, and, so the young conqueror believed, vast treasure, arms for a quarter of a million men, and the high roads to Constantinople and India. But in the roadstead off the little port lay two British ships of the line, their rigging grimly rising against the spring sky. It was a spectacle with which he was to grow strangely familiar during the next seven weeks.

For, thanks to Phélypeaux's genius for fortification and the naval guns and crews with which Sidney Smith stiffened the Turkish garrison, Acre proved surprisingly formidable. The ubiquitous British warships even captured Bonaparte's siege train as it crept up the coast from Egypt, embarked in gunboats. Its guns were promptly used by the indefatigable Smith against the French. Without them the ridiculous little fort with its 3000 shabby Turks and handful of British tars could not be battered into submission. Frontal assaults, however dashing, produced no results but casualties. There was nothing for it but to sit down and starve the place out. And this, owing to British sea power, was more easily proposed than done.

• • • • • • •

In Europe and in India other armies were marching. On March 1st, 1799, the Directory, having received no answer from Austria to its ultimatum, launched its attack. The French crossed the Rhine with the old familiar confidence and, debouching from Switzerland, overran the Grisons. But on March 25th, advancing through the

Black Forest, Jourdan came up against the Archduke Charles at Stockach. He was repulsed with loss and forced to retreat.

The victory of the Imperialists broke the legend of Republican invincibility. During the next few weeks Bernadotte, Soult, Victor and Souham all suffered defeat in southern Germany, while Massena was forced to fall back in the Grisons. Since its defeat by Bonaparte, two years before, the Austrian Army had been reorganised: it now numbered a quarter of a million well-equipped men. The French Army, on the other hand, had been neglected and cheated by the politicians in Paris and subjected to the demoralising influence of living without war on a conquered countryside. With nearly 100,000 deserters from its colours and scattered over an immense area, it found itself faced for the first time by superior numbers.

Its weakness was greatest in Italy—the scene of its late glory—where Bonaparte's strategy of concentration had been abandoned for one of dispersal. The Directory's fiscal policy was defined in a memorandum on the occupied Papal States. "The Revolution at Rome has not yet been productive enough. The only course to take, so as to derive from it a more suitable return, is to consider and to treat the finances of the Roman State as the finances of the French Army."[1] The latter, to enforce this extortion, was dissipated in dozens of little garrisons cut off from one another by mountain ranges and almost impassable tracks. On April 5th old Schérer, who had taken the offensive with his depleted field army, was defeated by the Hungarian, Kray, at Magnano. Within a week the French had been driven across the Mincio and forced to retire behind the Adda.

Here they were assailed by a more formidable enemy. On March 3rd the Russo-Turkish Fleet had taken Corfu. Six weeks later the advance guard of the Russian Army reached the Italian front under the command of the world-famous Marshal Suvorof. This barbaric genius—a Muscovite Elizabethan of sixty-nine strayed into the eighteenth century, hardy, valiant, eccentric almost at times to madness, who had never known defeat and lived only for war and the adoration of his rough soldiers—at once attacked with a fierceness and speed hitherto only equalled by Bonaparte. Forcing the line of the Adda on the 27th, he entered Milan two days later amid the acclamations of the populace. The entire French Army in Italy was in deadly danger.

Already in the south the French Parthenopeian Republic was crumbling. At first the wise and conciliatory policy of the soldier

[1] *Cambridge Modern History*, VIII, 638.

Championet, had partially won over the fickle *lazzaroni* of the capital. But the intrigues of thwarted contractors and venal agents had soon brought about his recall in favour of a more complacent commander. Immediately a swarm of harpies had settled on the hapless Republic, robbing the inhabitants of houses, lands and churches, cash, treasure and livestock. Incited by a warlike Cardinal named Ruffo and supplied by British cruisers, the peasants took up arms. When the news of the Allied successes in the north reached the French General Macdonald, his hold on the country became precarious. To save himself from encirclement he abandoned Naples on May 7th and, leaving small delaying garrisons behind him in the principal fortresses, retreated northwards.

• • • • • • •

Three days earlier, more than four thousand miles to the east, a British-Sepoy army stormed Seringapatam, capital of the great Mahommedan Power of Mysore. Ever since the French had begun to talk of an eastern expedition Tippoo Sahib, its ruler, had been scheming to drive the British from the Orient. A premature and boastful proclamation by the French Governor of Mauritius with whom he had been corresponding, gave warning to the British authorities and led, in the summer of 1798, to the dispatch by Dundas of military reinforcements to the East. The alarm coincided with the arrival in Calcutta of a new Governor-General. An Irishman with an imperial vision rare among the English, the thirty-seven-year-old Earl of Mornington had at once resolved to abandon his predecessor's humdrum policy of non-intervention in Indian affairs and strike a resounding blow at Tippoo's French-trained army, before a Mahratta confederacy and the arrival of Bonaparte should bring the structure of Clive and Warren Hastings crashing to the ground. He therefore ordered General Harris to concentrate all available troops in Madras and prevailed on the Nizam of Hyderabad to join an alliance against Mysore.

By the end of 1798 Mornington had prepared a powerful and well-equipped army. He was fortunate in having the aid of his brother, Arthur Wellesley, who had been sent with his regiment to India a year earlier. This able and painstaking young man of twenty-nine possessed an unsuspected genius for planning war, perfectly adapted to a country without roads and normal means of supply. Too unassuming and well bred to arouse envy, the unknown Lieutenant-Colonel of the 33rd Foot was the brain behind the preparations for the long march through the jungle to Tippoo's capital. His methods were epitomised in a sentence from his official correspondence: "It is better to see and communicate the difficulties and dangers of the enterprise and to endeavour to overcome them than to be blind to everything but success till the moment of difficulty comes and then to despond."[1] He had learnt his lesson since his campaign with the British Army in Holland.

As soon as Mornington heard from Nelson's overland courier of the Nile victory, he abandoned his waiting game and insisted that Tippoo should receive a British envoy. But that subtle Oriental, playing for time until Bonaparte should come, put off the peremptory Governor-General with excuses. Accordingly on February 11th, 1799, Harris—a veteran of Bunker's Hill—crossed the Madras border into Mysore with 5000 British troops and 16,000 Sepoys. He was joined by an army of 16,000 natives from Hyderabad, which Colonel Wellesley, in recognition of "judicious and masterly arrangements in respect of supplies," was seconded to command. A third army of 6,000 under James Stuart started from Bombay.

Tippoo Sahib had 50,000 men and the advantage of interior lines. By forced marches he surprised and almost overwhelmed Stuart at Periapatam on March 6th. But the unexpectedly rapid advance of the main British force from the west compelled him to face about. On the 22nd, engaged by the combined armies of Britain and Hyderabad at Malavelly, he broke off the fight rather than risk the loss of his guns, and retired behind the formidable fortifications of Seringapatam. He knew that no army could long maintain itself hundreds of miles from its base in the heart of southern India.

By the beginning of May the British-Sepoy forces had no other choice but starvation or retreat. Fording a swift river 300 yards wide—one of the most remarkable feats in the annals of war—they flung themselves at the breaches. By nightfall on the 4th the British flag was flying over the town. Little quarter was given, for by Tippoo's orders all the prisoners within the fortress had been massacred. Next morning the body of a corpulent, short-necked man with delicate hands and feet was found under a heap of dead in one of the gateways. It was the end of the robber dynasty of Hyder Ali. His country—almost the size of England—was divided between Hyderabad and the East India Company, while a puppet representative of the old Hindu royal line was set to rule over the remainder. Arthur Wellesley stayed as Civil Administrator and Commander-in-Chief. His four years of rule—the beginning of British hegemony in southern India—was distinguished by an almost pedantic respect for native rights and customs and a welcome absence of plunder and exaction.

[1] *Supplementary Despatches and Memoranda of the Duke of Wellington*, I, 196.

While the British storming parties were fighting their way into Seringapatam the man who had sailed a year before to conquer an Indian empire was still sulkily surveying the ramparts of Acre. "The whole fate of the East," he said, "hangs from this little corner." Phélypeaux had been killed, a Turkish relief force routed at Mount Tabor and the handful of defenders thinned by casualties. But the flags of Turkey and England continued to fly over the fort and English warships to ride in the roadstead. In the first week of May the French made sixteen attempts to storm the place. On the 8th, spurred by the approach of a fleet of Turkish transports from Rhodes, they captured one of the towers. But Sidney Smith, throwing every seaman into the fight, saved the day. Two weeks later Bonaparte, having lost more than a quarter of his force in the sixty-two days' siege, made a final assault on the stinking, corpse-strewn ditches and, failing, threw his guns into the sea and retreated. The plague was in his camp and his men were mutinous. On May 25th he abandoned Jaffa, on the 29th Gaza, on June 2nd El Arish. At each place a trail of plague-stricken, dying Frenchmen testified to Smith's achievement. So did Bonaparte's angry gibes at the rash buffoon of a sea captain who had made him miss his destiny. "If it had not been for you English," he declared afterwards, "I should have been Emperor of the East. But wherever there is water to float a ship, we are sure to find you in the way."

. . . .

With the Russians and Austrians overrunning Bonaparte's conquests in Lombardy and Piedmont and French armies outnumbered on every front from the Rhine to the Campagna, the Republic was in greater danger than at any time since the dark days of 1793. The country was in the utmost confusion. In March, 1799, the flame of civil war had broken out again in the west and the Chouans had taken the field. The Directory were universally detested. In a despairing attempt to retrieve their fortunes, they sent Admiral Bruix, the brilliant young Minister of Marine, to Brest, where a fleet had long been preparing, with orders to put to sea at any cost and, entering the Mediterranean, to shatter the British supremacy that had brought all these disasters on the Republic and rescue from Egypt Bonaparte—the one man who could save it.

Had the British intelligence system been better or had the Commander-in-Chief of the Channel Fleet understood the full meaning of blockade, such orders would have been useless. But instead of keeping close to Ushant, Bridport, nursing his ships, kept station too far out. On April 25th he was driven a dozen miles west of the island by a north-easter. That evening Bruix with twenty-five battleships and ten frigates escaped in the haze and, taking the Passage du Raz, steered for the south.

Bruix's escape imperilled the whole structure of British sea power in the Mediterranean. On it depended Allied military operations from Syria to Genoa and the cohesion of the Coalition. While Bridport mobilised every ship in home waters to defend the Irish coast, the French Fleet appeared off Cadiz where Lord Keith, with fifteen sail of the line, was blockading a superior Spanish force. Fortunately Bruix, doubting his unpractised crews' ability to cope with a westerly gale on a lee-shore, ran for the Straits. Here, on May 5th, St. Vincent, watching from Gibraltar, saw his ships gliding by like ghosts through the mist.

At that moment half the British Mediterranean Fleet was at the French Admiral's mercy. Duckworth with four battleships was off Minorca, Ball with three blockading Valetta, Sidney Smith with two opposing Bonaparte at Acre, Troubridge with four watching Naples, and Nelson with a solitary ship guarding the Neapolitan Royalties at Palermo. But Bruix after a fortnight at sea had had enough. With the reverberation of the guns at Aboukir haunting him, he saw himself not as a hunter but as the hunted. Instead of sweeping eastwards with the wind to overwhelm St. Vincent's scattered squadrons, he made for Toulon.

When he arrived on May 14th he found the Republic's danger slightly lessened. For Russian temperament and Austrian greed had given the army of Italy a breathing space. Suvorof after taking Milan had unaccountably paused for a week of junketing. The Aulic Council, intent on acquiring Italian territory, had insisted that the reduction of Lombard fortresses should precede pursuit of the enemy. Consequently Moreau, superseding the defeated Schérer, had been able to withdraw to the Genoese hills to cover Macdonald's retreat from the south. Here at the beginning of June Bruix sailed to join him at Vado Bay.

But though he brought urgently-needed supplies to Moreau's hungry troops, the French Admiral achieved nothing else. By his flight to Toulon and his prolonged stay there he had given the British Fleet time to mobilise. Nelson, on receipt of St. Vincent's warning, had given immediate orders to his scattered ships to assemble in the channel between Sicily and Africa, barring the way to Egypt. "I consider the best defence for his Sicilian Majesty's dominions," he wrote, "is to place myself alongside the French." St. Vincent, with Spanish connivance—for the wise old Admiral had been showing every courtesy to the weaker of his two enemies and intriguing with them against their bullying ally—managed, despite the easterly gale, to get an overland message to Keith to join him at Gibraltar. He was thus able to sail on May 25th with sixteen ships of the line to retrieve Duckworth from Minorca. Thence cruising midway between that island and the Catalan coast he waited for the attempted junction of the French and Spanish Fleets.

Having failed to strike the blow which could alone have turned the tide of defeat in Italy, Bruix on June 6th sailed for Cartagena to join the Spaniards who had entered that port after Keith's withdrawal from Cadiz. But for St. Vincent's illness he would have encountered that which, when divided, he might have destroyed but which now, united, would undoubtedly have destroyed him—the British Fleet off Cape San Sebastian. Fortunately for Bruix, the old Admiral's health, long ailing, at that moment failed him. On June 2nd he handed over his command to Keith and returned to Gibraltar. Keith, a good sailor and a brave fighter, lacked St. Vincent's moral stature. Haunted by fears for Minorca, he abandoned his cruising station to protect his base. When, three days later, after being reinforced from England, he returned, the French had passed. On the 22nd they entered Cartagena, sailing again on the 29th with sixteen Spanish battleships which they bore off as hostages for Spain's good behaviour. A week later, St. Vincent, waiting at Gibraltar for a ship to take him to England, saw Bruix's fleet for the second time passing the Straits.

• • • • • • •

Even before Bruix left the Mediterranean further disasters befell the French armies. On May 27th Suvorof surprised Turin, capturing more than 250 guns, 80 mortars and 60,000 muskets. By the end of the first week of June the Russian outposts had reached the head of the Alpine passes looking into France. A week later the Calabrian patriots, supported by a British fleet, captured Naples. Then on June 17th Suvorof, marching at high speed to cut Macdonald's line of retreat on the Trebbia, defeated him in one of the hardest-fought and bloodiest battles of the war. During the pursuit over the mountains the Russians took 13,000 prisoners, including four Generals.

In Germany and Switzerland also the fortunes of France were crumbling. Here, as in Italy, the Aulic Council had forbidden a vigorous pursuit in order to secure fortresses. For Thugut and his Emperor had learnt nothing from the defeats of four years. They had still to grasp that the first fruits of victory depended on destroying the enemy's army. Yet despite these handicaps the patient Archduke was ready by the beginning of June to attack the lines of Zurich. Though his first assault was repelled, he forced Massena by the 7th to fall back, leaving the city and immense stores of arms in his hands. As the French withdrew and the puppet Government of Swiss traitors fled in their wake, the peasantry rose in the hills.

. . . .

Such was the position at midsummer, 1799, less than eleven months after the deliverance of the Nile. Now 200,000 tired Frenchmen, dangerously spread out on a failing front from the Texel to Genoa, faced half again as many assailants commanded by two great masters of war. The Republic's attempt to restore the naval balance in the Mediterranean had failed, and beyond the narrow seas on her northern flank the untried Army of England was waiting its chance to attack.

For the conviction was growing that the hour for England's return to the Continent had come. Four years had passed since a British soldier had set foot on the European mainland save as a fugitive raider. During that time much had been done to make the Army a more effective force. By 1799 the folly of mortgaging the flower of the nation's manhood for sugar islands had at last dawned on the authorities. In five years 100,000 young Britons had been killed or permanently disabled by the Caribbean climate. But in 1797 General Abercromby had laid the foundation of a less wasteful policy by raising a dozen negro regiments to garrison the islands. When the planters threatened to flog all who joined, the shrewd old Scot succeeded in obtaining Dundas's authority to enfranchise negro recruits—an important step in human betterment achieved, not for the last time in British colonial administration through the exigencies of war and the courage of a liberal-minded soldier.

The Government, taught by bitter experience, endorsed the new system in defiance of vested interests. In the following year a thirty-eight-year-old Brigadier, Thomas Maitland, having taken over command at Mole St. Nicolas, entered into negotiations with the negro chieftain, Toussaint l'Ouverture, for a British evacuation of Santo Domingo. He had the sense to recognise that Toussaint and his dusky followers were as little friendly to the Republican authorities as they had been to the Royalist planters. By ceasing to make war on them and extending a hand of friendship, he won their gratitude and separated them from the French and Spaniards. His withdrawal from the island in October, 1798, was fiercely criticised by the West Indian slaveowners. But it saved the country thousands of precious lives.

Cornwallis's conciliatory Irish policy also lessened the strain on British man power. For the first time since the war began th

Government was able to use its forces where it wanted instead of being compelled to hurry them where they were needed. In December, 1798, General Stuart, after his conquest of Minorca, had proposed the formation of a Mediterranean force to operate against the enemy's southern flank. Striking at French communications on the Genoese Riviera in the summer of 1799, it might have engulfed the armies of Moreau and Macdonald in irretrievable disaster.

But the Government, having other plans, ignored Stuart. Political and naval considerations demanded the employment of the Army nearer home. Russia and Prussia, whose active co-operation was the major concern of British diplomacy in the winter of 1798-9, were both traditionally interested in the former United Netherlands. To win over Prussia Britain had offered its Sovereign a preponderant influence in Dutch affairs and, in the last resort, even annexation. And when Prussian cowardice and jealousy of Austria could not be overcome, Britain, with her eye on Russia, continued to make the expulsion of the French from Holland her first objective. For not only was it a natural meeting ground for British and Russian troops, but the menace of the Dutch coast still haunted the Admiralty.

On June 22nd, 1799, a treaty was signed by Britain and Russia for an immediate Anglo-Russian invasion of Holland. Britain was to provide 30,000 troops and find the money for 18,000 Russians. The hereditary Stadtholder of Holland and his son, the Prince of Orange, both exiles on English soil, assured the Cabinet that their countrymen would rise as one man against the French.

The project was linked up with a wider one for regrouping the Allied armies for a major offensive in the autumn. In Italy and Switzerland co-operation between Russia and Austria had been proving increasingly difficult. The half-crazed dictator of Russia, now in one of his recurrent moods of universal benevolence, was haunted by grandiloquent visions: of a holy league of all sovereign States to liquidate the Revolution, restore the pre-war international *status quo* (except in partitioned Poland) and re-unite Christendom. Alarmed by these, the *realpolitik* rulers of Austria, who neither wished to restore Piedmont to its Royal House nor exchange Venetia for Belgium, had forbidden the indignant Suvorof to press down the Alpine valleys into Savoy until he had reduced Mantua and the other Italian fortresses they coveted. In retaliation the Marshal had threatened to resign his command.

To resolve these discords it was decided to transfer Suvorof and his Russians to Switzerland where they were to join a second

Russian army, subsidised by England, which was due there in August under Korsakof. The Italian theatre was to be left to the Austrians, while the Archduke Charles was to march north to the defence of the Lower Rhine and so draw off French forces from Holland before the Anglo-Russian invasion.

This general post of commanders and armies in the middle of a campaign—bitterly opposed by the Archduke—was adopted at the moment that the French, rendered desperate by peril, were beginning to recover something of their old spirit. The murder of two of the French delegates to the dissolving Congress of Rastadt in the spring by a troop of drunken Austrian hussars had roused a frenzy of hatred against Germany. During the summer the French Government fell and a new Directory—in reality as corrupt as the old—was set up to prosecute the war more vigorously. The defeats on the Trebbia and at Zurich led to a renewal of Jacobin terrorism, a fresh conscription and the appointment of Bernadotte as War Minister. Under his regimen a forced loan was levied on property and 200,000 conscripts called to the colours.

. . . .

Such was the position in August, 1799, when the British prepared to launch their invasion of the Continent. As was inevitable in a parliamentary country the pros and cons of doing so had been widely discussed. Public opinion strongly supported the idea; despite Britain's achievement at sea there was a feeling that she was not pulling her weight and must rouse herself from sloth to renew the laurels of Agincourt and Blenheim. Two years of drilling against invasion had made the country martial-minded; the scarlet coat and bugle call had become natural to Englishmen. They had even founded a Military Academy, and established a Royal Staff Corps to train sappers in the science of reducing Continental fortresses. On June 4th the King on his sixty-second birthday took the salute in Hyde Park as 10,000 London Volunteers and Militia marched past with the precision of Prussians. The little monarch, erect on his white charger and making great sweeps with his hat, was beside himself at the sight, chuckling repeatedly over the gibe of a French General about a nation of shopkeepers. "Call them the Devil's Own!" he cried as the Inns of Court Volunteers swung past, "call them the Devil's Own!"[1]

All that Britons asked at that moment was to test their mettle against the enemy. The thought consoled them for the perpetual rain and cold of that cheerless, barren summer, relieved the shortage of coal and vegetables and even reconciled them to the new income

[1] Wheeler and Broadley, II, 244.

tax forms. Since the beginning of the year one after another of the Fencible regiments, had been voluntarily relinquishing their immunity to foreign service. For like the haughty seamen, they too wanted to have a crack at Johnny Crapaud. They had no doubt as to the result. At midsummer Canning recorded his belief in the imminent collapse of "the monstrous fabric of French crimes and cruelties and abominations."

Almost the only people who did not share the popular enthusiasm for an invasion of the Continent were the senior officers of the Regular Army. They knew too much of the might of the French armies and the haphazard methods of supply and transport employed by British politicians and administrators. Behind them was a long succession of disasters, surrenders and evacuations extending for nearly a quarter of a century over the present and American wars. Advanced in years, sobered by misfortune, long accustomed to fighting at a disadvantage, their minds lacked resilience.

Early in June the Government had summoned Sir Ralph Abercromby from Edinburgh to take the principal command. The brave old Scot, who was sixty-five, expressed the strongest disapproval of the project, which he predicted would be attended by the usual disasters. It was not, however, in his soldier's creed to refuse a professional task committed to him by the civil authority. The wisest course would have been to have passed him over for a younger man who believed in victory. But neither Stuart nor Moira—the two best general officers for a bold offensive—possessed the necessary seniority, and neither was popular with the Cabinet. Instead, the Duke of York was seconded from the Horse Guards to take command with Abercromby as chief adviser.

By its treaty with Russia the Government had committed itself to a larger expeditionary force than was immediately available. It therefore had recourse to the Militia. On July 12th, a month before the "secret armament" was to sail, an Act was hurried through Parliament to draft Militiamen into Regular regiments. In the prevailing mood of enthusiasm tens of thousands took the £10 bounty and volunteered for foreign service. Of their fine, soldierly appearance and potential fighting capacity, there could be no dispute. But of their readiness for Continental warfare, there was justification for a good deal.

While British cruisers harried the European coastline from Brest to the Texel, alarming the French authorities, a great military encampment was formed on the Kentish Downs between Canterbury and Deal. Here the advance guard of the invasion force assembled under Abercromby. And here, in growing numbers and in every degree of intoxication, came the bounty men from the Militia. The difficulty of absorbing them into their regiments in time to take the field never troubled the Government.

To supervise the great departure the Prime Minister and Secretary for War took up residence at Walmer Castle. Both were strongly impressed with the urgency of the venture. The summer was well advanced, the gale season approaching and the Continental campaign at a crucial stage. In September the Russians, moving to their new positions, were to strike in Switzerland, and the Archduke Charles was to take the offensive on the Lower Rhine. If Suvorof could smash Massena in the Alps as he had smashed Moreau in Lombardy, October might see a Slavonic invasion of France through her vulnerable Swiss frontier. The delivery of the British blow before the French levies could be mobilised might well prove decisive.

Pitt, therefore, showed impatience at Abercromby's interminable litany of obstacles. The fine old soldier, who under his shaggy eyebrows gave contemporaries the impression of a good-natured lion, was always raising difficulties in his slow, Scottish manner. He pointed out that the Army was almost entirely without facilities for moving its guns, sick, stores and provisions. "The Emperor of Russia," he wrote, "may make a general into a private man by his fiat, but he cannot make his army march without their baggage. It is only in a free country like ours that a Minister has absolute power over an army. . . . An army is not a machine that can move of itself; it must have the means of moving."[1] The complaints led to the hasty formation on August 12th of a Royal Wagon Train of five troops—increased in September to eight—each of four officers and seventy drivers, mostly retired cavalrymen: the first germ of an Army Service Corps.

But to Pitt all this was trifling: the ill-timed pedantry of an old woman in a red coat. "There are some people," he murmured, "who have pleasure in opposing whatever is proposed." Advised by the Foreign Office and Orange partisans, he was so obsessed with the idea that the Dutch would rise that it never occurred to him that the Army would have any difficulties of supply and communication. "The operation," wrote Grenville to Dundas, "will be rather a counter-revolution than a conquest." The politicians forgot that refugees are not the best judges of a country from which they have been expelled, and that there is a wide difference between sympathy with a foreign cause and revolutionary action to support it.

[1] *Fortescue*, IV, 646.

Just as the advance guard was preparing to embark, news arrived that the combined Fleets of France and Spain were returning from their fruitless Mediterranean foray. Though Keith was in close pursuit, there was always the possibility that they might sweep up the Channel and attack the assembled transports. But on August 12th it became known that Bruix had put into Brest. With a Grand Fleet of more than fifty battleships based on Torbay and "the whole naval power of France and Spain under lock and key,"[1] all danger passed. On the 13th, Abercromby was hurried to sea.

It was left to the General and Admiral Mitchell to decide whether the expedition should occupy Walcheren and the islands at the mouth of the Meuse or make a landing farther north on the tip of Holland called the Marsdiep between the North and Zuyder Seas. On the ground that Walcheren was too bare for concealment and that the Marsdiep isthmus, being long and narrow, was unlikely to be defended in force, Abercromby chose the latter. An initial success here would cut off the naval base of the Helder and endanger the Dutch fleet at the Texel. It would also enable the British, after forcing an entry into the Zuyder Zee, to advance southwards down the isthmus with both flanks protected by warships. The disadvantage was that the Marsdiep was some distance from the main centres of population where a rising was expected, and that before these could be reached the French might have time to organise strong resistance.

The initial wisdom of the decision was quickly proved. For on the first day at sea the almost incessant rain of the past few weeks turned to a south-wester. The transports would have fared ill among the islands. As it was they remained in danger for a week before the wind abated sufficiently to make a landing possible. During that time the country was in the greatest alarm, for no one had anticipated storms of such intensity and duration so early in the year.[2]

But the Navy did its work well. The two hundred vessels of the Fleet kept together, and on the 21st the wind fell. That night the low Dutch coast could be clearly seen in the moonlight. But next day, after the Dutch Governor of the Helder had been summoned to surrender, the storm again freshened. Not till the 26th, nearly a fortnight after leaving England, could the transports resume their station in-shore. By that time water and provisions were dangerously low. And owing to the Admiral's premature summons, the defenders were expecting a landing.

[1] *Spencer Papers*, III, 112.
[2] See *D'Arblay*, III, 188.

Abercromby, however, decided to persist. At dawn on the 27th disembarkation began at a point about four miles south of the Helder in the face of determined fire. It was covered by a tremendous barrage from the guns of Duncan's battleships which the old Admiral had placed at the disposal of the expedition. The first tow consisted of 3000 men. Daendels, the Dutch commander, had nearly twice as many. The flat-bottomed barges for which Abercromby had asked had not been provided and several boats overturned in the surf. But the fire of the great ships and the fierce persistence of the landing parties wore down the defenders, many of whom were in secret sympathy with the invaders. By nightfall the bulk of Abercromby's 10,000 troops were ashore, the sandhills of Groot and Klein Keten in their hands, and the Helder cut off from the rest of Holland. The British suffered about 500 casualties; the French and Dutch nearly three times as many.

Had old Abercromby, who had been in the heat of the fire all day,[1] been less exhausted, enemy losses would have been still heavier. By not pushing his outposts to the edge of the sandhills, where the marshy meadows to the Zuyder Zee could be overlooked, he allowed the garrison of the Helder to escape in the night along the solitary road running under the dunes. Early next morning John Moore, who had commanded the northernmost landing party, occupied the town without opposition.

Two days later Admiral Mitchell, entering the channel between the Helder and Texel Island, captured the Dutch fleet at anchor. At sight of the British ships the seamen forced their officers to haul down the Republican flag and hoist that of the House of Orange. Seven Dutch ships of the line—the survivors of Camperdown—and eighteen smaller warships with 6000 seamen passed into British keeping without firing a shot. "Thus," wrote John Moore in his diary, "the greatest stroke that has perhaps been struck in this war has been accomplished in a few hours and with a trifling loss. The expedition . . . began with every appearance against it. . . . It showed great enterprise in Sir Ralph to persevere in the attempt, and he has met with the success he deserved. The chances of war are infinite."[2]

Abercromby's victory of the 28th had struck panic into the doubting Dutch and filled the French authorities with dismay. In all Holland there were only 10,000 French troops, of whom 5000 were concentrated in Zeeland to prevent a landing in the islands. At any moment the Dutch army, another 20,000 men, might follow the

[1] Duncan to Spencer, 28th Aug., 1799.—*Spencer Papers*, III, 178.
[2] *Moore*, I, 343.

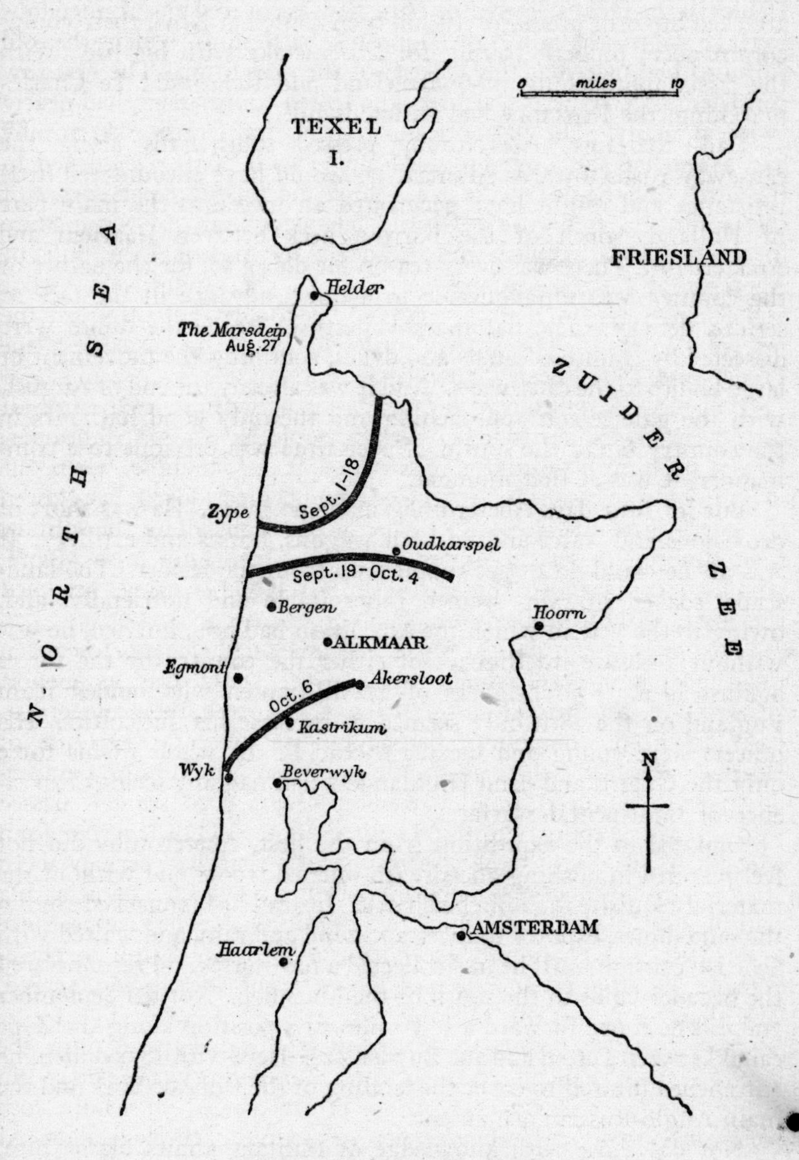

The Helder Campaign, 1799.

fleet's example. It was idle to hope for aid from Paris. A fortnight before the French in Italy, attempting to relieve Mantua, had attacked Suvorof prematurely and been routed at Novi, their young commander, Joubert, paying for his mistake with his life. With the crisis approaching in Switzerland and the Archduke Charles marching, the Directory had its hands full.

Had, therefore, Abercromby pressed southwards along the causeway roads towards Alkmaar he would have encountered little resistance and might have penetrated at once into the main part of Holland, south of the narrow neck between Haarlem and Amsterdam. There was every reason for doing so, for the nature of the country was unfavourable to a quick advance in the face of serious defence. The flat marshy pastures inside the dunes were dissected by countless canals and dykes, confining the movement of large bodies to the causeways. And it was already the end of August, with the gale season approaching and the only good harbours in the country far to the south. If ever time was precious to a commander, it was at that moment.

But for four days Abercromby made no move. He was short of provisions and water and without wagons, horses and artillery. It was all he could do to get supplies up from the Helder. The landscape, soaked in rain, seemed inhospitable and unfriendly, and, owing to the way in which the expedition had been hurried, he was without accurate intelligence of either the country or the forces against him. Two brigades of ex-Militiamen who landed from England on the 28th only seemed to increase his difficulties. His officers were young and inexperienced. In the whole of his force only the Guards and 92nd Highlanders had had any serious experience of Continental warfare.

Opposed to the expedition from the first, Abercromby did not feel justified in pushing ahead with untried troops and without the material requisite for a pitched battle. Instead he bivouacked among the sand dunes, exposed to incessant wind and rain, and waited with Scottish caution until he had collected a few horses and reconnoitred the broader lands to the south of the Marsdiep. Not till September 2nd did he move forward a few miles to a position along the Zype canal between Petten and the Zuyder Zee. Here with 18,000 men, he entrenched himself to cover the landing of the Duke of York and the main Anglo-Russian armament.

Nor did those with knowledge of military affairs blame him. The King, when the news reached him at Weymouth on September 1st, wrote that it would be best to follow up the initial success with caution and wait for reinforcements to make the next move decisive.

The country was thrilled by the landing, the bloodless capture of the Dutch fleet and the news of Suvarof's victory at Novi: the thought of an early peace made up even for the summer's deluge and ruined crops. Soon the gallant Russians from the Baltic would be emulating among Dutch water-meadows and windmills the exploits of their countrymen in Italy. Meanwhile every day witnessed the departure of more splendid-looking regiments from the great camp on Barham Downs and the arrival of more Militiamen. That the latter were in such a state as to be unable even to turn out for a review which the Prime Minister wished to hold after Abercromby's victory, worried no one: the eighteenth century expected soldiers to be drunk when they had money in their pockets. And the moment seemed one for legitimate intoxication. Pitt confidently expected that the Army, having freed Holland, would soon be at liberty for a still more glorious operation. For with French Royalists in arms and the combined navies of France and Spain bottled up in Brest, a wonderful possibility floated before British minds. Plans for a new expedition to Brittany were preparing in the Admiralty and War Office, and there was even talk of a Russian landing on the banks of the Seine.[1]

Meanwhile the naval and military commanders in the field continued to wait on events. Not being engaged with the enemy, they fell to quarrelling with one another. Precautions, born of earlier experience, had been taken to prevent this: before the expedition sailed Vice-Admiral Mitchell had issued an Order of the Day recommending all under him "to behave with that good fellowship and cordiality towards the troops they are about to serve with as shall cause them to meet a return of a like esteem, by which they will be mutually endeared to each other and the better enabled to act with zeal and energy in their Sovereign's cause." Such co-operation, he added, could not fail to ensure success.[2] But by September 4th Mitchell was complaining of Abercromby and Abercromby of Mitchell. The latter—described by St. Vincent as a "bull-necked Centurion"—seemed to think that his own part in the invasion had ended with the surrender of the Dutch fleet. For though the General repeatedly urged him—"in the strongest terms" —to fit out gunboats and use them in the Zuyder Zee against the French right and rear, Mitchell did not even trouble to answer his colleague's letters. The truth is that both officers had reached an age when they found it difficult to take the initiative.

General Brune, Commander-in-Chief of the French forces in

[1] *Spencer Papers*, III, 117-25.
[2] *Spencer Papers*, III, 156.

Holland, had no such difficulty. He was thirty years younger than Abercromby: an active, impulsive man, typical of his country and the Revolution that had made him. He used the breathing-space given him by the cautious invaders to assemble his troops and hurry them into the threatened peninsula north of the Haarlem isthmus. By September 9th he had got together 21,000 men, a force slightly superior to Abercromby's but, being two-thirds of it Dutch, of uncertain sympathies. But as Abercromby so unaccountably did nothing, Brune assumed—what the former never seemed to assume—that his foe must have grave difficulties of his own. He therefore attacked him at dawn on the 10th.

In this he erred. All along the line he was repelled with heavy loss. The Militia lads from the English shires, fighting in prepared defensive positions, showed a steady courage worthy of Burrard's Brigade of Guards. The Dutch, aware that their hereditary Prince was in the British lines, took to their heels at the first chance, and the French were forced to retreat. Had Abercromby under his stolid Scottish courage possessed the imagination to realise the effect of his victory on the Dutch mind, he might—with support from Mitchell's gunboats—have been in Amsterdam in two days.

But instead of thinking of Brune's difficulties, which at the moment seemed to that volatile Frenchman wellnigh desperate, Abercromby could think of nothing but his own. Nearly two thousand of his men, landed on an inhospitable shore without greatcoats or adequate tent equipment, were sick; fuel, food and water were short; transport hopelessly deficient and communication with the ships constantly interrupted by the surf. The shivering troops could not even obtain spirits, since no sutler had been sent from England. As for the Dutch, all that Abercromby could see were stolid, sullen farmers who lounged about his lines with their pipes in their mouths like passive spectators of an unpleasant disturbance and chaffered with his commissariat officers for their cattle and boats.[1] They were very unlike the ardent patriots whom the Prince of Orange had painted in such glowing colours before the expedition sailed. "I believe the Prince has been deceived," wrote the old soldier, "in thinking that he has more friends than enemies in this country. If we can advance, every one will be on our side, but there are few who will risk anything."[2] He failed to see that in this he condemned himself.

But Abercromby's period of sole responsibility was nearing an end. On the night of September 12th the Duke of York landed and

[1] Bunbury, II, 41.
[2] *Fortescue*, IV, 668.

during the next few days 8000 more British arrived and 12,000 Russians. The latter were escorted from the Baltic by Captain Sir Home Popham. They were men of an incredible toughness, "all hoffs, choffs and koffs," who slept on bare decks, lived on boiled grain and quas and even ate with relish the tallow which they scraped out of the ships' lanterns and washed down with train oil. On one British frigate the Russian captain, who was much liked for his jovial courage, never took his boots off the whole voyage and spent much of his time sharpening his spear on the ship's grinding-stone, swearing he would sacrifice every Frenchman he met.[1]

No attempt was made to use the newcomers in a landing farther down the coast in the French rear—the nightmare that haunted Brune. But the return of Lord Duncan from sick leave and the arrival of Home Popham stimulated Admiral Mitchell to a certain activity. Popham was full of ideas, even bombarding the First Lord with them: he was aware, he apologised, that he was forward in projects but, since they were sure to be modified by steadier military heads, they could do no harm. Meanwhile he prepared gunboats to harry the French flanks.

The Duke of York was now at the head of an army of more than 40,000 men, three-quarters of them British: as large a force as any Englishman had commanded on the Continent since Marlborough. But it was understood that, as a constitutional prince, he was to be guided by the advice of his senior Lieutenant-Generals—Abercromby, David Dundas, Pulteney and Lord Chatham. As his strength was nearing its maximum he decided to attack without delay—a resolve which, in view of the purpose of the expedition, his advisers could scarcely challenge—and fight his way to the defile of Holland and thence to Amsterdam. He divided his force into four columns: 12,000 Russians among the North Sea sand dunes on the right under General D'Hermann, and 12,000 British under Abercromby on the left, with two smaller columns under Dundas and Pulteney in between. For the first time in the war the artillery was to act under a single command, the guns being withdrawn from the battalions and massed in "brigades" or batteries with their own drivers. Among them was one to become famous: the new "Chestnut" Battery.

On the evening of September 18th Abercromby set off to cover the fifteen miles to Hoorn on the shores of the Zuyder Zee, where he was to guard the Allied left and utilise any success won by the main forces to the west. Before dawn on the 19th he had surprised

[1] *Gardner*, 207; *Spencer Papers*, III, 17.

and captured the town. Here his tired men lay down to rest and await events. On the right the Russians, two hours before the scheduled time, had already commenced their attack. Advancing down the road under the sandhills they pushed forward in a solid mass at immense speed, heroically oblivious to their losses. Storming the village of Groat they poured through the enemy's entrenchments and forced their way into Bergen, two miles behind his lines. Had there been a reserve close behind to follow up their success, the battle would have been won by eight in the morning.

But owing to their having started two hours too early, Dundas's column was not yet in position to support them. As soon as they entered the town the Russians, who by this time were little more than a brave mob firing wildly in every direction, lost impetus and began to straggle after plunder. When Brune, throwing in his reserve, counter-attacked, they proved no match for the clever and experienced French. General D'Hermann was killed, his second-in-command taken prisoner and the survivors driven back in confusion. Their panic, following hard on their incredible valour of the dawn, communicated itself to the untrained British Militia, and the situation on the right was only saved by the steadiness of the Artillery and Brigade of Guards. When one of the Duke's staff called on a hard-pressed battalion of the First Guards, nearing the end of its physical powers and ammunition, to hold a village, one of the Grenadiers lifted his chin from the muzzle of his rifle and growled: "Give us some more cartridges and we will see what can be done." And they held it.

While Dundas's wearied men struggled to retrieve the Russian débâcle, Pulteney's column—of which nothing much had been hoped—was steadily pushing ahead across dykes and canals. By two in the afternoon it had carried the village of Oudkarspel, midway between Bergen and Hoorn. An hour later the Dutch troops facing it began to yield before its steady volleys. Daendels, their commander, was carried away in the flying stream and only narrowly escaped capture. The battle which had been all but won in the morning and even more nearly lost at noon, trembled again in the balance as the scales tilted towards a British victory. Had Abercromby resumed his march from Hoorn and appeared, as intended in such an event, on the flank of the shattered Dutch at Alkmaar, he might have converted the defeat of the enemy's centre into a rout. But he spent the day resting and waiting for information. The virtual immobilisation of 12,000 British troops a dozen miles from the battlefield robbed the Allies of their numerical superiority. At dusk the Duke of York, shaken by the failure of his right, broke off the battle and recalled Abercromby to his lines.

Such was the Battle of Bergen: "the unfortunate 19th," as Admiral Mitchell described it in an indignant dispatch to the Admiralty. It cost the British 1450 men and the Russians 2600 men and twenty-six guns. The French and Dutch lost sixteen guns and about the same number of men. But as they remained in possession of their lines and the Allies failed to force their way to the defile of Holland, the French claimed the victory. The most serious consequences was the bad feeling roused between Russians and British. The former, forgetting their disregard of the time schedule, attributed their defeat and the loss of their commander solely to their allies' failure to support them. The latter were equally shocked by what they regarded as Russian ill-discipline and barbarity. "The Russians is people," wrote one scandalised Militiaman, "as has not the fear of God before their eyes, for I saw some of them with cheeses and butter and all badly wounded, and in particular one man had an eit day clock on his back and fiting all the time which made me to conclude and say all his vanity and vexation."[1] Matters were not improved by the Duke of York, who enjoyed a Hanoverian talent for mimicry and who, though the kindest of men and the soul of tact in his official letters, was apt in his cups among his familiars to indulge it at the expense of the Muscovite generals.[2]

Direct attack having failed to dislodge the French, a council of war was held to consider other possibilities. The Duke proposed that 4000 more Russians from Kronstadt and some fresh troops from England should be used with part of the forces already landed either in a descent on the North Sea coast behind the French lines or in an attack from the Zuyder Zee on Amsterdam, where the Dutch were reported to be spoiling for a rising. But both Abercromby and David Dundas opposed amphibious operations of any kind—a prejudice which they seemed to share with Admiral Mitchell. The Duke therefore reluctantly abandoned the idea in favour of a second frontal attack.

Planned for September 29th, the attempt had to be postponed till October 2nd owing to another appalling bout of storm and rain. This time the main assault on the French left was undertaken by Abercromby with the pick of the British Army. Advancing rapidly along the beach, he reached the village of Egmont seven miles down the coast before encountering serious opposition. But here, lacking trained riflemen capable of dealing with the French sharpshooters, he suffered heavy casualties, including his second-in-

[1] Colburn's *Military Magazine*, Feb., 1836, cit. *Fortescue*, IV, 677.
[2] *Bunbury*, II, 44.

command, Major-General Moore, who was dangerously wounded. It was the skill and gallantry shown that day by this young hero—now thirty-seven—which laid the foundations of that reputation as the first soldier of the new army which he retained till his death at Corunna.

Meanwhile the other three columns were held up by the main French lines around the village of Bergen, three miles away, largely through the refusal of the Russians to obey orders. Had Abercromby been able to march to Dundas's assistance he might have cut off the main enemy force and won a decisive victory. But his men were exhausted, parched with thirst and short of ammunition. He again forgot that his opponent's plight might be still worse. After dusk Brune withdrew unmolested, leaving the British in possession of Alkmaar and the Egmonts.

The hopes of those inclined to hope—of the politicians at home and the younger officers on the spot—now rose again. Spencer described Egmont as a "glorious and important victory"; Popham thought that after the "wonderful gallantry of the British troops" the French would soon be pushed beyond the Meuse. But the generals did not share the prevailing optimism. Even the news of the Archduke's speedy capture of Mannheim failed to cheer them. They were oppressed with the lack of transport, the soaking ground and endless dykes under the lowering Dutch skies and the pitiless surf that endangered their precarious communications with England. They pushed on slowly after the enemy, but they did so with heavy hearts. Yet had they been able to read the letters passing between the French commanders and their Government in Paris, they might have felt—and behaved—differently.

For after Egmont even Brune abandoned hope. He wrote on October 4th that if the British continued to attack, lassitude among his troops might cause disaster, that Dutch desertion was growing, and that the Batavian Government, impressed by the Allied successes, was showing unmistakable signs of hedging. Like the Duke of York, he was short of provisions, his bread wagons having been taken for the wounded and large supplies having been abandoned at Alkmaar. Such was the position when on October 6th the Allies cautiously resumed their advance, with the intention of reconnoitring the new French-Batavian line from Wyk on the North Sea through Kastrikum to Akersloot, about half a dozen miles south of Alkmaar. Beyond it lay the narrow defile, scarcely four miles wide, between the ocean and an inlet of the Zuyder Zee, through which the interior could alone be reached.

That morning Abercromby, advancing along the North Sea

beach, found himself at the outskirts of Wyk, some way in front of the general Allied movement and within easy striking distance of the defile. On the left of the line Dundas also moved rapidly, capturing Akersloot and pushing on towards Uitgeest, half-way between that place and the Zuyder Zee. But in the centre Brune, opposed by a Russian column outside Kastrikum, called up his reserves and with characteristic impetuosity counter-attacked. Within a few minutes what had been intended by the Allied Command as an affair of outposts became a general engagement. The Russians, their discipline undermined by suspicion, were only saved from disaster by a brilliant charge of the 7th Light Dragoons under Lord Paget, sixteen years later to command the cavalry at Waterloo. Abercromby, abandoning all hope of seizing the defile, was also forced to hurry to their aid.

For several hours a desperate fight continued round Kastrikum. It was pelting with rain, the country was confused and intricate, and clouds of smoke hung like fog in the trees. The Duke, trying to follow the course of events from the church tower of Alkmaar, completely lost control of the battle. Both he and his advisers were deceived by the vigour of Brune's counter-attack into believing that the French had received reinforcements from the interior—a fear which had grown during the melancholy weeks of waiting into an obsession.

The feelings of the opposing commanders on the morrow of the battle were, therefore, curiously similar. Brune, whose outnumbered soldiers, though temporarily successful against the Russians, had been worsted by nightfall at every point by the stubborn patience of the British, felt that any renewal of the fight would result in the rout of his army and an Orange rising. Abercromby and David Dundas, appalled by their casualties and the inexperience of their young Militiamen—"all powerful if attacked but without resource if beaten"[1]—and baffled by problems of supply and transport, multiplied tenfold by the weather, felt that the only safety lay in a strong defensive line. They, therefore, represented to the Duke the necessity for an immediate retreat to the Zype canal. The young Commander-in-Chief, realising the gravity of the decision, asked them to put their reasons in writing. This they did in a compendious "Appreciation of the Situation" which enumerated all their own difficulties and dangers and omitted those of the enemy. They appreciated everything except the situation "on the other side of the hill."[2]

[1] Abercromby to Dundas, Oct., 1799—*Fortescue*, IV, 699.

[2] See two brilliant articles by Colonel Alfred Burne in the *Army Quarterly* and the *Fighting Forces* for October, 1939.

To the dismay, therefore, of the British rank and file, who imagined in the words of one of them that they had given the French a "complete drubbing,"[1] and to the even greater astonishment of the enemy, the Allied Army on the evening of October 7th began to retreat. By the 9th it was back in its old lines behind the Zype. Some of the supply wagons took two days to cover the nine miles of mud. Ironically, as soon as they reached safety the weather cleared for the first time that autumn and grew so mild that the troops were able to bathe. Their spirits, however, did not recover.

The retreat was the subject of mutual reproaches between the Services. Admiral Mitchell announced that what he had always dreaded had come to pass: the army had missed a glorious opportunity and should have been in Amsterdam long ago. "You'll pardon my ideas of a soldier," he wrote to the First Lord, "I hope that your Lordship does not think that I mean to criminate." It is just to add that his more enterprising subordinate, Home Popham, did not share his views. As an experienced transport officer he had grown deeply impressed with the badness of the army's communications, the inadequacy of its single port and the shortage of shipping. He felt, too, that the expedition had been sent to the wrong place.

. . . .

Two days after the retreat all hope of using the army against any other part of Holland was dashed by the news from Germany. The departure of the Archduke Charles from Zurich and the arrival of Korsakoff's Russians had been followed by a succession of disasters. From the first the latter had shown a dangerous contempt for the enemy and a disregard of all normal precautions. Where the Archduke advised the posting of a regiment, Korsakoff only placed a company, remarking scornfully: "I understand you; an Austrian battalion or a Russian company!" The convergent movements from widely separated mountain valleys by which the Russians were to drive the French from Switzerland would have been perilous if directed against undisciplined barbarians: in the face of Massena it was madness. Before Suvorof, battling his way over the Alps with incredible hardihood, could emerge from the St. Gothard, the French had flung their main force against Zurich. By the night of September 24th Korsakoff's army was surrounded.

Russian heroism redeemed Russian folly, but failed to avert disaster. Korsakoff, disdaining Massena's summons to surrender, fought his way out of the trap, but at the cost of all his horse, guns and transport. Suvorof drove his army over goat-tracks along the

[1] Surtees, *Twenty-five Years in the Rifle Brigade*, 28.

edge of precipices to the rendezvous, only to find that his countrymen and the Austrians had been forced to retreat. To escape destruction he had to break through a ring of foes and lead his exhausted and starving veterans over desolate passes of ice and snow. Achieving what to any other man would have been impossible, he lost 13,000 men, every cannon and waggon he possessed, and all but broke his heart. It was the first time the old hero had ever been defeated.

• • • • • • •

The Cabinet reviewed these events on October 15th. In view of the uselessness of further campaigning, the mounting toll of British sick and the reports of the Admiralty on the difficulties of maintaining supplies on that windswept coast, they resolved—Grenville alone protesting—to abandon the idea of holding the Helder during the winter. Three days later the Duke of York agreed with Brune for an armistice. Each side still under-estimated the other's difficulties. Brune was haunted by the fear of a Dutch rising and by news of Chouan successes on the Loire. The invaders, who had only three days' bread left, were therefore to their surprise allowed to depart in peace. Eight thousand French prisoners were to be repatriated, but not the Dutch fleet. "Whatever the British do, they always succeed in adding to the number of their ships," an Austrian observer noted.

The evacuation was completed early in November though at a loss of four ships and several hundred men. The Russians were landed at Yarmouth, where they alarmed the inhabitants by drinking the oil from the street lamps.[1] The country after its high hopes was bitterly disappointed. Pitt tried to explain the failure away by the weather, contending—falsely—that the diversion had enabled the Russians and Austrians to triumph at Novi. "It ought," he added, "to be a source of satisfaction to us that our army has been restored to us safe and entire." But the country took no pleasure in the thought, and the Opposition made full use of its opportunity. Sheridan, imitating Pitt's Jove-like complacency, pointed out that, besides the capture of the Dutch fleet, the nation had gained some useful knowledge. It had been found that no reliance could be placed in the Prime Minister's knowledge of human nature, that Holland was a country intersected by dykes, that the weather in October was not so good as in June. The question was whether the price paid had not been too dear.

The worst consequence of the débâcle was that the country lost its reviving faith in the Army. The bounding confidence of the summer was succeeded by an extreme pessimism about Continental

[1] *Fortescue*, IV, 701.

operations. Sheridan expressed the general view of Dundas's offensive policy by describing it as "nibbling at the rind of France." From this moment until Arthur Wellesley's first victories in Portugal nine years later, the British people, as opposed to their Prime Minister, took up a *non possumus* attitude as to their ability to rescue Europe from itself. They concentrated their efforts instead on saving themselves.

Before the sailing of the expedition Windham had predicted that it would destroy in the bud, and before it came to its full strength, an Army that with a little delay might have exceeded anything yet known by England.[1] But what it destroyed was not the Army but the nation's faith in its ability to use it. Pitt's airy notion of doubling it with further drafts from the Militia faded into nothing. Dundas's project for capturing the Combined Fleets by a landing on the Brest peninsula—something that "by its brilliancy and importance might surpass the battle of the Nile"[2]—lost its appeal. And though in pursuit of Windham's Chouan crusade the now thoroughly disgruntled Russians were moved to the Channel Islands—where their impact on the islanders appears to have been much like that of Peter the Great on Evelyn's holly hedges—the preparations for a descent on France were pursued with little vigour. The insurgents, instead of receiving the troops they had hoped for from England, only saw their enemies reinforced, for, as soon as the British had departed, Brune's army set off at full speed for the Loire.

• • • • • •

As the hopes of England, so high for the past year, fell, those of France rose. On the day that the British regained the lines of the Zype, Napoleon Bonaparte landed at Frejus. When the people of the little town heard the news they swarmed down to the waterside, breaking quarantine, and bore the hero ashore. For the stature of the absent General had been steadily rising in the French imagination. All others who had taken his place—soldiers and politicians alike—were knaves and bunglers: he alone was invincible, patriotic and virtuous. The people knew nothing of his failures: everything of his successes. His return was preceded by the news of an astonishing victory in July when, following his withdrawal from Syria, he had routed an army of 15,000 Turks landed by a British squadron at Aboukir. Scarcely a man had escaped his terrible recoil.[3] Now, hearing of the plight of his war-racked country from some newspapers which Sidney Smith had sent him,

[1] *Windham*, II, 113.
[2] *Spencer Papers*, III, 128.
[3] One of the very few to reach the British ships was an Albanian private, thirty years later to become famous as Mehemet Ali.

he had run the gauntlet of the British cruisers and after a thrilling six weeks' voyage reached France.

The pear was ripe for his plucking. The French people were longing for a deliverer. To them Bonaparte appeared as the heir of the Revolutionary dream. All the way to Paris, vast crowds surrounded his carriage, acclaiming him as their saviour. Only the corrupt Directors and politicians did not want him, and they were divided among themselves. Within three weeks of his arrival he had cast in his lot with the strongest faction and by armed force had overthrown the Constitution. It was the most popular thing that had happened in France since the meeting of the States General.

But to the English, wearily watching these events from the other side of the Channel, it was only another sordid Paris revolution. On the whole, so far as ruined hopes and crops enabled them to rejoice at anything, they welcomed it, for they felt that the new regime could not last. Canning thought it portended a restoration of the Bourbons: the two Dictators, Bonaparte and Sieyès, linked only by their common treachery to others, would soon betray one another. Windham was not so hopeful: to him the only lesson to be learnt from the latest display of illegality across the Channel was that all intercourse or compromise with the evil thing must be shunned. "A Government such as the present, dropt from the clouds or rather starting from underneath the ground, is in no state to offer anything. It cannot answer for its own existence for the next four-and-twenty hours."[1]

Accordingly when, having been elevated under a brand new Constitution to the rank of First Consul, Bonaparte on Christmas Day, 1799, addressed a personal letter to King George proposing peace, it was treated with scant courtesy. Couched in reasonable terms and asking whether the war between the two countries which had ravaged the earth for eight years was to continue until it had destroyed civilisation, it was viewed in England merely as a trick to upset the financial treaty impending with Austria in return for that country's agreement to restore the King of Piedmont. It was also regarded—from an upstart like Napoleon—as an impertinence. No reply was therefore returned. A memorandum, sent by the Foreign Secretary to Talleyrand, stated in frigid terms that His Majesty saw no reason to depart from the forms long established for transacting business with foreign States and that the French people's best hope of peace, if they wanted it, was to restore their ancient rulers. A surer way of rendering the Bourbons unpopular could scarcely have been devised.

[1] Windham to Pitt, 18th Nov., 1799.—*Windham Papers*, II, 143.

Yet British statesmen were right in believing that Bonaparte's motives were not genuine. "What I need," he told Junot at a New Year's Eve reception, "is time, and time is just the one thing that I cannot afford. Once conclude peace, and then—a fresh war with England!" His aim was to drive a wedge between the Allies and pose to his countrymen as the apostle of reason and moderation. The Foreign Office's foolish reply enabled him to prove to the French people, who were longing for peace, that peace was made impossible by the selfish, grasping islanders and their dupes, the Austrians. Already the Russians, furious at the Austrian intrigues which had robbed them of victory, had virtually dropped out of the war. The soldier Bonaparte, wanting to give Europe peace, was denied it by foreign usurers and mediocre politicians. The only thing left him was to teach these blunderers how to wage war.

So the man who had been raised to supreme power to give France peace, was able to ask his countrymen for new armies. He recalled the exiled Carnot to the War Office and raised a quarter of a million men. In the utmost secrecy he built up a great reserve. It was his intention—though he was debarred from doing so by Sieyès's bogus Constitution—to lead it in person. For it had not been to keep Cromwell from the battlefield that the Self-Denying Ordinance had been passed.

France's recovery was too sudden and miraculous to be yet apparent to the outer world. Despite Russia's defection, the Dutch fiasco and the reverses in Switzerland, the odds still seemed to favour the Allies. Austria, aided by a new British loan, had concentrated an enormous army in Italy, where all but the last vestiges of French conquest had been eliminated. The British Navy, stronger than ever, commanded the Atlantic, the North Sea and the Mediterranean. Malta and Egypt were still locked in an iron ring.

Moreover, Britain still had an Army. With 80,000 Regular troops and a large force of Militia and Volunteers for home defence, she could play her part in the coming land campaign if she chose. "Bring me back as many good troops as you can," Dundas had told Abercromby after the decision to evacuate the Helder, "and before next spring I will show you an army the country never saw before."[1] In December Stuart had again urged that the 6000 troops of the Mediterranean Command at Minorca should be brought up to sufficient strength to strike in the rear of the struggling French on the Genoese Riviera. With 15,000 more men he guaranteed his ability to cut their communications at any point between Genoa and Toulon.

[1] *Fortescue*, IV, 775.

But the Government's military nerve had been shattered. For six weeks it returned no answer to Stuart's proposals. Not till the beginning of February, 1800, and then only to hearten its Austrian ally, did it approve his plan in principle. But it proceeded to cut down the proposed reinforcement from 15,000 to 10,000, and in March from 10,000 to 5,000. And even these were not ready to sail till April.

For the Cabinet was now hopelessly divided. Dundas on the whole was in favour of Stuart's expedition. But Windham still passionately advocated the Chouan cause, which neither he nor his colleagues were aware was already lost. He represented the obligation to help the Royalists before they were overwhelmed as a first call on Britain's honour and was so persistent that he carried his point. Six thousand troops were set apart for an operation off the Brittany coast, and in May were dispatched under Thomas Maitland to seize Belleisle. They found the place far too strongly held to be taken and spent five precious weeks in transports off the Breton coast waiting for new orders from England.

By the time that the other 5,000, after idling for nearly a month at their anchorage, sailed under General Pigott for Minorca at the end of April, Stuart, worn out by fretting and disappointment, had resigned. The cause of his final breach with Dundas was his refusal to accede to a Cabinet decision—taken in an eleventh hour attempt to placate Russia—to hand over the brave people of Malta to the despotism of the Tsar. In this he was politically right: the decision was dishonourable and in any case useless, for Russia had already resolved to withdraw from the Coalition. But as Dundas said: "If officers are to control our councils there is an end to all government," and Stuart had to go.[1] He died eleven months later, one of the great soldiers England has wasted.

He was succeeded in the Mediterranean Command by Abercromby. The instructions given to the old man by the Cabinet mark the nadir in British strategy. With a total force of 12,000 he was to reinforce the besiegers of Malta, provide 4000 for the defence of Minorca, assist the Austrian armies in Italy, co-operate with any rising in the south of France, protect Naples and Portugal and, if possible, attack Tenerife.

Abercromby sailed in the frigate *Seahorse* on May 15th, 1800, accompanied by Major-Generals Moore and Hutchison. Before he reached Minorca on June 22nd, the Continental campaign in which he was to have taken part was over. At the beginning of April the Austrians, concentrating more than 100,000 men in northern Italy,

[1] *Fortescue*, IV, 777.

had taken the offensive under old Melas. By the middle of the month they had cut the French army in two and driven Massena into Genoa. At that moment Lord Keith's fleet had complete command of the sea. Had any British troops been available they could have been landed at any point on the French or Italian Riviera.

But the sands of Allied opportunity were running out. On April 25th the French, ostensibly concentrating their main forces in southern Germany, crossed the Rhine under Moreau. Within a fortnight they had defeated Kray at Moesskirch and forced him back to the Upper Danube. This was Bonaparte's moment. On May 15th, having made the most careful preparations, he began the passage of the Great Saint Bernard with 50,000 men. A week later he emerged on the north Italian plain in the rear of the Austrian army.

Thereafter events moved at the usual dazzling speed. On June 5th, three days after Bonaparte entered Milan, Massena, reduced to his last rat, surrendered Genoa. On the same day Lord Keith sent an urgent summons to General Fox at Minorca for British troops to hold the port, since every Austrian was needed to meet the threat of Bonaparte's army to the north. But Fox, though Pigott's 5000 from England had now joined him, could do nothing—save assemble transports—until his new Commander-in-Chief arrived from England. "For God's sake," Grenville had written to Dundas two months before, "for your own honour and the cause for which we are engaged, do not let us, after having by immense exertions collected an army, leave it unemployed, gaping after messengers from Genoa, Augsburg and Vienna till the moment for acting is irrevocably past by."[1] It was precisely what the Secretary-for-War had done.

It was Britain's last chance to liquidate the Revolution before it turned into something more terrible. On June 14th, 1800, the main armies met at Marengo. It was one of the most closely contested battles in history. At one moment disaster faced Bonaparte. Had the troops Stuart had begged for been fighting by the side of the Austrians it must have ended in an allied victory. As it was, Bonaparte's reserves, flung into the scale at the eleventh hour, gave France the decision. Next day Melas, his communications cut, signed a convention abandoning all northern Italy west of the Mincio.

From the battlefield on June 16th the victor addressed a letter to the ruler of Austria: "I have the honour of acquainting your Majesty with the desire of the French people that an end be put to the war that lays waste our two countries. English craft and

[1] *Pitt and the Great War*, 386.

cunning have repressed the effect which this simple and candid wish must have on the heart of your Majesty. On the battlefield of Marengo, amidst the dying and wounded, surrounded by 15,000 dead bodies, I beg your Majesty to lend ear to the cry of humanity and not to permit the younger generation of two powerful and courageous countries to murder one another in the interest of causes with which they have no concern."[1] At that moment the British Secretary-for-War was dispatching new orders to Maitland off Belleisle to send 4000 men to Minorca for important operations on the Italian Riviera.

A week later Abercromby reached Port Mahon. On reading Keith's appeal for troops to hold Genoa, he at once sailed with 10,000 men in the transports Fox had prepared. Before he could arrive the French were in the town. Two hundred miles to the north of the Lombard plain where Bonaparte again ruled, the French under Moreau, having defeated Kray near Ulm, were entering Munich. The Austrians, fighting alone, had been beaten on every front. "Our own army," wrote the Foreign Secretary, "could not have done worse!"

[1] *Frischauer*, 100.

CHAPTER THIRTEEN

Of Nelson and the North

1800-1

"The meteor flag of England
Shall yet terrific burn
Till danger's troubled night depart
And the star of peace return."

Campbell.

THE transformation wrought by Marengo and Moreau's victories on the Danube left the combatants a little breathless. The proud Austrian armies, which a short while before had threatened France with invasion, were still in being, but their prestige had been shattered. Bonaparte, on the other hand, was back where he had stood after Rivoli. His humiliations in Egypt and Syria were wiped out. Marengo, so near at one moment to being a defeat, had decided his destiny. His charter to rule was clearly writ in its blood.

Immediately after the battle he returned to Paris. His first thought, as always in the hour of success, was to consolidate his position. From the royal palace of the Tuileries he opened a diplomatic offensive. To Austria he proposed peace on the tacit understanding that she should abandon her alliance with Britain. To the Tsar of Russia he offered Malta, where the French garrison of Valetta still precariously held out against its besiegers. To Spain he offered an Italian kingdom for the Queen's brother and dropped a hint to the dictator, Godoy, of a Lusitanian throne when the English should be driven from Portugal.

To his own people he proffered new laws and regulations, lucid, rational and beneficent: extended trade and glory; everything, in fact, except liberty. The Revolution, he explained, was over; the time had come to enjoy its fruits. He gave the peasant security in his lands against the feudal lords, the right to attend his parish church—so long as the priest kept out of politics—and an assured market for his produce. He gave the new rich and the bourgeoisie pomp and an ordered society. He ended the cruel dissensions of the past ten years and raised the proscription on more than a hundred thousand exiles. With the same unresting energy that he showed in battle, he established a new national administration. For all this he asked one thing only; absolute and universal obedience to his will. Those who were unwise enough to oppose him he subjected to a purge of death or deportation. Even over Fouché's police he set a secret police of his own with spies and informers everywhere. It was a price which France was ready to pay. "Gentlemen," declared Sieyès, "you have a master over you. Bonaparte wants everything, knows everything and can do everything!" The country rejoiced in its new-found despotism.

The truce in Italy was followed by another in Germany. The French armies in both theatres of war were to continue to live at large on the territories they had conquered, while the encircled Imperial garrisons were to be re-victualled every fortnight for two weeks only. With the liquidation of the Revolution by a Cæsar, the war had suddenly become unreal to the tired peoples of Europe. They were ready for a new order. An Englishman lodging at Frankfurt-on-Main had left a description of the arrival of the French there that July. They did not seem to come as enemies but merely as friendly conquerors. The young officer who was billeted on the house did not even resent the fact that his fellow lodger was an Englishman. On the contrary he discussed poetry with him and shared with relish in the delights of the new German—and revolutionary—dance, the waltz.

On July 21st, 1800, an Austrian plenipotentiary arrived in Paris to discuss peace. After a week of tempestuous flattery, insinuation and veiled menaces, the First Consul prevailed upon him to sign formal preliminaries giving France everything she had won by the Peace of Campo Formio three years before. But this was too much for the Aulic Council and the Imperial Chancellor. With all his faults Thugut was an inflexible patriot. He refused to ratify terms based on an agreement dictated when the French armies were at the very gates of Vienna.

Thugut was moved, too, by other considerations. His Government, in return for a loan of two millions sterling free of interest, had just made a formal compact with Britain not to conclude a separate peace. Britain had behaved with undeniable generosity. Not only had she overlooked an unredeemed former loan, but, putting the interests of Europe before her own, she had offered in any joint negotiations for peace to offset her colonial conquests against France's territorial claims in Germany and Italy. The extent of her good faith had been shown after a Turkish-French agreement had been signed in Sidney Smith's flagship for the evacuation of Kléber's army from Egypt to France. Nelson, with his strong sense of political ethics, had sternly pointed out to his erring subordinate "the impossibility of permitting a vanquished army to be placed by one Ally in a position to attack another," and Lord Keith on his return to the Mediterranean had promptly repudiated the Convention. Thus, to assist Austria, Britain deliberately jeopardised her eastern dominion and her friendship with Turkey by leaving a French army in Egypt.

Accordingly on August 15th Austria notified France of her inability to ratify the Paris preliminaries or to make peace without England. At the same time she expressed the readiness of both countries to negotiate concurrently. At this the First Consul, whose object was to separate the Allies, affected a great rage and threatened to end the Armistice and carry immediate war into the Hapsburg hereditary domains. But as his prime purpose was still to consolidate his internal position in France before extending his conquests, he used the Allied reluctance to negotiate separately as a means of filching advantages from England which he could not otherwise hope to obtain. For, despite all his conquests on land, he was still confronted by another's mastery of the sea. Through that dominion Britain had robbed France of her colonies and trade and even—and this was particularly bitter to the First Consul—of those Mediterranean conquests which had been his own peculiar achievement. Her stranglehold on the world's seaways not only withheld from the French people the prosperity which he had promised them in return for their liberty, but at that moment was threatening to starve his armies out of his last stronghold on the route to the Orient.

For this reason Bonaparte instructed Monsieur Otto, the French agent-general for the exchange of prisoners in London, to demand a naval armistice from Britain as the condition of any extension of the military convention with Austria. The Cabinet at first demurred on the ground that such a thing was unheard of. But on the First Consul threatening an immediate renewal of the war in Germany and Italy they gave way. There seemed no alternative if they were to retain their ally. They therefore proposed on September 7th that Malta and Egypt should be put on the same footing as the beleaguered Imperial garrisons and revictualled once a fortnight, that the blockade of Brest should be lifted, but that the right to sail should only be extended to merchant ships and not to men-of-war.

This did not suit Bonaparte, for he was determined, even if he could not save Malta, to put Egypt out of danger of capture. He needed it both for the fulfilment of his eastern ambitions and as a bargaining counter. In counter-proposals on September 20th he demanded that the ban on warships should apply only to capital ships and that six French frigates should sail for Alexandria at once without being searched by British cruisers. It was his plan to cram these with troops and munitions. Simultaneously he attempted to double-cross the Allies by using the new manual telegraph to instruct Moreau to insist on the immediate surrender of Ulm, Ingolstadt and Philipsburg as the price for renewal of the Austrian armistice.

In this he was successful. Austria yielded to obtain a respite till December and the full fall of winter. But over Malta and Egypt Bonaparte overreached himself. For, with the Imperial fortresses in his hands, the need for Britain to make concessions at sea on her behalf ceased. She flatly refused to allow the cunning Corsican to revictual Egypt. As for Malta, the starving garrison of Valetta, after a two years' siege, had surrendered that month to a small force of British soldiers under Colonel Thomas Graham. The chief heroes of the siege had been the Maltese themselves—"a hardy, brave race," wrote General Abercromby, "animated and, eager in the cause in which they were engaged"[1]—and the calm, philosophical Gloucestershire sea captain, Alexander Ball, to whom Nelson had entrusted the blockade of Valetta and who became, a little incongruously, the subject of their passionate devotion. So close had been the Navy's watch that for nearly a year not a single vessel entered the port. Since his assumption of power, Bonaparte had given repeated orders to revictual it, but in vain. In February, 1800, one of the two survivors of the line-of-battle at the Nile, the *Généreux 74*, with three frigates and 3,000 troops from Toulon, had had the misfortune to encounter Nelson on one of his rare excursions to Valetta, and had at once been captured. A month later the remaining Nile battleship, the *Guillaume Tell*, attempting to escape from the doomed port, suffered the same fate.

But Nelson, back in his Sicilian bondage, was not there to see it. Nor, for all the entreaties of his friends and sad-eyed captains, did he receive the surrender of Valetta. Vexed in his vanity by the return of Lord Keith to the Mediterranean, and caught up in an unwonted sensual web, he had insisted on being relieved of his command on the grounds of ill-health. "My career of service," he assured the faithful, protesting Troubridge, "is at an end." On the day of Marengo he had arrived at Leghorn with his siren—"Rinaldo in the arms of Armida"—on the first stage of his journey home. Four weeks later he had struck his flag and set out for Vienna with the Queen of Naples and the Hamiltons who had been recalled to

[1] *Moore*, I, 369.

England. It was a strange ménage: "They sit," wrote Lady Minto "and flatter each other all day long." Another eyewitness described Emma as cramming the Admiral with trowelfuls of flattery which he swallowed quietly like a child taking pap. At Vienna, as one after another of the laurels of the Nile were plucked by the new Cæsar of the West, Nelson, tricked out with ribands and stars like the hero of an opera, received the plaudits of an idle multitude and sat at faro with Lady Hamilton while Haydn played unregarded.[1]

Yet, for all his rival's triumph, one fruit of the great Admiral's victory remained. His country still rode mistress of the Mediterranean. Here during the summer months of 1800 a British army wandered vainly up and down in its transports seeking employment. From Minorca to Leghorn, from Leghorn to Malta, from Malta back to Minorca and from Minorca to Gibraltar, its path was guided by the successive and varying instructions of the Cabinet, always sent several weeks after the event which prompted them and always arriving too late to effect the purpose for which they were sent.

For, despite the now unmistakable impatience of the public with all its military ventures, the Government in its contest of manœuvre with Bonaparte was again making use of the Army. At midsummer, after the failure of the attempt on Belleisle and the final liquidation of the Chouans, it resolved to employ it to knock Spain out of the war. For France's junior partner, after three ruinous years, hoped only for peace. Relations between blockader and blockaded off the Iberian ports had for long been far more friendly than those between the Spaniards and their bullying French masters: high-flown compliments, presents of wine and cheese and even more substantial services had been continuously exchanged by British naval officers and the courtly Dons. It was only Godoy who seemed to be keeping Spain in the war at all.

The capture of Spanish naval bases became, therefore, the Government's first objective. In July 13,000 of the troops which Stuart had vainly demanded for operations in Italy were sent under General Pulteney and a naval escort to seize the great naval arsenal of Ferrol. No attempt had been made to reconnoitre the ground or obtain information about the strength of the Spanish garrison and defences: a little vague talk by sanguine naval officers was quite enough for Dundas. When the troops landed on the Galician coast in the third week in August they found the place impregnable. After a brief skirmish with Spanish outposts they re-

[1] "It is really melancholy," wrote John Moore in July at Leghorn, "to see a brave and good man, who has deserved well of his country, cutting so pitiful a figure."—*Moore*, I, 367.

embarked, much to the fury of the Navy which had set its heart on prize money. The public, which was now ready to blame the Army for everything, ignorantly endorsed this view.

It mattered little. For at the beginning of August the Cabinet had reached a further decision: to concentrate its entire available force for an attack on Cadiz. In accordance with its latest orders 22,000 British soldiers, drawn from Pulteney's abortive expedition and from Abercromby's Mediterranean command, were assembled at Gibraltar in September. With the hurrican season approaching, they were to make a sea-borne descent on one of the strongest places in Europe: the principal naval port of a proud people who, however lukewarm towards their ally's cause, were famed for valour in defence of their own soil.

It fell to Abercromby, supported by Pulteney and Moore, to command the expedition. It sailed from Gibraltar on October 3rd, 1800, in more than a hundred and fifty transports escorted by Lord Keith and the Mediterranean Fleet. For the next three days, while the crowded ships tossed up and down in a heavy swell, a spirited dispute raged between the General and Admiral about the latter's ability to guarantee the Army's communications once it was ashore. This, the Admiral, though unaccountably refusing to give a definite reply, was naturally unable to do at such a time of year. Accordingly, after half Moore's Division was already in its boats, Abercromby took it on himself to abandon the venture. How right he was, was shown next day when a tempest arose which, driving the Fleet far out into the Atlantic, kept it at sea for more than a fortnight. It was a fitting end to an ignominious summer. "Twenty-two thousand men," wrote Lord Cornwallis, "floating round the greater part of Europe, the scorn and laughing-stock of friends and foes."[1]

When the sea-sick army at last regained Gibraltar on October 24th it was to find new orders from England. In view of the worsening international situation Abercromby was to proceed to Malta for an attack on Egypt before the French were able to reinforce their forces there; Pulteney was to defend Portugal from an impending attack from Spain. For, while the military forces of Britain were groping their way round the shores of Spain in hopes of delivering a knock-out blow, Bonaparte had turned the tables on the fumbling islanders. On the first of the month he had concluded with the Court of Madrid the preliminary Treaty of San Ildefonso. In return for an Italian throne for the Queen's brother, Spain was to transfer to France six ships-of-the-line and secretly

[1] *Fortescue*, IV, 798.

cede the great colonial province of Louisiana in North America—a first step to the restoration of the French empire that Chatham had destroyed. And in order to deprive the common enemy of her oldest ally, the chief source of supply for her Mediterranean Fleet and the emporium for her South American trade, a Spanish army was to invade Portugal at the earliest possible moment. "Notify our Minister at Madrid," the First Consul wrote to Talleyrand on September 30th, "that our troops must be masters of Portugal before October 15th. This is the only means by which we can have an equivalent for Malta, Mahon and Trinidad."[1]

It was not in Bonaparte's nature to be thwarted. He represented the embodied will of an invincible Revolution. By her mastery of the sea Britain was thwarting the consummation of that Revolution. Since for the moment his fleet could not challenge that mastery, he would choose another way: by expelling the islanders from every port in Europe, he would ruin their trade and force them to make peace. That, at least, lay within his power.

Though the uneasy armistice with Austria still held for the moment, Bonaparte was free to move against the smaller clients of the failing Coalition. On October 15th his troops poured into the capital of Tuscany. At Leghorn he seized forty-six English ships, close on a million quintals of wheat, barley and dried vegetables, and every penny of British capital in the town. Meanwhile at the other end of Europe he prepared an unexpected blow.

Since the French flag had been driven from the seas, the maritime neutrals had had a growing incentive to run the gauntlet of the blockade and gain the Republic's carrying trade. To Denmark, Sweden and the United States—the chief of these—the First Consul offered in the summer and fall of 1800 the most advantageous terms. Reversing the harsh policy of his predecessors, he raised the embargo on their ships—impounded for carrying British merchandise under Jacobin decrees—waived the customary rights of blockade and invited them to come and go as they chose. He had almost everything to gain by doing so, nothing to lose. If, in contrast to his liberal policy, England continued to use her ancient international rights of search and confiscation—her only remaining weapon against France—she would incur the odium of mankind.

Once before during the American war, when Britain was contending single-handed against the chief naval Powers of Europe, the Baltic States had combined to claim a novel immunity from the rights of search. The flag, they maintained, covered cargo: neutral ships sailing under convoy were immune from inspection and

[1] Mahan, *Sea Power*, II, 67.

capture. In her then extremity Britain had been unable to do more than protest. Since that time, however, all the contracting Powers had either themselves enforced the customary rights of search in their own wars or expressly renounced their unwarrantable claim in friendly treaties with England. But during the early part of 1800, encouraged by France and impelled by commercial cupidity, Denmark had revived it. In July one of her frigates, attempting to protect a convoy, was fired on in the Channel and carried into the Downs.

This time Britain, all-powerful at sea, did not hesitate. She sent to Copenhagen an Ambassador backed by the guns of a powerful naval squadron. While the defences of the Danish capital were still incomplete, she extracted a recognition of her ancient rights pending full consideration of the matter at a conference to be held in London after the war. The Danes abandoned their claim to convoy ships to France and admitted their liability to search, while Britain undertook to repair the damaged frigate.

But at this point Bonaparte intervened. Ever since his accession to power he had been carefully courting the crazy autocrat of Russia. To inflame him against his former allies he had offered to hand over Malta to his troops. Later, affecting immense indignation at a somewhat ungenerous British refusal to exchange French prisoners in England for Russians taken in Holland, he had sent the latter back to Russia in new uniforms accompanied by a flowery letter. This display of chivalrous sentiment was perfectly calculated to arouse the childlike enthusiasm of the Tsar, already full of venom towards the cowardly, selfish English and Austrians who had caused his invincible soldiers to be defeated.

The news of the capture of Malta—which Paul now viewed as his private property—and of the British expedition to the Sound set a match to the train which the First Consul had so carefully prepared. On November 7th in a fit of homicidal rage the Tsar placed an embargo on all British ships in Russian ports. When some succeeded in escaping, he had a number of the others burnt and marched their crews in chains into the interior.

Bonaparte's project was taking shape. With Muscovite aid the decision of Nelson's guns in Aboukir Bay could be reversed, the position in the eastern Mediterranean transformed and a new road to the Orient opened through Persia. On December 2nd Dundas sent warning to Keith and Abercromby to be prepared to repel an attack from Russia—still nominally Britain's ally—through the Dardanelles. On every horizon on which the Cabinet in London looked out that autumn of 1800, storms were rising. The Tsar's embargo, followed by his impetuous approach to Sweden, Denmark and Prussia to revive the Armed Neutrality of the North, threatened both to break the blockade of France and to close the Baltic to British trade. Already in November Prussia, angered by the seizure of one of her ships carrying contraband, had marched into Cuxhaven, a port of the free city of Hamburg and one of the chief channels of British commerce with central Europe. The First Consul's purpose was plain. It was to make the sea useless to the country which ruled it.

Similar threats had been made against England before. But they had done her little harm because, so long as the Baltic, with its all-important trade in grain, timber and naval stores, remained open to her ships, the closure of the remainder of the European coastline hurt Europe more than it injured Britain. Controlling the ocean routes, she could deny the colonial produce of the New World and the East to her foes while extending her own imports and supporting her elaborate structure of usury through trade with the Hanseatic and Scandinavian towns. On this basis the long war, which many had thought would be her ruin, had actually enriched her. So soon as she had established complete command of the seas over the combined fleets of France, Spain and Holland, her wealth and financial power, instead of contracting, had expanded. "Our trade," Pitt told the House of Commons in the summer of 1799, two years after Cape St. Vincent and Camperdown, "has never been in a more flourishing situation." By the turn of the century British exports had reached a declared annual value of nearly forty millions, or half as much again as at the outbreak of war, while imports had doubled. Despite privateers the tonnage cleared from Great Britain to North Germany in the same period had trebled. The destructive effect of the war and Revolution on the Continent was making Britain the manufactory as well as the warehouse of the world.

These increases were reflected in the revenue returns, which, notwithstanding the vast sums sunk in free loans and subsidies to the Allies, remained as buoyant as the Prime Minister's spirits. By 1800 the nation was raising thirty-six millions a year on an estimated trade of between seventy and eighty millions. The conquest of the French, Spanish and Dutch islands in the West and East Indies had raised the Custom receipts by as much as fifty per cent. "If," Pitt proudly declared, "we compare this year of war with former years of peace, we shall in the produce of our revenue and in the extent of our commerce behold a spectacle at once paradoxical, inexplicable and astonishing."

But there was one flaw in the imposing structure of British commercial supremacy, and Bonaparte saw it. Owing to the national passion for individual liberty and the utter inadequacy of the antiquated administrative machine, the prosperity of the populace had not kept pace with the country's expanding trade. The war had enriched the wealthy and enabled them to bear its financial burdens with comparative ease. But though it had increased the purchasing power of the landed and commercial classes, it had only as yet indirectly and very partially raised that of the peasant and labourer. The rise in prices far outran the rise in wages: a Suffolk labourer earning 5s. a week in 1750, and 9s. a week plus 6s. from the parish in 1800, needed £1 6s. 5d. in 1800 to buy the equivalent of 5s. worth in 1750.[1] And by restricting the flow of certain essential commodities, the war had created shortages in real wealth which had fallen almost exclusively on the poor. By further contracting vital imports by an extension of his continental blockade to the Baltic, Bonaparte intended to strike at the stubborn rulers of England through the bellies of the poor. He would bring the Revolution home to them in the form they most feared.

It seemed in the autumn of 1800 as though the heavens were fighting on his side. The terrible rains of the previous summer had been followed by a black season of high prices and food shortage. In July wheat, which had averaged 45s. a quarter before the war, touched 134s. Parliamentary Acts, compelling bread to be baked twenty-four hours before sale and establishing a wholemeal loaf, failed to alleviate the scarcity. At Dorking Fanny D'Arblay reported that respectable journeymen's children were begging from door to door for halfpence, and at the other end of the country Dorothy Wordsworth at Rydale noted the same alarming phenomenon.[2]

A prolonged midsummer drought and a charming August had been followed by a sudden downpour just when the harvest was beginning. For the second year in succession the crops were ruined. By October the people in many districts were literally starving. A succession of bread riots, aggravated by the repressive measures of narrow-minded "anti-Jacobin" magistrates and judges, brought home the danger in the situation. To keep order in the industrial towns troops had to be recalled in November from Portugal.

So far as the state of educated opinion in economic matters permitted, the Government did its best. A special emergency session of Parliament was called and large additional bounties were offered for imports of wheat. But though the country had the wherewithal to buy, the markets from which it could do so were

[1] Mathieson, 87. [2] *Journals of Dorothy Wordsworth* (ed. W. Knight, 1934), 32.

perilously narrow. The value of wheat imports for the year touched the record figure of £2,675,000, nearly three times the pre-war normal. But the population of the British Isles had risen since 1791 from thirteen to fifteen and a half millions—an increase in mouths which even the farming improvements brought about by enclosures could not meet. Indeed, by reducing that individual attention to the lesser fruits of good husbandry which the family holding stimulates in times of scarcity, enclosures aggravated rather than solved the immediate problem.

Thus Bonaparte's threat to conquer the sea by the land was a very real one for the rulers of England in the closing months of 1800. In the villages at their park gates and in the towns through which they passed they saw men and women starving. The Tsar's embargo and the impending stoppage of the Baltic grain fleets placed them in a terrible dilemma. On December 16th Russia and Sweden signed a treaty of alliance by which they bound themselves to revive the heretical maritime code of the Armed Neutrality and to enforce their claims against any dissenting belligerent by naval action. A few days later Prussia and Denmark, despite her recent treaty with Britain, gave their adherence to the "League of the Armed Neutrals."

. . . .

Before this was known in London, Britain had lost her last effective allies. On November 28th, 1800, the French armistice with Austria expired. Within less than a week the Imperial field army in southern Germany had been destroyed. With incredible folly the Aulic Council had deprived the Archduke Charles of his command in favour of an inexperienced boy. As a result the one fighting force in Europe capable of checking the French Army had been exposed to Moreau's counter-attack in the snow-clad forest of Hohenlinden. Thereafter, though the great Archduke was hastily recalled to his former command, nothing could withstand the French advance. On Christmas Day an armistice was signed at Steyer, less than a hundred miles from Vienna. Thugut, his policy shattered, resigned, and the re-acceptance by a defeated Austria of the terms of Campo Formio became inevitable.

Meanwhile the kingdom of the Two Sicilies was seeking peace with the conqueror. After the occupation of Tuscany the Queen had hurried to St. Petersburg to beg the Tsar to intercede for her husband's throne. Bonaparte had gladly acceded to his new friend's request: it was his present policy to refuse him nothing. But he accompanied his forbearance with a servile treaty by which the Neapolitan Government bound itself to close its ports to British ships and merchandise and to admit French garrisons to its fortresses. Save for Portugal, now once more in deadly peril from Spain, the proud island which eighteen months before had led all Europe in a triumphant crusade against France had not a friend in the world.

. . . .

One resort only remained to Britain in the ruin of her hopes: her command of the sea. This still stood, dominating the angry winter waves beyond every rocky promontory of the Continent and setting bounds to the conqueror's dominion. Since St. Vincent had been appointed to the Channel Fleet a year before, it had become far more formidable. For in place of old Bridport's lax watch on Brest and the Atlantic ports, the new Admiral had imposed a rigid blockade of his own devising that spared neither man nor ship but allowed nothing that floated to enter or leave France's naval arsenals. In front of Brest, where the Combined Navies of France and Spain now lay an inert mass, the duty division of the blockading Fleet was increased from the customary fifteen to thirty sail. During easterly winds five ships-of-the-line were always anchored between the Black Rocks and Porquette Shoal, ten miles from the entrance to the harbour, and the frigates and cutters plied day and night in the opening of the Goulet. The main fleet rode well in with Ushant, seldom more than two or three leagues from the island. To prevent further escapes through the shoals to the south, a detachment of from two to four ships-of-the-line was stationed permanently at the southern entrance of the Passage du Raz, while cruisers ranged the Bay of Biscay intercepting every attempt to move along the coast and making periodic cutting-out expeditions on French roadsteads.

The strain imposed by these methods on ships and seamen was terrific. Collingwood, wintering off that rocky coast with only occasional spells in Cawsand Bay or lonely Torbay to break the monotony, complained bitterly to his wife of his irksome life and of a system which increased instead of softening the rigours of the sailor's unremitting service. Others of coarser clay murmured openly at the Admiral's attempt to apply the stern discipline of the Mediterranean to the Channel Fleet. But where the interests of his country were concerned, St. Vincent admitted neither humanity nor pity. "I am at my wit's end," he wrote, "to meet every shift, evasion and neglect of duty. Seven-eighths of the captains who compose this fleet are practising every subterfuge to get into harbour for the winter." They met with scant success. Even when driven by storms to Plymouth or Falmouth, no officer on blockade duty was allowed to sleep on shore or take his ship to the dockyards without leave from the Admiral. It was not surprising that the longing for peace among all ranks grew as their one hope of release from a life of slavery.

But the results justified the policy. The threat of the forty-eight battleships in Brest to Ireland and the West Indies diminished week by week as the shortage of naval stores and supplies in the congested port grew. The primitive and disorganised road services of western France were quite inadequate to take the place of the coastal carrying trade that St Vincent's stranglehold had destroyed. Nothing could evade his unceasing vigilance. Repeated orders from the terrible First Consul for part of the French Fleet to put to sea—to relieve Egypt or to harry British commerce—were unavailing, for the fleet could not move. It had not even food enough for its crews.

. . . .

Bonaparte's delight in the success of his plot to involve the Baltic Powers in the war can therefore be imagined. Between them they possessed 123 ships-of-the-line with an immediate potential of 24 battleships and 25 frigates while the hulks in harbour were being fitted out. With such a force, operating from a semi-inland sea, the British blockade could be outflanked and broken in the spring; then with a combined fleet of perhaps a hundred sail-of-the-line the threat to Ireland and of a direct invasion of England could be renewed. The shortage of naval stores which was crippling every effort to restore the French Marine would then be reversed. Faced, as always at the end of a long war, by a serious domestic timber shortage, Britain in turn would lose the source of supply from which five-sixths of her imported masts and timbers were derived. Her defeat would then be certain.

It is not surprising, therefore, that Bonaparte felt that his alliance with the Tsar far outweighed his victory over the Emperor. For it would enable him to "dominate England"; to do what had proved impossible after his earlier victory in '97 and without which he could not rule the world. His ascendancy over the mind of the autocrat of Russia was now complete. "Whenever I see a man," Paul addressed him, "who knows how to govern, my heart goes out to him. I write to you of my feelings about England—the country that champions the rights of all peoples yet is ruled only by greed and selfishness. I wish to ally myself with you to end that Government's injustices." His Ambassador paraded the scene of Suvorof's conquests with the French and Russian flags interlocked, announcing that the two great nations of the Continent should henceforward be eternally united for the peace of mankind. The Napoleonic myth was taking shape: of a heaven-born deliverer sent to re-unify Europe and save its civilisation from the perfidious dividing usurer of the seas.

It was not in this light that the people of Britain saw their country. Friendless and alone against a world in arms, the lion, as Collingwood put it, took his stand at the mouth of his cave.[1] At the beginning of February, 1801, Austria made her formal peace at Lunéville in a treaty which secured to France in perpetuity the Rhine and Adige frontiers, and an increase of a sixth in her population. The conqueror was thus free to concentrate his entire force against England. "Thus," he told his slaves, "will that nation which has armed itself against France be taught to abjure its excessive pretensions and learn at length the great truth that, for peoples as for individuals, there can be no security for real prosperity but in the happiness of all."[2]

As always in the hour of adversity, Pitt's spirit—for months past oppressed by gout—soared into a serener air. His reply to threats was to attack. On January 14th, when the full extent of the Baltic League became realised in London, the Cabinet gave immediate orders for an embargo on the ships of the contracting Powers. At the same time letters of marque were issued to seize all Russian, Swedish and Danish ships on the high seas. So promptly did the Navy act that nearly fifty per cent. of the tonnage of the Baltic States at sea was brought in the next few months into British ports.

Already the Cabinet was committed to an offensive in the Mediterranean. In the autumn of 1800, as soon as the weakness of Austria and the trend of Russian policy had become apparent, Dundas, with his eye on India, had urged that no effort should be spared to destroy the French army in Egypt while there was still time. On October 6th orders had been given for a joint expedition against that country from Malta, India and the Cape of Good Hope. The plan was wildly sanguine, took little account of the difficulties of co-operation over such vast distances and grossly underestimated French strength. It was largely based on wishful thinking about a few defeatist and homesick letters found in a captured mailbag and subsequently given immense publicity in England. Yet it also showed a certain imperial vision which Dundas, prosaic journeyman though he was, inherited from Chatham. And it displayed—what Britain most needed at that moment—courage and daring.

On November 24th Abercromby and Moore had reached Malta. A month later they sailed, under the majestic escort of the Mediterranean Fleet, with 16,000 troops for Marmaris Bay in Asia Minor to co-operate with the Turkish authorities for a landing near Alexandria and to purchase supplies, of which they were in great need. Dundas's letter to Lord Wellesley (as Mornington had now

[1] Collingwood, 82. [2] *Alison*, V, 472.

become) reached India early in 1801 and was followed by the dispatch of a force under Major-General David Baird to the Red Sea, where a squadron had already been sent by Spencer from the Cape under Home Popham. The Government was pitting concentric sea power against a purely military force operating on interior lines—a trial of strength on a small scale foreshadowing greater conflicts to come.

In her bold and realist policy of anticipation Britain carried her offensive against the First Consul into even remoter places. Early in 1800 the great Governor-General had sent the thirty-year-old John Malcolm on a twelve months' journey to Teheran and Bagdad to exclude the French from Persia and Mesopotamia and forestall Bonaparte's plans to march on India. Nothing could have been more timely. For when Malcolm was setting the seal on his laborious mission with an Anglo-Persian treaty of commerce, the First Consul was perfecting a grandiose scheme with his ally, the Tsar, for a French march along the Danube to the Black Sea and Caspian and a junction with a Russian army at Astrakhan for a joint drive on India.

. . . .

Before these brave measures could bear fruit, the Cabinet which had conceived them had dissolved. At the beginning of February, 1801, the country was shaken by the greatest political crisis of the war. Ever since the Irish Rebellion Pitt and the new Viceroy, Cornwallis, had been pushing forward plans for a Union of the British and Irish Parliaments. The measure, however mistakenly, appeared to them to offer the only means of ending the fatal unrest of Ireland and freeing the Empire from a constant peril at its heart. All through 1799 and 1800, with the war at a critical stage and the combined fleets lying at Brest, 50,000 British regulars had remained in Ireland to guard against the joint dangers of invasion and revolution. Survival, let alone final victory, depended on a solution. "Something must be done," wrote Lord Carlisle, "or we must fight for Ireland once a week."

Union seemed the one way out. By removing the fatal dualism that poisoned every attempt to alleviate the lot of Ireland, a sane and honest administration of Irish affairs might become possible. It would be the British reply to that policy of centralisation which in a few years had transformed the old, weak, federal constitution of France into the most powerful single unit of government in the world. The disappearance of selfish commercial and fiscal barriers between the two countries would bring prosperity to the "distressful island." Above all it would be a step, as Cornwallis said, to a real partnership with the Irish nation instead of with a corrupt ruling faction which only represented a tithe of it.

The measure was bitterly opposed by the fanatic Protestant minority and the graceful and dissipated aristocracy which regarded its governing monopoly and its freedom from the pedantic control of Westminster as an inalienable personal property. Such opposition could only be overcome by coercion or bribery. It was the English way to choose the latter. "I despise and hate myself every hour for engaging in such dirty work," wrote Cornwallis, "and am only supported by the reflection that without an Union the British Empire must be dissolved."[1] The place-holders and borough-mongers were bought out lock, stock and barrel: there was no other way. As the young Irish Secretary, Lord Castlereagh, put it, it had become necessary "to secure to the Crown the fee simple of Irish corruption" in order to end it.

On January 1st, 1801, the Act of Union, passed by both Parliaments, became law. The new Union Jack, with the cross of St. Patrick superimposed on those of St. George and St. Andrew, floated over Dublin Castle and Westminster. But there was one further measure which Pitt and Cornwallis regarded as essential to a lasting settlement. In September, 1800, the Cabinet, with three dissentients, had secretly agreed that the oath which still excluded Catholics from Parliament and supreme office must be revised to bring all Irishmen within the Union. A common Parliament with Protestant England and Scotland would give the Protestant interest in Ireland a perpetual majority over the dreaded Papists. "A broad and inclusive basis" in Church and State had at last become compatible with the security of the minority; without it there could be no permanent peace or safety in Ireland. Justice to the Irish majority, obligation to the Catholics who had helped Cornwallis and Pitt to carry the measure in the confident hope of a wider toleration, and Britain's supreme peril alike demanded it.

But there was one formidable and dreaded last fence in the race against religious fanaticism—the King's conscience. He came of an alien line which had been entrusted with the British Crown on certain conditions of which the exclusive Protestant Constitution was the first. To the contractual obligation of 1689 and 1714 he had given his coronation oath in his impressionable youth, and nothing could erase the memory of it from his narrow but tenacious mind. When the tactful Dundas tried to prepare it for a more tolerant interpretation of the law, he had been met by the royal rejoinder: "None of your Scotch metaphysics, Mr. Dundas! None of your Scotch metaphysics!" Warned by Loughborough, the treacherous Lord Chancellor, of the Government's intention, he

[1] *Pitt and the Great War*, 424.

appeared at the Levee on January 29th, 1801, in a state of intense excitement, openly upbraiding Ministers and declaring that he would reckon any man who proposed such a measure as his personal enemy. For he saw it as a plot to destroy the Church and Civil Order: the most Jacobinical thing, he said, he had ever heard of. Two days later he sounded the Speaker, Addington, as to the possibility of his forming an Administration.

Against such royal obstinacy there was no contending, for the Government on a question which touched Protestant fanaticism could not look for solid support in the country. On the last day of January Pitt accordingly wrote to the King commending to his consideration the measures for Catholic Emancipation agreed by the Cabinet and begging to be allowed to resign if they were not approved. During the next three days further letters passed between Sovereign and Prime Minister, the one expressing his unalterable resolve to preserve the Constitution unimpaired and the hope that his Minister would not quit him, the other respectfully affirming the necessity for his resignation. On the 4th it was agreed that Pitt should go, and by the 5th Addington had consented to form a new Administration.

When the country learnt the news it was profoundly shaken. The uneducated urban populace had no love for Billy Pitt, whose name it associated with high prices and war restrictions and whose shy, reserved bearing was little calculated or designed to win the love of multitudes. But the thinking and propertied minority, the City and rustic England generally—the solid core of 18th century public opinion—had come to look on Pitt after sixteen years in office as an unchangeable institution: "the Atlas," wrote Minto, "of our reeling globe."[1] The man chosen to succeed him was an amiable nonentity: the son of the great Chatham's physician and one who owed the Speakership and his political career to the friendship of the Pitt family. That such a mediocrity should take the helm at an hour when the country was facing a world in arms caused consternation. Even the collection of second-rate Tory noblemen whom Addington assembled round him—for Dundas, Grenville, Windham and Spencer all resigned with their chief on the Catholic question—scarcely believed in him. Several of them publicly expressed the hope that the experiment would be short-lived.

The situation was only made possible by Pitt's behaviour. While all around him were sunk in gloom, he appeared quietly cheerful, gave his unqualified support to Addington and uttered no reproach against his Sovereign, whose sincerity of purpose he praised warmly.

[1] *Windham Papers*, 171.

At the moment when he was being relegated—shabbily and needlessly—to private life, he had only one thought: the good of his country. It was characteristic of his conception of public duty that, though he was almost penniless and heavily in debt through his long neglect of his own affairs, he declined to allow his admirers in the City to subscribe to a free gift of £100,000 and refused a royal offer of £30,000 from the Privy Purse. It was only with difficulty that a few intimate friends prevailed upon him to accept a loan of £11,000 to avoid a distraint on his furniture.

To quiet the public mind and prevent a slump in the Funds, the great Minister agreed to remain in office until he had introduced the Budget. He did so on February 18th, making provision for an Army of 220,000 Regulars and Fencibles and 80,000 Militia, a fleet of 220 ships of the line and 250 frigates and an expenditure, including debt charges, of sixty-eight millions. It was the biggest Budget in the nation's history.

Three days later the King, who had contracted a chill while attending divine service on the National Fast and Supplication Day, developed alarming symptoms of his old insanity. The agitation of the past few weeks had proved too much for his excitable mind. At the end of the month his life was despaired of.

The situation of the country could scarcely have been more gloomy. Within a few days Pitt was to lay down his office, while the Sovereign's death or prolonged insanity would bring to the head of the State a prince of deplorable habits and levity, whose favourite counsellor was the irresponsible Fox, a man who was regarded at that time by the overwhelming majority of his countrymen as little better than a traitor. Every nation on the Continent save Turkey and Portugal was either a willing or a passive accomplice of Bonaparte in his crusade against England. A great fleet was known to be preparing against her in the Baltic ports and a new army of invasion was gathering on the Channel shore. The *corps d'elite* of the Regular Army, after its many humiliating experiences, was embarked on a remote and risky venture at the far end of the Mediterranean; to crown public anxiety it became known about this time that seven French ships of the line, after three months of vain endeavour, had evaded St. Vincent's blockade in a storm and, crowded with troops, had sailed southward, presumably for Egypt. At home the price of wheat stood at four times its pre-war figure and the 6d. loaf at 1s. 5d. The leader of the Opposition calculated that one-sixth of the population was living on charity: Crabb Robinson wrote in his diary that the sun of England's glory was set.

On March 3rd, however, the King took a turn for the better. By the 6th he was well enough to resume his functions. The nightmare of a change on the throne passed, but the country's danger remained unimpaired. On March 14th, having given his agitated Sovereign a promise that he would never again raise the Catholic question during the royal lifetime, Pitt ceased to be Prime Minister.

. . . .

As the weak hands of his successor fumbled at the reins of office, England, confronting the three corners of the world in arms, launched her attack. At each end of a vast hoop of ocean—at the centre of whose arch stood the blockading fleet off Brest—enclosing the North Sea, Atlantic and Mediterranean shores of Europe, she struck simultaneously at her foes. On February 22nd, 1801, the day the King was placed under restraint, Abercromby sailed from Marmaris Bay for Egypt. At the same time a great naval expedition, secretly ordered three weeks earlier by Pitt's Government, began to assemble at Yarmouth to forestall the plans of the Armed Neutrals.

. . . .

Abercromby's venture seemed to his cautious, experienced mind if possible even more forlorn than that on which he had set out for Holland eighteen months earlier. With 15,000 troops, ill-equipped and without cavalry, he was going to invade an unmapped country occupied by an experienced enemy of unknown strength who had had several months to prepare for his coming. Actually the French in Egypt numbered 24,000, or 8000 more than the Cabinet had calculated. Only a few weeks before, some frigates from Toulon had run the gauntlet of Keith's fleet with ordnance and stores for Alexandria; and, though Abercromby did not know it, Ganteaume's relieving battle squadron had already entered the Mediterranean. In a semi-tropical climate the British army was to land on an open beach with no water but what it could draw from the fleet and little hope of regular supply until it could capture a walled town. The Turks, to whom Abercromby had been told to look for help and military collaboration, had proved a broken reed: Moore, who visited their army at Jaffa in January, had found it a "wild, ungovernable mob" decimated with plague and, under corrupt, supine leaders, incapable of action.[1] It was no wonder that Abercromby confided to his friend, the Military Secretary, that he could see little hope of success. "There are risks in a British service unknown in any other," he wrote.

On March 2nd the expeditionary force, in close on two hundred

[1] "They are in general a stout, active and hardy people, and are allowed to be individually brave. They are certainly material of which excellent soldiers might be formed; but under a Turkish government everything becomes debased."—*Moore*, I, 396.

transports, escorted by Keith's fleet, anchored in Aboukir Bay on the scene of Nelson's victory, facing the east or Aboukir Castle end of the long narrow strip of land on which Alexandria lies. For five days, during which time the French had ample time to make preparations, a gale made landing impossible. But on the afternoon of the 7th the wind dropped and orders were given for an attack at dawn.

The Army was in a grim mood. It had been drifting aimlessly about the Atlantic and Mediterranean for the greater part of a year. The men felt the injustice of the undeserved ignominy which had befallen them. They were fighting fit after their six weeks training in Marmaris Bay, and, as is often the way with Englishmen overlong oppressed by adversity, had developed a feeling of contempt for their enemy. One of the young colonels waiting in the transports, Edward Paget, wrote to his father on the 7th: "You may depend upon it there is a certain devil in this army that will carry it through thick and thin. It is the first fair trial between Englishmen and Frenchmen during the whole of this war, and at no former period of our history did John Bull ever hold his enemy cheaper."

The operation began with the firing of a rocket at two o'clock on the morning of March 8th. By dawn most of the waiting troops in the boats were at the rendezvous some miles from the Fleet and opposite a high sandhill which John Moore, who was in charge of the first division, had marked in his mind as the dominating point of the enemy's defences. But the work of assembling and arranging the boats could not be completed in the swell till after eight o'clock, the French remaining spectators of the curious scene. The flotilla then moved towards the shore in four carefully dressed lines, the first consisting of fifty-eight flat-bottomed boats, while supporting fire was given by naval gunboats and launches.

As soon as they came within range of the French guns on the sand dunes and the batteries of Aboukir Castle, a storm of shot, whipping up the waters of the bay, drenched the soldiers who, packed fifty into a boat, sat patiently waiting with their firelocks between their knees. Many were killed, and several of the boats were sunk. But the sailors continued rowing swiftly until, as the keels grounded, the men sprang ashore and formed up in the order so often rehearsed in Marmaris Bay. Assembling the Fortieth, Twenty-third and Twenty-eighth Foot, Moore led them at the charge up the great sandhill. Scrambling up its two hundred feet of seemingly almost perpendicular side without firing a shot, the men surprised and overwhelmed the French Sixty-first Demi-

Brigade. Accustomed to warfare against undisciplined Turks and Arabs, the latter had never anticipated such a method of assault. Its men fled, leaving their guns in the victors' hands. Meanwhile the Coldstream, 3rd Guards and 42nd Highlanders distinguished themselves by repelling cavalry on the beach.

The whole action was over in little more than half an hour, the British losing 600 men killed and wounded. The rest of the army landed in the afternoon and, on Sidney Smith's suggestion, set to work digging for water under the date trees that dotted the desolate landscape. Its position was precarious in the extreme. With Aboukir Castle untaken in its rear and dominating the only point at which it could draw supplies from the fleet, it had to advance along twelve miles of narrow isthmus under a burning sun towards Alexandria, a walled city held by an unknown number of French veterans. If repulsed, it must either perish of famine or take to its boats in the presence of a victorious enemy. On March 12th, having landed his guns, Abercromby, leaving two regiments to blockade Aboukir Castle, set out to fight his way to the port.

. . . .

While these events, unknown to Englishmen, were proceeding in the Orient, the armament which was to strike at the other end of Britain's long sea reach was assembling amid snow and easterly gales at Yarmouth. Its command had been entrusted to a dapper, pedantic, highly-strung little Admiral of sixty-two years of age, with more seniority than active service. Sir Hyde Parker, who had recently returned from four years on the lucrative Jamaica station, was known to his contemporaries as "old vinegar." Apart from personal bravery and his place on the Navy List, there was little to commend him for his appointment, for, as his friend, the Governor of Gibraltar remarked, "he was getting old, getting rich and had married a young wife."[1] But with the curious unreason of Government Departments the Admiralty tried to offset these defects by appointing as his second-in-command the youngest and most daring Vice-Admiral in the Service, the forty-two-year-old Baron Nelson of the Nile.

This enigmatic character had arrived at Yarmouth after his long Continental tour three months earlier, attended by the now inevitable Hamiltons. At that time his reputation was much sunk from the meteoric height that it had reached two years before: the general belief in official and political quarters was that his career was over.[2] He seemed to common eyes only "a little man without dignity." After a chilly meeting and a rather painful attempt to

[1] *Dyott*, I, 146. [2] Mahan, *Nelson*, II, 42.

endear his new friends to her, he had parted with Lady Nelson to the tittering scandal of London Society. At the only Levee he attended, the King, after the briefest greeting, turned his back on him. The fallen hero had spent his Christmas in the appropriately histrionic atmosphere of Fonthill Abbey, where the eccentric Beckford had assembled a cosmopolitan party including, of course, Lady Hamilton who displayed her attitudes. An artist present noticed that she was bold and unguarded, drank freely and had grown fat. He was unaware—as was every one else including probably her husband—that she was about to present her infatuated lover with a child.[1]

From this painful milieu Nelson was rescued by the exigencies of the Service he loved. After reporting fit for duty, he was appointed on January 17th, 1801, to a command in the Channel Fleet under his old chief, St. Vincent. A few days later every available man and ship was mobilised to meet the storm from the north. The effect on Nelson's spirit was electric. "We are now arrived," he wrote, "at that period we have often heard of but must now execute—that of fighting for our dear country." To Spencer he expressed his readiness to sail for the new theatre of war in anything, from a first-rate to a sloop.

On March 6th he reached Yarmouth, flying his flag in the *St. George*. He found his Admiral "a little nervous about dark nights and fields of ice. But we must brace up," he reported, "these are not times for nervous systems. I hope we shall give our northern enemies that hailstorm of bullets which gives our dear country the domination of the seas. All the devils in the north cannot take it from us if our wooden walls have fair play." For Nelson viewed England's new enemies with the same pugnacity and intensity as the old. "Down, down with the French!" had been his repeated cry in the Mediterranean, and he now applied it to their allies. "I am afraid," he had once truly written of himself, "I take all my services too much to heart."

Sir Hyde, worthy man, did not. His chief interest at the moment was a farewell ball which his young wife was preparing to give at Yarmouth on the 13th. Nelson, who knew that every minute was precious if the Baltic Powers were to be disarmed in detail before they had time to prepare and unite their forces, was beside himself with impatience. "Strike home and quick," he urged. He dropped a hint of Parker's preoccupation to his old friend, St. Vincent, now suddenly called to the Admiralty to strengthen Addington's embryo Administration. Whereupon the Fleet received orders to sail at once,

[1] *Farington*, I. 307

the ball was abandoned and the two Admirals started on their mission on decidedly strained terms.

But when Nelson made up his mind, there was no resisting him. Between the sailing of the Fleet on March 12th—two days before Pitt ceased to be Premier—and its arrival on the 19th at the Skaw, the northernmost point of Denmark, he had already half won over his superior—tradition has it with a timely turbot. There was something about Nelson's ardour and, when his imagination was aroused, his limitless dedication to his country's service that touched even the coldest heart.

Not that he had yet succeeded in inspiring Parker with his own spirit. Eighteen miles north of Kronborg Castle and Helsingor (Elsinore), where the Kattegat narrows into the Sound between Sweden and the Danish island of Zealand, the fleet anchored to await the return of Vansittart, the Government envoy, who had been sent on in a frigate to Copenhagen with a 48-hour ultimatum. Nelson was for pushing on at once into the Baltic before the Danes and their Russian and Swedish allies were ready. "I hate your pen and ink men," he wrote; "a fleet of British ships are the best negotiators in Europe. . . . While negotiation is going on, the Dane should see our flag waving every time he lifts up his head." But until Vansittart had a chance to accomplish his mission Parker would not face the double guns of the Elsinore Straits and the responsibility for precipitating war with countries still technically neutral. Nelson's strong, realist mind told him diplomacy was now useless, that the Danes having gone so far would not draw back without the compulsion of force and that they would merely use the delay to make themselves stronger. Every minute lost meant the certain death of more brave men and the endangering of England's purpose.

It was a sombre moment. The weather was bitterly cold and half the fleet seemed to be coughing.[1] "Everything wears so dismal an appearance," Captain Fremantle had written a few days earlier to his wife on the political changes in England, "that I submit to Fate for the decision of this contest with all the world; I think the man or minority who can extricate us from such difficulties will be more than human." Certainly the new Prime Minister had little hope of doing so, for on March 21st, despairing of success, he and his Foreign Secretary, Lord Hawkesbury—known to the elect as "young Jenky"[2]—made secret approaches to Bonaparte for peace.

The day chosen for this abasement was an ironic one, for unknown to Ministers the tide set in motion by their predecessors was

[1] *Wynne Diaries*, III, 31. [2] Afterwards Prime Minister as Lord Liverpool.

already changing in England's favour. At that very hour a British army had just vanquished in equal encounter a picked force of French veterans outside the walls of Alexandria, and Abercromby, falling in a blaze of glory, was reading mankind a lesson—to be conned more closely in the next age—that, given a fair field, the soldiers of England were a match for the conquerors of Europe. And three days later Nelson, prevailing over the timid spirit of Parker, brought about the decision which led to the shattering of Bonaparte's hopes. On the same night, struck down by the hand of his own subjects, England's enemy, Paul of Russia, was assassinated in the Michael Palace at St. Petersburg.

. . . .

On March 23rd Vansittart returned to the Fleet with the Crown Prince of Denmark's rejection of the British ultimatum. Nelson was thereupon summoned to the flagship. "Now we are sure of fighting," he wrote in jubilation to Lady Hamilton, "I am sent for!" He found all in the deepest gloom, Vansittart expatiating on the strength of the Danish defences, and Parker, appalled by his account of great batteries erected by multitudes of defiant Danes, in favour of anchoring in the Kattegat till the united Baltic navies emerged to give battle. Nelson thereupon set to work, quietly and cheerfully, to argue the Council of War round: "to bring," as he put it, "people to the post." Pacing up and down the flagship's stateroom he pressed his reasons for attacking and, lucidly, persuasively, yet with a flame which shamed all fears, showed how it might be done. After learning that the Copenhagen defences were strongest in the north where the Trekronor Battery barred the approach from the Sound, Nelson suggested that the Fleet should follow the longer route by the Great Belt round Zealand and so fall on the enemy where he was least expecting attack, in the rear. The manœuvre would have had the additional advantage of placing the British between the Danes and their Russian and Swedish allies. But the great thing, he insisted, was to attack at once. "Go by the Sound or by the Belt or anyhow," he said, "only lose not an hour."

It was not Nelson's habit to leave anything to chance. He had talked the Council round, but as soon as he returned to his ship he sat down to write a long letter to Parker emphasising the reasons for action. This document, dated March 24th, is the very quintessence of Nelson: daring, sagacious, winning. "The more I have reflected, the more I am confirmed in opinion that not a moment should be lost in attacking the enemy. They will every day and hour be stronger; we shall never be so good a match for them as at this moment. . . . By Mr. Vansittart's account their state of preparation exceeds what he conceives our Government thought possible, and the Danish Government is hostile to us in the greatest possible degree. Therefore here you are, with almost the safety, certainly with the honour of England more entrusted to you than ever yet fell to the lot of any British officer. On your decision depends whether our Country shall be degraded in the eyes of Europe or whether she shall rear her head higher than ever. . . . I am of opinion the boldest measures are the safest."

Parker's yielding nature could not resist such strength. He would not, as Nelson urged, press boldly on against the Russians—the heart of the Armed League—and smash half their fleet at Reval while it was still separated from the remainder by the ice. The thought of leaving the Danish ships in his rear was too much for his conventional mind. But he agreed to pass through the Belt and attack the Danes: on that point he argued no more. On the 26th, as soon as the wind allowed, the Fleet weighed and steered towards the Belt. But on learning from his flag-captain something of the danger of those intricate waters, the Admiral changed his mind and decided to brave what he had refused before, the narrow entrance to the Sound between the Danish and Swedish guns. The one thing he would not face now was Nelson's scorn: he went on. As often happens when men boldly grapple with difficulties, the initial obstacles vanished as soon as tackled. When, after being detained by head winds for three days, the Fleet entered the dreaded Straits of Elsinore on the 30th, the passage proved absurdly easy. Finding little opposition from the Swedish shore, where the batteries of Kronborg were not yet ready, the fleet inclined to the east of the channel and sailed southward with the Danish shot splashing harmlessly short of it.

That afternoon eighteen British sail of the line and thirty-five smaller vessels anchored five miles south of Copenhagen. The two Admirals at once made an inspection of the town's defences in a schooner. They found that they had been still further strengthened during the days of waiting. But Nelson showed no sign of dismay. "It looks formidable," he wrote to Emma, "to those who are children at war, but to my judgment with ten sail of the line I think I can annihilate them; at all events I hope I shall be allowed to try." Next day at the Council of War he got his way, and when he asked for ten battleships, Parker gave him twelve. For the old gentleman, in spite of his longing for ease and quiet, was almost coming to love Nelson.

How great was the need for speed was shown on the day the

British passed the Sound. A hundred miles away Danish troops entered the Free Town of Hamburg, while the Prussians, scenting plunder, cast in their lot with the Baltic Powers and closed the mouths of the Elbe, Ems and Weser to British commerce. A few days later they invaded Hanover. Hesitation at that hour would have been fatal; England could only hold her place now in the world by courage and resolution.

At a second Council of War Nelson's plan was adopted for the destruction of the Danish fleet and floating batteries. About two miles to the east of Copenhagen the water in front of the city was broken by a great shoal known to pilots as the Middle Ground. Between this and the shore flats ran a swift current of deep water called the King's Channel, along the western or inner side of which nineteen hulks and floating batteries with a host of smaller vessels were anchored in an unbroken line whose head was protected by the famous Trekronor Battery. Instead of attacking it from its strongest end, Nelson proposed to take the twelve lightest battleships and the smaller vessels of the Fleet round the Middle Ground and so sweep up the King's Channel from the south with the current. This would enable him, after crippling the enemy, to rejoin the rest of the Fleet without turning. It involved, however, an intricate and dangerous piece of navigation, for the shoal waters round the Middle Ground ran like a mill race and the Fleet had no charts. But Nelson spent the icy, foggy nights of March 30th and 31st in an open boat taking soundings, and he felt confident of his ability to take the battle fleet through the shoals. It was by now his only chance of overcoming the defences.

While Parker with the reserve moved up to the north end of the Middle Ground about four miles from the city, Nelson on the afternoon of the 1st skirted the west of the shoal and anchored at sundown some two miles to the south of the Danish line. That night he entertained his captains on board his temporary flagship, the *Elephant*—for the *St. George* was too large for his business—and afterwards, exhausted by his efforts of the past two nights, lay in his cot for several hours dictating orders while his flag-captain, Hardy, took soundings round the head of the Danish line. Nelson's instructions, unlike those issued before the Nile, were of the most detailed kind. There would be no room for manœuvring on the morrow and little for individual initiative. Every ship was therefore allotted an exact task.

During the night the wind veered to the south as though to reward Nelson for his pains. He was up long before dawn making final preparations. At eight the captains came aboard for their

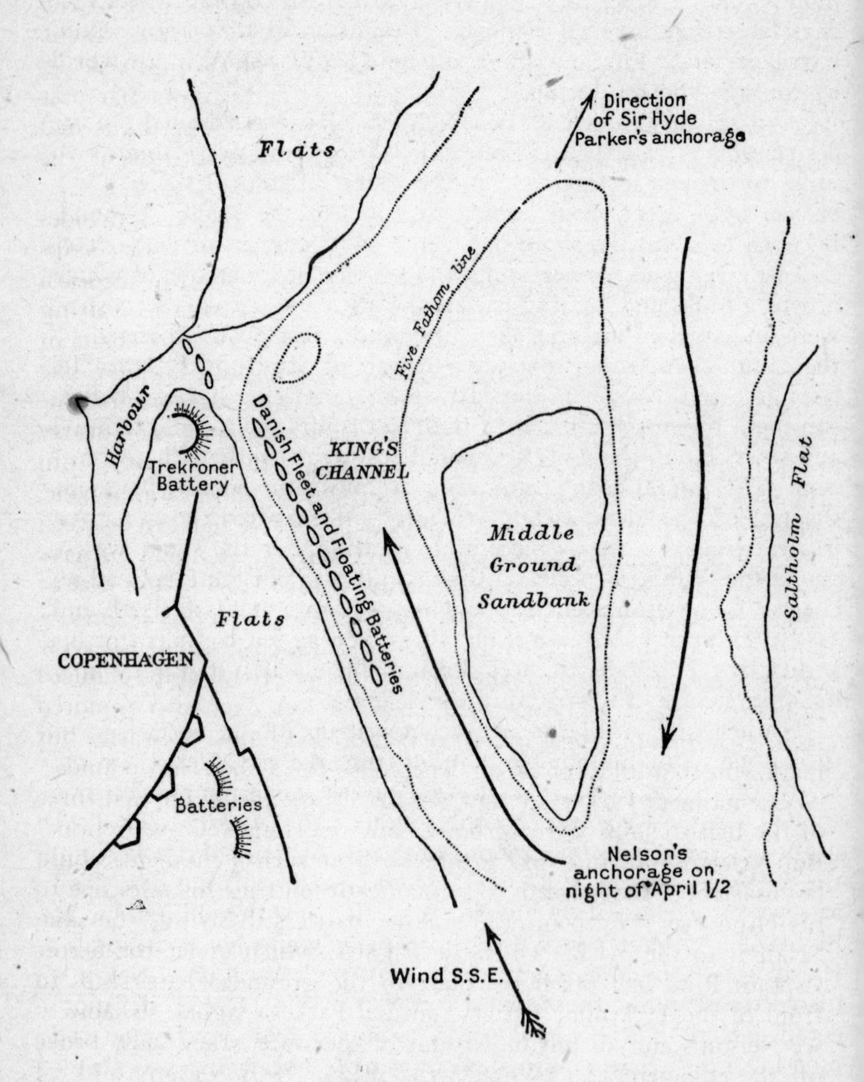

Battle of Copenhagen, 1801.

final orders: at nine-thirty the Fleet weighed. At the last moment the pilots panicked: masters of small Baltic traders, the thought of taking great battleships through such narrow, shallow waters was too much for them. In the subsequent confusion three of the four leading ships—or a quarter of the main British force—went aground. Disaster was only averted by Nelson's promptitude in putting the *Elephant's* helm a-starboard and so bringing her past the grounded *Russell* into the main channel which the pilots had lost. The rest of the Fleet, following him, steered clear of the shoal.

As usual the British entered action without a sound. Both sides seemed to be awed by the solemnity of the scene: the great ships like enormous white birds, with rows of cannon bristling beneath their canvas, bearing down on the Danish line, and the waiting city tense with expectation. In that brooding silence the chant of the pilot and helmsman sounded to one listening midshipman like the responses in a Cathedral service. Then, as the leading ship came into range of the enemy batteries, the thunder began. For nearly four hours the Danes, with successive relays of volunteers from the shore taking the place of the fallen, kept up the cannonade. Along a mile and a half of water, with only a cable's length between them, fifteen hundred guns pounded away at one another: "I have been in a hundred and five engagements," wrote Nelson, "but that of to-day is the most terrible of them all." Twice the Danish Commodore was forced to shift his flag: in the *Dannebrog*, 270 of the crew of 336 were struck down. One or two of the British ships endured casualties almost as heavy: the *Monarch* lost over two hundred men. "Hard pounding," remarked Nelson to Colonel Stewart, "but mark you, I would not be anywhere else for a thousand pounds." At one moment Parker, seeing from his distant anchorage that three of the British ships were aground, flew the signal "Cease Action." But Nelson, knowing that to break off at such a moment would be disastrous, disregarded it, symbolically putting his telescope to his blind eye. "Keep mine for closer battle still flying," he said. "Nail it to the mast." Only the frigates, which under the heroic Captain Riou had taken the place of the grounded battleships in front of the Trekronor Battery, noticed Parker's signal. Unable to see Nelson's and all but blown out of the water, they sadly broke off the engagement. "What," cried Riou, "will Nelson think of us?" Almost as he spoke a raking shot cut him in half.

About two o'clock in the afternoon, the Danes' fire slackened. Taken at a disadvantage by the unexpected direction of the attack, and, for all their courage, overborne by the deadly accuracy of the

British fire, they could do no more. Nelson's own position was almost as precarious with the undefended Trekronor batteries dominating the treacherous channel between his battered ships and the main Fleet to northward. With the sure psychological insight which was part of his greatness, he at once penned a letter addressed: "To the brothers of Englishmen, the Danes," and sent it under a flag of truce to the Crown Prince. For his instinct told him that he could now obtain what he had come for without further bloodshed.

The weariness of his foes and his glorious bluff did the rest. While he referred the terms of the proposed armistice back to the *London*, he cleared his ships from the shoals under the silent guns of the Trekronor batteries and drew off his prizes. His reputation as much as his crew's gunnery had broken the enemy's will to resist. The truce, prolonged from day to day, ended, thanks to Nelson's exquisite skill as a negotiator, in a permanent armistice. The Danes were to suspend their alliance with the Russians and leave their warships in their existing unmasted state for fourteen weeks, during which time they were to supply provisions to the British Fleet. In return the British were to refrain from bombarding Copenhagen.

Nelson had gained his purpose. The hands of Denmark were tied, and his Admiral was free to proceed against the Russians without fear for his rear. On April 12th the Fleet entered the Baltic. But to Nelson's horror, instead of proceeding to Reval with a fair wind, Parker waited off the Swedish coast for new instructions from England. A blow at Russia, Nelson saw, would destroy the whole northern Coalition, for Denmark and Sweden were merely intimidated by their mighty neighbour. And so long as the ice in the Gulf of Finland prevented the Russian squadron at Reval from retiring on its inner base at Kronstadt, Britain by striking could either destroy it or exact terms from the new Tsar. When Parker objected that too rapid an advance up the Baltic might expose the fleet to a superior Russian and Swedish combination, Nelson replied: "I wish they were twice as many: the more numerous, the easier the victory!" For he knew that their inability to manœuvre in large bodies would place them at his mercy.

Not till May 5th did fresh instructions arrive from England. They recalled Parker and left Nelson in command. Immediately the latter left for Reval, but too late. Three days before, the ice had melted sufficiently to enable the threatened Russian squadron to retreat to Kronstadt. There was nothing for Nelson to do but to make as firm and dignified an exchange of letters with the Tsar's Minister, Count Pahlen, as circumstances admitted, and then retire.

But his work, if incomplete, was done. The shattering effect of the Battle of Copenhagen, coupled with the Tsar Paul's death, had destroyed Bonaparte's prestige throughout the North. The First Consul, on hearing the news, expressed his feelings by stamping and shouting with rage. The new Tsar, Alexander, like his subjects, had no wish to preserve a quarrel with a former ally of such strength and courage as Britain. When Nelson went ashore at Reval, the populace hailed him with cries of "That is him! that is him!—the young Suvorof!" "The Baltic people will never fight me if it is to be avoided," he commented. On May 16th, 1801, Russia raised her embargo on British ships, and a month later a Convention between the two countries affirmed the full legality both of the right of search and the seizure of hostile goods in neutral bottoms. Already Prussia and Denmark had withdrawn their troops from Hanover and Hamburg. The northern threat to Britain's security was dispersed.

. . . .

The tidings of Nelson's victory filled the country with relief. For the second time he became the hero of England: Parker was everywhere reviled or forgotten. And though the new Government, with galling mediocrity, replied to Nelson's explanation of the Armistice with Denmark that "upon a consideration of all the circumstances, his Majesty has thought fit to approve," those most competent to judge his achievement did not spare their praise. "Your Lordship's whole conduct," wrote St. Vincent, "is the subject of our constant admiration. It does not become me to make comparisons: all agree there is but one Nelson."[1]

England's cup of rejoicing was not yet full. At the beginning of May news arrived from Egypt of a victory won by Abercromby on March 21st. At the outset of his advance along the isthmus, he had driven the French from a strongly fortified position but had then fallen into his old fault of not following up his success. Had he done so he might have seized Alexandria before the main French army under General Menou arrived from Cairo. For that officer, like all the French in Egypt grossly underrating the quality of their adversary, had been in no hurry. Not till the 19th did his field army, 10,000 strong, march into Alexandria.

By that time the British, pushing forward cautiously, had taken up a new position about three miles short of the port, with their right on the Mediterranean on the site of a ruined Roman palace and the left on the inland lake of Aboukir. About 3000 of those who had landed a fortnight earlier were sick, but the fall of Aboukir

[1] Mahan, *Nelson*, II, 104.

Castle on the 18th had secured Abercromby's base. The two armies were equally matched numerically, but the French had the advantage of 1400 cavalry and a slight superiority in guns. Relying on the superior quality of his troops, all of whom were veterans of Bonaparte's first Italian campaign, Menou decided to attack before dawn on the 21st and drive the invaders into the sea before an expected Turkish army could arrive from Syria. He had no doubt whatever of his ability to do so.

The attack began with a feint against the British left at half-past three in the morning. John Moore, who was Major-General of the day, was only deceived for a minute, and, after investigating, galloped to the right, where he was convinced the real attack was impending. Almost immediately the British pickets in front of the Roman palace were driven back by strong forces, and the French advanced out of the darkness. But the 58th Foot, posted in the ruins, were not in the least perturbed by the beating drums and shouts of "Vive la France! Vive la République!" set up by the victors of Lodi. They held their fire till their enemies' glazed hats could be clearly distinguished and then discharged at them several volleys so well directed that they broke in confusion.

Meanwhile a more serious attack had developed on the left of the Roman camp, where French cavalry had infiltrated in the darkness into the rear of the position held by the 28th Foot and the 42nd Highlanders. While these two regiments were engaged in repelling an infantry attack, they were charged in rear by a large body of armoured horse. But the twenty-five-year-old colonel of the 28th, Edward Paget, calmly gave the order: "Rear rank, right about, fire!" and the men, though completely encircled, repelled the Dragoons while continuing to engage the enemy's attack to the west.[1] Though the Highlanders were temporarily broken by the weight of the French horse, they continued fighting as individuals. All along the right and centre of the British line the story was the same: calm and resolute resistance by units surrounded but clinging grimly to their positions till the British reserves moving to their help could take the French cavalry between two fires. Much of their success was due to the careful, individual training which Moore had previously given the troops of his division; everybody knew what he ought to do and did it.

In the course of this engagement, General Abercromby, supervising the elimination of the French dragoons between his closing lines, had galloped forward to the Roman ruin. Here, while almost

[1] The 28th, to-day the Gloucestershire Regiment, still wear the Regimental badge on the back as well as the front of their caps.

alone, he was attacked by a small detachment of French horse. Before his assailants were driven off, the brave old man, striking at them with his sword, was wounded in the thigh. Until the battle was won he took no notice of his own condition; only when at ten o'clock the French began to withdraw towards Alexandria did his spirit yield. As he was borne from the field, an officer placed a wrapping over his litter with an apology that it was only a soldier's blanket. "Only a soldier's blanket," replied Abercromby. "A soldier's blanket is of great consequence; you must send me the name of the soldier to whom it belongs."

The British lost 1,500 men or fifteen per cent. of the force engaged. The French casualties were far heavier, amounting to nearly forty per cent. in killed, wounded and prisoners, including a divisional General. The 42nd, who had already lost 200 men in the two earlier engagements, lost 300 more in the battle, or more than half their strength. Moore, whose skill and coolness was beyond praise, testified that he had never seen men more determined to do their duty, while veterans of the Lombardy campaign declared that till that day they had scarcely known what fighting was.[1]

The new British Army had proved itself. After many sufferings and vicissitudes, it had shown its ability not merely to take punishment but to give it. By a curious irony of fate, James Stuart, the man who, given a chance, might have led it to a greater victory, died at Richmond Lodge three days after the battle at the age of forty-eight. Abercromby followed him swiftly. Gangrene set in on March 26th and he died on the 28th universally mourned by his men. His epitaph was published by his old comrade-in-arms, the Duke of York, in a General Order of the Day:

> "His steady observance of discipline, his ever-watchful attention to the health and wants of his troops, the persevering and unconquerable spirit which marked his military career, the splendour of his actions in the field and the heroism of his death are worthy the imitation of all who desire, like him, a life of honour and a death of glory."

Alexandria did not fall to the British with the victory. The French retired behind its walls and, lacking a siege train, the victors had no alternative but to starve the town out. But their communications with the fleet were now secure, and with the arrival of 4000 Turks on March 25th they were able to institute a siege of Rosetta at the mouth of the Nile. The place fell on April 19th, opening the way to Cairo and the conquest of Egypt.

[1] *Fortescue*, IV, 843.

CHAPTER FOURTEEN

A Truce of Exhaustion

1801-2

> "No one fights with more obstinacy to carry a contested point, yet, when the battle is over and he comes to the reconciliation, he is so much taken up with the shaking of hands that he is apt to let his antagonist pocket all they have been quarrelling about. . . . It is difficult to cudgel him out of a farthing; but put him in a good humour and you may bargain him out of all the money in his pocket."
>
> *Washington Irving, John Bull.*

THE tide had turned and—despite the odds against her—in England's favour. The First Consul had lost the initiative. So long as Britain fought with Continental allies France had found it easy to divide and destroy their cumbrous combinations. But whenever the great island Power had been left alone, as in 1798, the offensive had passed to her. "We have at this moment in the wreck of surrounding nations," Pitt declared in defence of the new Government, "the glory and satisfaction of maintaining the dignity of the country. We have kept our resources entire, our honour unimpaired, our integrity inviolate. We have not lost a single foot of territory, and we have given the rest of the world many chances of salvation."

For, unchallenged as was Bonaparte's mastery of western and southern Europe, the martial power of Britain was as tremendous. In eight years of war the strength of her Navy, losses notwithstanding, had grown from 15,000 to 133,000 men, and from 135 ships of the line and 133 frigates to 202 and 277 respectively. According to Bonaparte's estimate of a fleet of 30 sail of the line as equal to 120,000 troops on land, Britain had a sea force equivalent to a Continental army of nearly a million. Against this the French navy had been reduced by more than fifty per cent: by 1801 she had only 39 battleships and 35 frigates left and few of these in condition to take the sea.[1] Britain had almost as many building. In the same period the British Army had grown from 64,000 to 380,000 men with more than another 100,000 Volunteers.

For all this Englishmen were proud and glad. Yet they were not

[1] Mahan, *Sea Power*, II, 73; *Rose*, I, 481.

happy. On May 3rd, 1801, Mrs. Fremantle, whose husband commanded the *Ganges* in Nelson's fleet, noted in her diary the glorious news from Egypt contained in that day's papers. But her only comment was: "I wish all these victories may lead to peace." For more than eight years Britain had been struggling to achieve her aims. But still the war went on. And the country, weighed down by taxes, high prices and bloodshed, was weary of it.

That spring the sixth bad harvest in succession, accompanied by the stoppage of the Baltic grain trade, brought popular discontent to a head. In Buckinghamshire Mrs. Fremantle found the Swanbourne villagers starving; in the West Country every family was on a ration of one quartern loaf per week per head.[1] For the poor, who depended on bread for their main support, it was a terrible deprivation. As a whole they had borne their distress with noble patriotism; their patience during the winter of 1800-1801 matched Nelson's constancy among the Baltic fogs and ice. But though in the smaller villages, where ancient patriarchial conditions of life still lingered, much was done by their richer neighbours to alleviate their lot,[2] in districts where the new economics had supplanted personal responsibility for the common weal, the industrial workers and the starving peasants, deprived of their patrimony by enclosures, took the law into their own hands. In Somerset and Devon village mobs put ropes round farmers' necks to make them reduce the price of their corn;[3] the Mendip miners marched into Bristol and held the town up to ransom. At Plymouth the dockyard men became so threatening that the Commissioner had the cannon spiked. The workers of the manufacturing north were equally sullen and explosive.

These things were reminding the class in whose hands political power rested of the price that had to be paid for Pitt's prolonged war against the Revolution. The martial progress and financial resilience of the country on which he had dwelt so often in his speeches could not conceal the dark social reverse. "A very pretty state we are reduced to," was the characteristic comment of a London merchant towards the close of his Administration, "Our pockets filled with paper and our bellies with chicken's meat!" Taxes, rates and prices could not always go on rising: a halt would have to be called some time to the appalling extravagance of the war. Since its start the national debt had more than doubled. The thought

[1] *Ham*, MS.

[2] Elizabeth Ham's father and his fellow South Dorset farmers during the bad period bought up barrels of imported rice and sold it to the poor at three-halfpence a pound, while their wives and daughters served daily in its distribution.

[3] *Hester Stanhope*, 20.

of that swelling incubus made prudent, honest men shake their heads and even—in their weaker moments—share the defeatist Fox's gloomy fears for the future.

Pitt had repeatedly reminded his countrymen that they were at war with armed opinions. So long as the Revolution continued on its bloody course, they needed no reminding: one horror and outrage after another shocked and steeled them for the fight. It was not France as a nation or the abstract speculations of a School they were then fighting, but a fanatic national horde who were turning all the resources of civilisation into a fearful instrument to destroy the laws, manners, property and religions of their neighbours. So long as "this strange, nameless, wild thing" raged in the middle of Europe, consuming and threatening, Britain was forced to contend against it. The existence of everything Englishmen held dear plainly depended on her doing so.

But eighteen months of Bonaparte's rule had changed the face of affairs. "This last adventurer in the lottery of revolutions," as Pitt described him after his rape of power, had not gone the way of his furious predecessors. Whatever else might be said of his Government, it was proving stable. Internally at any rate the revolution of destruction seemed over. While he was still climbing, the First Consul had committed as foul atrocities as any other Jacobin chief: plundered churches, mutiliated tombs, "burnt the town of Benasco and massacred eight hundred of its inhabitants," murdered his prisoners in Syria, shot the municipality of Pavia. He was a liar, a perjurer and a robber. But once he had extinguished his rivals, he established some sort of justice and enforced it. And he professed as much desire for external tranquillity as for internal. He was—or appeared to be—coming to terms with the old order. He had made peace with the Emperor of Austria. He was the ally of the Court of Spain, the friend of the Tsar and the patron of the King of Prussia.

His attempt to force England to make peace by blackmailing her with a Baltic League—a thing no Englishman would brook—had now been defeated. Britons had proved to their own satisfaction and every one else's that Bonaparte could not beat them. But they seemed as far away as ever from liquidating the new regrouping of Europe he had stabilised. The Dutch ports, which the Guards had sailed to protect in 1793, had been in French hands for more than six years; the Austrian Netherlands had been incorporated in France for even longer and had been twice formally renounced by the Austrian Government. The task of conquering the European mainland was as manifestly beyond the English as that of conquering the British Fleet was beyond France. There was no common ground on which they could attack their adversary. And in the meantime they were ruining themselves by their refusal to listen to the First Consul's appeal for peace. By doing so they ran the risk of precipitating in their own country the same social cataclysm that had plunged the Continent into misery and war.

Such was the growing feeling: an expression of war weariness which had spread even to the Fleet. "Would to God that this war were happily concluded," wrote Collingwood from his vigil off Brest, "nothing good can ever happen to us short of peace." No longer was the first question when officers met, "What news of the French?"; it was now, "What prospect of peace?". Everywhere men and, above all women, were longing for an end to the interminable business of killing, hatred and sacrifice. It was only, perhaps, a mood, but it was become a very powerful one. "Wearied out," as Coleridge recorded, "by overwhelming novelties; stunned by a series of strange explosions; sick of hope long delayed, and uncertain as to the real objects and motive of the war from the rapid change and general failure of its ostensible objects and motives, the public mind had lost all its tone and elasticity. . . . An unmanly impatience for peace became almost universal."[1]

A nation which had never had a very clear grasp of first principles had temporarily forgotten what it was fighting for. The changes of the European scene had been so dazzling, the exhaustion of the war so great, that the British people were in a state of bewilderment. Again and again Pitt had told them they were contending for security, but, an empirical Englishman and not a philosopher like Burke, he had never made it clear in what their security consisted. They supposed that it had been achieved because the French Revolution had been liquidated. They forgot that it was not the Terror and the red Cap of Liberty—the propagandist's bogey—that had endangered Britain's existence and her sober philosophy of law and liberty, but the Revolutionary thesis that there was no law but the untrammelled will of a single Party or Nation and the Revolutionary practice which threatened at the cannon's mouth all who opposed that will. A people unversed in abstractions failed to see that, though the First Consul had succeeded the pitiless Tribunes of the mob, French claims and practice remained unchanged. There was no law or morality in Europe but the will of the "Great Nation" and its leader. There could be no security for libertarian England in such a Europe.

The Government failed to make this clear. Addington was a

[1] *The Friend*, Section I, Essay 10.

weak, well-meaning, inexperienced mediocrity, little given to examining, let alone enunciating first principles. He was merely a stop-gap. His Cabinet of second-rate peers and sons of peers contained no one who commanded the slightest confidence except the sailor, St. Vincent. Such an Administration was incapable of controlling the new tide of public opinion. On the contrary, conscious of its own weakness, it tried to anticipate it. In the dark days of the Baltic League when it first took office it had put out peace-feelers through Bonaparte's agent in London, Monsieur Otto: an approach which the First Consul treated with contempt so long as he thought there was a chance of obtaining his ends by smashing instead of tricking Britain. And when Nelson's and Abercromby's unexpected achievements and the death of the Tsar changed the face of affairs, the Cabinet resumed its overtures. Like good Mrs. Fremantle, it welcomed British victories chiefly because they made peace possible.

For it could see no other end in them. To an unimaginative mind like Addington's it now seemed impossible that Britain could win the war. The fate of the First and Second Coalitions had shown that though she could annihilate every fleet France and her allies sent to sea and seize their colonies at will, she was powerless to prevent the French armies from over-running the Continent. On the *terra firma* of the old world—the home of traditional civilisation—Bonaparte with his forty million slaves and dupes could not be challenged. The balance of power had gone and the hegemony of France, against which Dutch William and Marlborough had fought, was become an established fact. There was no further point in struggling against it. Continental nations could not be saved in their own despite: in yielding they had signed away their right to Britain's protection. And perhaps it was better for the world that Europe, like France, after so much useless anarchy and destruction, should pass under Bonaparte's strong, orderly, unifying rule. It would be good for trade and might conceivably make for ultimate progress.

Material security, in fact, which had formerly depended on waging war, now seemed to such rootless minds to depend on making peace. A prolonged war always brings in its train of exhaustion and unnatural sacrifice a feverish aftermath of materialistic longing. France experienced it under the Directory; Britain under Addington. A cant phrase—"the blessings of peace"—became much in vogue about this time. The nation, it was felt, having proved itself unconquerable and given an unparalleled if useless example to the world, had earned a respite from alarm, starvation prices and high taxation. It could now reap the rich reward to which its manufacturing skill and commercial enterprise entitled it.[1]

In other words materially-minded Englishmen were already anticipating the peaceful harvest of wealth and empire which was to fall to their children and children's children in the golden reign of Victoria. Even in the midst of war's alarms their trade had passed all previous bounds and their dominion had been enlarged, not only by their conquests from France and her allies but by their colonising and imperial activities elsewhere. In India the great State of Mysore had passed under their beneficent control, and Lord Wellesley, by his proconsular gifts, had already transformed and nearly doubled the territories of the old East India Company. In Australia a new continent and in Canada a new half continent were quietly and imperceptibly entering upon the first stage of their wondrous march to imperial nationhood. The spectre of the Revolution militant having been exorcised, a race of shopkeepers could enter upon its peaceful and boundless heritage.

On this basis, therefore, the Addington Government approached the First Consul and proposed a business deal. Its principle was to be that of *uti possidetis*. France was to keep her Continental conquests, Britain her colonial, or at least the more important of them: Malta, Ceylon, Trinidad, Martinique and the Cape. The rest might be returned as the price of the restitution of Egypt to Britain's ally, Turkey. In view of the fact that France had incorporated Belgium, Westphalia and Savoy and increased its European population to nearly three times that of Britain, while establishing suzerainty over the adjoining Batavian, Cisalpine, Ligurian and Helvetic Republics, it seemed a reasonable enough proposal.

. . . .

But there was a dragon in the path. Bonaparte also wanted peace. But he wanted it only to gain the power to destroy England. So long as her fleets remained intact he could not achieve the mastery of the world. So long as she maintained her merciless stranglehold on his ports, he could not even consolidate his power over France and her neighbours. The peoples of western Europe, deprived by the British blockade of colonial products and seaborne goods, were growing increasingly restive. Illogically they laid the blame, not on England but on the "Great Nation." Russia, Prussia and Austria were still formidable military Powers: a third Coalition and a general rising against France might reverse the decision of Marengo and Hohenlinden. Without a pause for commercial and

[1] See Southey's interesting summary of this view in his *Letters of Espriella*, I, 131.

industrial recovery the French people could not yet sustain such renewed war. More strained and exhausted than their island adversaries by an unbroken decade of revolution, anarchy and battle, they had raised Bonaparte to supreme power to give them peace. He was First Consul only for a term: his consolidation and continued lease of rule depended on his ability to fulfil that promise. More quick victories on land would be useless, if he could not first end the interminable resistance of the British. Only when that bulldog grip was relaxed would the French people be able to recover the buoyant enthusiasm and vigour he needed of them for grander projects.

After the Tsar's death and Nelson's shattering blow at Copenhagen, Bonaparte knew that he could not, so long as the present war continued, destroy Britain at sea. No further naval combination against her was possible for no other fleets anywhere remained. Since 1793 she had sunk, burnt and captured 81 sail of the line, 187 frigates and 248 sloops. New navies could neither be built nor equipped while the ports and arsenals of France, Spain and Holland were blockaded and denied naval stores. Whereas the First Consul, for all his Continental victories, could do little more to injure Britain, every day that the contest continued weakened France's commercial position and diminished her wealth and ultimate strength. Already she had lost her entire colonial empire except Guadeloupe and Mauritius: and these could be taken from her whenever the British chose to concentrate their military forces, now released by Bonaparte's own conquests from continental commitments. The greater part of the rich Dutch empire had passed into British hands. So had the more valuable of Spain's remaining possessions in the West Indies. It was only a matter of time before the omnipresent islanders seized on the greatest prize of all: the restless Spanish colonies of South America.

Bonaparte therefore did not reject the secret British peace overtures. Like a good negotiator, he hid his eagerness and instructed Monsieur Otto to take a high line with the inexperienced Hawkesbury. He was to insist that it was beneath the dignity of the Republic to yield any of France's pre-Revolutionary possessions, whether in Europe or overseas. Only on such terms, the British Government was to be informed, was peace obtainable. Neither of the chief protagonists could be expected to give up anything permanently theirs. But if they chose to negotiate on the *uti possidetis* principle for the conquered possessions of each other's allies, that was another matter.

Having established this basis of negotiation, the First Consul took immediate steps to increase his own bargaining power by attacking Britain's remaining allies and protégés. With the threat of a French Army of Observation he forced Spain to invade Portugal and extort an abject surrender from the helpless court of Lisbon. In pursuance of his recent treaty rights with the terrified Kingdom of the Two Sicilies, he garrisoned Brindisi, Otranto and the ports of Calabria with French troops. He sent another force from the Italian mainland to Elba to drive the British garrison from Porto Ferrajo. And he tightened his grip on the satellite Republics at France's gates, particularly Holland. From all, as from Portugal and Naples, British trade was rigidly excluded. For within the watery line which the British cruisers kept round his dominion in western Europe Bonaparte could do as he chose.

Meanwhile he made desperate efforts to restore the situation in Egypt. For here Abercromby's success threatened to rob him of his most valuable card. Earlier attempts to send help by sea to the beleaguered French army of the Orient had ended in the usual frustration. Admiral Gantheaume's escape from Brest at the end of January had merely proved the effectiveness of the British blockade. For so short were his ships of naval stores that only one of his seven battleships was sea-worthy by the time they reached the Mediterranean. With their crews starving and in rags, they were forced to run for Toulon. Twice in the spring and early summer of 1801 Bonaparte's wrath drove Gantheaume again to sea but each time with the same humiliating result. At the beginning of June the harried Admiral almost succeeded in putting 4,000 troops ashore at Derna to finish the last four hundred miles of their journey to Alexandria on foot. But even this desperate expedient—which must almost certainly have ended in a Western Desert tragedy—was forestalled by the appearance of British sails on the eastern horizon.

Foiled, the First Consul tried again. During Gantheaume's race from Brest to the Mediterranean the British blockading squadrons had left their posts off Ferrol and Cadiz to pursue him. This enabled Bonaparte to concentrate twelve Spanish ships of the line at Cadiz under a French Admiral. A further three from Gantheaume's ill-fated force were ordered to join them for a new attempt to provision and reinforce Egypt. But before they could do so a British squadron under one of Nelson's Nile captains—Rear-Admiral Sir James Saumarez—had taken its station off the port. On June 21st, operating on interior lines, Saumarez with five battleships attacked the French division from Toulon in Algeciras Bay as it waited for a chance to run the blockade of Cadiz.

The attack failed, for the wind dropped while it was still only half-developed. A British battleship, the *Hannibal*, ran aground, and, exposed without support from her wind-bound consorts to the Spanish shore-batteries, was forced to surrender. Paris magnified the incident into a major naval victory.

But even before it had been announced, Britain in her terrible fury had struck back. After five days working day and night to refit his ships, Saumarez sailed again on July 12th, the entire population of Gibraltar turning out to cheer as the Admiral's musicians sounded "Heart of Oak," and the massed bands of the garrison replied with "Britons, strike home!" That night the five British seventy-fours came up with nine French and Spanish sail of the line, including two 112-gun ships, who were slowly returning to Cadiz from Algeciras with their prize. In the darkness and confusion the Spanish three-deckers opened fire on each other and after a fratricidal duel blew up in a single awful explosion with nearly 2000 men. Meanwhile the French *Antoine* struck her flag to the *Superb*. The remainder of the Franco-Spanish force, badly damaged, fled next morning under the guns of Cadiz, leaving the victors, as Lord St. Vincent put it, "upon velvet." The fierce, unconquerable spirit of the British seamen was shown by the captives in the hold of the French *Formidable* who, undismayed by the threats of their jailors, at every broadside directed at their prison's sides broke into triumphant cheers.

In Egypt itself Bonaparte's plans went equally awry. Early in May, General Hely-Hutchinson, Abercromby's successor, set out to cover the hundred miles from Rosetta to Cairo. He had only 5,000 British troops and 4,000 ill-disciplined Turks and he was without siege guns. But by June 27th he had received the surrender of the Egyptian capital together with more than 13,000 dispirited and homesick French soldiers and 320 cannon. Other British forces from India, crossing the desert from the Red Sea port of Kosseir to Keneh and Thebes, overran Upper Egypt, while the remainder of the French army was closely invested in Alexandria. Twenty-four thousand veterans with more than 600 guns had been routed at every point by an invading force with inferior numbers and equipment based on control of the sea. It was the most humiliating reverse to French arms on land since 1793.

. . . .

Everywhere that Bonaparte encountered the forces of Britain that spring and summer of 1801 he was thwarted. Even the minute garrison of Porto Ferrajo in a five months' siege successfully defied 6,000 veterans supported by the entire resources of the French army of Italy. But though unable to defeat his adversaries in the field, the cunning First Consul was more than a match for them in the Cabinet. While stubborn redcoats closed in on the despairing Republicans in the fly-blown, plague-stricken furnace of Lower Egypt and fierce Jack Tars poured their shattering broadsides into French and Spanish galleons, Bonaparte steadily manœuvred Hawkesbury and Addington from position to position. He wanted peace for the moment as much as they; he needed it far more. But his motives, being the exact opposite of theirs, gave him an enormous advantage. His object was to blackmail them into yielding as many strategic and commerical vantage-points as possible for his next leap. Theirs was merely to secure the minimum essential to a rich country's security.

All, therefore, he had to do was to make them think that almost any price was worth paying for peace and quiet. Entering with uncanny precision into their innocent minds, he concentrated a bogus army of invasion on the Channel shores. He was under no illusions as to the feasibility of a successful crossing now that the Northern battle-fleets had been scattered. But he was at great pains to suggest that such a venture was imminent. The Paris newspapers, anxiously scanned by British politicians, were filled with boastful proclamations, the harbour works of Boulogne were enlarged and batteries erected along the coast from the Garonne to the Scheldt to drive off British cruisers. An ordinance of July 12th divided the still largely legendary flotilla of invasion barges into nine divisions and posted all the artillerymen of the Armies of the Rhine and Maine to its gunboats.

These Napoleonic feints served their purpose. A strong Government would either have suspended negotiations until they had ceased or temporised while it gathered in new spoils overseas to offset French threats in Europe. But that of Addington, like a rabbit in the presence of a boa-constrictor, became unable to think of anything but the intended invasion. Had it chosen, it could have snapped its fingers in Bonaparte's face. Instead, a body of well-meaning, honourable but not very astute English gentlemen swallowed the wily Corsican's line and let him play it. It never seemed to occur to them that he was bluffing. Once more Volunteers drilled on every village green and paraded in Hyde Park before their Sovereign. In July a secret circular was directed to District Commanders warning them on the imminence of a French descent; Parson Woodforde in Norfolk attended a parish meeting to consider what was to be done in the event of an enemy landing. As with such overwhelming British superiority at sea a full-scale conquest was hardly possible, the Cabinet decided—as the First Consul meant it to do—that a swift and ruinous raid on London was to be made at the Empire's commercial heart. To his inexpressible disgust, Nelson, home from the Baltic, was appointed to the command of a miscellaneous force of light craft to guard the Channel. When, pining for a quasi-domestic interlude ashore, he protested, the Prime Minister explained that nothing else could quiet the public mind.

But once again when Bonaparte's boasted projects encountered the solid fact of British sea power, they proved wholly insubstantial. Nelson, after his initial disgust, threw himself with his innate enthusiasm into the task of defeating the French invasion plans, real or imaginary. On the assumption that a flying force of 40,000 picked troops in 500 gunboats and barges would be used for a simultaneous landing in Kent and Essex, he worked out his usual minutely careful dispositions for dealing with them. His hope was to encounter Bonaparte in mid-ocean and make him "feel the bottom of the Goodwins." Once at sea, the enemy was to be harried by every vessel under his command and allowed no rest. "The moment they touch our coast, be it where it may," he ordered, "they are to be attacked by every man afloat and ashore."

Almost immediately the initiative in the Channel passed from France to England. With a young officer, Commander Parker, whom he had singled out for promotion in the Baltic, Nelson set in train plans for attacking the French flotilla in its own ports. On August 4th he bombarded Boulogne harbour for sixteen hours. Eleven nights later he resumed the attack with a force of fifty-seven boats. His object was to capture the enemy's barges and tow them back to England.

In this he was disappointed. The French shore-batteries, Latouche-Treville's gunboats moored off Boulogne pier, and above all the Channel tides and currents were too strong. The operation was technically a failure; forty-four lives, including that of the gallant Parker, were lost to little apparent purpose. But the event, by showing the impracticability of landing operations in the treacherous and intricate water of the Channel, even when conducted by only a few picked vessels, under a superlative naval commander, removed all real fear of invasion. Nelson returned convinced of its impossibility. "The craft which I have seen," he wrote, "I do not think it possible to *row* to England; and sail they cannot."[1]

. . . .

But by this time the First Consul had secured all he could have hoped for when negotiations started. He had discovered that, once

[1] Mahan, *Nelson*, II, 138.

the slow-witted English had been brought to concede a point, they regarded themselves as unalterably bound by whatever subsequently happened. Of this unaccountable and, as it seemed to his Italian mind, childlike and pedantic affectation, he took full advantage. Nor was it difficult to obtain colonial concessions, one by one, from the English milords. For they were by now so obsessed with the supposed advantages of peace that they were reluctant to risk missing it by standing out for trifles. And unlike their predecessors, the new Ministers seemed to regard colonial possessions as trifles compared with Continental concessions. This naturally suited Bonaparte, who wanted colonies and could dispose of the Continent as he chose.

For to such barndoor statesmen as Addington and Hawkesbury, Bonaparte's latest *faits accomplis* in Europe—the annexation of Piedmont, the occupation of the Neapolitan ports, the subjection of Portugal and the re-Gallicising of the Batavian Republic—seemed so vast and threatening that to obtain some modification of them they were ready to sacrifice any number of remote colonial conquests. Noblemen of the *ancien régime* with minds that moved only in well-worn grooves, they regarded Naples as far more important than outlandish Cape Town and a petty German or Italian principality as worth all Canada. They did not share the imperial vision of Dundas or the new commercial horizons of Pitt: theirs were bounded by the capitals and courts of eighteenth century Europe: the narrow world of the past and not the oceanic world of the future. For a little transient ease and popularity they not only agreed to restore to France all her pre-war possessions—Martinique, St. Lucia and Tobago in the West Indies, her forts and factories in India, Goree and Senegal in Africa, and the North Atlantic islands of Miquelon and St. Pierre—but conceded, step by step, the return to the puppet Batavian Republic of the Cape of Good Hope, Demerara, Berbice, Essequibo, Surinam, Curacoa, Malacca, Cochin China, Negapatam and the Spice Islands. Of Britain's conquests from Holland they retained only Ceylon and of those from Spain—in deference to the City—Trinidad. In the Mediterranean they relinquished the last remaining fruits of Nelson's victories: Malta to the Knights of St. John, Minorca to Spain, and Elba to France.

In return for all this Britain obtained from the First Consul the restoration of Egypt to Turkey, a guarantee of Portuguese territorial integrity and a promise to withdraw the French garrisons from the south Italian ports. The importance of the first concession was dwindling daily as a result of British triumphs in the desert, while the rest depended on Bonaparte's good faith and readiness to refrain from future aggression. But on one point, at least, the Government had cause to be proud: the restitution which its protection secured for its helpless allies. England might have asked too little for herself, but she had not betrayed those who had trusted her: the character of the country, as Pitt said afterwards, remained on high ground. In the autumn of 1801, for all her adversary's power, it is doubtful if her credit on the Continent had ever stood higher. In every country the English name was held in respect while the French were universally detested for their spoilations.[1]

Such was the position reached by the middle of September—a month after Nelson's attempt on the Boulogne flotilla. Bonaparte, impressed by the almost limitless elasticity of the English mind when in an appeasing mood as contrasted with its obstinacy in battle, was still standing out in the hope of further concessions, and the few in England who knew of the secret negotiations were growing hourly more depressed. On September 17th, Lord Cornwallis, representing the view of a little minority of tired, disillusioned leaders of the older generation, wrote that he could see no prospect of peace or of anything hopeful. "We must, I am afraid," he added, "lose many more good men in Egypt."

But on that very day Bonaparte, from his geographical vantage-point in Paris, received news that his garrison at Alexandria was at its last gasp. Within a few weeks at the outside the British Government and the world would learn that France's arms and prestige had received a shattering blow and that her chief concession to England was become valueless. Unless the First Consul could conclude the negotiations at once, all he had gained might be lost. For all his bold front, peace for a time was essential to him: unlike the British Ministers who did not live in Europe and feel its effects, he was only too conscious of the power of the blockade. Its continuance for another winter might ignite the whole Continent.

He showed no weakness. As on the field of battle, when things were going against him, he acted with speed and decision. He at once instructed his agent in London to conclude the preliminaries by October 2nd: before, that is, the British could receive news of their final triumphs in Egypt. Unless an armistice was signed by that date, he was to inform Hawkesbury that negotiations would be broken off.

The bluff succeeded. As he had done so often before, Bonaparte snatched victory out of defeat. In its haste to retrieve the vanishing mirage of peace the Cabinet forgot every card in its hand: the

[1] *Farington*, I, 338.

blockade, the victories in Egypt, the imminent fall of Alexandria, the control of the Channel. It fell into the trap, grasping peace while it could. Vital points which were still unsettled it left, on a few vague verbal assurances from Monsieur Otto, to further discussion after the cessation of hostilities. Nothing could have suited Bonaparte's purpose better. On the night of October 1st, 1801, Hawkesbury signed the Preliminary Treaty.

Next morning news arrived that the last French garrison in Egypt had begun to negotiate a surrender. Simultaneously the announcement of a general armistice was made to England in an Extraordinary Gazette. It came as an overwhelming surprise. In the popular joy and relief every other consideration was forgotten. As mail coaches, decked with laurels, bore the tidings into market-towns and villages, cheering crowds filled the streets; at Torbay, where Collingwood was about to sail for Brest, his servant, running in as he sat at breakfast, could only stammer out the ecstatic words: "Peace! Peace!"

The general view was that the terms were as good as could be expected, and that no mere territorial gains could have been worth the continuance of the war. It was put by a London lady who wrote to a country correspondent of those who found fault with the Treaty and said it should have been better: "I only say it should have been sooner, yet better late than never!" [1] For the moment the country did not feel dishonour or fear future danger: the victories of Nelson, Saumarez and Abercromby had made too deep an impression in men's minds for that. Alone among the nations who had contended against France Britain had lost nothing: on the contrary she had increased her territories. The hungry mob, believing that peace spelt plenty, welcomed the envoy who brought Bonaparte's ratification with hysterical delight: surrounded his carriage, took out the horses and dragged it from Portman Square to Downing Street. Cheers were even given for the First Consul, whose picture was sold in the streets; by one of those bewildering transformations endemic to English politics, "the Atheistical Usurper" and "Corsican Adventurer" of yesterday became the "Restorer of Public Order," "the August Hero" and even—on one solitary inscription—"the Saviour of the World."[2] Nelson could not restrain his disgust at this ignorant exultation. "There is no person rejoices more in the peace than I do," he wrote, "but I would sooner burst than let a damned Frenchman know it!"

Only a few refused to welcome a peace which their reason told

[1] Bamford, 214.
[2] *Crabb Robinson*, I, 105-6.

them could not endure. The King, after reading the Preliminaries, lifted his hands and eyes to Heaven, heaved a sigh and thereafter kept silence on the matter.[1] Grenville and Windham, in their new freedom from official ties, declared that Britain had "given up everything everywhere," and described the Treaty as the death-warrant of the country. But the official Opposition under Fox supported it, its most patriotic member, Sheridan, speaking of it as a peace "which every man ought to be glad of but no man can be proud of." It was defended in the Commons by Addington, Wilberforce and Pitt, and in the Lords by Hawkesbury, Nelson and St. Vincent. Pitt argued that the security for which he had so long contended had been achieved, that the financial situation made peace necessary and—on surer ground—that a period of rest had become indispensable to England. Though he regretted the loss of the Cape, he welcomed the retention of Trinidad and Ceylon as permanent keys to the West and East Indies and the two most valuable acquisitions that could have been chosen. In the Lower House no Division was taken, and even in the Upper, where Grenville and Spencer stood out fiercely, the resolution approving the Treaty was carried by 114 votes to 10. The gift of peace seemed too precious after so many years of war and suffering to be scrutinised over closely.

But those who sup with the devil need a long spoon. It fell to the Government—as it deserved—to be the first to test the truth of this. After the official cessation of hostilities and the raising of the blockade on October 22nd, the preliminary Armistice had to be turned into a definitive Treaty of Peace. The questions left indeterminate on Monsieur Otto's verbal assurance in the eleventh-hour hurry to sign had now to be adjusted. There was the question of compensation to Britain's protégés, the Prince of Orange and the King of Sardinia, the delimitation of the Newfoundland fisheries and the recognition by Spain and Holland of the retention of Trinidad and Ceylon. There were the provisions for securing the absolute independence of Malta and its guarantee by a third Power. Most important of all there was the negotiation of the commercial facilities on the Continent to which British merchants looked forward as the fruits of the peace for which their statesmen had sacrificed so much. Given the same good will and good faith on the French side as on the British, little remained but a few formalities. It was not anticipated that they would take long.

The task of negotiating them was entrusted to that most distinguished soldier and proconsul, the Lord-Lieutenant of Ireland.

[1] *Windham Papers*, II, 176.

The Marquis of Cornwallis had taken little part in the war; he was a hero—if a somewhat tragic one—of an earlier contest. He had always been held in reserve as a national trump card to be played at supreme moments: in 1794 Pitt and Grenville had proposed him to the strangely unimpressed Austrian General Staff as a possible Commander-in-Chief to save the First Coalition from disruption and defeat. Needless to say, he shared the Government's views about the necessity for peace: American defeats, a decade of campaigning in India and his experiences at Dublin Castle had made him at sixty-two a profound pessimist. He described himself in September, 1801, as "out of sorts, low-spirited and tired of everything."[1] He was a great gentleman and a great patriot. But his vision of England's place in the world derived not from the sunrise over Aboukir Bay but from the melancholy twilight of Yorktown.

He set out for Paris on November 3rd, in order to be present, at the First Consul's express wish, at the Festival of Peace. The Festival turned out to be nothing but fireworks in the mud and the French capital, to Cornwallis' saddened eyes, a dreary place without society or liberty, the women largely whores and the men ill-looking scoundrels "with the dress of mountebanks and the manners of assassins." Almost at once he encountered difficulties. The First Consul, who gave him two brief audiences, was impatient, imperious and plainly unaccustomed to being contradicted. At the start he asked after the King's health, spoke of the British nation with respect and declared that so long as the two peoples remained friends there need be no interruption to the peace of Europe. But the moment Cornwallis raised the question of the retention of Tobago, whose planters were petitioning the Cabinet against a return to French rule, Bonaparte stigmatised the suggestion as scandalously dishonourable and indignantly refused to recognise the obligation to refund the sums which the British Government had expended on the maintenance of French prisoners and which it had offered to cancel in exchange for the little island.

For when it came to tying up the untied ends of the Treaty and converting verbal promises into formed agreements, Cornwallis found he could do nothing. The First Consul and his shameless Foreign Minister, Talleyrand, either blandly denied ever having made them or treated them as the occasion for new and outrageous French demands. Truth and honour were virtues unknown to them; nothing they said could be depended upon. Even Bonaparte's brother, Joseph, who had a reputation in Paris for moderation and honesty, and who on the peace conference's removal to Amiens in

[1] *Cornwallis*, III, 382.

December became the chief Republican negotiator, proved wholly unreliable. "I feel it," Cornwallis complained, "as the most unpleasant circumstance attending this unpleasant business that, after I have obtained his acquiescence on any point, I can have no confidence that it is finally settled and that he will not recede from it in our next conversation."[1]

In any case Cornwallis's hands were tied. For by concluding an armistice the Government had unloosed such a torrent of pent-up longing for peace that there was now no controlling it. In a nation ruled by public opinion the discipline and united purpose of war cannot be maintained when war is over. A parliamentary country, by laying down its arms before it has won a complete victory, loses the power to bargain. However prudent or necessary it might now appear to the Cabinet to insist on the performance of verbal promises given before the preliminary Treaty, they could no longer enforce them by breaking-off negotiations. The country would never have permitted an immediate renewal of the war, or even the threat of it, save under the most overwhelming and unmistakable necessity. When France promptly took advantage of the cessation of the blockade to fit out an enormous expedition, including twenty-two battleships and 25,000 troops, to reconquer Santo Domingo from the negro Toussaint l'Ouverture, Britain could only feebly protest. The Admiralty could not even strengthen the West Indian Squadron, because seamen who had been pressed in time of war refused to serve abroad until the ships had been re-manned by volunteers.

The First Consul saw that the British Government was in a trap, and he acted accordingly. He refused all satisfaction on matters not already formally concluded and instructed his brother to refuse even to discuss the affairs of Germany, Italy or Switzerland. "All these subjects," he wrote, "are completely outside our deliberations with England." That country had foolishly relaxed the blockade and made peace: its reward was to have the door of the Continent slammed in its face. Even its trade was not to be admitted there: on this point Bonaparte now remained absolutely adamant. He announced that he would sooner have war than "illusory arrangements." He had regained his own colonial empire and the freedom of the seas, but his rival's commerce was still to be excluded from western Europe.

Simultaneously he sought new strategic advantages for the day when he should be able to renew the war. At the end of the old year he put out a counter-project, amounting almost to a new

[1] Cornwallis to Hawkesbury, 30th Dec., 1801, *Cornwallis*, III, 420.

treaty, claiming extended fishing rights in Newfoundland, the restoration of the fortifications of Pondicherry at British expense, an establishment in the Falkland Islands and the abolition of the right of salute at sea. In the same document, as though the matter were still open, he omitted all reference to Spanish and Dutch recognition of the cession of Trinidad and Ceylon and calmly proposed to substitute the King of Naples for the Tsar of Russia as the guarantor of Malta.

Cornwallis and Hawkesbury had the utmost difficulty in resisting these claims. They were accompanied by every sort of trickery: the Spanish representative, when at last he was appointed, turned out to be a man who either was or pretended to be ill at Padua. The suggestion that the future independence of Malta should depend solely on the weak Kingdom of the Two Sicilies would give France, with its prepondering influence over the smaller nations of the Continent, the power to betray Britain's interests in the island at any moment. The difficulty was to get Bonaparte to see this or, at least, to admit that he saw it. Yet even while the negotiations were proceeding, he provided an illustration of what was likely to happen in the future. For after a visit to Lyons in January, 1802, to meet the Deputies of the Cisalpine Republic, he calmly announced that he had accepted its supreme office under the style of President of the *Italian* Republic. Yet the independence of the Cisalpine, Ligurian, Helvetic and Batavian Republics had been one of the chief conditions of the Treaty of Lunéville signed less than a year before.

In this Bonaparte almost overreached himself, for the more informed part of the British public showed signs of strong resentment. "The proceedings at Lyons," wrote Hawkesbury to Cornwallis on February 12th, "have created the greatest alarm in this country, and there are many persons who were pacifically disposed and who since this event are desirous of renewing the war."[1] Even Hawkesbury expressed himself as shocked by the "inordinate ambition, the gross breach of faith and the inclination to insult Europe" shown by the First Consul. But with the Powers prostrating themselves at his feet and the great mass of the British people still stubbornly set in its new mood of good-humoured indolence, there was little the Government could do. As Coleridge put it, "any attempt to secure Italy, Holland and the German Empire would have been preposterous. The nation would have withdrawn all faith in the pacific intentions of the Ministers if the negotiations had been broken off on a plea of this kind, for

[1] *Cornwallis*, III, 457.

it had taken for granted the extreme desirableness, nay, the necessity of a peace; and this, once admitted, there would have been an absurdity in continuing the war for objects which the war furnished no means of realising."[1]

Had it not been for the necessity of passing the annual estimates through Parliament and of knowing whether to budget for peace or war, it is doubtful whether Cornwallis would have ever completed his mission. But on March 14th, when a decision could no longer be postponed, the Government, roused by the First Consul's perpetually-rising demands, embodied the latest of them in a formal treaty which it instructed its plenipotentiary to present for immediate acceptance or rejection. If no answer was returned in eight days, he was to leave France.

Yet, even after this, Bonaparte was able to wring a few small, final concessions from Cornwallis. For though the latter longed to be gone from Amiens and its dismal society, he remained acutely conscious of what he called "the ruinous consequences of . . . renewing a bloody and hopeless war." Sooner than risk this, he took it upon himself, to Addington's subsequent intense relief, to modify the tone of his instructions. And at three o'clock on the morning of March, 25th, after a five hour midnight session he brought his mission to an end and signed the Treaty, leaving the most important question—that of Malta—still indeterminate. The British forces were to be withdrawn within three months and their place taken for a further year by a Neapolitan contingent. The Order of St. John was to be reconstituted—no one knew how—so as to be free from external influence, and the island's independence was to be guaranteed by the six major Powers, Britain, France, Russia, Austria, Prussia and Spain. The consent of the last four however, had still to be obtained. "Nothing surely can be worse," wrote Pitt's confident, George Rose, "than loose stipulations in a treaty of peace that may occasion strife and ill-blood." As another shrewd observer put it, the Treaty of Amiens bore the seeds of a just and durable war.

But as the country had by now settled down to peace, the Government had no choice in the matter. It demanded a definitive Treaty and was prepared to wait no longer for it.[2] Had Addington refused to give it, political power might well have passed to the pro-Bonapartist Fox. The thought temporarily silenced even the strongest opponents of appeasement.

In April, 1802, London celebrated the official Proclamation of

[1] *The Friend*, Section I, Essay 10.
[2] See *Collingwood*, 90.

Peace. The general, unthinking view was expressed by Southey's landlady who, after struggling in the crowd till two in the morning in a vain attempt to see the illuminations outside the French Consulate in Portman Square, execrated all who disliked the Treaty, congratulated herself on the fall in the price of bread, hoped that Hollands' gin and French brandy would soon fall too, and "spoke with complacency of Bonniprat."[1] The crowd was prodigious, the principal streets as bright as day with rows of candles blazing in all the windows in twin, interminable, tapering lines of light, the fashionable gaming-houses in St. James' Street resplendent with lamp-lit crowns and patriotic inscriptions and transparent pictures "emblematical of peace and plenty."[2] And far away in Grasmere, Dorothy Wordsworth by the lakeside watched the moon travelling through the silent skies, the stars growing and diminishing as the clouds passed before them. The sheep were sleeping and all things quiet.

. . . .

A few weeks later Bonaparte received from his people the price of the settlement he had given them. By a plebiscite of three and a half millions to eight thousand they affirmed that he should be Consul for life. From that day he called himself Napoleon. The era of the Cæsars had returned to Europe.

Yet the masterpiece of knavery and cunning by which the great Corsican had won his ends from England laid the foundations of his own destruction. He had tricked the stubborn, stupid islanders, who did not know their own strength and the power of the terrible weapon their sea-captains had forged, into relaxing their stranglehold on his ports and restoring his colonies. He had gained eighteen months to revictual and refit the armed camp in which he chose to live, and with it twelve years of dominion and triumphant war. The sea winds with which France now filled her exhausted lungs fanned the distant camp-fires of Austerlitz, Jena and Friedland.

For, through the ultimate justice of the moral law that governs the destinies of this world, Bonaparte had begun to defeat himself. He could have had his boasted New Order of European unity and progress had he chosen. Only one thing at that moment could have prevented it. That one thing the First Consul in his arrogance and reckless cynicism elected to do. By cheating and bullying the most confiding but stubborn folk in the world, he forged the weapon

[1] *Espriella*, II, 50.

[2] "This was a transparency exhibited this night at a pot-house in the City, which represented a loaf of bread saying to a pint of porter, I am coming down; to which the porter-pot made answer, So am I."—*Espriella*, I, 90.

that was to destroy him. He united the British people as they had never been united before. He united them in a single passionate resolve to put an end to him and all his purposes.

Even as they rejoiced at the peace they had made, they began to perceive instinctively that there was no peace. As is the way with a free country, the knowing few—and more especially those who were untrammelled by office and the still stronger bonds of loyalty and personal friendship—were the first to voice their protest at what Grenville called "unnecessary and degrading concessions," and Canning the "gross faults and omissions, the weakness and baseness and shuffling and stupidity of the Treaty." But there was something more than Party feeling in the growing wave of criticism. Even Pitt, still flawless in his support of his old protégé, Addington, spoke strongly in favour of increased armaments at the very moment that the negotiations were being concluded. "I am inclined to hope everything that is good," he declared, "but I am bound to act as if I feared otherwise."

"Peace, Sir, in a week and war in a month!" was Malmesbury's reply to the Duke of York's request for the news when they met in the Park in March, 1802. When Addington spoke of "a genuine reconciliation between the two first nations of the world," Britain already knew in her heart that he lied. For there was no room for her free spirit to exist beside the imperious, despotic philosophy that breathed on the other side of the Channel.

The first to realise it after the dissentient Windhams and Grenvilles were the merchants whom Bonaparte had shut out of the Continent. If there had been no other failure in the Treaty, this omission would have sufficed to prove his bad faith and to ensure Britain's renewed hostility. For it robbed a trading people of the chief advantage they had promised themselves from the peace. Its effects, at first confined to the rich, were soon felt by the entire nation, even by the ignorant multitude who had hailed the peace because it would bring cheap food and plenty.

A stronger Government, and one closer to the country's deeper feelings and historic destiny, would have known this from the first. Addington, ten years out of date, had mistaken war weariness for an expression of inability to wage war. As the sequel was to show, nothing could have been further from the truth. He misunderstood the character of his countrymen. He preceded them where in the mood of the moment they fancied they wanted to go instead of steeling them to stand firm in the place dictated by their own unalterable temperament. So long as despotic power reigned on the Continent, something in the English heart forbade

Englishmen to rest. It was a betrayal of that heart to let them think otherwise.

Yet it may have been inevitable. Lack of social unity and the failure of the governing class—so fit for rule in other ways—to give the nation guidance in the great internal revolution through which it was passing had weakened Britain's war effort. So long as there was any shadow of doubt as to the nature of the Revolution militant and the intentions of Bonaparte, the popular mind remained divided. The weak Administration of Addington was the expression and price of that division: nations get the Government their failings as well as their virtues earn.

Bonaparte, like Hitler after Munich, resolved Britain's dilemma. His actions—unmistakable in their intent—were to restore to the British people "popular enthusiasm, national unanimity and simplicity of object . . . attaching to the right objects and enlisting under their proper banners the scorn and hatred of slavery, the passion for freedom, the high thoughts and feelings"[1] which were their birthright and which bound them to the great names of their own past: to Milton and Hampden, to Latimer, Falkland, and Sidney and the reeds at Runnymede. After the First Consul had betrayed the peace, had trodden down every remaining liberty in western Europe and, scorning his own promises, had insulted, threatened and cheated the only people save the Russians who had never flinched before him in the field, no Briton was ready to trust his word again or to believe that perjured France had anything better to offer mankind than had his own imperfect but dear country. The Peace of Amiens deserved the name of peace, wrote Coleridge, because it gave unanimity at home and reconciled Englishmen with one another. The young rebels of yesterday became the patriots of to-morrow, bringing to the embattled cause of freedom a passion and fire unknown in the earlier years of grim endurance. Henceforward the British people were to follow and deserve great leaders: Pitt and Fox, Nelson and Wellington, Collingwood, Moore and Cornwallis, Castlereagh, Perceval and Canning. In the final stage of their victorious struggle against despotism, Wordsworth and Scott were to be their poets, and Southey and Coleridge their philosophers.

[1] Coleridge, *The Friend*, Section I, Essay 10.

EPILOGUE

Light Out of the Past

"YET now," said Mr. Valiant-for-Truth, "I do not repent me of all the trouble I have been at to arrive where I am." After nine years of harsh, unremitting war England had achieved parity with her adversary, made peace with her under a misconception and found, in the hour of making it, that there was no peace.

As always, she had started to fight at a disadvantage. Our ancestors in 1793 were as unprepared for war as we in 1939. They were handicapped by all the defects of their libertarian virtues and institutions: by Party divisions, long-ingrained commercial habits, Treasury pedantry and incorrigible amateurishness. Their politicians, being more used to compromises than decisions, were ill-fitted to choose between rival courses: to make that option of difficulties which Wolfe defined as the problem of war. Having far-flung commitments and inadequate forces, they were weak at every point and strong at none. They left the initiative to the enemy and were unable to regain it. Their one asset was their courage. In the face of repeated disappointment and disaster they showed, in common with the people they led, an astonishing resilience.

Such statesmen, like the British leaders of 1939, failed to grasp the strength and speed of the forces they had challenged. Facing men who were using a new dynamic of power to dominate the world, they put their trust in a victory based on financial resources. They forgot that the symbols of past commercial activity—favourable trade returns, accumulated bank balances and credits—could not avail on the battlefield. Economic like military strength is not the cause of human achievement but the result. It is not weapons which decide wars in the end but men, for it is men who make the weapons and then marshal and use them.

For all their apparent bankruptcy, the Jacobins enjoyed an enthusiasm and cohesion unknown to their opponents. They felt that they were fighting for a way of life which offered them and their children a dignity and usefulness more in keeping with the eternal needs of human nature than the old dispensation. When, operating from interior lines under young and revolutionary leaders, they struck with concentrated force at the Allies' defensive cordons, the slow and confused *sitzkrieg* of the first year was succeeded by a lightning war of movement, terror and calamity. The monarchical States of the *ancien régime* proved no match in battle for the vigour and fanatic unity of Revolutionary France. They were routed by their own slackness, inefficiency and selfish divisions almost before a shot had been fired.

As in 1940, Britain was driven back to her last line of resistance, the sea. Her expeditionary force, deserted by its allies, was expelled from the Continent, the flanks of her trade routes exposed to attack and the ports of Western Europe closed to her ships. Her people suffered a food shortage as grave but far less equally borne than in the present war. Even her vaunted financial system came within a few hours of bankruptcy.

But those who thought that Britain was defeated were proved wrong. In adversity her real strength became apparent. It lay not in her gossamer web of trade and usury and amorphous commercial empire—as the Jacobins, like their Nazi prototypes, supposed—but in the character of her people. Against that rock the waves of conquest broke in vain. In the hour of danger our ancestors closed their ranks. They made many mistakes but they never bowed under the consequences. They learnt from them and went on.

By 1797 they had discovered where their strength resided. Forced by adverse circumstances to concentrate on the sea, they made the destruction of the enemy's naval power their first objective. In doing so they reaped the advantage geography and history had given them. They learnt what Raleigh and Pepys, Cromwell and Chatham had taught by precept and example: that an island Power wastes and dissipates its strength unless it controls the sea. Only by an absolute command of the ocean trade routes—such as to-day involves mastery of the air above as much as of the sea itself—could Britain secure her shores, obtain the sinews of war and sustain her allies. Without it her armies were mere immobilised spectators of Continental battles like the *Culloden* on her shoal at the Nile.

By putting first things first this country, within eighteen months of the fall of her last ally and the naval mutinies that marked her nadir, established a command of the sea so complete that, so long as she retained it and fought on, defeat was impossible. Discarding seniority-encrusted Admirals who used sea-power as a defensive weapon till it all but broke in their hands, she evolved under younger and more daring leaders a new offensive technique. Cape St. Vincent, Camperdown, the Nile and Copenhagen not only saved her from destruction but placed an unborn century of human destiny in her hands. It was then decided that Pitt's—and Jeremy Bentham's—England and not France's New Order was to shape the human future. Henceforward the seas remained a ring of steel round the tyrant's conquests. He had to break it or perish.

But the colleagues of Pitt and Addington did not yet realise it. They had saved England; they had yet to learn how to save Europe. Though Nelson's glorious counter-attack and Russian victories awoke universal hopes of a second front, the army which Britain had raised behind the shelter of her fleets struck too late and too far from the main theatre of war to break an enemy acting on interior lines. Its troops were insufficiently trained in the new warfare and its commanders so oppressed by their own difficulties that they forgot those of their enemies. Instead of pushing boldly on and snatching victory, they consolidated minor gains while the odds against them hardened. When a few months later Bonaparte smashed Austria at Marengo, Britain, having shot her bolt, remained a helpless spectator of events on land. By her sea offensive she had enclosed the armed Jacobin in a cage. She had still to find out how to enter it and destroy him.

Discouraged by that failure and the collapse for the second time of all her allies, Britain relaxed her stranglehold. When out of necessity she resumed it, she did so without seeing any rational way of destroying the titanic power she had challenged. Time had still to teach her that, so long as she kept the sea routes closed to the conqueror, his New Order was denied the means of enduring life, while her own growing industrial strength, freely nourished through those same watery channels, could become, like that of America to-day, a potent force for liberating Europe. She had still to learn, too, how a British army, based on the sea and enjoying perfect freedom of movement, could exert an influence out of all proportion to its size[1] and could prove to an enslaved and restless Continent that the Grand Armée was not invincible.

. . . .

Yet military prowess alone could scarcely have conquered Napoleon's France. It needed a human agency with its own superlative efficiency even to resist it. Only one with a greater spiritual force could break it. After Nelson's victories and the resumption of war Britain, having repaired her early defects and omissions, faced France at last on something approaching equal terms. The struggle

[1] "An army supported by an invincible navy possesses a strength which is out of all proportion to its size."—G. F. R Henderson, *The Science of War*, 26.

then became a contest not merely between physical forces but between rival principles.

That of Jacobin and Napoleonic France had one ineradicable weakness. With all its immense vitality and military virtue and efficiency, it tended to worship itself. It lacked humility and therefore understanding of the laws that ultimately govern the universe. Even at the outset the Revolutionary effort was impaired by human failings. The besetting vices of the men who set out to build a new heaven and earth in a day were impatience and arrogance. The resulting lack of discipline brought them into trouble as soon as they encountered an orderly and cohesive people like the British. The fleets which put out of Brest and Toulon with wild boasts and unharnessed enthusiasms were no match for the patient, hard-trained men who sailed under the "meteor flag of England."

But the vitality which sprang from the new philosophy of freedom gave the French people the honesty and vigour to correct these early faults. They learnt the first lessons of the harsh school of war more quickly than their foes. They subjected themselves to discipline to achieve unity. Yet here again they fell into moral errors which impaired their victories. In their impatience for victory they condoned cruelty and injustice. Because of this, the Terror which united France ended by dividing her.

From the worst frenzies of hatred and fear and their corrupt reaction the young Napoleon rescued Revolutionary France. He ended the persecution of party by party, annulled the proscription of religion and stemmed the ugly internal flow of blood. Yet, though as a result he shattered France's enemies, the fatal flaw in the Revolution remained: that human reason was divine and that the sum total of human reason, as expressed either by the majority vote of an assembly or by some other man-made device for testing the aggregate will, was divine too. Having seen the divinity of majority rule culminate in the Terror, France substituted the rule of a single national representative. But the belief persisted that the aggregate reason of the nation and, therefore, of its representative, was above moral law.

The folly of this assumption lay in the failure to see that, though human reason may partake of the divine, human nature, through which reason has to operate, is perpetually vitiated by faults of passion and selfishness which blind and distort it. Napoleon, like Robespierre and the Terrorists before him and Hitler and Mussolini since, came to believe that what he wanted as a fallible man was synonymous with the promptings of his divine and infallible reason: in other words, that he was not liable to error. He not only supposed that what he wanted was right but that he was bound—so long as he wanted it enough—to get it. The greater his triumphs, the more deeply he fell into this insane error.

. . . .

In the course of a century of misplaced endeavour that industrious, intelligent but obtusely pedantic race, the northern Germans, built a similar thesis around a study of the Revolutionary and Napoleonic wars. The Prussian general and historian, Clausewitz, basing his judgment on Napoleon's practice, applied to the new national States of the nineteenth century the maxim that a nation can achieve whatever it fights for irrespective of the morality of its object. The extent of his blindness is illustrated by a sentence of one of his pupils, Field-Marshal Von der Goltz. "The statesman who, knowing his instrument to be ready and seeing war inevitable, hesitates to strike first is guilty of a crime against his country." But what, one asks, recalling August, 1914, if the blow outrages the conscience of mankind and rouses in opponents spiritual forces more tenacious than the "will to victory" of the aggressor? For this is what the practice of Von der Goltz's text achieved when the German General Staff marched into Belgium in defiance of treaty obligations and human decency. And the result was not the triumph of Germany but her eclipse. She was indeed stabbed in the back, as Hitler said, but not by profiteers and defeatists in 1918 but by her own statesmen in 1914. It is not the first impact which decides wars but the last. It is not the United States which will suffer most from Japanese treachery at Pearl Harbour but the people of Japan. It is not Poland and Norway, Holland, Belgium and Russia which will be the final victims of Hitler's conceptions of *blitzkrieg* but the people of Germany.

For what Clausewitz failed to see was that the qualities needed to achieve victory derive from moral laws which exist independently of human will and lust. A self-centred man or nation, however efficient in the short run, must fail in the long, for its balance is in the wrong place. The England of Pitt and Wellington rested on a juster and more enduring base than the France of Robespierre and Napoleon. The Great Nation, whose military and totalitarian virtues Clausewitz held out as an example to his countrymen, was defeated in the end by a nation with a far smaller population. He overlooked the more enduring strength of a people who subordinated self-will to the decencies of the human conscience. It never seemed to occur to him that there were any such decencies.

For in the light of our own apocalyptic experience, we can see that Britain's supreme asset was the innate respect of her people for moral law. Despite many shortcomings neither they nor their leaders were capable of substituting for the rule of individual conscience the monstrous abstractions of the aggregate mind. Incapable of Napoleon's activity and genius, they were equally incapable of his immorality and ultimately insane mistakes. For initial complacency, refusal to plan ahead, mental and moral laziness they paid dear. Unhampered by Irish resentment, the evils of unregulated enclosure and industrialism and the greed and sloth that battened on the Slave Trade, they might have defeated the armed Jacobin in 1799 or even earlier. But as, learning from reverses, they corrected their grosser mistakes, two things emerged: the slowly-growing moral stature of Britain and the dwindling strength of France. An infidel dictator might act as though he were above moral law and therefore infallible; a Christian people could not. Acknowledging

> "Laws that lay under heaven's ban
> All principles of action that transcend
> The sacred limits of humanity",

they waged war in conformity with the dictates of the individual conscience and individual common sense. Theirs was that saving humility and wisdom called by the Hebrew seers "the fear of the Lord" and by the old Greeks justice. "Upon the morality of Britain," wrote Coleridge, "depends the safety of Britain." Not only her safety, he might have added, but the triumph of her cause.

INDEX

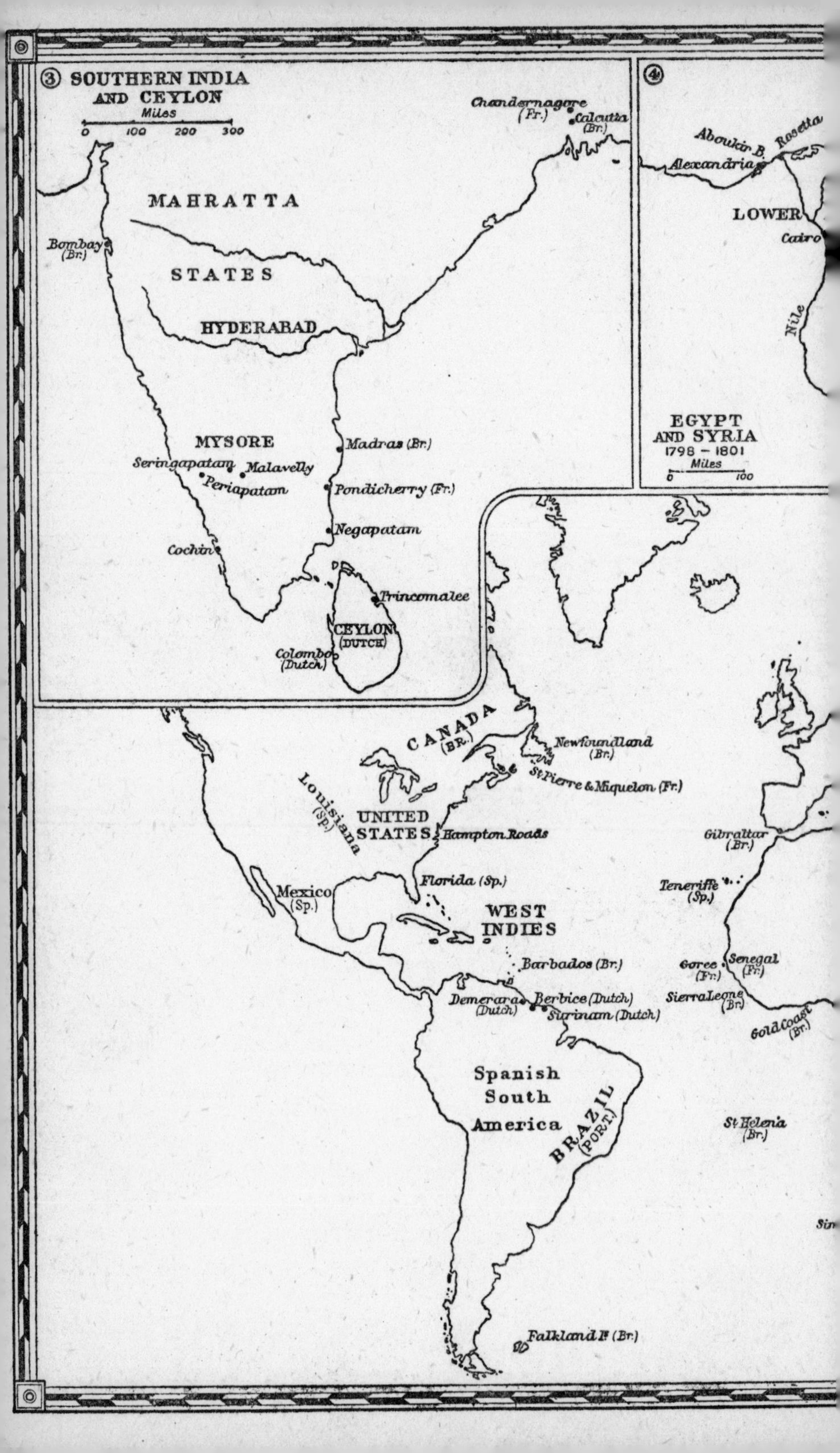

③ SOUTHERN INDIA AND CEYLON
Miles
0 100 200 300
Chandernagore (Fr.)
Calcutta (Br.)
MAHRATTA
STATES
Bombay (Br.)
HYDERABAD
MYSORE
Seringapatam
Malavelly
Periapatam
Madras (Br.)
Pondicherry (Fr.)
Negapatam
Cochin
Trincomalee
CEYLON (DUTCH)
Colombo (Dutch)
④
Aboukir B.
Rosetta
Alexandria
LOWER
Cairo
Nile
EGYPT AND SYRIA
1798 – 1801
Miles
0 100
CANADA (BR.)
Newfoundland (Br.)
St. Pierre & Miquelon (Fr.)
Louisiana (Sp.)
UNITED STATES
Hampton Roads
Gibraltar (Br.)
Mexico (Sp.)
Florida (Sp.)
Teneriffe (Sp.)
WEST INDIES
Barbados (Br.)
Goree (Fr.)
Senegal (Fr.)
Sierra Leone (Br.)
Demerara (Dutch)
Berbice (Dutch)
Surinam (Dutch)
Gold Coast (Br.)
Spanish South America
BRAZIL (PORT.)
St. Helena (Br.)
Falkland Is. (Br.)